ECONOMIC GROWTH AND FOREIGN TRADE RELATIONS AMONG INDIA, CHINA AND ASEAN

ECONOMIC GROWTH AND FOREIGN TRADE RELATIONS AMONG INDIA, CHINA AND ASEAN

V.B. JUGALE

SERIALS PUBLICATIONS
NEW DELHI

First Published - 2009

ISBN: 978-81-8387-159-4

Published by

SERIALS PUBLICATIONS
4830/24, Prahlad Street, Ansari Road
Darya Ganj, New Delhi-110002 (India)
Phone: 23245225 Fax: 91-11-23272135
E-mail: serials@satyam.net.in

CONTENTS

PREFACE

There are varieties of externalities generated by the economies for accelerating the domestic growth rates. This has puzzled the economic theorists all the time to explore the fact that why some economies grow much faster than others? Similarly, what is the rationale and mandate remains to the growth rate of developing countries as compared to the developed economics? This quality & quantity of growth rates adherence to the developing economies, no doubt, but developing economies are required to look into the development rates rather than growth rates. However, to confine the boundaries of development rates and their summation of macro variables is very difficult. But, obviously, it is essential to diagnose the quality of the development. Otherwise the material or physical growth has no scope to justify the case of development. Consequently, development indices of some of the macro economic variables are being developed and assessed; for example, human development index, human poverty index, social indicators of development etc. During 1970s poverty eradication programmes become the goal of development of most of the developing economics. During 1980s moral, ethical values are considered alongwith environment aspects in the development process. During 1990s the quality of life and human resource development became the thrust of the development paradigm. Self-esteem, freedom from servitude and sycophancy and fetching the basic needs become the development indicators. Of late freedom, rationality, social choices, democratic set up are becoming the indicators of development.

Taking into account the charges in the development paradigms, we thought to focus these views and to expose the issues for the use of fellow readers & researchers and the experiences replicated into the regions, countries and sectoral growth either convergence or divergence in nature is in fact the main rationale of bringing this volume in the market.

Since the classical paradigm, foreign trade is one of important activity insisting the countries to grow. Of course, some trade is better than no trade; with this vision numbers of replicative endeavours are discussed in the volume.

The Indian cases are explored & compared in various fronts (Rajashekar Bahu, Abdus Salam). The issues of trade with ASEAN, SAARC, China with reference to some sectors or sub-sectors were considered by the paper writers (e.g. M. Bhanmathi, R.Meenakshi, R.P.Pradan, Ashir Mehta, Christoper Gan, Karasu and Ozdemir, Sandeep Kumar, Jased Alltar etc.)

The HDR issues, (Choudhury) SMEs (Saiful Islam), AoA (Cyril Kunmony), demographic parameters (Islam & Ali), public health (Asif & Wali) and Sarkar), child labour (Sharma) and business development (Harahap) are the imperative and comparative issues discussed in the volume.

The Indian case studies obviously are given justice in the volume. Agriculture technology (Mishra), forestry, (Sunder), inter-state poverty and waste management (Ramesh) are the main thrust areas discussed in the volume.

The contributions of foreign experiences are one of the specific features of this volume. Such experiences orient the policy matters towards a favourable step for the common cause. We are sure, this volume will fetch the academic and research needs of the universe.

V.B. JUGALE

IMPACT OF GLOBALIZATION ON INDIAN ECONOMY

M. Raja Sekhara Babu

For the last 40 years after independence, the performance of the Indian economy has been dominated by a reigme of multiple controls, restrictive regulations and wide ranging state intervention. Instead of enforcing fiscal discipline, the Government restored to adopt the soft options of printing additional notes and borrowings heavily from within the country. The crisis situation built up in the Indian economy, left no choice for the government than to act fast and bring about major economic reforms, which are popularly known as structural adjustments or liberalisation or Globalization. For a long time businessmen every where believed that home markets were adequate and safe. The scenario is different now. Globalise are perish is the slogan now-a-days.

The Indian economy needs to be totally transformed to solve its basic problems of poverty, unemployment and unednality Liberalisation or Globalization of the economy is a remedy for all these ills. Therefore, India decided to participate in the process of Globalization. In this context, an attempt is made here to analyse the connotion of Globalization arguments for and against Globalization.

Russi Mody views globalization as a two way thing. First it envisages free competition, high productivity using the state of the art of technology and second, selling in one single market place of the whole market. "Globalization of the economy may be defined as the global dimension of the evolving world economy. In current economic literature the term Globalization is used to mean a more liberal "outward-oriented" policy which includes eliminating anti-export biases, lowering of very high import tariffs and quantitative restrictions on imports. In simple economic terms, Globalization refers to the process of integration world into one huge market. Against this brief background this paper attempts to study:

1. The impact of Globalization on foreign investments in India, and
2. The effect of Globalization on agriculture and Industry.

The growth of world exports in between 1990-99 is 64 per cent, but the Indian Exports have increased to 103 per cent during the same period. In 1990 the share of India's share in world's Commercial value is 0.55 per cent but, now it is increased to 0.8 per cent. Now the Foreign Investments to India is floating very much. After 1991 every year on an average 4 billion dollars of Foreign Investment is coming to India. In 2002-03 alone the direct foreign investment to India is 3.6 Billon Dollars and 2 Billon Dollars is indirect investment. Up to December 2004 the indirect Foreign investment came to India is 8 Billion dollars.

In order to attract foreign Investment on a large scale the Government has taken several steps to remove the barriers and irritants which hindered the flow of Investment on a large scale. FERA and MRTP restrictions have been lifted, Foreign investment promotion board has been set up, bureaucrat hurdles have been removed and infrastructural facilities have been stepped up. The results of all these efforts are encouraging. The numbers of approvals and the amount of Foreign Investment have been increasing from year to year. This is shown in Table 1.

Table 1
Foreign Direct Investment Actual Flows Vs. Approvals

	1991	*1992*	*1993*	*1994*	*1995*	*1996*	*1997*	*1998*	*Total*
Approvals Rs. Crore	739	5,256	11,189	13,590	37,489	39,453	57,149	28,783	1,93,648
US $ million	325	1,781	3,559	4,332	11,245	11,142	15,752	6,975	55,111
Actual Inflows Rs. Crore	351	675	1,786	3,009	6,720	8,431	12,085	9,116	42,173
US $ million	155	233	574	958	2,100	2,383	3,330	2,230	11,963
Actual Inflows as % of Approvals (in US $ Terms)	47.7	1301	16.1	22.1	18.7	21.4	21.1	32.0	21.7

Source: Economic Survey and RBI Annual Reports, 2000-01 and 2001-02.

Foreign Direct Investment in India has grown considerably since the process reform began in 1991 through 1997, with FDI flows from approximately $ 154 million in 1991 increased every year, peaking at more than $ 3.6 billion in 1997-1998. FDI inflows declined from peak level in 1997-1998 to US $ 2.5 billion in 1998-1999. The declining trend continued in the next two years. However, inward stock grew from $ 1.8 billion in 1991 to US $ 16.4 billion by 1999 in India.

The growth in FDI investment in India was as low as around 6 per cent per annum between 1948 and 1992 while it grew at around 30 per cent for the next six years. The surge in foreign private capital stock clearly began after 1991. During 1970s, cumulative inflows of FDI was about US $ 454 million or 0.20 per cent of gross domestic investment (GDI). FDI inflows reached $ 9.8 billion during during the 1990-1997 period from just over a billion $ during the 1980s.

GLOBALIZATION OF INDIAN AGRICULTURE

Agriculture today holds a third position in India's GDP, the highest proportion in the developed and developing world, and without fail, it will continue to be the back bone of the economy for the years to come. Almost 70 per cent of India's population depends on agriculture but an unfortunate dichotomy is

Table 2

Foreign Investment Flows by Different Cateories (India), US $ Million

	1992-1993	*1993-1994*	*1994-1995*	*1995-1996*	*1996-1997*	*1997-1998*	*1998-1999*	*1999-2000*	*2000-2001*	*2001-2002*	*2002-2003*
(A) Direct Investment	315	586	1314	2144	2821	3557	2462	2155	4029	6131	4660
RBI Automatic route	42	89	171	169	135	202	179	171	454	767	739
SIA/FIPB route	222	280	701	1249	1922	2754	1821	1410	1456	2221	919
NRI	51	217	442	715	639	241	62	84	67	35	—
Acquisition of shares $	—	—	—	11	125	360	400	490	382	881	916
(B) Portfolio Investment	244	3567	3824	2748	3312	1828	-61	3026	2760	2021	979
(a) FIIs	1	1665	1503	2009	1926	979	-390	2135	1847	1505	377
(b) Euro equities	240	1520	2082	683	1366	645	270	768	831	477	600
(c) Offshore funds & others	03	382	239	56	20	204	59	123	82	39	02
Total (A+B)	559	4153	5138	4892	6133	5385	2401	5181	6789	3152	5639

Source: Reserve Bank of India Annual Reports , 1999-2000 and 2000-01,2001-02,2002-03.

that while in terms of total output India stands in the global markets favourably, in terms of yield it is extremely low. In Rwanda the restructuring of the agricultural system has precipitated the population into abject poverty and destitution.

After entering new era of globalization and economic liberalisastion, Indian agriculture stands hoisted to prominent commercial riche and foresees increased track in global markets external liberlisation which seeks to integrate the economy with global market is all set to open new vistas for agricultural exports. The opening of the economy has brought varied changes in the agricultural sector. Infact, globalsiation compelling Indian agriculture to shift its focus from being "supply driven" to "market driven". Any inability to adopt the changing need may limit farmers market and income opportunities. In that case, commericialisation of agriculture is not only necessary but also essential. Commercialisation of agriculture promises a boost both in productivity and income to farmers.

The record production of 181 MT of food grains during 1992-93 is a testimony to the resilience of Indian agriculture. Though the year year's production fell marginally short of the targeted 183 MT. It has been lauded a credible achievement by policy markers. The shortfall was due to poor rains. It is a remarkable recovery from the previous year's performance which was about 171 MT and it has bettered the previous best production of 176.4 MT in 1990-91. The Sterling performance on the farm front and the reforms have helped the boost of Rs. 7,600/- crores in 1992-93, as against the previous year's Rs. 6,200 crores. The subsidies for agrilututal in developed countiers have incrised after the W.T.O. agreement. In 2001 thery are 311 US billion $. And now they stand today at $325 billion as against $276 billion before 1994.

With the initiation of NEP, the Indian agriculture is poised to enter the wonderland of global markets. It has made good strides in the past years. It has shown remarkable resilience due to concessions given to the allied segments of agriculture under the NEP. Indian farms produces have a price advantage in the international trade and India should try to cash in such advantageous environment. Some 24 developing countries with three Billion people have doubled their ratio of trade to income over the past the three decades The more gobalised developing countries have increased their percapita growth rate from 1 per cent in the 1960's, to 3 per cent in the 1970's, 4 per cent in the 1980's and 5 per cent in the 1990's.Their growth rates now substantially exceed those of the rich countries.

INDUSTRY

Improvements in transportation, communications and manufacturing technology, however provided companies with a way to reduce costs by dividing production into part processes and relocating the less skilled and more labour-intensive segments in low wage areas. Jet air craft, container ships and super tankers more reliable communications through fibre optic cables facsimiles and the internet and the increased use of numerically controlled machines and robots all played a part these changes have four important consequences. First, there has been a steep decline in industrial employment in all OFCD (Organisation for Economic Co-operation and development). Countries and this has had an adverse impact on the trade unions.

Second, the ability of firms to easily shift their production facilities overseas underscores a fundamental difference between companies and governments. Third, the weakening of government control over the economy underminded the effectiveness of trade unions and social democratic parties forged during the age of industrial capitalism. Finally, since the wider distribution of industrial production leads to a reduction of profit margins ion the manufacturing sector.

Now the question arises whether the Globalization of Indian Economy will help in achieving the desired results, i.e., higher production, higher exports, greater employment. There are some challenges which are to be faced. Firstly it is said, "Globalization is mutually beneficial when capital labour technology and goods flow between equals when the country is ready to face the world competition on equal terms, otherwise, any attempt by the ruling elite in the third world to globalise its economy can rebound adversely on the vast majority of the people".

With regard to increasing production of exports, it is for granted that it will considerably go up and will maintain increasing tempt, as producers are free from different types of restrictions and regulations. With regard to employment, increase in investment, number of production unit, inflow of foreign capital will lead to increased production and ultimately will have a high demand for human resources, but foreign investor may prefer automation as well as sophisticated machinery manufactured by their own country. It may result in making the present skilled force in our country redundant and on the other hand, they may be free to bring skilled labour of their own country. In such a situation, a significant part of earnings may go back to foreign countries in the form of dividends and profits. Now, it is clear that in the process of Globalization only those can compete in material market as well as global market who can produce and deliver goods and services of high quanlity by making best use of the latest technology at competitive cost. It is based on Darwinian selection and survival of the fittest theory. Further more, Globalization leads to consumerism.

On the other hand, Globalization will lead the developing countries to cut-throat foreign competition which will weaken their political, social and economic independence. Multinationals might be in position to manipulate things to their advantage which will prove detrimental to the interests of the poor nations. It has further been criticised that globalization which implies consumerism of western type, has actually led to nation to a higher priority for luxury cars over mass transport and five star hotels over the low-cost indigenous housing. Moreover, in a country like India, where there is a high income inequality and huge sum of unaccounted money in the hands of a few people it is very difficult to control imports by a devaluation accompanied by import liberalisation. In the words of J.D.Sethi that Indian liberalisation is at the wrong time and from the wrong end.

In Conclusion the FDI flows to developing countries showed a sharp rise during 1990s and emerged as an important instrument of global integration since the 1980s. This reflects the growing recognition of the role of FDI in the development process. The surge in FDI flows has been facilitated to a great extent by the changes in the policy environment in many developing countries.

Our approach to WTO and agriculture is based on the conviction that the emerging world trade regime is both a challenge and opportunity for India. There is no gain saying the fact that the liberalization of world trade in agriculture has opened up new vistas of growth.

REFERENCES

Russi Mody, (1992), "Globalization Efforts with Accent in Export" The Economic Times, April 21.

Choossudovsky, Michel (1997), Economic Reforms and in Developing Countries, Economic and Political Weekly, July 19th , p. 1786-87.

Oxfam. International; (2002).

Barnet, A . (2001), 'Revealed: How Britan's Richest Man Takes a Pound 3 Million tax Hand-out', The Observer, May 20.

The Hindu : New waves of Globalization and its Economic Effects.

Venkata Ramani, G. (1994), "Good years of Foodgrains", The Hindu Survey, p. 5.

Thiru Venkatachari, K. (1992), "On Globalization", Economic and Social Science Review, Vol. 1, No. 2, pp. 67-71.

Kurien, C.T. (1993), Indian Economic Reforms in the Context of Emerging Global Economy–Economic and Political Weekly, 10th April.

Malcom S. Adiseshaiah (1992), "Globalization of the Economy " Indian Association of Social Science Institution (IASSI), Vol. II, No. 1.

Pradhan, S. (2000), Foreign Direct Investment—Risk, Return and Host Country's Strategy, *Journal of Management Research*, September–December, pp. 18-30.

A COMPARATIVE STUDY OF GROWTH PATTERN IN INDIA AND CHINA: A REVIEW

Md. Abdus Salam

The attainment of sustained high economic growth is a necessary condition for improving the quality of life of the people throughout the country. China and India both the countries are undergoing through economic transitions during last many years. The central objective of transition through economic liberalization is to improve the competitive efficiency of the economy in the global market to sustain accelerated rates of economic growth and thereby continuously improve welfares of the people. India launched its market-oriented economic reforms in 1991. China launched similar reforms from 1978 and is now well ahead of India in integrating its national economy with the global economy. The contrast in the experiences of these two countries with economic reforms under different political systems with sharp inter-party differences on many issues is remarkable. This paper tries to make a comparative study of growth pattern in India and China during post reforms periods of both the countries. For this Some Important Indicators of economic and social development like GDP, life expectancy, literacy rates, the proportion of population employed in different sectors etc. are being used to characterize the difference between the two countries.

THE PERFORMANCE OF THE INDIAN ECONOMY

Two-thirds of India's population work in agriculture and agriculture, forestry and fishing accounts for around 25% of GDP. The paradox of the problem of the country is that the majority of farming families live below the poverty line. A policy of import substitution in the decades after independence encouraged the development of a broad industrial base. But a lack of competition contributed to poor product quality and inefficiencies in production. India in its more than fifty-seven years of independence has waged a long battle against hunger and poverty. To remedy this situation, India's economy went through several episodes of economic liberalization in the 1970s and the 1980s under Prime Ministers Indira Gandhi and, later, Rajiv Gandhi. However, these attempts at economic liberalization were halfhearted, and often self-reversing in parts. India suffered a major economic crisis in 1991, due largely to the effects of oil price shocks (resulting from the 1990 Gulf War), the collapse of the Soviet Union (a major trading partner and source of foreign aid), and sharp depletion of its foreign exchange reserves .The economic crisis led India to implement a number of economic reforms, including cut in the budget deficit, sharp cuts in tariff barriers, liberalization of FDI rules, exchange rate and banking reforms, and dismantling of the industrial licensing system etc. The principal aims of Industrial reform process were (I) the removal of capacity controls by "dereserving" and "delicencing" industries, or abolishing the requirement to obtain a license to create new capacity or substantially expand existing capacity; (ii) the dilution of provisions of the MRTP Act, so as to facilitate the expansion and diversification of large firms or firms belonging to the big business groups and (iii) foreign investment regulation. The thrust of the reforms in all areas has been to open India's markets to international competition, remove exchange rate controls, and encourage private investment and participation in industry and the finance markets. Several sectors have now been opened up to foreign participation under India's liberalizing reform programme, contributing to a significant expansion in the production of durable consumer goods, including cars, scooters, consumer electronics and computer systems. Services have proved India's most dynamic sector in last few years, registering rapid growth in telecom and information technology (IT). Services like airlines, banks and construction etc. accounted for over 48% of GDP in 2002. The major structural reforms carried out by several state governments include: (i) Measures to improve quality of life through improvements in basic public services such as primary health, primary education, and rural infrastructure services such as electricity, water, and roads. (ii) Clustering high-tech industries and services (for example, in software parks). (iii) Setting up Special Economic Zones and Agric-Economic Zones to promote exports. (iv) Formulating state-level industrial policies to attract investments. (v) Power-sector reforms that restructure state Electricity Boards by separating generation, transmission and distribution activities, encouraging independent power producers in the private sector to invest in the power sector, and setting up independent state Electricity Regulatory Authorities.

However, the most notable weakness of the reform process has been in fiscal consolidation. Indian governments at both the central and state levels have failed miserably to reign in growing revenue deficits and reduce the overall fiscal deficit. The foundations for a sustainable high growth rate in any economy lie in maintaining fiscal discipline. Indian policymakers have not adequately achieved this. The structure of revenue expenditure and political obstacles to any reduction of subsidies and downsizing the government at all levels has been primarily responsible for the lack of progress on fiscal reforms. India's record on social development expenditure has been poor considering Indian requirements and poor also in relation to many developing countries. India has some of the lowest human development indicators in the world, particularly in rural areas. At the other end of the scale, India also has a large number of highly qualified professionals, as well as several internationally established industrial groups. As according to Prof. Ahluwalia larger investment in the social sectors is 'necessary not only because social development is an end in itself, but also as a precondition of accelerating growth'. Therefore, there is a need to turn the pattern of government expenditure in favour of social sectors and infrastructure on the priority basis.

THE PERFORMANCE OF THE CHINESE ECONOMY

China had introduced market-oriented reforms in 1978 that is a decade earlier than India. As a consequence during the 1980s, industrial and agricultural output in China grew by an average 10 per cent per year. Between 1982 and 1990, per capita income tripled and by 2002, it had grown by about 40 per cent. China now accounts for about 4 per cent of the world's economic output. Exports of China rose by about 35 per cent in 2003,Imports were up by 40 per cent in the same period. Trade contributes an estimated 40 per cent to China's GDP. In 2003, the Chinese economy was the sixth largest in the world, at $5.989 trillion. The power behind the growth of Chinese economy is manufacturing, which provides more than half of China's GDP and is expanding by more than 12 per cent per year, on average; in 2003, industrial production rose by 16 per cent. Heavy industries such as steel and chemicals are a mainstay of the Chinese economy. Wages that average only $0.60 per hour have made China the low-cost producer in fields from textiles to telecommunications auto parts. This has also attracted large-scale investment from foreign companies to cash in on cheap labor. In 2002, foreign direct investment in China reached at an estimated $52.7 billion. Trade contributes an estimated 40 per cent to China's GDP. Economic growth has allowed China to emerge as one of the most growing economies of the world.

INDIA AND CHINA: A COMPARISON

China and India both are going through economic transitions. Fundamental concerns in India include the massive overpopulation, poverty, unemployment and environmental degradation. India's economy has shown relatively healthy growth since 1991 when an economic crisis caused the government to implement various economic reforms. China launched similar reforms from 1978 and is now well ahead of India in integrating its national economy with the global economy. However, India is slowly but steadily competing in this race. China and India are similar in relative population size and affluence. In 2001 China had a population of 1.276 billion and a GDP per capita of US$909, while India's population was 1.029 Billion and GDP per capita US$496. According to H. E. Mr. Robert D Blackwill (2002), the two countries china and India launched their economic reform programs from different historical experiences. Nonetheless, the fact remains that in the last 10 years, China has forged ahead on most economic measures. He has examined the economies of India and China respectively with the following statistics:

1. Over the last 20 years, China's GDP has grown at about 10% a year, compared with India's 6% growth rate.

2. A decade ago, India and China had close to the same per-capita income. Today China's per-capita income is about $900, roughly twice that of India.
3. In 1991, China produced 670 billion kilowatt hours of electricity, India 290 billion. In 2001, China's production was 1.14 trillion kilowatt hours while India's was about 450 billion.
4. In 1991, China's receipts from tourism were $2.8 billion. This had grown to $14.10 billion by 2001. The comparative figures for India were $1.4 billion in 1991, and $3.04 billion ten years later.
5. In 1991, India and China started off from about the same base, with less than one computer for every thousand individuals. By 2000 China's rate is three times India's, with more than 15 computers for every thousand persons, compared to 4.5 in India.
6. In 1990, manufacturing in China was about 37% of the economy; today that relative weight has increased to about 45%. China now produces 50 % of the world's cameras, 30 % of the air conditions and televisions, 25 % of the washing machines and 20 % of the refrigerators. In the last 12 years, manufacturing as a percentage of the Indian economy has decreased, falling to about 24% of the economy from 30%.
7. China's trade in goods and services as a percentage of GDP grew for 35% in 1991 to 49% in 2000. During the same period, India's percentage rose from 18% to 30%.
8. Since 1980, China has welcomed over $336 billion in foreign investment; India has received only $18 billion.
9. In 1990, China's exports were $62 billion, which were three-and-a-half times greater than India's. Today China's annual exports are over $266 billion, and the comparative gap has widened to over five-and-a-half times India's current exports.
10. And we all know what an enormous investment China is putting into its domestic infrastructure-airports, roads, port facilities, telecommunications, and so forth.

Many studies reveal that India's economy has failed to live up to its potential, especially relative to other developing countries like China, which has a comparable population size, but has enjoyed far greater economic development. The relative position of China and India in different fields is reflected in Table 1. As Table 1 indicates that both (down loaded from website: http://fpc.state.gov/documents/organization/23389.pdf) India and China experienced significant growth in population, GDP and per capita GDP (both measured on a PPP basis), exports, imports, and FDI during post reform periods. But on almost all the economic fronts, India lost significant ground to China. In 1990, India's economy (GDP, PPP basis) was about three-quarters the size of China's, but by 2002 it was less than half. India's living standards (per capita GDP, PPP basis) was slightly greater than China's in 1990, but by 2002 it had fallen to 55.5% of China's. India's exports relative to Chinese exports fell from 28.9% in 1990 to 15.7% in2002, while imports dropped from 55.3% to

19.8%. India made small gains in FDI flows relative to China over this period (rising from 2.3% to 5.9%), however, the total level of FDI stock in China was substantially higher than that going to India in both periods. In fact, FDI flows to China in 2002 alone (nearly $45 billion) were approaching the twice of the cumulative stock of FDI in India through 2002 ($26 billion). Many economists attribute the sharp widening economic gaps between India and China to differences in the pace and scope of economic and trade reforms undertaken by each country, where China has substantially reformed its trade and investment regimes (which has contributed to sharp rises in GDP growth, trade, and FDI flows), India's economic reforms have been far less comprehensive and effective. In the post reform periods the GDP growth rate of China was maintained at a pace that made for a wide gap with India's. In 1952, China's population was 57 per cent higher than India's. In the 1990s it was just 28 per cent higher. At present, China's population is growing at 0.57per cent while India's population is expanding at 1.44 per cent. At this rate, India's population will overtake China's by 2025. An editorial of The Hindu (December 8,2004) highlighted that "despite the fairly high Gross Domestic Product growth over the past decade, India has not been able to mobilize anything like the kind of FDI or domestic investment needed to build world-class infrastructure. FDI annual inflow into India has touched $4.7 billion. For an economy of India's size, given the huge investment requirements in core areas such as telecommunications, highways, power, mining, airports and seaports, this is still minor league considering the stunning achievement of China. It has been able, in recent years, to attract FDI to the extent of $50 billion a year. Despite India's political diversity and sharp inter-party differences on certain issues, the Centre and the States need to work in tandem to create attractive investment destinations. With private investment, domestic or foreign, tolls will become the order of the day. Many States feel this will be unpopular. Some States, notably in the west and south of the country, have done very well in developing infrastructure and attracting FDI. But all this is only a fraction of what is needed to achieve Chinese-type rapid industrial expansion,

Table 1
Selected Comparative Data for India and China: 1990-2002

	India		*China*		*India's Size Relative to China*	
	1990	*2002*	*1990*	*2002*	*1990*	*2002*
Population (millions)	850	1046	1139	1284	74.6%	81.5%
GDP, PPP basis ($ billions)	1189	2732	1583	6032	75.1%	45.3%
Per Capita GDP in $PPPs	1400	2610	1390	4700	100.1%	55.5%
Exports ($millions)	17975	46232	62090	293753	28.9%	15.7%
Imports ($millions)	23438	55035	42354	278151	55.3%	19.8%
FDI Stock ($millions)	1592	26255	68513	445287	2.3%	5.9%

Note: PPP refers to purchasing power parity. Such data reflect the purchasing power of foreign data in U.S. dollars.

Source: Economist Intelligence Unit.

Table 2
Selected Comparative Data for India and China

	CHINA	*INDIA*
Area:	Total: 9,596,960 sq km land: 9,326,410 sq km water: 270,550 sq km	Total: 3,287,590 sq km land: 2,973,190 sq km water: 314,400 sq km
Natural resources:	Coal, iron ore, petroleum, natural gas, mercury, tin, tungsten, antimony, manganese, molybdenum, vanadium, magnetite, aluminum, lead, zinc, uranium, hydropower potential (world's largest)	Coal (fourth-largest reserves in the world), iron ore, manganese, mica, bauxite, titanium ore, chromites, natural gas, diamonds, petroleum, limestone, arable land
Land use:	Arable land: 15.4% permanent crops: 1.25% other: 83.36% (2001)	Arable land: 54.4% permanent crops: 2.74% other: 42.86% (2001)
Irrigated land:	525,800 sq km (1998 est.)	590,000 sq km (1998 est.)
Environment-current issues:	Air pollution (greenhouse gases, sulfur dioxide particulates) from reliance on coal produces acid rain; water shortages, particularly in the north; water pollution from untreated wastes; deforestation; estimated loss of one-fifth of agricultural land since 1949 to soil erosion and economic development; desertification; trade in endangered species	Deforestation; soil erosion; overgrazing; desertification; air pollution from industrial effluents and vehicle emissions; water pollution from raw sewage and runoff of agricultural pesticides; tap water is not potable throughout the country; huge and growing population is overstraining natural resources
Environment-international agreements:	Party to: Antarctic-Environmental Protocol, Antarctic Treaty, Biodiversity, Climate Change, Climate Change-Kyoto Protocol, Desertification, Endangered Species, Hazardous Wastes, Law of the Sea, Marine Dumping, Ozone Layer Protection, Ship Pollution, Tropical Timber 83, Tropical Timber 94, Wetlands, Whaling signed, but not ratified: none of the selected agreements	Party to: Antarctic-Environmental Protocol, Antarctic-Marine Living Resources, Antarctic Treaty, Biodiversity, Climate Change, Climate Change-Kyoto Protocol, Desertification, Endangered Species, Environmental Modification, Hazardous Wastes, Law of the Sea, Ozone Layer Protection, Ship Pollution, Tropical Timber 83, Tropical Timber 94, Wetlands, Whaling signed, but not ratified: none of the selected agreements
Population:	1,298,847,624 (July 2004 est.)	1,065,070,607 (July 2004 est.)
Birth rate:	12.98 births/1,000 population (2004 est.)	22.8 births/1,000 population (2004 est.)
Death rate:	6.92 deaths/1,000 population (2004 est.)	8.38 deaths/1,000 population (2004 est.)
Infant mortality rate:	Total: 25.28 deaths/1,000 live births male: 21.84 deaths/ 1,000 live births live births female: 29.14 deaths/live births (2004 est.)	Total: 57.92 deaths/1,000 live births male: 58.52 deaths/ 1,000 female: 57.29 deaths/1,000 1,000 live births (2004 est.)

	CHINA	*INDIA*
Life expectancy at birth:	Total population: 71.96 years male: 70.4 years female: 73.72 years (2004 est.)	Total population: 63.99 years male: 63.25 years female: 64.77 years (2004 est.)
Literacy:	Definition: age 15 and over can read and write total population: 90.9% male: 95.1% female: 86.5% (2002)	Definition: age 15 and over can read and write total population: 59.5% male: 70.2% 48.3% female: (2003 est.)
GDP:	Purchasing power parity-$6.449 trillion (2003 est.)	Purchasing power parity-$3.033 trillion (2003 est.)
GDP-real growth rate:	9.1% (official data) (2003 est.)	8.3% (2003 est.)
GDP-per capita:	Purchasing power parity-$5,000 (2003 est.)	Purchasing power parity-$2,900 (2003 est.)
GDP-composition by sector:	Agriculture: 14.8% industry & construction: 52.9% services: 32.3% (2003)	Agriculture: 23.6% industry: 28.4% services: 48% (2002 est.)
Investment (gross fixed):	43.4% of GDP (2003)	23.1% of GDP (2003)
Population below poverty line:	10% (2001 est.)	25% (2002 est.)
Inflation rate (consumer prices):	1.2% (2003 est.)	3.8% (2003 est.)
Labor force:	778.1 million (2003 est.)	472 million (2003)
Labor force-by occupation:	Agriculture 50%, Industry 22%, Services 28% (2001 est.)	Agriculture 60%, Industry 17%, Services 23% (1999)
Public debt:	30.1% of GDP (2003)	59.7% of GDP (2003)
Agriculture-products:	Rice, wheat, potatoes, sorghum, peanuts, tea, millet, barley, cotton, oilseed, pork, fish	Rice, wheat, oilseed, cotton, jute, tea, sugarcane, potatoes; cattle, water buffalo, sheep, goats, poultry; fish
Industries:	Iron and steel, coal, machine building, armaments, textiles and apparel, petroleum, cement, chemical fertilizers, footwear, toys, food processing, automobiles, consumer electronics, telecommunications	Textiles, chemicals, food processing, steel, transportation equipment, cement, mining, petroleum, machinery, software
Industrial production growth rate:	30.4% (2003 est.)	6.5% (2003 est.)
Electricity-production:	1.42 trillion kwh (2001)	533.3 billion kwh (2001)

Contd....

	CHINA	*INDIA*
Electricity-consumption:	1.312 trillion kwh (2001)	497.2 billion kwh (2001)
Current account balance:	$31.17 billion (2003)	$3.41 billion (2003)
Exports:	$436.1 billion f.o.b. (2003 est.)	$57.24 billion f.o.b. (2003 est.)
Exports-commodities:	Machinery and equipment, textiles and clothing, footwear, toys and sporting goods, mineral fuels	Textile goods, gems and jewelry, engineering goods, chemicals, leather manufactures
Exports-partners:	US 21.1%, Hong Kong 17.4%, Japan 13.6%, South Korea 4.6%, Germany 4% (2003 est.)	US 20.3%, China 6.3%, UK 5.2%, Hong Kong 4.7%, Germany 4.3% (2003 est.)
Imports:	$397.4 billion f.o.b. (2003 est.)	$74.15 billion f.o.b. (2003 est.)
Imports-commodities:	Machinery and equipment, mineral fuels, plastics, iron and steel, chemicals	Crude oil, machinery, gems, fertilizer, chemicals
Imports-partners:	Japan 18%, Taiwan 11.9%, South Korea 10.4%, US 8.2%, Germany 5.9% (2003 est.)	US 6.7%, Belgium 5.9%, UK 5%, China 4.5%, Singapore 4.2% (2003 est.)
Reserves of foreign exchange & gold:	$412.7 billion (2003)	$102.3 billion (2003)
Debt-external:	$197.8 billion (2003 est.)	$101.7 billion (2003 est.)
Exchange rates:	Yuan per US dollar-8.277 (2003), 8.277 (2002), 8.2771 (2001), 8.2785 (2000), 8.2783 (1999)	Indian rupees per US dollar-46.5806 (2003), 48.6103 (2002), 47.1864 (2001), 44.9416 (2000), 43.0554 (1999)

world-class infrastructure development, increased trade, and higher levels of growth. Prime Minister Manmohan Singh's target of securing $150 billion FDI in 10 years is not beyond reach but it asks for tremendous work from the system." The Global Competitiveness Report 2003-04 of the *World Economic Forum* has ranked India several notches above China. In the Business Competitiveness Index (BCI), India's rank is 37 out of 102 countries as against China's 46. The BCI is an index of a country's micro-fundamentals and focuses on the quality of the business environment as well as the sophistication of companies in the country. India is the world's top-ranked country when it comes to the presence of a large number of competitive firms. On the availability of engineers and scientists, it is third in the rankings, and No 6 in terms of its policy on allowing foreign technology. Both India and China, however, have slipped on the Growth Competitiveness Index—which measures the long-term sustainability of growth. The reason for the fall in India's case, is a very sharp deterioration in the Macroeconomic Environment Index—India's ranking fell from 18 in 2002 to 52 in 2003. India's economy has also successfully moved into a higher trajectory of growth and displayed strong dynamism in selected sectors. This encouraging performance brightens the prospects for stepping up India's growth rate and improving the competitive edge in the years to come through further appropriate economic reforms. Local manufacturers are learning to innovate and compete globally, and the middle class is expanding. India's foreign-exchange reserves have reached about $130 billion. But this is not a lot compared with China's $403 billion. From table 2 and graphs from1 to 3,which are drawn with the help of table 2,in a nutshell, it can be observed that China is relatively in a much better position than India. However, given the comparative advantage of a skilled workforce available at low costs, backed by huge foreign exchange reserves India has a potential to compete in the world economy.

Graph 1

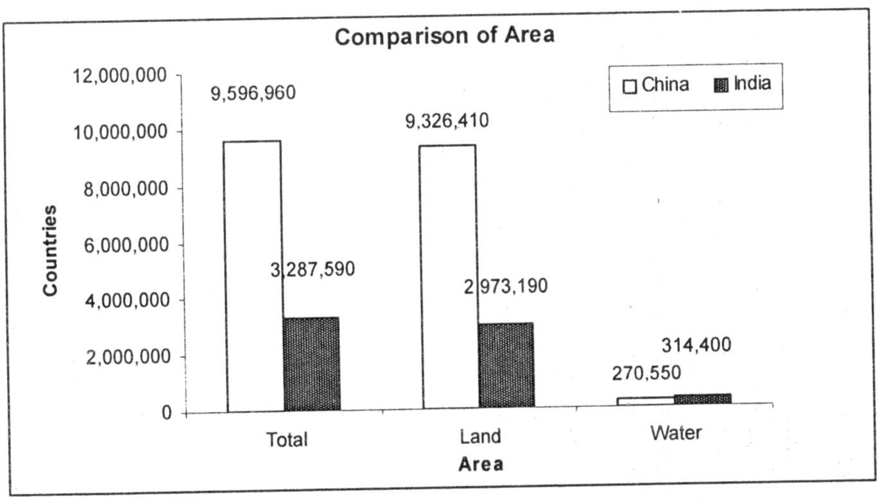

Graph 2

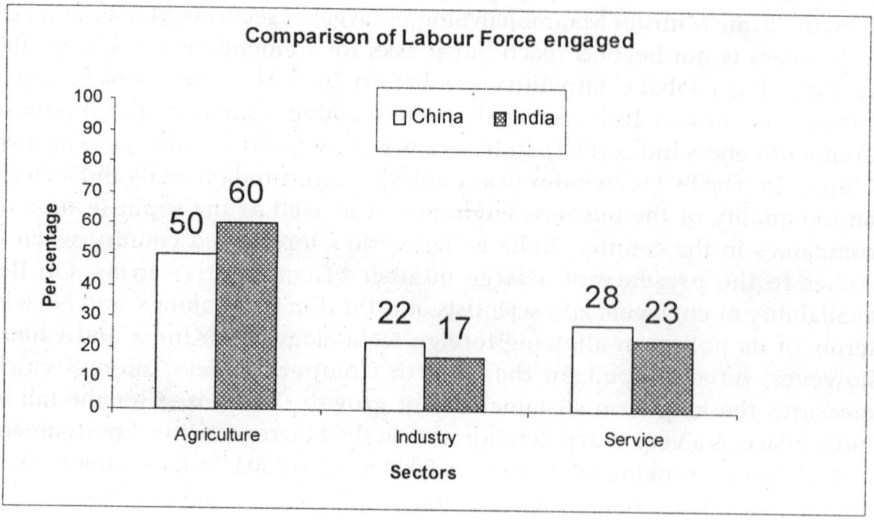

Graph 3

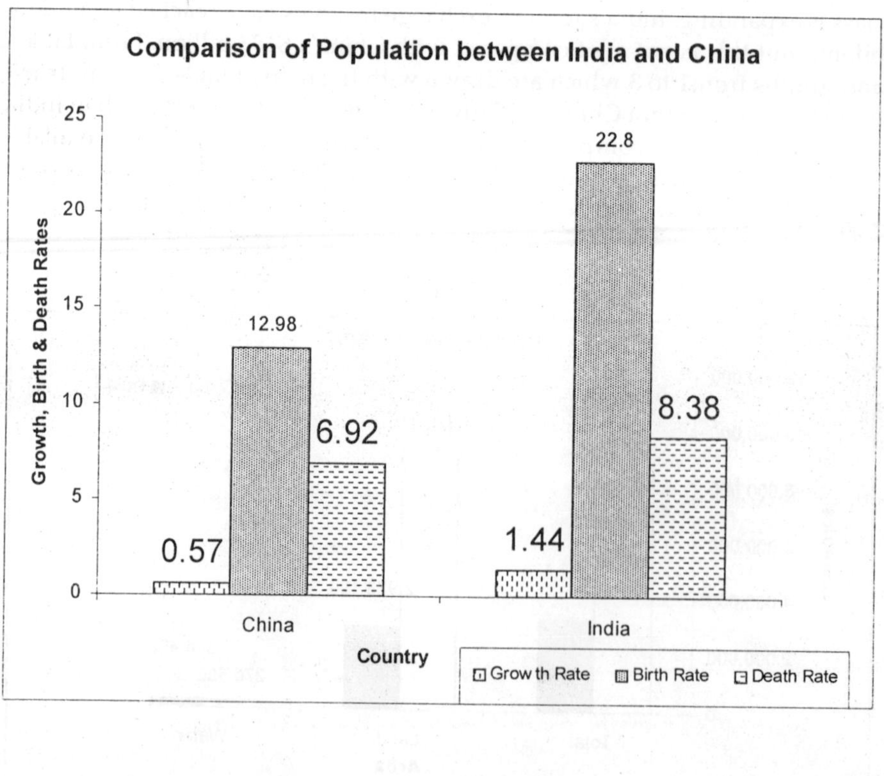

CONCLUSIONS

The major structural economic reforms carried out since 1991 have been primarily in the areas of Trade, Industry, Infrastructure, Finance, and Foreign Direct Investment etc. Through reform, India overcame its worst economic crisis. In post economic reforms, where the dismantling of the industrial licensing system, free investments by foreign companies, lowering of import tariffs on capital goods all contributed to the gross national product (GNP) to improve from an average of about 5.7 per cent in the 1980s to an average of about 6.5 per cent in the Eighth and Ninth Plan periods. It makes India one of the ten fastest growing developing countries. Literacy increased from 52 per cent in 1991 to 65 per cent in 2001. Software services, entertainment and information technology-enabled services emerged as new sources of strength, creating confidence about India's potential to be competitive in the world economy. The share of India's trade as proportion of GDP rose from 13.1 per cent in 1990 to 20.3 per cent in 2000. India's growing middle class of more than 350 million people, with a reasonably affluent standard of living, provides a huge market for foreign corporations, especially since April 2003, when all quantitative restrictions on imports were lifted. Along with its fairly good growth rate (which is far below the potential growth rate of eight per cent targeted by India's Tenth Five-Year Plan), India has been successful in reducing poverty. The poverty ratio that is people below the poverty line as a percentage of the population as estimated by the Planning Commission at the national level came down from 36 per cent in 1993-94 to 26.1 per cent in 1999-2000. The poverty ratio during this period declined both in rural areas and in urban areas. The Planning Commission has set a poverty ratio target of 19.3 per cent by the end of the Tenth Plan period (to March 2007). An important indicator of gains from economic reforms, reflecting the attractiveness of India as an investment destination, is shown by the increasing inflows of both FDI and Foreign Institutional Investment (FII) into India. Several measures to boost FDI have been taken. Projects for electricity generation, transmission and distribution as also roads and highways, ports and harbors, and vehicular tunnels and bridges have been permitted foreign equity participation up to 100 per cent. India's economy clearly is on the move and most certainly has the potential to emerge as a global economic power in near future. But, despite the above all progress in the economy India is still far away from china. Investment as a proportion of GDP is low in India compared with what it is in China even though the requirement is higher, particularly for infrastructure. The bottleneck to infrastructure investments is not a shortage of funds but a lack of clarity on regulatory issues.

In order to achieve the objective of transforming the economy into global economic power in near future as well as to compete with Chinese economy, the need of the hour is that India must accelerate spending on physical and human infrastructure, raise investment in agriculture in the areas like irrigation; watershed development; rural infrastructure; drinking water; housing and sanitation etc. promote information technology, make efforts to substantially liberalise trade and investment and lastly but not the least eliminate corruption from the economy. Therefore, future Indian economic policies drastically redesigned in the light of Security, Sincerity, Nationality, Accountability, Productivity and Profitability (SSNAPP).

REFERENCES

Abhijit Roy (2003), India set to Rank third by 2040, The Hindu, Dec. 29.

Chandrasekhar, C.P. and Jayati Ghosh (1999), "Financial Crises and Elusive Recovery: Lessons from Thailand and South Korea, Economic and Political Weekly, February.

Government of India, *Export Import Policy 2002-07*, New Delhi: Ministry of Commerce 2002.

Government of India, *Tenth Five Year Plan 2002-07* (in three volumes) (New Delhi: Planning Commission, 2002).

Ghosh, Jayati (1997), "India's Structural Adjustment: An Assessment in Comparative Asian Context", Economic and Political Weekly, May.

Ghosh, Jayati, Abhijit Sen and C. P. Chandrasekhar (1996), "Southeast Asian Economies: Miracle or Meltdown?" Economic and Political Weekly, October.

http://hrd.undp.org

http://www.bisnetworld.net/bisnet/index.htm

http://populationcommission.nic.in/cont-en1.htm

http://economist.com/countries/India/profile.cfm?folder=Profile-Economic % 20 Structure.

http://www.countrywatch.com/cw_country.asp? Vcountry=37

http://www.ucalgary.ca/~sici/2004shastri/PDF/Environment_policyconsultation.pdf

http://www.ilo.org/public/english/employment/strat/publ/etp55.htm

http://www.adb.org/Documents/Books/Key_Indicators/2004/default.asp

http://www.adb.org/Documents/Books/Key_Indicators/2004/pdf/IND.pdf

Jean Dreze and Amartya Sen (1995), *India: Economic Development and Social Opportunities,* (New Delhi :Oxford University Press).

Krugman, P. (1994), "The myth of Asia's miracle", Foreign Affairs, Vol. 73, No. 6 November/December).

Little, I.M.D., T. Scitovsky and M.F.G. Scott (1970), Industry and Trade in Some Developing Countries: A Comparative Study, OUP for the Development Centre of the OECD.

Ozler B., Datt G. and Ravallion M. (1996), "A Database on Poverty and Growth in India", World Bank, January.

Patnaik, P. and C.P. Chandrasekhar (1996), *Investment, Exports and Growth: A Cross-Country Analysis,* Economic and Political Weekly, Vol. XXXI, No. 1, January.

Special Address by H.E. Mr. Robert D. Black will, US Ambassador to India on "Doing Business With India" October 29, 2002, New Delhi.

Sen A. and Patnaik U. (1997), "Poverty in India", CESP Working Paper, JNU, Delhi.

Singh, Ajit (1995), *How Did East Asia Grow So Fast? Slow Progress Towards an Analytical Consensus,* UNCTAD Discussion Paper, No. 97, February.

World Trade Organization (1997), Annual Report, Volumes 1 & 2, Geneva: WTO.

Young, A. (1994), *Lessons from the East Asian NICs: A Contrarian View*, European Economic Review, Vo. 38, No. 3/4 (April).

http://fpc.state.gov/documents/organization/23389.pdf

INDIA'S TRADE WITH SOUTH EAST ASIA

M. Bhanumathi

INTRODUCTION

India's foreign trade took a westward orientation during the colonial period. The British rulers looked at India, as indeed at all their colonies, as a source of raw materials for the growing industries in their country and as a captive market for their manufactured products. Things started changing after independence. Diversification of trade and also significant changes in the commodity composition of trade started taking place. The UK, which accounted for the bulk of its trade before independence, today accounts for no more than 5% of India's exports and 4% of its imports. Trade is spread over a large number of countries, with no country accounting for more than 18% share. Likewise, dramatic changes have taken place in the commodity composition of the country's trade. At the time of independence, roughly 75% of the country's exports consisted of agricultural commodities and industrial raw materials but today manufactured goods account for nearly 80% of its exports.

The above transformation, which is largely due to deliberate policy measures adopted in the last 50 years, is commendable indeed. But a great disappointment is that India's share in world trade plummeted during this period: from more than 2% in 1947, the country's share in world trade slipped steadily, standing at 0.8% today. The simple message from this is that the growth rate of India's exports has been far below that of most other countries during this period. Due to a variety of reasons including its inward-looking economic policies, India failed to make use of the growth opportunities provided by the burgeoning world trade.

The year 1990 marked a watershed in Indian economic policy. As part of the process of economic liberalization and integration with the world economy, India started adopting policy measures and action plans to raise its share of world trade. The current Foreign Trade Policy aims at doubling India's share in global trade to 1.5% by the year 2009. One of the several government initiatives formulated in 1991 for the purpose of achieving this goal is the Look East Policy which aims at enhancing the country's diplomatic, cultural, economic and trade relations with the countries of South East Asia. These countries in our backyard have seen remarkable growths in economy and trade in recent decades and could have provided us with vast opportunities for exchange of goods and services, The Look East Policy, however, is a highly potent instrument for growth in India's foreign trade, though late in coming.

This paper attempts to assess India's trade with seven of the countries which are classified by Asian Development Bank as South East Asian: Indonesia, Malaysia, Singapore, Thailand, Myanmar, Philippines and Vietnam. As our trade with Laos and Cambodia is very small, these two countries have been omitted.

ECONOMIC PROFILES OF THE COUNTRIES

It is necessary to understand the structure and growth of the economies of these countries, in order to appreciate their potential as India's trade partners. (Table-1)

Of the seven countries in the list, one (Singapore) belongs to High Income Group, another (Malaysia) belongs to Upper Middle Income Group, two (Thailand and Philippines) belong to Lower Middle Income Group and remaining three (Indonesia, Myanmar and Vietnam) are Low Income countries, the category to which India belongs.

Table 1
Population and GDP

Country	*Population in Millions (Year: 2001)*	*Total GDP in PPPD (Year: 2001)*	*GDP Per Capita in PPPD (Year: 2002)*
Indonesia	209	591	2830
Malaysia	24	188	7910
Singapore	04	94	22850
Thailand	61	381	6230
Myanmar	48	NA	NA
Philippines	78	319	4070
Vietnam	80	164	2070
India (for comparison)	1032	2913	2820

Source: World Bank World Development Indicators 2003.

Structure of Economy

As may be seen from Table-2 with the exception of Singapore in which service sector dominates and Myanmar which, because of its closed economy, continues to remain a predominantly agricultural country, all the others are fast industrializing their economies.

The decline in the share of agriculture and the increase in the share of industry and services may be noted.

International Trade

The decade beginning with 1990 showed a remarkable expansion of foreign trade of these seven countries, all of them with few exceptions showing growth rates much above the world average, partly reflecting their liberalized economic and trade policies. Table-3 illustrates the point.

Table 2
Contribution to GDP, Per cent

Country	*Agriculture*		*Industry*		*Manufacturing*		*Services*	
	1990	*2001*	*1990*	*2001*	*1990*	*2001*	*1990*	*2001*
Indonesia	20	16	38	47	18	26	42	37
Malaysia	15	9	42	49	24	31	43	42
Singapore	0	0	34	32	27	23	65	68
Thailand	12	10	37	40	27	32	50	49
Myanmar	57	57	11	10	8	7	32	33
Philippines	22	15	34	31	25	22	44	54
Vietnam	39	24	23	38	12	20	39	39
India (for comparison)	31	25	28	26	17	16	41	48

Source: World Bank World Development Indicators, 2003.

Table 3
Annual Average Percentage Growth

Country	*Export Trade*		*Import Trade*	
	1980-1990	*1990-2000*	*1980-1990*	*1990-2000*
Indonesia	-0.9	8.1	2.6	2.7
Malaysia	8.6	12.2	7.7	9.5
Singapore	9.9	9.9	8.0	7.8
Thailand	14.0	10.5	12.7	5.0
Myanmar	-7.6	14.4	-4.7	22.6
Philippines	3.9	18.8	2.9	12.0
Vietnam	NA	NA	NA	NA
India (for comparison)	7.3	9.5	4.2	10.1

Source: World Bank World Development Indicators, 2003.

Integration with World Economy

The indicators given in Table-4 go to demonstrate the high level of integration of the national economies with the global economy.

Table 4
Integration With Global Economy

Country	*Trade in goods as % of GDP*		*Gross foreign direct investment as % of GDP*	
	1990	*2001*	*1990*	*2001*
Indonesia	41.5	60.1	1.0	3.2
Malaysia	133.4	184.0	5.3	5.6
Singapore	309.5	277.6	20.7	22.0
Thailand	65.7	110.9	3.0	3.5
Myanmar	NA	NA	NA	NA
Philippines	47.7	88.9	1.2	2.7
Vietnam	5.1	36.4	1.7	3.1
India (for comparison)	13.1	19.5	0.0	0.6

Source: World Bank World Development Indicators, 2003.

It needs to be noted that the rates of growth in both foreign trade and foreign direct investment of the South East Asian countries far outstripped those of India, whose own performance has not been insubstantial during this period.

Direction of Trade

Between 1990 and 2002, very significant changes took place in the direction of exports of the seven countries under study. The most significant changes were: (a) reflecting their own growing manufacturing industry and the pull of the great manufacturing power house that is China, every one of these countries registered a remarkable growth in exports to China; (b) Japan as an export destination showed a marked decline in importance; (c) exports to Developing Member Countries (of Asian Development Bank) showed impressive gains. The USA and EU, the traditionally important export destinations for these countries were losing their importance, the exports of the major exporters of this group of seven countries (Singapore, Malaysia and Thailand) registering decline. Table-5 shows the destination-wise export share of the seven countries to the different destinations, illustrating the above points.

Table 5
Direction of Exports (% of Total)

Country	*DMCs**		*China*		*Japan*		*USA*		*EU*	
	1990	*2002*	*1990*	*2002*	*1990*	*2002*	*1990*	*2002*	*1990*	*2002*
Indonesia	18.4	30.3	3.2	5.1	42.5	21.1	13.1	13.2	12.0	13.9
Malaysia	40.0	37.8	2.1	5.6	15.3	11.3	16.9	20.2	15.4	12.4
Singapore	34.7	43.9	1.5	5.5	8.8	7.1	21.3	15.3	15.0	12.5
Thailand	19.3	28.7	1.2	5.2	17.2	14.5	22.7	19.6	22.7	14.8
Myanmar	49.0	50.5	8.1	4.8	6.9	3.8	2.3	13.2	6.9	13.8
Philippines	14.2	26.5	0.8	3.9	19.8	15.0	37.9	24.7	18.5	18.1
Vietnam	25.3	18.0	0.3	6.4	13.5	14.6	0.0	14.9	6.8	24.2
India (for comparison)	11.3	16.4	0.1	4.2	9.3	3.8	15.1	22.9	27.7	22.9

Source: Asian Development Bank Outlook 2004.
*DMCs stands for Developing Member Countries of ADB.

It may also be seen from the table that India has slightly increased its share of exports to the Developing Member Countries of ADB. Its performance with the South East Asian countries under study will be dealt with in a later section of this paper.

Conclusions from Part II

The presentation made above in this part of the paper clearly establish that:

- the economies of the group of seven countries under study have undergone much liberalization and increased degree of integration with the global economy;
- the foreign trade of the countries in question have not only grown at a vigorous rate but also have undergone significant changes in their composition and direction;

- trade with China has registered an impressive rise, reflecting perhaps the role of many of the countries under study as suppliers of components or parts to the manufacturing industries of China.(The Economist, 2-8 October, 2004)

INDIA'S TRADE POLICY TOWARDS AND VOLUME OF TRADE WITH SOUTH EAST ASIA

Till the beginning of the last decade, India's efforts to promote its foreign trade were focused on the west, mainly Europe and the USA. Even the diversion of markets was taking place mainly in these regions. Historical connections were an important reason for this. Besides, it was these regions which were able to meet the capital goods and technology requirements of India during the period of its rapid industrialization. The external trade of the South East Asian countries were also west-oriented, again mainly due to historical reasons, with the possible exception of Singapore which has all along been a major centre of entrepot trade. Six of the seven countries were colonies of European powers. The only country which did not come under any colonial power was Thailand.

Myanmar was a province of British India till its independence in 1948. The present Malaysia was a British colony from 1794 until 1948. Vietnam was a French colony for long. Indonesia was ruled by the Dutch from 1816 to 1945. And Philippines, which carries the name of the Spanish King Philip, was a Spanish colony till it was transferred in 1898 following the Spanish-American war to the US who ruled it till its independence in 1946. It was towards the end of the 1970s that the countries in the region started organizing for increasing economic co-operation among themselves. The conclusion of Preferential Trading Agreement (PTA) among the ASEAN members in 1979 was a major step in this direction.

It was not until 1992 that India established special relationship with the ASEAN. In that year India was accepted by ASEAN as a Special Dialogue Partner in the trade, investment, tourism and science and technology sectors. The position got upgraded in the year 1996. In July, 1996 India was admitted as a member of the ASEAN Regional Forum which is concerned with matters relating to security. A milestone in relations with ASEAN was reached when India-ASEAN summit meeting was held in Phnom Penh in November, 2002. The relationship was taken a step higher with the signing of a Framework Agreement on Establishment of Free Trade Agreement between ASEAN and India at the second ASEAN-India summit held in October, 2003 in Bali, Indonesia. The agreement envisages liberalization of trade in gradual stages, culminating in the establishment of free trade by the year 2012. India also committed to aligning its peak tariffs to East Asian levels by 2005.

Simultaneously India is engaged in upgrading its trade relations with selected members of the ASEAN on a one-to-one basis. A Framework Agreement for creation of a Free Trade Area between India and Thailand was signed in October, 2003. In terms of this agreement India agreed to reduce its import duties by 50 % by April, 2004 on a Early Harvest List of 84 items.

Negotiations for concluding a Comprehensive Economic Co-operation Agreement with Singapore are underway.

India has taken several other initiatives to deepen its economic relations with countries in the region. These include the Mekong-Ganga Co-operation and BIMST-EC, which provides the framework for cooperation between India and five South East Asian countries, viz., Bangladesh, Indonesia, Myanmar, Sri Lanka and Thailand.

The policy measures and new initiatives taken by India have resulted in a significant increase in the two-way trade between India and the seven countries in question. The values of merchandise trade over the period 1991-92 and 2003-04 with each of the seven countries, year wise, are given in the tables given in Annexure-I to this paper. The graphs illustrate the trends.

It may be noted from the above that both India's exports to each of the seven countries and imports from each of them registered an impressive increase between 1991-92 and 2003-04, although the rising trend was interrupted in varying degrees in the three years starting with 1998-99. These were the years of the South East Asian financial crisis which had a severe impact especially on Indonesia, Malaysia, Singapore and Thailand. The two-way trade crossed US$ 4 billion in the case of Singapore, US$ 3 billion in the case of Indonesia and Malaysia and US$ 1.5 billion in the case of Thailand. Trade with the remaining four countries, with whom the trade was negligible in 1990-91, has also grown significantly.

The list of major commodities exchanged is given below.

Exports from India:	Imports into India:
Gems and Jewellery	Vegetable oils
Iron and Steel	Electronic goods
Oil meals	Wood and wood products
Electronic goods	Organic chemicals
Drugs and pharmaceuticals	Transport equipments
Dyes	Non-electrical machinery
Manmade yarn and fabrics	Pulses
Other metals	Ores and metal scraps
Inorganic, organic and agro chemicals	Coal

PROBLEMS AND PROSPECTS

In assessing the performance of India's trade with South East Asia in general and with the seven countries under study in particular, the stupendous difficulties faced by India should be borne in mind. Till the 1980's, apathy was mutual. For the South East Asian countries, India was a difficult country because of its slow pace of economic reforms, lack of consistency in policies, indecisive and lethargic bureaucracy and a high level of corruption. As far as India was concerned, the fast pace of globalization and economic liberalization in the ASEAN group of countries were not something suited to India. The validity of this view was demonstrated by the devastating financial crisis which gripped many of the ASEAN and some other Far Eastern countries in the late 1990's. As a result, trade and other economic exchanges between the two sides were far below potential.

The tariff differential between India and the seven South East Asian countries was too wide to facilitate growth in trade. The Table-6 illustrates the point.

Table 6
The Tariff Differential Between India and The South East Asian Countries

Country	*Year*	*All Products*	*Primary Products*	*Manufactured Products*
Indonesia	1989	13.2	59.	15.1
	2000	5.4	2.8	6.6
Malaysia	1988	9.9	4.6	10.8
	1997	5.8	10.0	5.5
Singapore	1989	0.5	2.5	0.6
	2001	0.0	0.0	0.0
Thailand	1989	33.0	24.3	34.9
	2000	9.7	7.7	10.1
Myanmar	-	NA	NA	NA
	-	NA	NA	NA
Philippines	1988	22.4	18.5	23.4
	2001	4.0	5.9	3.4
Vietnam	1994	18.4	46.5	12.9
	2001	15.1	21.7	9.3
India	1990	56.2	25.4	70.8
	2001	28.2	28.5	29.0

Source: World Bank, World Development Indicators, 2003.

The difficulties involved in India establishing free trade arrangement with the ASEAN can be easily imagined. Bringing down the duties to the level of ASEAN has serious implications for Indian economy in general and the manufacturing sector in particular. Even the reduction of tariffs by 50% on a selected list of 84 items under the Framework Agreement with Thailand in the current financial year has led to vociferous protests from Indian manufacturers of automobiles components and parts. They apprehend that, because of the very low duties on raw materials, the auto component manufacturers in Thailand will enjoy advantages to such an extent that Thailand will turn out to be the low-cost base for Indian automobile manufacturers and others to import both components and finished products like steering assemblies. (Tom Yam Swamp by Arindan Mukherjee, Outlook 18 Oct. 2004). The fear is that the Indo-Thai Free Trade Agreement may similarly affect several other sectors like consumer durables, consumer electronics and textiles. The anticipated migration of manufacturing activities in some sectors from India to Thailand may, of course, have very adverse consequences on industry and employment in India.

The problem, therefore, boils down to one basic question: Is India prepared to go the whole way towards bringing its tariff rates down to those of the South East Asian countries? The difficulties involved in India taking such a step are numerous. The experience with FTA concluded with Sri Lanka readily comes to one's mind. To alleviate the hardships experienced by Indian producers of tea, rubber, etc., India had to hike the duties on these items, which happened to be the very same items of interest to Sri Lanka. This is not an argument for eliminating or slashing the duties whatever the consequences for Indian industry and economy. It only highlights the need to identify what are sensitive items to India preparatory to trade negotiations and to skillfully negotiate the FTAs. But it should be realized that India cannot have it both ways. To argue, in the context of BPO outsourcing by the Western countries to India, that such movement of jobs is inherent in the process of economic integration and globalization and, then, to bemoan the movement of any jobs from India to other countries brought about by FTAs that it voluntarily chooses to sign, is incongruent. What is needed is adoption of a give-and-take policy with built-in safeguards to protect against any socially or economically disastrous consequences that may flow from any trade agreement. For this purpose, the Government of India will have to involve Indian industry and trade in an increased measure in the course of preparatory work for all trade agreements and also at the negotiation stage.

A view is sometimes expressed that the scope for achieving any notable increase in trade with South East Asian countries is limited by the absence of complementarities among the economies concerned. This view has been invalidated by the increasing trend towards outsourcing on a global scale. In many cases, countries no longer manufacture a product 100 % within their respective national borders; parts and components are outsourced from countries with low costs and the finished products are sold all over the globe. What is currently happening in South East Asia and the Far East is a striking example to illustrate this trend. Table-5 of this paper showed how China is beginning to account for a rapidly increasing share of the exports of the seven countries under study. Asian Development Bank's Outlook 2004 clearly brings out (page 5) the increasing scale of production -sharing, or vertical specialization, in the East and South East Asian region. Referring to China's increasing import of components and parts from other countries in the region, the Report states that, "the structural trade balances between PRC and its major trading partners clearly show its role as an assembly centre for many exports from Asia to the US and EU". It adds that production-sharing is expected to become more important to regional trade, facilitated by improvements in transportation and communication and falling trade and investment barriers.

India, as another fast-growing large economy in Asia, has to be prepared for similar changes if it is to fully participate and gain from the forces of globalization. The process may adversely affect some sectors but the government has to take steps to ameliorate the sufferings of people so affected and to encourage growth in other areas with a view to maximizing the gains to the economy.

CONCLUSION

South East Asia and East Asia are regions of high economic growth and burgeoning foreign trade. India stands to gain tremendously by establishing closer cooperation with the countries in the region. India's efforts in recent years to upgrade its economic relations with the ASEAN countries are in the right direction and have in fact produced highly satisfactory results. But the path has many pitfalls and, hence, needs to be treaded with care.

Trade in merchandise, with which this paper was concerned so far, is only one part, albeit a major part, of the economic exchanges among the ASEAN countries and India. Trade in services like travel, tourism, health care and, of course, information technology hold great opportunities for India. Such exchanges will help promote not only economic prosperity but also social and political stability among the people of this region who historically share so much in common in terms of culture and civilization.

REFERENCES

Bhattia R.C. (2001), *International Business with Asian Countries*, Deep & Deep Publications.

Jayapalan N. (2004), *Foreign Policy of India*, Atlantic Publishers and Distributors.

Vibha Mathur (2003), *Foreign Trade of India Policy and Developments 1950-2000*, New Century Publications.

Asian Development Bank Outlook 2004.

World Development Indiculurs (2003), World Bank Publication.

Economic Survey (2003-04), Government of India Publication.

CMIE Report (2004), "Foreign Trade and Balance of Payments", Publication of Centre for Monitoring Indian Economy Pvt. Ltd.,

RBI Annual Report (2004), Reserve Bank of India Publication.

Rahul Sen, Mukul G. Asher, Ramakrishna S. Rajan (2004), "ASEAN-India Economic Relations Current Status and Futures Prospects", *Economic and Political Weekly*, July 17, 2004.

Raja Mohan G. (2004), "India and China: A Shifting Paradigm", *The Hindu*, 29th July 2004.

Jon E. Hilsenrath (2000), "India's Economy is set to Beat China", *Asian wall Street Journal*, 27th April 2000.

Kupppuswamy C.S. (2003), "India's Look East Policy: Gaining Momentum with the Prime" *South Asia Analysis Group Paper, 819*, 20th October 2003.

Sultan Shahin (2003), "India's "Look East" Policy Pays off", *Asia Times*, 11th October 2003.

Chandan Irom (2000), "Whatever Happened to India's Look East Policy? The Mekong-Ganga Co-operation, *The Hindu*, 28th November 2000.

Raja mohan C. (2002), "Looking East: Phase Two" *The Hindu*, 11th April 2002.

Amit Baruch (2000), "Looking East the Launch of the Mekong-Ganga Co-operation in Laos Signals a new beginning in India's Foreign Policy, but will it Gather Momentum?" *The Front Line*, Vol. 17, Issue 24, Nov. 25-Dec. 8, 2000.

TRENDS IN FOREIGN TRADE OF SEVEN COUNTRIES

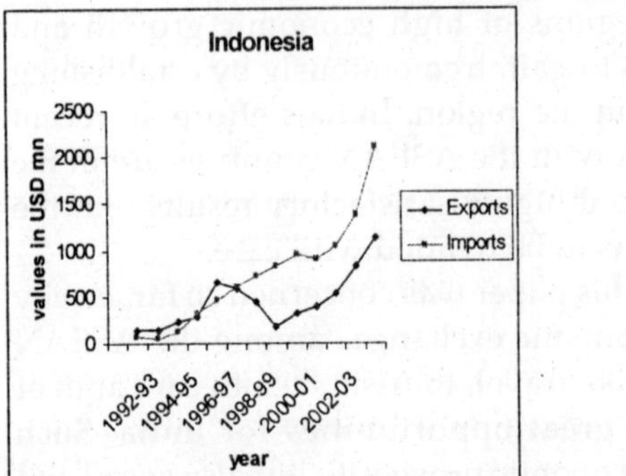

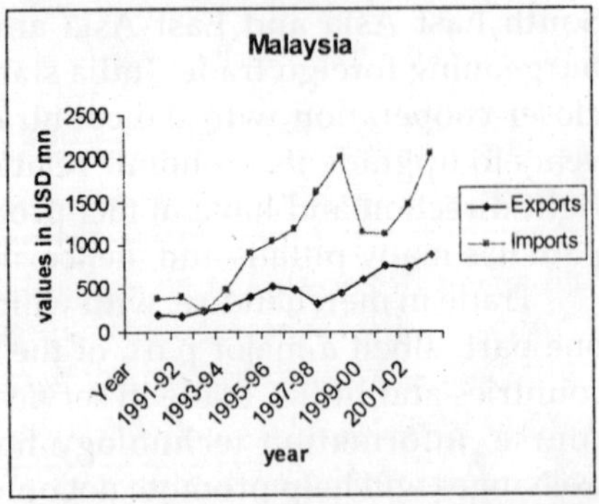

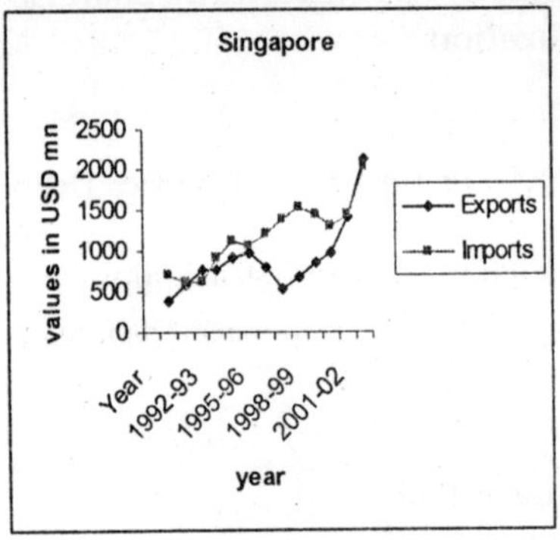

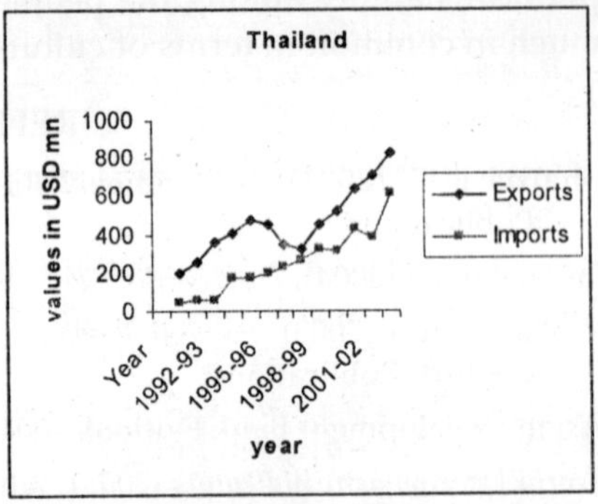

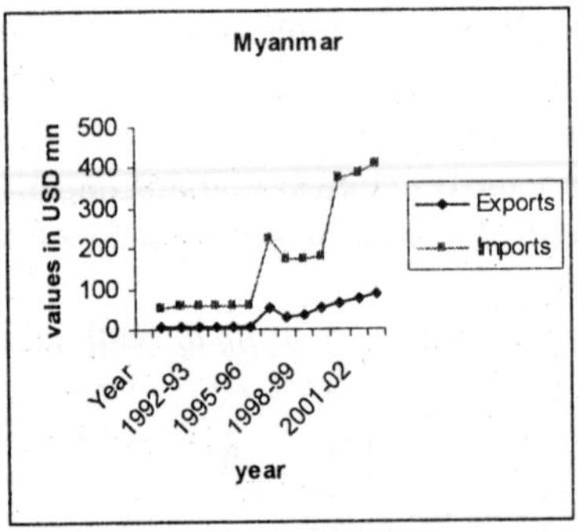

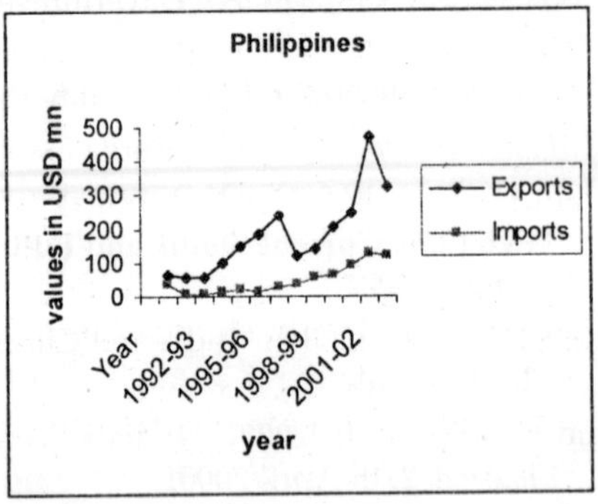

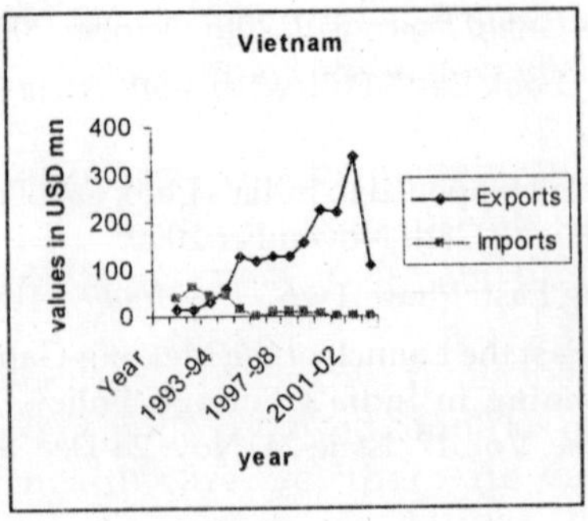

ANNEXURE - I
TRENDS IN FOREIGN TRADE OF THE SEVEN COUNTRIES

	Indonesia			*Malaysia*	
Year	*Exports*	*Imports*	*Year*	*Exports*	*Imports*
1991-92	149	67	1991-92	204	392
1992-93	138	60	1992-93	190	406
1993-94	235	120	1993-94	247	249
1994-95	277	322	1994-95	287	490
1995-96	663	462	1995-96	394	904
1996-97	592	599	1996-97	531	1042
1997-98	438	733	1997-98	491	1180
1998-99	185	829	1998-99	321	1610
1999-00	325	960	1999-00	447	2021
2000-01	395	904	2000-01	601	1152
2001-02	535	1039	2001-02	776	1137
2002-03	828	1384	2002-03	751	1469
2003-04	1126	2102	2003-04	891	2051

	Singapore			*Thailand*	
Year	*Exports*	*Imports*	*Year*	*Exports*	*Imports*
1991-92	391	696	1991-92	200	49
1992-93	589	632	1992-93	254	58
1993-94	751	626	1993-94	356	57
1994-95	770	900	1994-95	407	172
1995-96	903	1115	1995-96	474	170
1996-97	978	1064	1996-97	448	197
1997-98	781	1199	1997-98	345	234
1998-99	517	1384	1998-99	321	273
1999-00	670	1536	1999-00	450	328
2000-01	862	1436	2000-01	529	315
2001-02	976	1299	2001-02	635	425
2002-03	1425	1439	2002-03	713	380
2003-04	2122	2035	2003-04	830	611

	Myanmar			*Philippines*	
Year	*Exports*	*Imports*	*Year*	*Exports*	*Imports*
1991-92	4	51	1991-92	65	32
1992-93	4	56	1992-93	55	10
1993-94	4	56	1993-94	58	6
1994-95	4	56	1994-95	100	12
1995-96	4	56	1995-96	145	22
1996-97	4	56	1996-97	184	17
1997-98	49	224	1997-98	239	28
1998-99	30	174	1998-99	119	37
1999-00	34	172	1999-00	144	56
2000-01	51	181	2000-01	202	63
2001-02	61	376	2001-02	249	92
2002-03	75	387	2002-03	473	124
2003-04	89	410	2003-04	322	122

	Vietnam	
Year	*Exports*	*Imports*
1991-92	13	39
1992-93	17	61
1993-94	28	44
1994-95	59	44
1995-96	125	16
1996-97	118	2
1997-98	127	9
1998-99	125	9
1999-00	154	12
2000-01	225	7
2001-02	219	0
2002-03	338	0
2003-04	109	0

ROLE OF ASEAN IN INDIA'S DEVELOPMENT

R. Meenakshi

INTRODUCTION

The forerunner of ASEAN is the Association of South East Asia proposed by the Malayan Prime Minister Tunku Abdul Rahman in 1959. Currently ASEAN includes Brunei, Indonesia, Cambodia, Laos, Malaysia, Myanmar, Philippines, Singapore, Thailand, and Vietnam with longstanding and successful regional grouping for economic integration and peaceful coexistence. The founders of ASEAN envisioned it as eventually bringing together all the countries of Southeast Asia and getting them to cooperate in securing the region's peace, stability and development. ASEAN has emerged as an important institution permitting an increase in the share of the developing countries in the world trade with a significant improvement in their growth. While the 20th century economy was driven by capital accumulation, manufacturing technologies and labor power, the 21st century is defined by knowledge and human capital giving strength to the Asian identity.

INDIA-EMERGING PARTNER OF ASEAN

The relations between India and the ASEAN have been rising as a sectoral dialogue partner in Trade, Investment, Tourism and Science & Technology. But hitherto India's role in world trade has been insignificant. This has been the result of pursuit of autarchic import-substitution policies since independence, continuing well beyond the period for which they may have been effective. India embarked on a course of radical economic reform, restructuring the domestic economy to promote greater efficiency, productivity, and competitiveness, and opening up the economy to international competition bringing Indian economy into international trade and investment considerations. Consequent to the economic reforms India's annual growth rate has averaged 5.9% during 1992-93 to 2002-03 periods due to the growing involvement of Indian companies abroad. Since the initiation of India's Look East Policy in the early 1990s, bilateral relations between India and ASEAN have progressed rapidly. India-ASEAN trade constitutes about 6 per cent of India's total trade. The important trading partners among the ASEAN nations are Indonesia, Singapore and Malaysia but trade with other ASEAN countries too has been growing steadily. Thus, India became a sectoral dialogue partner of ASEAN in 1992; full dialogue partner in 1995; and a member of the ASEAN Regional Forum (ARF) dealing with security issues in 1996. Subsequently the first ever ASEAN-India summit hosted by Cambodia in November 2002 represented another important milestone in bilateral relations.

THE ASEAN-INDIA SUMMIT, 2002

The following are the findings of the summit:

- Strong signals from Indian leaders of the desire to fortify relations with ASEAN through a series of bilateral visits by Indian leaders to other ASEAN members.
- ASEAN leaders in turn have recognized the need to actively engage India for developing a more balanced relationship with all the major Asian economies.
- The recognition that India's economic structure is largely complimentary to ASEAN economies with significant areas of mutual gain.

During the summit, India proposed negotiations for Regional Trade and Investment Agreement (RTIA), with ASEAN to operationalize it within a decade. India's current negotiations with Singapore and Thailand for closer economic cooperation framework would also make this task easier, as both are among the key economic partners in Asia. The progress could be even more rapid if such discussions also take place with the other two important partners, Malaysia and Indonesia.

INDIAN INTERACTION WITH OTHER ASIAN COUNTRIES

While India has been interacting with ASEAN for more than a decade, it has been formally cooperating with two of the JACIK (Japan, ASEAN, China, India and South Korea) members also from Northeast Asia, namely China and South Korea, as a part of the Bangkok Agreement concerning trade cooperation, which has been operational since 1975.

India and China have decided to focus on economic issues and leave political and security issues to be resolved at a later date. Both countries wish to focus on domestic tasks and require rapid economic growth and greater integration with the world economy. Thus, each side is now more focused on the opportunities for mutual gains than on competitive challenges from each other.

India's relations with South Korea have focused on realizing synergies between Korea's competitive advantage in electronics hardware, and India's in chip design and software. Both countries regard each other as an important partner in diversifying economic relationship to lessen the risk of over-dependence on the current major trading partners. India also regards South Korea as an important source of foreign investment, particularly in manufacturing and in infrastructure.

Additionally India and Japan have established a firmer basis for wide-ranging economic and political cooperation. The need to protect sea-lanes in the Indian Ocean and the Malacca Straits, combating international terrorism, stake in checking North Korea's nuclear ambitions, complementarities in developing advanced technologies, including in chip design, biotechnology, space and defense sectors, and the need to diversify their economic partners have contributed to this welcome development. Japan is a major bilateral aid donor to India; and a major investor, particularly in motor vehicles, electronics, and entertainment sectors.

India is aligning its tariff structure more and more with the ASEAN countries and is trying to forge regional trading agreements as well as entering into free trade agreements with individual countries. India realizes that ASEAN and the Far-East Asia could be the largest trading block by 2020 and is accordingly making efforts to increase its economic interaction with these regions.

THE PROBLEMS FACED BY ASEAN ECONOMIES AND THE ASIAN CRISIS

The East Asian crisis affecting many rapidly growing Southeast Asian countries like Thailand, Republic of Korea, Malaysia, Indonesia, and the Philippines was felt by neighboring countries also, including India. Till 1990 India was able to push exports into their markets. As a result, the growth rate of India's export to these countries was higher than that of the rest of the world. But, the crisis brought about a turnaround in this trend affecting the trade on oil meals, gems and jewelry, machinery, iron ore and semi-finished iron ore, leather and leather goods and project exports. India's rupee depreciated by 17.6 per cent, between the onset of the Asian financial crisis in July 1997 and till it was over in February 1999. But, this depreciation is quite modest compared to the other Asian countries.

The financial crisis in Southeast and East Asia, in fact, should have been seen as an opportunity for enhanced economic and commercial interaction. Unfortunately, India was slow to appreciate the nature and extent of the crisis and failed to make use of this opportunity to explore new avenues of partnership. While China and the other major regional powers not only demonstrated solidarity with ASEAN by providing financial support (bailout package) as also specific bilateral cooperation measures, India did not come up with any meaningful proposals. The crisis could have hastened and helped ASEAN investment flows and trade with India. In the end, ASEAN investments and trade with India decreased.

It is very important to note certain changes in the International economy with the recent developments in South and East Asian countries. The South East Asian countries have received continuous inflow of capital and as a result the exchange rates have been very good. Due to this the interest rates in these countries have been kept lower. The stock markets have picked up because of high inflows. This situation leads to a stage where inflation rates are high, interest rates are low, the stock market witnesses boom and the exchange rate is kept overvalued. This results in the fundamental disequilibria in these economies and a crisis has set in.

This crisis is mainly because of the fact there has been an improved US economy against that of Japan. Japan has been losing exports to China. It could not have sufficient domestic monetary expansion. The growth in exports of China also has not been satisfactory. All these have led to enormous depreciation of their currencies. In spite of this the Indian economy has not been affected against the direct consequences of the developments in South East Asian economies. However some impact in Indian economy was noticed because foreign financial inflows were becoming negative and the situation in the domestic economy was seen with inflationary expectations. International Monetary Fund (IMF) has said that a very positive aspect of India's recent economic performance is that it avoided the worst of the Asian financial crisis, and growth has been maintained at a rate close to the average seen over the previous years.

ECONOMIC RELATIONS BETWEEN ASEAN AND INDIA

Over the last 50 years India's foreign policy with the ASEAN region has gone through three distinct phases—the first was the pre-Independence period when the two regions were linked together through the de-colonization process unique to the region. The second phase encompasses a period from the early 1960s till about the early 1990s. The international scenario was dominated by the Cold War and it was within this background that the ASEAN was formed in 1967. In the early 1990s, a policy shift occurred in India with regard to its relations with the ASEAN region. Third, the most recent agreement to host annual India-ASEAN summits is a very significant step as it leads to the institutionalization of the (ASEAN plus one) as a formal structure of the ASEAN's annual processes. Past assessments of the ASEAN reflect the fact that the process of institutionalization is a significant step in the development of its ties with its summit partners.

The "Look East" policy of Indian Government in 1992 to strengthen the country's economic ties with the ASEAN has helped India improve its trade and investment relations with the region significantly during the 1990s. Similarly, ASEAN investments in India also picked up considerably over this period. India's budgets have enunciated poverty eradication, infrastructure development, fiscal consolidation, agriculture and related aspects, and enhancing manufacturing sector efficiency. This has brought India's average tariff levels closer to some of the ASEAN economies improving its cost competitiveness. Hence ASEAN provides a growing market to India with a significant role to play. Just as for India, ASEAN has emerged as a major economic space, for ASEAN too India has emerged as an attractive destination for export of goods, services, technology and capital. Faced with growing difficulties in accessing and sustaining growth in traditional markets, both players see opportunities to develop a mutually beneficial partnership.

Agriculture, Bio Technology and Food Security

Indian economy is largely based on agriculture. Bio Technology represents one of the knowledge based new technologies and is expected to benefit the rural poor. There are a number of activities namely agricultural crops; medicinal plants, floriculture, sericulture, dairy and poultry farming can be taken up by rural people due to congenial climatic conditions. India is on the threshold of a biotechnology revolution. Promotion of mutual cooperation through the exchange of information amongst scientists, institutions and Indian industries and ASEAN countries has great potential. India is the world's second largest producer of food next to China. Agriculture is a very important sector for the sustained growth of the Indian economy. ASEAN countries like Malaysia, Myanmar, Singapore and Thailand have the largest markets for their exports to India to provide the food security in course of their trade.

Energy Sources

Energy is another area of promise for India - Malaysia partnership. There is already active collaboration between Indian Oil Corporation and Petronas in certain areas with potential to cover the entire range of hydrocarbon business enabling the member countries to optimize the use of energy resources. India, the largest economy of the region, is also energy starved. India's neighbors have surplus energy sources like huge reserves of gas and India is the most suitable market for it. If the political climate is favorable such energy sources can be tapped profitably. Pakistan has surplus hydro electricity, which can be gainfully exported to the northwestern India. Nepal and Bhutan also have suitable conditions for production of hydro-electricity.

Information and Communication Technology

The Indian IT industry has grown impressively in the last 10 years. Indian software industry employs nearly 550,000 employees, a third of which is employed in software exports. India is expected to have around 4 million IT professionals by 2008. The Indian IT industry is approximately 2.8 per cent of India's GDP and is expected to become 7 per cent by 2008. Software exports constitute more than 16 per cent of the total exports from India in terms of revenue. India is the fourth largest telecom market in Asia after China, Japan and South Korea.

The Indian telecom industry is the eighth largest in the world and the second largest among emerging economies. Teledensity has more than doubled from 2.3 per cent in 1999 to 4.8 per cent in 2002 expecting to increase three-fold by 2012. Based on the above facts ASEAN countries are likely to benefit from India in this field. Indian IT enabled services create multiple opportunities for collaboration in embedded software or joint development of industry specific solutions. ASEAN countries can outsource their operations to quality Indian service providers at competitive prices. Today, South East Asian countries import most of their IT products from the West, which are actually developed by Indian human resources and talents working in Western countries. The irony is that most of these products are actually created by Indian sub-contractors. The result is a double disadvantage that ASEAN pay much more and India gets much less.

Tourism, Entertainment and Multimedia Sector

Indian entertainment business has benefited from deregulation and export opportunities. Joint ventures for animation software exports present attractive opportunities for India and ASEAN. The amazing diversity offers tourists everything they would want from a holiday. Actual foreign tourist arrivals were 2.54 million in 2001, projected to increase by 68 per cent by 2007 and a further 45 per cent between 2007-2012.Opportunities for collaboration abound in Eco-tourism, Leisure tourism, including cruises, Packages for promoting intra-regional and inter-regional tours, Creation of theme parks and Tourism Infrastructure development.

Pharmaceutical and Healthcare Services

The Indian pharmaceutical industry has achieved global recognition due to its low cost and high quality generics and branded and patented medicines. ASEAN can source its imports from India, or shift manufacturing base to India. Since healthcare is dependent on the people served, India's huge population of a billion people represents a big opportunity. . Using the latest technical equipment and the services of highly skilled medical personnel, healthcare services are available at competitive prices encouraging patients not only from developing countries but also even from a number of developed ones to come to India for specialized treatment. This can be exemplified by Indian medical expertise being utilized for specialty treatments of people from Pakistan, Bangladesh, and recently Iraq.

Infrastructure Development

India has placed special emphasis on infrastructural development to stimulate rapid economic growth. This includes de-regulation of all segments of our telecom industry and up gradation of highways, railways, bridges, ports, airports and convention centres. Many ASEAN companies are already present in these and other sectors which have enormous potentials. Specific opportunities include feasibility studies, detailed project preparation, construction supervision, project management and construction of facilities.

India has trading partnership with Malaysia in providing contracts for roads and highways in India. In turn India is hopeful of getting security contracts for railway sector for Malaysian Government. Next to Malaysia, Singapore has become increasingly integrated with Indian economy in the development and management of ports.

Space Technology

Space technology namely satellite communications, remote sensing and geographic information systems (GIS) play both a complementary and supplementary role to conventional technologies in the different types of applications. It has been instrumental in providing the means to extend the reach of ICT services to even the most remote and isolated regions of any economy irrespective of the status. With meager financial resources for space related activities India has sent 13 satellites in orbit and has also produced world's best imaging satellites. India is using satellite technology for predicting natural calamities; provide medical care for remote villages and reclaiming farmland. India is also having plans to send a satellite to moon by 2008. ASEAN countries for their development can effectively utilize this Indian expertise.

Educational Services

Educational services are another area of potential cooperation between ASEAN and India. APTECH India-Ascent Network Solutions has a franchise agreement for opening of IT educational institutions in the Philippines to operate four training schools. NIIT-Mind Stream Ltd is having a franchise agreement for opening of IT educational institutions in the Philippines to operate five such schools. Thapar Institute of Technology, Pune and Asian Institute of Management, Philippines provide for collaboration between the two institutions for providing management education in India. Two Indian schools, namely Bhavan's Indian International School, operate in Indonesia and Delhi Public School is operating in Singapore and Indonesia, which provide education in medical and life sciences and management and information technology.

Financial Services

The Indian financial services industry is growing rapidly, driven by deregulation of insurance and investment in the banking sector by private companies and foreign banks. ASEAN investors will find attractive opportunities in personal financial services, insurance and corporate banking. India is poised to emerge as an additional global hub for financial transactions.

CONCLUSION

India's relations with ASEAN have grown considerably over the last decade, but a vast potential still remains untapped. ASEAN has considerable strengths in the old economy and ambitions in the new economy. India has needs in the old economy and competence in the new economy. India's economic structure is highly complementary to that of East Asia's as evidenced by the strength of East Asian countries that lies in IT Hardware & Electronic Equipment, Heavy Engineering, Product Development & Marketing, Underutilized Capacity in Construction and Need & Ability to invest in R & D, compared to India's potential for Computer Software, Light Engineering and pharmaceuticals, Process Development, Huge Potential Demand for Infrastructure and well developed R & D Infrastructure & Manpower.

REFERENCES

"India's Economy at the Midnight Hour: Australia's India Strategy", East Asia Analytical Unit, Department of Foreign Affairs and Trade

Mukul G. Asher and Sadhana Srivastava (2003), "India and the Asian Economic Community, Paper Prepared for the volume on Asian Economic Community, RIS.

Rahul Sen, Mukul G. Asher, Ramkishen S. Rajan, "ASEAN-India Economic Relations-Current Status and Future Prospects".

Nagesh Bhushan (2003), "India's Response to China's Emerging Role", *The Indus Telegraph.*

Prime Minister Sri. A.B. Vajpayee's (2003), Speech at Asean Business and Investment Summit October 7, Bali, Indonesia.

Nagesh Kumar (2002), "Towards an Asian Economic Community: The Relevance of India": July, Research and Information System for the Non-aligned and Other Developing Countries New Delhi.

INDIA'S FOREIGN TRADE WITH SAARC IN THE GLOBALIZATION ERA: FACTS AND POSSIBILITIES

Rudra Prakash Pradhan

INTRODUCTION

Globalization has become very fashionable and extensively used today in all over the world. It means diverse things to diverse people and has set in a path of far-reaching change that affecting everybody (ILO, 2004). It defines as a process that draws countries out of their insulation and makes them join the rest of the world in its march towards a new world order (Kapila, 2002). It is nothing but an extension of economic transactions and the association of economic activities across the political boundaries of the states (Nayyar, 2002). Globalization is treated as a total mind-set in which the entire world becomes a single market so that the corporate strategy is based on the dynamics of global business environment.

Globalization essentially means expanded free trade and investment opportunities across the world. Economists, by and large, tend to view that free trade and open investment policies are the positive forces and expect those countries pursuing these policies to benefit significantly (Ramakrishna, 2003). However, there is no doubt about that an increasingly integrated global economy presents policy makers with both opportunities and challenges. Global economic integration in all its manifestation aimed at improving allocation of resources, promoting technology transfer, enhancing market size, creating a fair competition, reducing poverty (Mathur, 2003) and finally improving the livings standard of the people. Simultaneously, economic integration has frequently been held to be responsible for growing trade imbalances, increased financial market escalations, growing economic inequalities and lack of more or less effective domestic macroeconomic policies (Shariff, 2003).

The process of global economic integration is not something new. It has been underway since the inception of the modern world system in the 16th century. However, the basic framework of global economic integration has been in place since the nineteenth century. In today's context, globalization means homogenization of prices, products, wages, rates of interest and profits to become the same all over the world. But in reality, there are several differences between globalization today and globalization in the past. First, an obvious difference is its scale. There are subsequent flows of trade and capital, as a percentage of GDP. Second, there is the speed of communications, which makes for a much higher degree of integration and has led to the enormous increase in short-term capital flows, which, unlikely long-term capital flows, were previously very limited. Short-term capital flows have played a very important role in the instability that we have seen in the last 25-30 years. Third, globalization today has to do with the use of force. There is one final way in which the process of globalization has changed, and that is related to the process of democratization. There is much more public scrutiny now of what is going on. That is why there is a stronger globalization debate today than 100 years ago. It is also viewed as a natural process of historical change and the only possible path for the future world economy, which supposedly will increase wealth and prosperity for all countries and around the globe (Stiglitz, 2002).

In India, the first phase of globalization started in the decade 1980s during the Prime Ministership of Rajiv Gandhi (Bhuimali and Sarkar, 2004). However, this phase of globalization was assumed as half-hearted and self-reversing in nature. But, globalization was an eventual in terms of policy changes in the decade 1990's and these changes have been taking place at three different levels such as global, national and sectoral level. But the first and foremost development is the globalization process at the international level. This ensures a closer integration of the countries and peoples of the world and has been brought about by enormous reduction in costs of transportation and communication. This has also been breaking down of artificial barriers to the flows of goods, services, capital, knowledge and to a lesser extent people across the borders (Wadhva, 2003).

More specifically, globalization manifests itself in three various forms such as an increase in international trade, financial flows and foreign direct investment (Loots, 2002; Nayyar, 2002; Majumdar, 2003). However, the flows of trade and finance bore the testimony to radical metamorphosis in its total scope and spectrum on account of the onset of globally coined business jargon. Again, among the many changes in foreign trade are noticeable. This is because multilateral trading has gained currency under the aegis of World Trade Organization (WTO). Although, the contradictions are galore with respect to multilateralism amidst the surfacing of inter, intra and regional trade gaping, yet the hard reality is that besides the multilateral trading, regional and Free Trade Accord (FTA) have come to stay on the global economic plane. The basic philosophy and tenet behind this is to promote inter and intra regional trade among the countries and thereby, to faster economic cooperation, growth and development (Azad and Fayaz, 2004).

South Asian Association of Regional Cooperation (SAARC) is one such regional trade grouping, which consists of seven South Asian countries such as India, Pakistan, Sri Lanka, Nepal, Bhutan, Bangladesh and Maldives. They have been working together since 1985 and trying to find out their common problems in a spirit of trust, mutual understanding and cooperation based on equity, justice and shared benefits. The primary objective of this regional trading is to promote and strengthen trade among the member countries. Keeping in above view, the paper examines India's foreign trade with other SAARC countries during the globalization era.

The rest of the paper is organized into five different sections including the earlier introduction. Section II discuses the importance of foreign trade in the economy. Section III highlights the India's foreign trade in the pre-and post-globalization era. Section IV discuses India's trade with SAARC nations. In section VI, the paper concludes with some possibilities for establishing better trade with SAARC nations.

FOREIGN TRADE: THE IMPORTANCE IN THE ECONOMY

Foreign trade plays a paramount role in the economic development of the country and treats as an engine of economic growth (Robertson, 1949). It accelerates economic growth by bringing new ideas, new technologies and new tastes. That, in turn, stimulates innovation in the economy. As per the empirical investigation, it has been confirmed that there exists a positive and significant relationship between exports and economic growth and accordingly, suggested that there is export promotion, trade liberalization and outward looking strategy because of multidimensional favourable effects of exports (Afzal, 2004; Ram, 1987; Salvatore, 1983). Foreign trade is a treasure house of static and dynamic gains for the economy. It enables an economy to compliment development of industrial or agricultural structure and ensures diversified consumption for its people. It is instrumental in equalizing factor prices and results, in a more efficient allocation of resources. Foreign trade promotes capital formation and brings sectoral and external economies in the industrial activities of a country (Ram, 1987; Feder, 1983; Balassa, 1978).

It bestows a number of economies of scale and enables a country to produce those goods, which are economical, competitive and are based on rational cost proportions. It strengthens relationship (both economically and politically) with other trading countries and provides an opportunity to enter into customs union, which bring forth trade creating and trade diverting benefits. It promotes the hidden talents on entrepreneurs and thus, augments the comparative advantages in the country. Foreign trade provides access to scarce resources needed to promote economic growth such as raw materials, machinery, capital goods and intermediary producer goods that are indispensable for economic growth.

Foreign trade is supposed to ban indirect transmitter of capital often through MNCs. It improves the allocative efficiency of nations through international specialization in the production of goods and services. It provides and promotes an atmosphere of healthy competition among trading nations by checking monopolies and restrictive trade practices. Foreign trade widens the horizons of consumption possibility frontiers of the countries far in excess of domestic production constraints. There is increasing choice of the consumers in the trading regime, as different varieties for the same good (differentiated products) are available in an open economy. Foreign trade is supposed to bring growth oriented structural changes in the economy by changing the composition of GNP, employment and consumption. In fact, trade is considered as a better alternative to foreign aid, foreign direct investment and portfolio investments. This is because the latter are mostly political vulnerable (Krishnamoorthy and Reddy, 2002).

Apart from the above mentioned benefits accruing to individual countries, the world as a whole also benefits from international trade. The world production of every commodity is maximized, through international allocation of resources. There is greater international equality in real incomes, factor prices and consumption levels and consequently in welfare levels across countries of the world. The relative wage levels would increase in a labour abundant country and fall in a capital abundant country. This would equalize real wages of labour in all the trading nations. In view of these reasons, the classical and neoclassical economists considered free trade as the first best policy to promote economic growth. Over and above, foreign trade plays a multilateral role in economic growth and thus, there is urgent need for the country to boost the trade and integrating the same with rest of the world. Moreover, trade openness promotes economic growth and raising economic growth in a sustained manner reduces poverty in the economy (Mathur, 2003).

Trading between countries is not a new concept and in fact, it was traced back since the inception of human civilization. However, these relations were limited during those days because of lack of infrastructure besides host of other factors. With the passage of time, trading between and among the countries gradually developed with respect to technological advancement. In fact, after the World War II, trade volume increased by leaps and bounds and world trade witnessed an extraordinary growth. The increase in the value and volume and the diversification of world trade were mainly due to the advancement of technology, better infrastructure and indeed, by the effect of globalization. Most interestingly, developing countries were not able to derive benefits by this growth till 1972 on account of lower growth rate in their exports. As a result, the share of developing countries in world exports declined. India also felt these worldwide changes and the revolution in the sphere of technology and thus, adopted a steady policy to enhance its trade relation with the countries of the world (Khan and Fayaz, 2004). One of such policies is the effect of globalization in the decade 1990s. Accordingly, in the subsequent section, we examine India's foreign trade in the globalization regime.

INDIA'S FOREIGN TRADE: THE PRE-AND POST-GLOBALIZATION ERA

The fundamental objective of globalization in India, which was initiated in the decade 1990s, is to boost economic growth and reduce poverty. However, Indian post-globalization regime has been somewhat evolutionary and incremental in nature. There had been cases of delays and reverses, resulted stalling of reforms in India in some areas for some times. This was probably due to interplay of forces of democratic politics and coalition governments and the existence of different pressure groups with their robed interests. Despite these problems, India has been very successful in moving ahead to open up its economy to the rest of the world and preparing itself to transform through further economic reforms for emerging as a significant player in the global economy by 2020 (Wadhva, 2003). However examining the performance of Indian economy during the globalization era, we have been observed that there is mixed picture of notable failures and achievements.

On the failure sides, there is growing revenue deficits as well as fiscal deficits, declining trends of tax revenue as a percentage of GDP, sluggish human development, low social sector expenditure (Dev and Mooij, 2004-05), wide income inequalities, slow growth of agriculture, regional variation in infrastructure, jobless growth (Bhide and Kalirajan, 2004), etc. So far as achievements are concerned, there is favorable impact on macro economic stabilization policies including the devaluation of rupee and other structural reforms (Ramakrishna, 2003; Singh, 2003). There are improvements in current account balance, inflows of external finance and accretion of foreign exchange reserves, moderate rate of inflation, sectoral diversification on economic growth, high trade-GDP ratio, etc. (See in Table 1).

Over and above, the effects of globalization can be studied through stabilization and structural adjustments. Stabilization involves measures relating to control of fiscal balance, the balance of payments and external payment deficits and maintaining a low rate of inflation. On the other hand, structural adjustment aims at improving efficiency and productivity and integrating the economy with the rest of world trade and capital movements. Most importantly, it is assumed that India's trade policies have been very effective in bringing imports and exports into an equilibrium path in the long run (Upender and Aruna, 2004). Accordingly, in this section, we examine the trends of India's foreign trade in the globalization period. That is to make comparison between pre- and post-globalization era. To establish the same, we have taken the data of 22 years from 1980-81 to 2001-02 and divided the same into two parts: one part is from 1980-81 to 1990-91 and is called as pre-globalization period; second part is from 1991-92 to 2001-02 and is called as post-globalization period.

The trade under pre-globalization period is presented in Table 2. The figures reflect that total exports of the country have grown from a low of Rs. 6710.7 crores in 1980-81 to a high of Rs. 32558.0 crores in 1990-91. However, there are wide fluctuations in its growth rate. The growth rate of exports is negative (7.2%) in the year 1985-86 and reached a high positive (36.7%) in the year 1989-90. On the average, the compound growth rate of export has increased at the rate of 16.14% during the entire pre-globalization period (i.e. from 1980-81 to 1990-19991). The compound growth rate of exports is also statistically significant at 1% probability level and is judged through the values of s-statistics (See Table 2).

On the other side, the amount of imports has been increased from a low of Rs. 12549.2 crores in 1980-81 to a high of Rs. 43192.9 crores in 1990-91 and its fluctuation varies from a low of 2.2% in 1986-1987 to a high of 26.9% in

Table 1
A Macro Economic Profile of India

Items	1990	1991	1992	1993	1994	1995	1996	1997	1998	1999	2000	2001	2002	2003	2004
X_1	5.6	1.3	5.10	5.9	7.30	7.30	7.80	4.80	6.50	6.10	4.40	5.60	4.40	6.0	6.3
X_2	6.76	-1.22	4.09	5.20	10.20	11.60	7.10	4.30	3.70	4.80	6.60	3.30	6.10	NA	NA
X_3	13.72	-12.32	9.28	5.83	22.92	11.10	-1.00	7.70	0.70	20.30	-1.40	3.00	NA	NA	NA
X_4	26.30	22.60	23.60	23.10	26.00	26.90	24.50	24.60	22.60	25.20	24.00	23.70	23.9	24.0	25.0
X_5	23.10	22.00	21.80	22.50	24.80	25.10	23.20	23.10	21.50	24.10	23.40	24.00	24.50	24.1	25.2
X_6	-3.50	-0.34	-1.71	-0.42	-1.05	-1.65	-1.19	-1.37	-0.96	-1.05	-0.54	0.29	0.6	0.10	0.20
X_7	2.27	1.46	1.59	3.54	2.84	1.31	2.96	2.47	2.01	2.48	1.86	1.99	2.57	NA	NA
X_8	-0.40	1.43	0.33	3.18	1.44	-0.82	1.52	0.94	0.95	1.38	1.31	2.46	3.35	NA	NA
X_9	11.81	15.71	11.58	9.63	12.5	8.1	4.6	4.4	5.9	3.3	7.2	3.6	2.8	5.0	5.0

Note: X_1: GDP growth; X_2: Industrial growth; X_3: Investment growth; X_4: Investment as a percentage of GDP; X_5: Saving as a percentage of GDP; X_6: Current account balance as a percentage of GDP; X_7: Capital account balance as a percentage of GDP; and X_8: Reserves accretion as a percentage of GDP; X_9: Inflation rate in percentage.

Source: RBI, Hand Books of Statistics, 2002-03; GOI, Economic Survey, 2003; Asian Development Outlook, 2003.

1988-89. However, the whole imports has grown at an average rate of 12.42% during the entire pre-globalization period and the growth rate is also statistically significant at 1% probability level. The Table 2 also reflects the trade balance of the country, which is all along negative during the pre-globalization era. This reflects that the magnitudes of import are substantially higher in contrast to the magnitude of exports. However, more interestingly, the trade balance is in declining trend in the Indian economy during the pre-globalization era. It is also inspiring to mention that both exports and imports as a percentage of GDP has been gradually increasing in the Indian economy. The exports-GDP ratio was 4.9% in 1980-81 and increased to 6.2% in 1990-91. On the contrary, import-GDP ratio has been fluctuating at an average of 9% during the pre-globalization era and substantially higher to exports-GDP ratio (See Table 2).

Table 2
India's Foreign Trade during the Pre-Globalization Era (Rs. In Crores)

Year	X_1	X_2	X_3	X_4	X_5	X_6	X_7
1980-81	6710.7	–	12549.2	–	-5838.5	4.9	9.5
1981-82	7805.9	16.3	13607.6	8.4	-5801.7	4.9	8.9
1982-83	8803.4	12.8	14292.7	5.0	-5489.3	5.1	8.9
1983-84	9770.7	11.0	15831.5	10.8	-6060.8	4.9	8.2
1984-85	11744.0	20.2	17134.2	8.2	-5390.5	5.2	8.1
1985-86	10895.0	-07.2	19657.7	14.7	-8763.1	4.4	8.1
1986-87	12452.0	14.3	20095.8	2.2	-7643.8	4.1	7.7
1987-88	15674.0	25.9	22243.7	10.7	-6570.0	4.9	7.7
1988-89	20232.0	29.1	28235.2	26.9	-8003.7	5.2	8.6
1989-90	27658.0	36.7	35328.4	25.1	-7670.0	6.2	8.9
1990-91	32558.0	17.7	43192.9	22.3	-10635.0	6.2	9.4
CGR	16.14		12.42				
t-statistics	11.99		12.11				
r^2	0.94		0.94				

Note: X_1: Amount of Exports (in Rs. Crores); X_2: Change in Exports (in percentage); X_3: Amount of Imports (in Rs. Crores); X_4: Change in Imports (in Percentage); X_5: Trade Balance (in Rs. Crores); X_6: Exports as a Percentage of GDP; X_7: Imports as a Percentage of GDP; CGR: Compound Growth Rate (in Percentage); r^2: Correlation Coefficient.
Source: Hand Book of Statistics on Indian Economy, Reserve Bank of India, Mumbai

India's foreign trade under post-globalization period is also in increasing trend (See Table 3). The amount of exports has been increased from a low of Rs. 44041.8 crores in 1991-1992 to a high of Rs. 209018.0 crores in 2001-02 and is about five-fold increase in the past 12 years. Similarly, the amount of imports also increased from a low of Rs. 47850.8 to a high of Rs. 245199.0 crores. There is also considerable variation in the annual growth rates of export and imports. The annual percentage changes in exports varied from a low 2.7% to a high of 29.9% and on the contrary, the annual percentage changes in import varies between a low of 6.2% to 36.4% during the entire post-globalization era. However, the compound growth rate of exports and imports during the entire periods are 16.56% and 17.97% respectively.

Table 3
India's Foreign Trade during the Post-Globalization Era (Rs. In Crores)

Year	X_1	X_2	X_3	X_4	X_5	X_6	X_7
1991-92	44041.8	–	47850.8	–	-3809.0	7.3	8.3
1992-93	53688.3	21.9	63374.5	32.4	-9686.2	7.8	10.2
1993-94	69751.4	29.9	73101.0	15.3	-3349.6	8.1	9.6
1994-95	82674.1	18.5	89970.7	23.1	-7296.6	8.1	10.9
1995-96	106353.3	28.6	122678.1	36.4	-16324.8	8.9	12.0
1996-97	118817.1	11.7	138919.7	13.2	-20102.6	8.6	12.3
1997-98	130100.6	09.5	154176.3	11.0	-24075.7	8.7	12.5
1998-99	139753.1	07.4	178331.8	15.7	-38578.7	8.3	11.5
1999-00	159561.4	14.2	215236.5	20.7	-55675.1	8.4	12.4
2000-01	203571.0	27.6	230872.7	07.3	-27301.7	9.8	13.0
2001-02	209018.0	02.7	245199.0	06.2	-36181.0	9.4	12.0
CGR	16.56		17.97				
t-statistics	17.0		18.06				
r^2	0.94		0.94				

Note: X_1: Amount of Exports (in Rs. Crores); X_2: Change in Exports (in percentage); X_3: Amount of Imports (in Rs. Crores); X_4: Change in Imports (in Percentage); X_5: Trade Balance (in Rs. Crores); X_6: Exports as a Percentage of GDP; X_7: Imports as a Percentage of GDP; CGR: Compound Growth Rate (in Percentage); r^2: Correlation Coefficient.

Source: Hand Book of Statistics on Indian Economy, Reserve Bank of India, Mumbai

There is as usual India's export and export growth, which is lagging behind that of imports during this period. As a result, trade balance is negative through out the years in the post-globalization era. However, most interestingly, the negative trade balance has also been increasing over the years both in absolute terms as well as in relation to total trade. Furthermore, the amount of exports and imports as a percentage of GDP has also been increasing in the post-globalization era. Export-GDP ratio has increased substantially from 7.3% in 1991-92 to 9.8% in 2001-02 and imports-GDP ratio varies from 8.3% to 13.0% in the entire period from 1991-92 to 2001-02.

INDIA'S FOREIGN TRADE WITH SAARC NATIONS

All in all, it is discernible from the above discussion that India's foreign trade has registered a wavering trend during the period of globalization. In other words, Indian globalization process has opened up more vistas for foreign trade. But, it is up to us that how we leverage our resources to derive more more-benefits from the changing economic world order. It is evident that India's trade performance in the globalization era is quite impressive. Both exports as well as imports (in rupees) have registered an encouraging trend. But, the trade deficit has also been increased simultaneously (Bhuimali and Sarkar, 2004). This is not a good sign for the economy and mostly due to growing demand for petroleum products and its inability to compete in the western markets despite the opportunities provided after the globalization of the Indian economy. Furthermore, its share in world trade has also gone down (Khan and Fayaz, 2004) and unfortunately, the trade share is very low in comparison to their many peers in Asia (Krishnamoorthy and Reddy, 2002).

Accordingly, in the subsequent section, we examine India's trade with other SAARC nations in the post-globalization era and to establish the same, we have taken seven years data from 1996-97 to 2002-03.

Examining India's trade with Bangladesh, it is inferred that India's export to Bangladesh has been in increasing trend over the years during the post-globalization regime except in the year 1997-98 and 1999-2000 (See Table 4). In case of imports, there is little bit variation between $ 50.81 million to $ 80.51 million. It is lowest ($ 558.15 million) in the year 1999-00 and highest ($ 1113.95 million) in the year 2002-03. The percentage share of exports to Bangladesh is varying between 2% to 3% of the overall trade of India. On the contrary, the percentage share of imports to total trade of Bangladesh is about less than 0.5% during the globalization era. However, the balance of trade has always in favour of India. This is because the growth of exports to Bangladesh is substantially higher in contrast to its amount of imports.

Table 4
India's Foreign Trade with Bangladesh

Items	*1996-97*	*1997-98*	*1998-99*	*1999-00*	*2000-01*	*2001-02*	*2002-03*
X_1	868.96	786.46	995.64	636.31	935.04	1002.18	1176.00
X_2	–	-9.49	26.59	-36.09	46.95	7.18	17.34
X_3	33469.94	34784.99	33218.72	36822.49	44560.29	43826.73	52719.43
X_4	–	3.93	-4.5	10.85	21.01	-1.65	20.29
X_5	2.59	2.26	3.00	1.73	2.10	2.29	2.23
X_6	62.23	50.81	62.40	78.15	80.51	59.12	62.05
X_7	–	-18.34	22.81	25.24	3.01	-26.57	4.96
X_8	39132.41	41484.49	42388.71	49738.06	50536.46	51413.29	61412.13
X_9	–	6.01	2.1	17.34	1.61	1.74	19.45
X_{10}	0.159	0.1225	0.15	0.16	0.16	0.11	0.10
X_{11}	806.63	735.63	933.24	558.15	854.54	943.06	1113.95

Note: X_1: Amount of Exports to Bangladesh (in US$ Million); X_2: Percentage of Growth of Exports to Bangladesh; X_3: India's Total Export (in US$ Million); X_4: Percentage of Growth of Total Exports of India; X_5: Percentage Share of India's Export to Bangladesh; X_6: Amount of Imports from Bangladesh (Us$ Million); X_7: Percentage of Growth of Imports to Bangladesh; X_8: India's Total Import (in US$ Million); X_9: Percentage Growth of India's Total Import; X_{10}: Percentage Share of India's Total Import from Bangladesh; and X_{11}: Trade Balance between India and Bangladesh (in US$ Million).

Source: Directorate General of Foreign Trade, Government of India, New Delhi

India trade with Maldives is substantially very low. The exports to Maldives have shown positive trend from a low of $10.36 million in 1996-97 to a high of $ 31.59 million in 2002-03. But, the percentage share of exports to Maldives has always been low and is about less than 0.07% in the period under reference. Similarly, India's imports from Maldives are also very negligible and vary from a low of US$ 0.05 million in 1998-99 to a high of US$ 0.40 million in 1999-00 and 2001-02 (See Table 5). The percentage share of imports from Bhutan to India's total imports is considerably very negligible. However, the trade balance is always in favour of India, as the amount of exports is above than that of the amount of imports.

Table 5
India's Foreign Trade with Maldives

Items	*1996-97*	*1997-98*	*1998-99*	*1999-00*	*2000-01*	*2001-02*	*2002-03*
X_1	10.36	8.74	8.38	7.30	24.61	26.88	31.59
X_2	–	-15.72	-4.11	-12.84	237.10	9.20	17.53
X_3	33469.94	34784.99	33218.72	36822.49	44560.29	43826.73	52719.43
X_4	–	3.93	-4.5	10.85	21.01	-1.65	20.29
X_5	0.0310	0.0251	0.030	0.020	0.060	0.060	0.060
X_6	0.17	0.24	0.05	0.40	0.19	0.40	0.33
X_7	–	39.10	-79.16	671.33	-52.63	108.73	-16.00
X_8	39132.41	41484.49	42388.71	49738.06	50536.46	51413.29	61412.13
X_9	–	6.01	2.1	17.34	1.61	1.74	19.45
X_{10}	0.0004	0.0006	0.000	0.000	0.000	0.000	0.000
X_{11}	10.19	8.50	8.32	6.90	24.42	26.48	31.25

Note: All notations and source are same, as mentioned in Table 4.

Coming to India's trade picture with Bhutan, it is observed that export to Bhutan shows a high volatile scenario with both highly negative and positive growth rates. The amount of exports to Bhutan is considerably low and varies from a low of US$ 1.08 million in 2000-01 to a high of US$ 39.05 million 2002-03 under the post globalization era. In contrast to the amounts of imports from Bhutan is substantially high in comparison to imports. The amount of imports is low in the year 1998-99 (is about US$ 6.13 million) and high in the year 1996-97 (is about US$ 33.37 million). The percentage share of exports to Bhutan is also very low and is about less that .07%. On the contrary, the percentage share of imports from Bhutan reflects highly fluctuating trends and varies from 0.01% to 0.09% in the post-globalization era (See Table 6). The trade balance is always in the favour of Bhutan, as the amount of imports is much higher in contrast to the amount of exports. However, it is only in the year 1998-99 and 2002-03, the trade balance is in the favour of India.

Table 6
India's Foreign Trade with Bhutan

Items	*1996-97*	*1997-98*	*1998-99*	*1999-00*	*2000-01*	*2001-02*	*2002-03*
X_1	21.98	13.33	9.56	7.57	1.08	7.60	39.05
X_2	–	-39.37	-28.28	-20.78	-85.78	605.38	413.89
X_3	33469.94	34784.99	33218.72	36822.49	44560.29	43826.73	52719.43
X_4	–	3.93	-4.5	10.85	21.01	-1.65	20.29
X_5	0.065	0.038	0.030	0.020	0.000	0.020	0.070
X_6	33.37	13.44	6.13	18.01	21.09	23.92	32.15
X_7	–	-60.22	-54.38	194.00	17.08	13.42	34.41
X_8	39132.41	41484.49	42388.71	49738.06	50536.46	51413.29	61412.13
X_9	–	6.01	2.1	17.34	1.61	1.74	19.45
X_{10}	0.086	0.032	0.010	0.040	0.040	0.050	0.050
X_{11}	-11.8	-0.11	3.43	-10.44	-20.01	-16.32	6.89

Note: All notations and source are same, as mentioned in Table 4.

India's trade with Pakistan is somewhat extraordinary in comparison to other SAARC countries and mainly due to the existence of high tensions between the countries. India's exports to Pakistan have registered a wide fluctuating trend and vary from a low of $101.01 million in 2000-01 to $ 206.16 million in 2002-03. The total exports to Pakistan as a percentage of India's total trade is about 0.5%. On the other side, imports from Pakistan is also showing fluctuating trend. It registered a high amount of $ 214.45 million during 1998-99 and a low amount of % 36.16 million during 1996-97. Indian imports accounted for less than half percent of total imports during the period under study. The trade balance is in favour of India except in the year 1998-99 (See Table 7).

Table 7
India's Foreign Trade with Pakistan

Items	*1996-97*	*1997-98*	*1998-99*	*1999-00*	*2000-01*	*2001-02*	*2002-03*
X_1	157.22	143.15	106.10	92.95	186.83	144.01	206.16
X_2	–	-8.95	-25.88	-12.40	101.01	-22.92	43.16
X_3	33469.94	34784.99	33218.72	36822.49	44560.29	43826.73	52719.43
X_4	–	3.93	-4.5	10.85	21.01	-1.65	20.29
X_5	0.35	0.33	0.32	0.25	0.42	0.33	0.39
X_6	36.16	44.45	214.45	68.21	64.03	64.76	44.85
X_7	–	22.93	382.45	-68.19	-6.14	1.14	-30.74
X_8	39132.41	41484.49	42388.71	49738.06	50536.46	51413.29	61412.13
X_9	–	6.01	2.1	17.34	1.61	1.74	19.45
X_{10}	0.924	0.1071	0.510	0.140	0.130	0.130	0.070
X_{11}	121.06	98.70	-108.35	24.73	122.81	79.25	161.31

Note: All notations and source are same, as mentioned in Table 4.

Investigating India's trade with Nepal during 1996-97 to 2002-03, we could highlight that exports to Nepal have shown a fluctuating trend and varies from a low of $122.41 million in 1998-99 to $ 350.36 million in 2002-03. The share of exports to Nepal is below half per cent of the total exports of India during these periods. On the contrary, the amount of imports from Nepal is in increasing trends. It is of US$ 64.07 million in 1996-97 and has increased to US$ 281.76 million in 2002-03. But, unfortunately, the amount of imports as a percentage of Indian total imports is substantially low and about less than 1%. Most interestingly, the trade balance is in the favour of Nepal except few exceptions (See Table 8).

India's trade with Sri Lanka is always in the favour of India, as the amount of exports is substantially higher in contrast to imports in the entire period under reference (See Table 9). India's export to Sri Lanka has registered a dithering trend. It has increased from a low of $ 437.13 million in 1998-99 to a high of $ 920.98 million in 2002-03. India's export to Sri Lanka as a percentage of total trade is about less than 2% in the globalization era. The low export to Sri Lanka is mainly ascribed to similarity of basket of goods and services and more or less concentration on exports to western countries rather than among the member nations. On the other side, the amount of imports from Sri Lanka is substantially low in comparison to the amount of exports. It varies from a low of US$ 30.21 in 1997-98 to a high of US$ 90.83 million in 2002-03. Interestingly, the growth rate of imports from Sri Lanka is negative in the year 1997-98. India's imports from Sri Lanka as a percentage of total trade are about less than 1% through out the years.

Table 8
India's Foreign Trade with Nepal

Items	*1996-97*	*1997-98*	*1998-99*	*1999-00*	*2000-01*	*2001-02*	*2002-03*
X_1	165.72	170.05	122.41	151.23	140.84	214.46	350.36
X_2	–	2.61	-28.02	23.54	-6.87	52.28	63.37
X_3	33469.94	34784.99	33218.72	36822.49	44560.29	43826.73	52719.43
X_4	–	3.93	-4.5	10.85	21.01	-1.65	20.29
X_5	0.4951	0.4889	0.370	0.410	0.320	0.490	0.660
X_6	64.07	95.16	144.85	188.63	255.08	355.94	281.76
X_7	–	48.51	52.22	30.23	35.23	39.54	-20.84
X_8	39132.41	41484.49	42388.71	49738.06	50536.46	51413.29	61412.13
X_9	–	6.01	2.1	17.34	1.61	1.74	19.45
X_{10}	0.1637	0.2294	0.340	0.380	0.500	0.690	0.460
X_{11}	101.65	74.89	-22.44	-47.40	-114.24	-141.48	6.89

Note: All notations and source are same, as mentioned in Table 4.

Table 9
India's Foreign Trade with Sri Lanka

Items	*1996-97*	*1997-98*	*1998-99*	*1999-00*	*2000-01*	*2001-02*	*2002-03*
X_1	477.41	489.23	437.0	499.27	640.14	630.89	920.98
X_2	–	2.48	-10.65	14.22	28.22	-1.45	45.98
X_3	33469.94	34784.99	33218.72	36822.49	44560.29	43826.73	52719.43
X_4	–	3.93	-4.5	10.85	21.01	-1.65	20.29
X_5	1.4264	1.4064	1.320	1.360	1.440	1.440	1.750
X_6	42.84	30.21	37.68	44.23	45.01	67.38	90.83
X_7	–	-29.49	24.73	17.40	1.75	49.71	34.80
X_8	39132.41	41484.49	42388.71	49738.06	50536.46	51413.29	61412.13
X_9	–	6.01	2.1	17.34	1.61	1.74	19.45
X_{10}	0.1095	0.0728	0.090	0.090	0.090	0.130	0.150
X_{11}	434.57	459.02	399.45	455.04	595.14	563.51	830.16

Note: All notations and source are same, as mentioned in Table 4.

CONCLUSION AND POLICY IMPLICATIONS

Over and above, as per the preceding discussion, the paper finds that there is substantial improvement in India's foreign trade in the globalization era. Both exports and imports are in increasing trend. However, the amount of imports is much higher in comparison to exports and thus, there is trade deficit in the Indian economy. There is also diversification of foreign trade in the Indian economy in the globalization era (Bhuimali and Sarkar, 2004; Majumder, 2003). In fact, this has also been substantially taken place with other SAARC countries and mostly due to the impact of globalization and establishment of South Asian Preferential Trading Agreement (SAPTA) during the reference period.

The main objectives of SAPTA are to promote and facilitate mutual trade and economic cooperation among the member states. The measures to be taken during this period to improve the trading among SAARC nations are tariff, non-tariff and direct measures. Some adjustments also made with respect to product-by-product basis, across the broad tariff reduction sectoral basis and also depending upon the circumstances prevailing in the SAARC in particular and world in general. However, the critics say that despite these substantial opportunities, trading among SAARC nations is about less than 4% of their total volumes. This mainly attributed diverse socio-economic status of SAARC countries, the emphasis of west policy to the member countries, same basket of commodities, tension between the member nations (especially Indian and Pakistan) and the comparative advantage enjoyed by India over the rest of the SAARC nations (Azad and Fayaz, 2004).

The paper accordingly suggests that these hindrances can be set off by liberalizing regional economies further and making effective peace between neighboring countries. Besides, under the WTO agreement, SAARC countries could assign Most Favoured Nation (MFN) status to each other. They should also cut their tariff rates. By doing so, India can channalise unofficial lucrative trade normally benefits of which are being enjoyed by the unauthorized agents and smugglers. India should come forward to implement Free Trade Agreement (FTA) with the neighboring countries on bilateral basis under the umbrella of SAPTA. The setting up of FTA will enhance trade between India and its neighbours in transportation, equipments, engineering goods and IT products and also the flow of investment, which will result in economies of scale through access to larger market. Mutual trade and understanding will help in improving the status of trade, generating employment opportunities, facilitating innovations, etc. (Mathur, 2003).

Furthermore, it will better, if SAARC countries focus their attention towards trade among themselves rather than with the west and develop their own capacities. This will ultimately provide them inner strength to fight the fierce competition in the global market. The steps like abolition of quota will adversely affect most of the member nations. Thus, in order to compensate them, multilateral trade among the group should be promoted. Besides, India and Pakistan should overcome their political differences and promote trade on priority among the member nations by shouldering their responsibility as being the bigger nation of the group.

In short, India can improve her trade with SAARC in particular and world in general by giving stress on its economy at a broad level. In this context, some of the possibilities, which, we can establish here as follows:

- To fall in line with the globalization process, India has already initiated removal of quantitative restrictions, simplification and rationalization of tariffs, reduced export restrictions and liberalized the trade and payments aspects. However, in this scenario, economy requires more openness and more transparency of their policies.
- Besides the operation of globalization since 1991, tariff rates are still high in India as compared to other developing countries. Thus, to enter to FTAs

with SAARC countries and Asian Countries, rate of tariff should be reduced further.

- There is need of internal economic reforms in the form of structural adjustment in a broad level to enhance the economic efficiency.
- There is need of encouraging Foreign Direct Investment (FDI). Most importantly, FDI related policies have to be rationalized to attract more FDI in export-oriented sectors of the economy. Further, to attract NRI funds, procedural simplifications have to be outlined properly.
- There is need of improving infrastructural base in the Indian economy, as it is a pace setter of economic growth and helps in integrating the economy through trade, investment and financial flows. Here, the step must be taken to encourage greater public investment as well as private investment in the infrastructural sector.
- There is need of boosting more and more bilateral and multilateral trade agreement under the regime of WTO. This is because under the WTO provisions there are enough opportunities for making Free Trade Agreements (FTA).
- Since Indian exports are more or less traditional in nature, steps should be taken by Indian corporate for making their export products more competitive by improving quality. New markets should be exploited and more commodities should be brought on the export list so that we can capture at least one per cent of global trade.
- Marketing information system should also be improved so as to know the size, nature, trend of consumer demand and the degree of foreign competition.
- There is need of introduction of new cost effective technology for improvement in productivity and export competitiveness.
- WTO agreements should be exploited as leverage for growth and development rather than impediments. New destinations for exports should be explored for Indian traditional and other goods.
- There is overall need for the simplification of export procedures in the light of WTO agreement.
- The position of Balance of payments (BOP) needs to be handling carefully. This is because invisible account balance is doing well in the globalization era and is due to high demand of IT professional and remittances by NRIs.
- Last but not the least, there is need of political stability. This requires political will and simplified trade procedural formalities in accordance with WTO agreements.

To conclude, India's trade with SAARC nations is not satisfactory. Thus, there is need of better trading with SAARC nations by integrating its economy with rest of the SAARC nations. The ongoing economic integration not only focus trade as a means of strengthening international competitiveness and as an engine of economic growth. This helps in alleviating poverty, curbing imbalances, reducing inequalities, plummeting backwardness, and ensuring terrorism free society with equity and justice.

REFERENCES

Afzal, M. (2004), "Export-Economic Growth Nexus: Pakistan's Experience", *Indian Journal of Economics and Business,* Vol. 3, No. 2, pp. 315-340.

Azad, I. And Fayaz, M. (2004), "India's Trade with SAARC in Globalized Trade Regime", Banking Finance, Vol. 17, No. 8, pp. 5-12.

Balass, B. (1978), "Exports and Growth: Further Evidence", *Journal of Development Economics,* Vol. 52, No. 2, pp. 181-189.

Bhide, S. and Kalirajan, K. (2004), "Impact of Trade Liberalization on Employment in Indian Manufacturing: Evidence from the Organized Sector", *Journal of Social and Economic Development,* Vol. 6, No. 1, pp. 1-19.

Bhuimali, A. and Sarkar, B. (2004), "India's Trade Performance in the Post-liberalization Era", *Indian Journal of Social and Economic Policy,* Vol. 1, No. 1, pp. 117-125.

Dev, S.M. and Mooij, J. (2004-05). "Patterns in Social Sector Expenditure: Pre- and Post- Reform Periods", in Parikh, K. and Radhakrishna, R. (eds.), *Indian Development Report,* Oxford University Press, New Delhi, pp. 96-111.

Feder, G. (1983), "On Exports and Economic Growth", *Journal of Development Economics,* Vol. 5, No. 1, pp. 59-73.

ILO (2004), "Report on World Commission on the Social Dimension of Globalization", *International Labour Organization,* Geneva.

Kapila, U. (2002), "Globalization and the Indian Economy", in (R. Kapila and U. Kapila, eds.) *India's Economy in the 21st Century,* New Delhi: Academic Foundation.

Khan, A.Q. and Fayaz, M. (2004), "Niche for Indian Foreign Trade in Globalizng Regime", *Banking Finance,* Vol. 17, No. 9, pp. 5-17.

Krishnamoorthy, D. and Reddy, V.V.S. (2002), "Growth and Instability in India's Foreign Trade: A Comparative Analysis of Pre and Post-Liberalization Periods", Artha Vijnana, Vol. XLIV, Nos. 3-4, pp. 349-366.

Loots, E. (2002), "Globalization, Emerging Markets and the South African Economy", *South African Journal of Economics,* Vol. 70, No. 2, March, Pretoria.

Mathur, S. K. (2003), "Trade Liberalization and the Poor: A Framework for Poverty Reduction Policies with Special Reference to Some Asian Countries Including India", Indian Development Review, Vol. 1, No. 2, pp. 179-230.

Majumder, B. (2003), "India's Trade-Link with The European Union: Facts and Possibilities", Management and Change, Vol. 7, No. 1, pp. 49-73.

Nayyar, D. (2002), Governing Globalization: Issues and Institutions. New Delhi: Oxford University Press.

Ram, R. (1987), "Exports and Economic Growth in Developing Countries: Evidence from Time Series and Cross Section Data", Economic Development and Cultural Change, Vol. 35, pp. 50-72.

Robertson, D. H. (1949), " The Future of International Trade", Readings in the Theory of International Trade, AEA & Co., Blankiston, p. 507.

Ramakrishna, G. (2003), "Globalization and Balance of Payments Experience of India", *Indian Development Review,* Vol. 1, No. 1, pp. 27-46.

Salvatore, D. (1983), "A Simultaneous Equations Model of Trade and Development with Dynamic Policy Simulations", Kyklos, Vol. 36, pp. 66-90.

Shariff, I. (2003), "Global Economic Integration: Prospects and Problems", *Inaıan Development Review,* Vol. 1, No. 2, pp. 163-178.

Singh, T. (2003), "Trade Flows, Trade Policy Regimes and Some Issues in Capital Account Liberalization in India", *International Journal of Applied Economics and Econometrics,* Vol. 11, No. 4, pp. 607-646.

Stiglitz, J. (2002), Globalization and its Discontents, Allan Lane, London: Penguin Press.

Upender, M. and Aruna, M. (2004), "Are Exports and Imports Drifting Apart from Each Other in India? An Application of Cointegration and Error Correction Modeling", *Indian Journal of Economics and Business,* Vol. 3, No. 2, pp. 397-407.

Wadhva, C.D. (2003), "Economic Reforms in India: In Retrospect and Prospect", *Man and Development,* Vol. 25, No. 3, pp. 17-62.

A CRITIQUE OF ECONOMIC GROWTH AND HUMAN DEVELOPMENT: POST ASIAN CRISIS

Masudul Alam Choudhury

OBJECTIVE AND STRUCTURE OF PAPER

We will undertake a critical investigation on the nature of interrelationships between Human Poverty Index (HPI) as a measure of incidence of poverty, GDP, HDI (Human Development Index) and GDI (Gender Development Index). These indices will be taken in their percentage change values so as to bring out the flux of relations among these critical indicators.

We will thus be searching for several conceptual results that can be expected to arise from a closer examination of Malaysia's performance with regards to her relationship between economic growth and poverty alleviation. We will examine two possible scenarios from the politico-economic and policy-theoretic viewpoints.

First, an enhancement of the two development successes would be in accord with Malaysia's continuous aspiration in her development plans to generate economic growth with equity. This leads to the study of factors that lie behind such a remarkable sustained relationship between the two variables. Here we can go and look for the existence of a complementary model of economic growth and development in the socio-economic sense.

The discovery of such a complementary model marks a major breakthrough over the usual neoclassical macroeconomic model of economic growth. The latter has been found to generate tradeoffs between the goals of economic efficiency (represented by growth, price stability and productivity) and distributive equity (represented by equitable income distribution and wealth, poverty alleviation and human development) (Okun, 1975). These representative indicators of the two camps of economic growth and development can be disaggregated to the microeconomic levels for purposes of identifying problems and questions relating to economic growth and poverty alleviation in both the neoclassical and the alternative models (Choudhury, Korvin & Seyyed, 2001).

The second result needing careful investigation is this. If development tradeoffs are found to exist, the neoclassical model of globalization and its various instruments may have had specific effects on the overall socio-economic progress of the nation. Here the argument of a neoclassical political economy of globalization can be expounded to affirm the causes that marginalize the poor.

SETTING THE PERIMETERS OF THE STUDY

Our starting point is to explain the perspective of poverty that we need to examine in the contrasting views cast upon development. One of these views arises from the side of the complementary model, which is essentially a politico-economic approach. This will be explained substantively in this paper. The other is the dynamic neoclassical model used now with regards to a neoclassical viewpoint of globalization.

In our theoretical model we will consider the change of poverty between absolute and relative poverty levels. Hence a dual labour market theory will be invoked along with its institutional implications. From this analysis certain policy perspectives will be generated.

On the applied side, since poverty data exist at the aggregate level we will use such data along with several explanatory variables appearing as indices that affect the poverty level. These selected variables will be Human Poverty Index (HPI), Human Development Index (HDI), Gender Development Index (GDI), Gross Domestic Product (GDP) for a cross-section of the 'medium human development countries'. We have chosen this group rather than the Southeast Asia and Pacific Region specifically for reasons of paucity of data in the latter case. On the other hand, the choice of 'medium human development countries' fits well with the case of Malaysia. From the resulting regression analysis we will compare the position of Malaysia with regards to her HPI, HDI, GDI and GDP.

The combination of the above two approaches is expected to throw light on the nature of tradeoff or of complementarities in the growth-poverty debate. The underlying model for poverty alleviation and economic growth will thus be determined and relevant policy-theoretic analysis will be brought out.

EFFICIENCY-EQUITY TRADEOFF IN THE NEOCLASSICAL ECONOMIC GROWTH MODEL

Macroeconomic tradeoffs between economic efficiency, economic growth and productivity on the one side and distributive equity with socio-economic development on the other side, have been well documented in the literature. Phelps (1989) has pointed out that the nature of neoclassical economic analysis does not permit the study of issues like social justice and economic efficiency within a complementary approach. The structure of neoclassical economic theory is not amenable to the study of complementary relations among socio-economic possibilities. This efficiency-equity tradeoff problem of neoclassical economics is deeply of a methodological nature.

Neoclassical economic theory is based on optimal allocation of scarce resources, whereby competition between opposing agents is both necessary and sufficient in determining the ultimate states of the competing variables. Examples of such competing variables and goals are economic efficiency versus social justice, economic growth versus socio-economic development, allocative efficiency versus distributive equity, price stability versus unemployment, and so on. In optimal allocation of scarce resources between such competing ends in neoclassical economics both at the level of the individual (household) and institutions (governments), competition, scarcity and optimization within the targeted criterion functions result in marginal rates of substitution between such opposite goals.

Thereby, the result of tradeoff, which is here seen as opposing state of the competing goals expressed by marginal rate of substitution between them, becomes endemic in the entire neoclassical theory of income distribution, production and consumption. Such a relationship is pervasive across consumers, firms and institutional levels. It is a situation implying that macroeconomic development tradeoffs between economic growth and social justice, allocative efficiency and distributive equity are repeated at the microeconomic level of preferences formed by individuals (households), firms (corporations) and institutions (governments and supra-governments).

Now to examine how the neoclassical economic growth model relates with the political economy of poverty alleviation we examine in this context the issues of entitlement and empowerment for the poor. The link between entitlement and empowerment is made through the allocation and distribution of resources in the neoclassical economic framework.

In Sen's model (1986) of deprivation and entitlement a starvation point is within the optimal production possibility frontier of a bundle of goods that should be socially dispensed to the poor. The existence of a starvation point causes entitlement failure by negating any one of the possibilities that must exist. Among many factors entitlement failure bundle comprises loss of access to market exchange for the goods and services of the poor, lack of human resource development, loss of entitlement enhancing policies for the poor, and loss of initial endowments needed to generate productivity of the poor. In the political economy framework these and many other entitlement related factors are interrelated in a complementary fashion. Thus, initial endowment for the productivity of the poor is linked with the use of land and tradable opportunities. Institutions combine in this entitlement enhancing relationship to move the starvation point from the interior towards the surface of the production possibility curve.

Now two problems arise in neoclassical economic methodology with regards to simulating the starvation point towards the production possibility frontier in order to attain the self-sufficiency objective of the poor. First, the interactions that occur among the various factors generating entitlement are so linked that participation in these either by means of agency, policies or relations among the variables will perpetually disturb the so-called optimal production frontier. Simulated points moved towards the frontier now belong to fuzzy domains because of knowledge induction (interaction). Consequently, the production possibility frontier becomes perturbed by the extent of polity-market interferences on the optimal allocation and distribution menus of the neoclassical genre.

Secondly, neoclassical growth model is permanently premised on the principle of marginal substitution among factor inputs. Among these inputs, technological change and institutions are either exogenous or if they are endogenized they fall in the category of marginal substitution between factor inputs. The latter case is explained by the neoclassical theory of endogenous institutions (North, 1981) and public choice theory (Buchanan & Tullock, 1962).

With exogenous technology and policy impact, the production possibility curve is shifted. Yet the intrinsic nature of tradeoff in the neoclassical growth model is not removed. Socio-economic environment such as a capitalist globalization order militates for capital and efficiency, growth and productivity against the social goals, such as, infant industry protection, subsidy for the poor, government and institutionally sponsored risk safety measures for the poor.

Contrarily, in the words of the *World Development Report 2000* (World Bank, 2000, p. 38), "Growth is essential for expanding economic opportunity for poor people—though this is only the beginning of the story of public action. The question is how to achieve rapid, sustainable, pro-poor growth." Between these two institutional viewpoints we note a wedge in the applicability of neoclassical economic growth model towards attaining its methodological conditions of efficient and optimal allocation of resources for attaining economic growth. The recognition of the tradeoff between social and economic factors is inherent in the World Bank's approach and in the emphasis on economic growth inherent in the IMF's economic approach. Between the two approaches we note that interactions between institutional and market forces cannot be answered by the conflicting and optimizing picture of organizing the poor within the neoclassical economic growth paradigm.

Upon returning to Sen's deprivation and entitlement failure model in the neoclassical framework we note many more methodological problems in it (Choudhury, 1993). Let us consider a point on the production possibility frontier that is 'optimally' attained by moving a starvation point through polity-market interventions. In such a case a Rawlsian state of original position (Rawls, 1971) is attained, for optimal equity and efficiency is assumed to have been attained through market-institution intervention. On the other hand, such a state of 'optimality' with respect to the Rawlsian case suggests that the agents of this state have become optimally individuated and thus non-corresponding with each other. Only in such a Kantian type original position of individualism of the altruistic individual can a rationalist doctrine of fairness be created in Rawls' original position. The rest of the trajectories signifying the movement of an interior starvation point onto the optimal production surface mark the 'difference principle' for attaining social wellbeing for the poor. Consequently, a contradiction arises from the functional meaning of participation and discourse with the market orientation towards economic distribution in such an entitlement model. Rawls' and Sen's ideas regarding equitable distribution conflict with each other and with the non-neoclassical model of pervasive learning (Choudhury, 1993 op cit).

Of late, the school of endogenous growth model argued that human capital induction in the growth model would make the tradeoff variables evolve in a codetermined fashion. The theory claims that it would then be possible to get out of diminishing marginal returns on resource use, which is a principle that underlies the tradeoff perspective (Romer, 1986).

Our contention against the endogenous growth model in the literature continues on in the neoclassical premise. We claim that since diminishing marginal rate of return and the marginal tradeoff are coterminous concepts, it is impossible to replace such a tradeoff by complementary relations without completely taking off the pre-condition of scarcity of resource allocation, and hence of competition and perfect or bounded foresight. All of these conditions are retained in the endogenous growth model. Endogenous growth model is like the public choice neoclassical theory of endogenous institutions (Buchanan, 1954). All these approaches translate a model of marginal substitution and diminishing marginal returns of production into a technologically induced one having conflicting market-polity interactions that we have discussed above. The attenuating methodological problems of the neoclassical economic paradigm persist in such approaches.

THE IMPORTANCE OF COMPLEMENTARY MARKET-POLITY INTERACTIONS FOR POVERTY ALLEVIATION

The World Bank (2000) has pointed out that among the several approaches to poverty alleviation are participatory mechanisms for the poor and a program of economic growth that is poor-oriented. The World Bank would like to utilize a combination of poor-oriented institutional policies with market friendly economic restructuring to attain the goal of poverty alleviation.

The following are some of the bold statements made by the World Bank (2000, p. 7) in this regard. It points out that in the various strategies of poverty alleviation, such as, promoting opportunities, facilitating empowerment and enhancing security "There is no hierarchy of importance. The elements are deeply complementary. Each part of the strategy affects underlying causes of poverty addressed by the other two." On the side of actions to alleviate poverty the World Development Report 2000 carries on to point out (p. 7), "There is no simple, universal blueprint for implementing this strategy. Developing countries need to prepare their own mix of policies to reduce poverty, reflecting national priorities and local realities. Choices will depend on the economic, socio-political, structural, and cultural context of individual countries—indeed, individual communities."

The political economy of poverty alleviation is thereby a complex study of many interacting factors. The question of poverty is thus a multidimensional problem in socio-economic development that recognizes the central importance of interaction generated by participation and consensual decision-making. In this regard the World Development Report 2000 points out (p. 12), "The way to deal with this complexity is through empowerment and participation—local, national, and international."

In what follows we will argue that a genuinely participatory model of development for poverty alleviation cannot be found in the entire neoclassical economic reasoning including its diverse forms found in endogenous growth models, public choice and social contract models of democratic institutions. An altogether different form of economic epistemology needs to be used within the perspective of interaction, co-determination and dynamic evolution realized through the process of participation, action and response within socio-economic development.

THE COMPLEMENTARY MODEL OF INTERACTIONS, INTEGRATION AND CREATIVE EVOLUTION AS THE NEW PARADIGM OF SOCIO-ECONOMIC DEVELOPMENT FOR ALLEVIATION OF POVERTY

The new economic reasoning for attaining complementary relations in the political economy of poverty alleviation within an appropriate development perspective needs a comprehensively interactive and dynamically complementary view of social and economic reality. This is brought about by the dynamic understanding of the episteme of unity of knowledge in a systems and process view of socio-economic development (Von Mises, 1960; Choudhury, 2000a).

Optimality Means the End of Learning Process

According to the participatory perspective of socio-economic development explained by continuous learning followed by actions and responses among agents, variables and their systems of relations, novelty perpetually denies optimum. We refer here to Shackle's (1972) incisive study rejecting the social realism of neoclassical meanings of equilibrium and optimality. He remarks in the following words that the neoclassical optimal points imply the end of novelty that comes with continuous learning. Hence if one were to depend upon a Marshallian type market clearing order, he will have to spend a lifetime, in the 'processual' sense, to ever come up with a market clearing equilibrium. Neoclassical economics thereby, does not provide the explanation as to how a system of resource allocation learns to attain the end states.

Shackle's (1972, p. 150) words on his criticism are as follows:

> *"Walras accordingly spoke of tatonements and Edgeworth of recontract. Both of these terms mean that sets of prices would be tried out until a set was found which taken together with the quantities that individuals would buy and sell at those prices, offer to each person that particular exchange of goods for goods he most prefers. When we examine this suggestion, we see that it is no more than a formal acknowledgement of a problem, the problem of how (by what institutional arrangement, by what organization of affairs) the equilibrium prices are to be discovered. Repeated trial and error, while the market stands in suspense awaiting the outcome, is not a practical resort. The number of distinct trials, even if confined to discrete steps of price and quantity, would be so immense that the necessary 'market day' would extend beyond human lifetimes."*

In reference to policy induction of optimal state-variables we now note that all learning would end at such optimal end-points. Besides, we are not even aware of the process of learning that goes prior to the attaining of the optimal-equilibrium points. In this intrepid universe of event and time moving together in consonance to each other, we cannot provide a substantive meaning to events. Neoclassical economics provides merely an exogenous meaning to time-independence. Hence, institution, policy, process and social contract remain linked with the independence of time-movement rather than with the endogeneity of knowledge induction (Holland, 1987).

When a new impetus is provided to the optimal-equilibrium end-point in the neoclassical optimal production frontier to change its position, the policy impact on such a point withers away, as market forces prevail and determine the mechanism of 'market exchange'. Thus between point to point of evolution under policy induction, institutional change and renewed social contracts, one finds no substantive theory of interactions, learning and process in neoclassical economics. Such policy, institutional and social interactions remain at best local and neutral in neoclassical economic theory. Their relevance withers away in the long-run picture of neoclassicism. This is the phenomenon that we refer to as the *exogenous* nature of policy, and thereby, of institutions and social contract in neoclassical economics.

Structural Embedding of Long-run Non-learning Neoclassical Resource Allocation Frontier

In order to study a new epistemological outlook of our economic science we must reject those conditions of the social economy that generate tradeoffs due to the existence of scarcity, competition, rationality of foresight (complete or bounded) and optimal-equilibrium methods of analysis. Indeed, the principal construction and meaning of the economic and social universe as an interactive whole are to be reinterpreted on the basis of the episteme of complementary relations among the agents, institutions, their preferences, and among the selected variables, policies and functions of such a social economy. This is the meaning of endogenizing the entire system of variables, policies, preferences, technology, institutions and social contracts by means of learning through pervasive interactions that cause consensus to arise and dynamic evolution of learning to continue.

Ethical Endogeneity and Resource Allocation: Entitlement Failure and Social Welfare

Our principle of ethical endogeneity states that resource allocation and social wellbeing are attained through interaction between agents, variables and their relations. The circular cause and effect relations between the endogenous variables explain such interactions in a dynamic sense. Such variables include policy variables, institutional variables and social contracts (Choudhury, 2000b). Since interactions within a relational order are essential for explaining the circular causation and continuity process, a pervasively learning process both among agents and variables ensues. The emerging model of resource allocation and social wellbeing now turns into a permanently knowledge-induced one on the basis of interactively sorting out policy, institutional, technological and social contractarian forms that bring about complementary relations among the endogenous variables. The principle of ethical endogeneity and the principle of universal complementarities are now coterminous.

The choice of variables that can be endogenized by a unifying (i.e. complementary) learning process is important in the ethically endogenous model. Let us explain by contrasting cases.

Interest rate in the Keynesian general equilibrium model is not amenable to such knowledge induction. That is because the presence of interest as a purely neoclassical consequence separates the real economic sector from the financial sector in terms of relative prices existing between goods and money, both seen as commodity. Such a relative price is the cause and effect of tradeoff between money and real economic activity. Such a relative price when subjected to knowledge induction within market-polity interactions must progressively replace the interest rate by the rate of return on real economic activities. The latter enhances microenterprise activity, whereas interest rate impedes it as a burden of financial collateral on the poor.

The choice of a rate of return on real economic activities establishes a circular endogenous interrelationship between this rate and the state variables, because they are cause and effect of each other. The emerging simulation model can now be interactively iterated to yield evolving levels of social wellbeing and values of the endogenized state and policy variables.

The social wellbeing criterion now assumes a meaning substantively different from the concept of social welfare as a neoclassical economic function. Social wellbeing is attained by means of complementary interrelations among the agents, knowledge-induced endogenous variables and their diverse relations. Hence its value represents a simulated measure of the degree to which complementarities among the chosen variables are attained. Market forces are now transformed conformably with respect to endogenous policy, institutional and social contractarian variables. Also the inherent preferences of consumers, the production menus and distribution of income and wealth are induced by the knowledge-flows arising from ethical interactions. Good examples of such complementary relationships between market and polity are ecological consciousness and community economic development (Korten, 1995).

The example of interest reduction followed by its abolition is an important approach to poverty alleviation at all levels. That is because poverty alleviation requires entitlement and empowerment formation and considerable social investment on outlets such as, education, enterprise development, human resource development, health care and subsidization of programs for the poor.

The theory of ethical endogeneity, that is of pervasively complementary relations among diversity of forms that are evolved and discoursed between market realities and institutional presence must logically reject all the assumptions of neoclassical resource allocation and social welfare. For instance, learning through pervasive interactions among agents, variables and their relations cannot accept optimal and steady state equilibrium points on any optimal resource allocation and social welfare frontier. There exists no such frontier. Thus there cannot exist relative prices that arise from marginal rates of substitution (supply side) and marginal utility (demand side), as is the case with neoclassical economics. In the end, our arguments presented earlier affirm that the only alternative view on resource allocation and social wellbeing now is to move along learning trajectories in diversity of forms, as knowledge induction with interaction intensifies within the market-polity domain, carrying with them interactive preference changes. A general ethico-economic system of political economy now emerges (Choudhury & Malik, 1992).

The endogenous theory of knowledge induction of social wellbeing simulation problem now implies that gains in Human Poverty Index (HPI), Gender Development Index (GDI), Human Development Index (HDI) and Gross Domestic Product (GDP) are possible from market friendly policies that are established through participatory discourse at the microeconomic level. Institutions now become grassroots participatory democracies, wherein possibilities for growth and equity are sought together through discourse. The social wellbeing function of the variables so formed by knowledge induction in market-polity framework is simulated to yield a post-evaluative position with respect to the effectiveness of the previously attained interrelationships among complementary agents, variables and their diverse relations.

In its simplest form such a knowledge-induced simulation model is given by (Choudhury, 2002),

$$\text{Simulate } \{\theta) \text{ SW } \{\theta, X(\theta)\}$$
$$\text{Subject to, } X(\theta) = f_1(\theta; \text{SW}(.))$$
$$\theta+ = f_2(\theta)-, X(\theta)-),$$

Thus proceding on interactively through recursions.

This simple form hides complex sequences of relations as of interactions across agents, states, policies and systems. X(θ) denotes a vector of market-polity variables endogenized by knowledge-flows through institution and market interactions. These knowledge-flows finally attain their temporary limiting values denoted by θ. Recursive feedback interrelations among the knowledge-induced market and polity variables are shown by the dependence of on attained values of θ. In turn, recursive θ-values (indicated by +) are determined by past θ-values (indicated by-). The circular causation and continuity proceed on between rounds of given recursive values of simulated SW, as shown. At the end, we have generated a truly process-oriented model of resource allocation and social wellbeing, explaining not optimality but simulation of this criterion with respect to resource allocation through interaction, consensus and creative evolution. This is the nature of the circular causation and continuity model of unity of knowledge underlying the principle of ethical endogeneity. In such a circular causation and continuity model of recursive learning and endogeneity, equilibrium states of the endogenized variables and the temporary equilibrium states of SW in simulation are formed by participation (interaction), consensus (complementary relations) and creative evolution (Choudhury & Korvin, 2001).

EMPIRICAL EVIDENCE ON THE EXISTENCE OF DEVELOPMENT TRADEOFF AT THE MACROECONOMIC AND MICROECONOMIC LEVELS

We use log-linear regression equations between rates of changes in HPI, GDP, HDI and GDI variables in order to explain the elasticities of the dependent variables in terms of the remaining independent variables by means of the coefficients of the log-linear regression equations. GEM (Gender Empowerment Measure) as an explanatory variable, could not be used because of paucity of data on this variable for the category of countries that we are examining. We define our meaning of the tradeoff or independence of relationship as follows:

(% rate of change in y)/(% rate of change in x) < 0 (tradeoff) or significantly small value (independence).

y denotes either HPIk/HPIk-1, HDIk/HDIk-1, GDIk/GDIk-1,

x denotes GDPk/GDPk-1,

k =1,2,... being the sequential values of the countries in the selected group as they appear in the Human Development Report.

The following results were obtained on estimating by multiple-OLS method the log-linear regression equations shown, using data on HPI, GDP, HDI and GDI. The data are given in the statistical appendix. The data are for the 'medium-HDI countries'. This particular selection was prompted by the need for having sufficient data not otherwise available for the Southeast Asian and Pacific Rim countries. The sample size comprised 50 selected countries in the entire group comprising industrialized, middle income and low-income countries. Malaysia is one of these countries occupying overall 61st place according to HDI ranking, but 5th place among the 50 medium HDI countries chosen.

In terms of GDI ranking Malaysia holds 6th place among these countries. In terms of GDP she holds 9th place. Yet in terms of HPI Malaysia holds 12th place among the selected countries. Such a status of Malaysia is expected to reflect the results on the relationship between rates of changes in the other variables as mentioned below on HPI-rate. The estimation is done circularly among the variables to establish causality amongst them.

1. HPI-GDP-HDI-GDI relationship

$\log(HPI_k / HPI_{k-1}) = 5.210E\text{-}02 + 2.709.\log(HDI_k / HDI_{k-1})$ -

t-statistics (0.921) (0.583)

significance levels (0.362) (0.563)

$1.655.\log(GDI_k / GDI_{k-1}) + 4.966E\text{-}02.\log(GDP_k / GDP_{k-1})$ (1)

(-0.619) (0.753) t-statistics

(0.539) (0.455) significance levels

R-square = 0.033

F-value = 0.517; Significance level = 0.672

2. HDI-HPI-GDI-GDP relationship

$\log(HDI_k / HDI_{k-1}) = -6.630E\text{-}03 + 2.706E\text{-}03.\log(HPI_k / HPI_{k-1})$ +

t-statistics (-4.367) (0.583)

significance levels (0.000) (0.563)

$0.271.\log(GDI_k / GDI_{k-1}) + 2.148E\text{-}03.\log(GDP_k / GDP_{k-1})$ (2)

(3.619)) (1.031) t-statistics

(0.001) (0.308) significance levels

R-square = 0.223

F-value = 4.412; Significance level = 0.008

3. GDI-HPI-HDI-GDP relationship

$\log(GDI_k / GDI_{k-1}) = -1.75E\text{-}03 - 4.990E\text{-}03.\log(HPI_k / HPI_{k-1}) - 8.200E\text{-}$

t-statistics (-0.561) (-0.619) (-2.370)

Significance levels (0.578) (0.539) (0.022)

$03.\log(GDP_k / GDP_{k-1}) + 0.818.\log(HDI_k / HDI_{k-1})$

t-stastistics (3.619)

significance levels (0.001) (3)

R-square = 0.297

F-value = 6.491; Significance level = 0.001

4. GDP-HPI-HDI-GDI relationship

$\log(GDP_k / GDP_{k-1}) = -6.120E\text{-}02 + 0.244.\log(HPI_k / HPI_{k-1}) +$

t-statistics (-0.486) (0.753)

significance levels (0.629) (0.455)

$10.504.\log(HDI_k / HDI_{k-1}) -13.269.\log(GDI_k / GDI_{k-1})$

t-statstics (1.031) (-2.370) (4)

significance levels (0.308) (0.022)

R-square = 0.129

F-value = 2.265; Significance level = 0.094

The above estimated results reveal that the relationships among social factors and among growth related factors are of a complementary nature individually taken in these groups. But the relations between growth-related variables and social variables are either too weakly positive to be accounted for any significant complementary relationship or are straight tradeoffs. The debate around the neoclassical tradeoff and thus the inability of such a premise to explain the human development perspective along with poverty alleviation, gender empowerment, entitlement and gender development through a complementary relationship between markets and institutions, is seen to appear for the medium human development countries.

We note from the structural equation (1) that there exists complementary relationship between the rate of change in GDI (same as $\log(HPI_k / HPI_{k-1})$) and poverty reduction indicated by a negative coefficient of the rate of change in GDI. As GDI increases (decreases) HPI decreases (increases). We obtain similar interrelationships from the structural equations of the circular processes (2) and (3). We note that the social variables (rate of change in HDI, rate of change in GDI) are complementary to each other.

Complementarities among the growth-related variables are also found between the rates of change in HDI (as a function of GDP) and GDP but are very weak in equation (1). The same implication also holds for equation (2).

Trade off or weak relationship is shown to exist between the rate of change in HPI and the rates of change in HDI and GDP per capita in expression (1). In expression (2) the relationship between the rate of change in HDI and the rates of change in HPI and GDP per capita is very weak. In expression (3) the rate of change in GDI is weakly related with the rate of change in GDP per capita, whereas the relationship with HPI is weak. In expression (4) the rate of change of GDP per capita has a tradeoff with the rates of change in HPI and GDI.

The reason for complementary relations between HDI, GDI and GDP per capita is the functional interrelationships among these variables, which all have the common variable, GDP per capita in them. When converted into rates of change, GDP per capita has the highest value among these variables. Thus a complementary relationship among these variables can be expected. Yet in the estimated equation (2) we note that the relationship between the rates of change in HDI and GDP per capita is weak. Likewise, similar relations are found to be weak in equation (3). In equation (4) there appears a tradeoff between the rates of change in GDP per capita and HPI and GDI. Equation (4), which is the most reliable one in the relations between the rates of change in the variables shows a tradeoff between the rates of change in GDP per capita and of HPI and GDI, and a complementary relation between the rates of change of GDP and HDI. The last result can be explained by the significant place of GDP per capita in the composite measure of HDI.

We also note that in all cases the results are accepted at high levels of significance, above 40 per cent, according to t-statistic. The circular relations among the variables are found to be well specified in terms of the variables included. However, the low values of R-square reflect that the log-linear form of the compound index model may not have been adequately specified in form. This is a valid reason for circular causation according to the model of complementarities that negates marginal substitution among variables in favour of complex phenomenon better amenable to estimation by simulation methods.

The above empirical results establish our case that the economic growth agenda of medium-HDI countries being of the neoclassical type, there exist significant tradeoffs or weak relations between economic growth and the social variables. The efficiency and equity tradeoff or independence of relationship is thus confirmed. The structural relations of circular causation in the composite index form a social wellbeing index, establishing thus the importance of such a system that can bring out the developmental tradeoffs and complementarities, as the case may be.

ANALYSIS OF RESULTS IN THE LIGHT OF SOCIO-ECONOMIC CHANGES IN MALAYSIA

The Malaysian Seventh Development Plan (1996-2000) continued to target economic growth *with* equity as its goal in line with the earlier development plans. The question that we started to address regarding the questionability of appropriateness of the neoclassical model of economic growth in the explanation of Malaysian economic growth now needs to be examined. Many of the well-known Malaysian policies of which is the New Economic Policy, aimed at distributing the national wealth towards empowering and mobilizing the very poor. The target groups comprised the Bumiputeras who lived off agricultural activity. Yet the experience of NEP has shown that this goal has not succeeded in attaining the kind of complementary relationship the development plan had in mind in combining economic growth *with* equity. We find that the human resource development of the very poor remained sluggish and the federal government had to undertake large expenditure to support the development efforts in unproductive transformation (New Economic Perspectives, 1991).

Mehmet (1988) has pointed out that NEP may have caused unwanted support of a rentier class among Bumiputeras. If such are the results of national resource allocation in projects like the Bumiputera Commercial and Industrial Community (BCIC) they establish the tradeoff nature of the neoclassical model and defeat the purpose of attaining economic growth with equity. Likewise, the program of Bumiputera Equity Ownership for increasing the participation and control of Bumiputera ownership in the corporate sector may run the risk of promoting a rent seeking economy. This can happen if the benefits of this program along with the effectiveness of human resource development of the Bumiputeras are not found to contribute to productive ownership of assets.

To the extent that economic growth is generated by export-orientation, capital flow liberalization, privatization, sectoral structural change, human resource development and total productivity, we then need to examine the Malaysian experience in these areas. We would then be able to infer the effects that they may have had on poverty reduction. Expectations of the Seventh Development Plan in the above-mentioned areas can be read off Table 1.

How do these compare with recent Malaysian performances? Table 2 shows comparative figures on relevant statistics.

From a comparative picture of Malaysia vis-à-vis neighbouring countries and the upper middle income group as a whole we find that she has done well on her growth performance and inflow of foreign direct investments and private capital. Yet none of these countries can be said to have done well on their debt performance. Besides, there appears to be comparatively higher *shift* in value added contribution from agriculture to other sectors for Malaysia than for the other countries and in comparison to the upper middle-income countries as a whole. Malaysia's record on labour/population ratio as an indicator of structural sustainability of labour-augmenting industry has been comparatively lower than the neighbouring countries by the year 1999. Such a trend could result in a growing labour-saving and capital-intensive economic growth menu for Malaysia.

The significantly growing volumes in private capital flows and FDIs point to a strong positive correlation between such capital flows and economic growth rates. This too is a sign of over-dependence of Malaysia on foreign investments to fuel her momentum of growth. In today's volatile capital markets it is necessary to ascertain that such capital flows are directed into real sectoral developments rather than into speculative portfolio investments.

Volatility of capital markets caused an outflow of accumulated short-term speculative portfolio investments in Malaysia, which was a major reason for the financial and economic crisis during 1996-97.

Table 1
Expectations under Malaysia Seventh Development Plan (by 2000)

Macroeconomic stability	Real GDP rate of 8 per cent annually will be targeted. Sustainable development will be targeted.
Monetary policy	Speculative capital inflow will be discouraged by keeping up interest rate levels domestically.
Fiscal policy	reinforce monetary policy in curbing price pressure
New investments	encourage savings
Balance of Payments	Current accounts deficits will be financed by FDIs brought in by foreign investors.
Poverty Alleviation	reduce disparity between ethnic groups and bring down the poverty rate to 5.5 per cent and eliminate hard core poverty.
	Bumiputera ownership will be increased as part of the complementary equity-efficiency development plan.
Productivity driven growth	total factor productivity growth will be targeted.
	Employment will grow at 2.8 per cent annually.
	Capital deepening technological change will be promoted.
	Science & Technology and Research & Development driven technological change in high value-added production promoting total factor productivity.
Competitiveness	Privatization within the globalization agenda will be enhanced.
	Global networking will be promoted.
Industrialization	export-led industrialization will be promoted as always in the face of globalization.
	Inter-industry linkages will be promoted.
Human resource development	Higher scale of training to be promoted to become competitive in the global environment.

Source: Malaysian Seventh Development Plan 1996-2000, Chapter 1.

The attractive growth performance and capital flows for Malaysia hold good prospects for privatization programs to pick up. The social and economic impact of such privatization programs will have to prove whether a neoclassical growth model will tilt resource allocation and ownership of assets in favour of the rent seeking class and short-term capital formation or otherwise. Contrarily, these opportunities can be used to enhance participatory frameworks of development among the small-scale, medium-scale and large-scale industries with market-polity interactions in place.

Poverty alleviation in Malaysia has been recorded as a significant achievement. Yet Johari (1991) has pointed out in his study on poverty in Sabah that the government statistics on which the count of poverty among households is computed are not reliable. He points out that government statistics on incidence of poverty or poverty-rates does not mention about the poverty line used for such estimates. Government data on poverty are confidential and often subject to contradictory inferences even between the development plans. On the basis of such problems with data and estimation on poverty levels in Malaysia some authors have shown that the incidence of poverty is higher than recorded in many areas. Among these are the provinces of Kelantan and Sabah.

Table 2
Comparative Statistics for Malaysia Development in Recent Years

Years	*Malay-sia*	*Indo-nesia*	*Thai-land*	*Singa-pore*	*Upper Middle Income*
Labour/population Ratio (percentage)					
1980	36.23	39.11	51.39	43.47	39.30
1999	39.65	47.82	59.96	62.50	44.15
Economic growth (average annual rate)					
1980-90	5.3	6.1	7.6	6.7	2.5
1990-99	6.3	4.7	4.7	8.0	3.6
Structure of Output (value added/GDP%)					
1990					
Agriculture	19	19	12	0	8
Industry	40	39	37	35	39
Manufacturing	26	21	27	27	24
Services	41	41	50	65	53
1999					
Agriculture	14	20	13	0	7
Industry	44	45	40	36	40
Manufacturing	35	25	32	26	23
Services	43	35	49	64	46
Financial flows (millions of dollars)					
1990					
Net private capital flow	769	3,325	4,399	–	–
FDI	2,333	1,093	2,444	5,575	–
External debt	15,328	69,872	28,165	–	–
1998					
Net private capital flow	8,295	-3,759	7,825	–	–
FDI	5,000	-356	6,941	7,218	–
External debt	44,773	150,875	86,172	–	–
Present value of Debt/GNP% 69	169	79	–	–	–

Source: World Bank, World Development Report 2001.

As long as regional disparities in poverty alleviation exist showing an increase in some against a decrease in other parts, the indications of economic growth with distributive equity may not have been truly attained. Urban sectors usually hide the incidence of poverty inter-regionally because of skewed income distribution in favour of the upper income bracket earners. According to Human Development Report 1999, between 1980 and 1994 Malaysia recorded 16.2 per cent in the bracket of the richest 20% to poorest 20%, in terms of real GDP per capita. This translated to 16 per cent of the population to be below the national poverty line. Similar statistics were 9.4 per cent of richest to poorest 20 per cent in terms of GDP per capita and 13 per cent of income earners being below national poverty line for Thailand. Similar statistics stood at 4.7 per cent and 8 per cent, respectively for Indonesia.

POLICY ANALYSIS

From our observations and empirical analysis on Malaysian relationship between economic growth and poverty alleviation we note that Malaysian development is mid-way between a neoclassical model and a complementary model of linkages. Yet some problems of neoclassical type tradeoffs have been noted. These need to be addressed in the framework of complementary developmental relations.

In addressing these problems of tradeoff we invoke our model of pervasive complementarities in the light of unity of knowledge. We note that manpower/population ratio along with strong sectoral linkages with the agricultural sector are needed for the benefit of generating entitlement and gradual productive transformation of the poor. To this arrangement must then be linked up other considerations. Among them are human resource development of the poor and a guided approach to globalization over and above a sheer role of FDIs in generating economic growth.

From our empirical results we note that a lower manpower/population ratio for Malaysia compared to other neighbours in the region may cause an eventual dependence on labour-saving and capital-intensive production menus. This will cause capital deepening in high-end technology for which the poor are not ready. Already the Malaysian Seventh Development has noted this transformation to happen and NEP showed that the human resource development was sufficiently reached out to the target group. But the transformation caused a rent seeking class among Bumiputeras. This is a reason why the BCIC could not be effectively realized even after the last two development planning periods.

Industrial structural shifts without linkages cause out-migration of labour from the rural to the urban sector in search of jobs. This runs the risk of an unsustainable agricultural sector by a dwindling of the service sector as support industry and a growing focus on the urban sector buildup. Privatization on capital deepening technology pursue the growth of the rural sector according to the demands of its own globally competitive technology serving as the medium of export-orientation for large-scale enterprises. In the midst of such a transformation, the alienation of technology falls upon those linked to agricultural activity. Consequently, the ratio of value-added contribution of the agricultural sector to total GDP declines. Consider the contrary technological change wherein the agricultural sector is also the processing sector of resource-based output and in it human resource development is attuned to train the rural sector manpower to man such a production menu. A resource-based agricultural sector is thus promoted side by side with the primary resource-based industry.

REORGANIZATION PRODUCTION RELATIONS ON THE BASIS OF PARTICIPATION AND CO-OPERATION

The complementary nature of resource-based manufacturing transformation and the human resource development for realizing it brings about community participation and institutional as well as trade-related entitlement in the rural population. Such trade-related entitlement formation in the rural sector is brought about by input-output relations among inter-sectoral flows of goods, services, resources and factors of production. An economy based on total factor productivity is thus established.

Retention of population in the agricultural sector is known to lead into population growth due to the nature of labour-market relations that the rural and resource-intensive sector creates. The result at the end is an increasing manpower/population ratio with a greater spread of capital across linked sectors. A capital-intensive technological change is replaced by a capital-widening transformation out of inter-sectoral linkages.

Human Resource Development

Human resource development with appropriate technological change in such a scenario of participatory community economic development is determined by the structure of inter-sectoral linkages and the importance of the rural sector. Consequently, FDIs, privatization and the export-orientation of the Malaysian economy find meaning in the milieu of such linked rural-urban sectoral development planning. The resulting employment causes entitlement and empowerment of the rural poor to increase. Reverse migration from the urban sector to the rural sector retains a viable manpower/population ratio in the rural sector. This movement frees the urban sector from the social expenditure pressure known to increase indebtedness of the national government. In this regard of accelerating government expenditure we note that Malaysia's external debt is embarrassingly high at this time as shown in Table 1.

Nation-wide Consciousness in Development Planning with Poor Focus

The importance of sustaining a comparatively better manpower/population ratio in conjunction with its consequential relationship with a capital widening technological change cannot be under-estimated. Such a demographic change would realize inter-sectoral linkages by giving importance to rural sector sustainability for community economic development. Its consequential participatory impact on poverty alleviation would then follow. Human resource development would then play a central role in causing labour market adaptation in the milieu of such a socio-economic transformation process. It is recommended that Malaysia's long held program of Bumiputera Commercial and Industrial Community as well as different areas of development planning should incorporate this important outlook of community-centered development focus within Malaysia in the new age (Tennyson, 1999).

Within this framework, the outlook on globalization along with its trade led-growth and capital flows is to be centered in community focus of socio-economic development. This can be done by appropriately restructuring the institutions of the public and private sectors to take account of such a sectoral diversification process. It would require development of appropriate financial packages and instruments that will sustain shares, such as unit trusts (*Amanah Saham*), to increase the empowerment of marginal shareholders. In this case, large companies may be allowed to hold resources on condition that there are contractual arrangement between the small-scale and large-scale enterprises with appropriate government policy to enforce these under the development plan, the BCIC establishment and investment guarantees with prorated government stake in such ventures.

Appropriate Fiscal and Monetary Policy Simulation

Financial arrangement should see to it that a sound monetary and fiscal policy simulation is maintained so that money circulation is brought in close link with the real economy through such instruments that can generate linkages between the financial sector and the real economy. In fact, one of the causes of volatility, which by itself erodes the sustainability of poor-oriented programs, is the independence of financial instruments from the real economic ventures. The result of such a competition and isolation between the financial and real economic sectors has been a steep increase in speculative portfolio investment component of FDIs. The undue benefits of such financial windfalls go to those who can stake large sums of money in highly risky ventures and often seek tax shelters on their financial losses.

Stakeholding with Shareholding at the Level of Rural Small-scale Enterprises

Stakeholding is another important way of increasing the participatory nature of projects and enhances the prospects of entitlement and empowerment for the poor. Stakeholding combined with shareholding supplies capital requirements of grassroots projects on shared basis or between labour (rural) and capital (urban) to finance projects that often are small-scale and thus fairly diversified in content in the agricultural, service and manufacturing sectors. A good example would be a project on developing the night market (*Pasar Malam*) system of vendor outlet using cooperative ventures among private entrepreneurs. *Pasar Malam* can be well developed and organized as a production, supply and consumer based system on the basis of linkages between the rural and urban sectors. In this system, the village suppliers have a chance to establish pawnshops and unit trusts for the marginal enterprises and in which the larger ones play a supporting role and the two share the benefits both as decision-makers and shareholders. Stakeholding has become a popular concept and practice even in the West. It is unfortunate that such an empowering instrument has not gained popularity in developing countries, where it is all the more required to realize the goals of poverty alleviation and community development.

Instruments for Shareholding, Stakeholding and Mobilizing of Resources at the Grassroots

Interest free Loans and Businesses

Interest free loans and businesses are meant not simply to grant access to resources for the poor and to help other businesses join hands in co-operative ventures. Besides, interest free transactions also help in integrating the fiscal and monetary policies cogently to mobilize resources in the most productive and fullest way while maintaining stable prices of goods. By so mobilizing the fiscal and monetary policies in a co-determined way with the joint demands and needs of the grassroots in cooperation with other businesses, an endogenous link is established between financial flows and real economic output. Money can now be thought of as a 'quantity in circulation' in accordance with the needs of the real economy. Such a real sector need is determined through interactions between clients and commercial banks, and thereafter between commercial banks and the central bank. Thus neither the central bank 'supplies' money nor the clientele demands money in such a case. Money supply and demand are determined by the 'circulation of a quantity of money' needed for meeting the demands of real economic activities. There now ceases to be an independent price for money, which is the rate of interest. The value of money instead, is measured in terms of the prices of real economic goods and services. When such prices assign the value to the goods and services we obtain the profit margin. From profits ensue profit sharing and cost sharing in the system of active cooperation between participatory production organizations.

Prices remain stable by the joint action of fiscal and monetary policy impacts when profit-sharing rates determine the mobilization of resources into increasing productivity of real economic activity. It has been shown for Malaysia that historically the low rates of interest and an active real economy caused the IS and LM curves of Keynesian macroeconomic analysis to be closely intertwined. Consequently, a continuously evolving trajectory of equilibrium is set between the quantity of money and the volume of goods and services produced (Choudhury, 1997). The case here is similar to the fullest impact of the multiplier at a low level of liquidity trap. The difference however is that we do not establish the evolutionary equilibrium of a money-real economy relationship from the side of liquidity trap. Rather, the argument is premised on the endogenous relationship between money and real economy giving the full expansionary capacity to the economy from the side of stable prices with expanded production. Total factor productivity in such an economy is thus the result of factor mobilization in the midst of production expansion and profit sharing with stable prices giving momentum to these consequences.

In the perspective of such endogenous relationship between money and real economic activity we recommend that Bank Negara should pursue conceptual research and application relating to such endogenous monetary transformation in the monetary and fiscal policy domains. The new arrangement should also conterminously transform the financial and capital markets away from speculative shares, bonds and stocks into linked shares between real economic activities and the quantity of money required to support them. Vouchers can be sold to the poor as claims on future profit shares as their productivity increases in the midst of the complementary process between money and production with stable prices enhancing the latter.

Zakat as a Specific Take on Wealth for Absolute Poverty Alleviation

Zakat is a mandatory Islamic take on the wealth of the needy to finance the needs of eight categories of social expenditure (*Qur'an*, 2:177). Instead of getting into details, here we are interested in the use of *zakat* for the uplift of the absolute poor. *Zakat* cannot be allayed to eradicate *relative* poverty. It is the objective of *zakat* to realize productive and dignified transformation of the needy. Thereby, panhandling on the part of the poor is considered to be against human dignity. This dehumanizing experience is replaced by a mandatory claim of *zakat* (and *sadaqah* meaning poor due) by the poor for productive purposes as a social need and right. The productive uplift of the absolute poor suggests a good use of *zakat* in expanding the activities of *Pasar Malam*. A whole range of marginal activities can be marked off. But with the advance of production diversity a natural indexation of *zakat* will follow to make it available at higher cost levels. Consequently, *zakat* would be spent on higher cost categories of human resources with the expansion of real economic activity.

Though *zakat* cannot be used for trading in shares and financial markets, the incomes gained by the productive use of *zakat* can be so allayed. Thereby, future volumes of *zakat* in society would depend upon generating income and wealth out of productive activity. Malaysia has a well-established *zakat* fund in the Prime Minister's Religious Department. The volume of collection and disbursement should attune to the linkage between *zakat*, productivity in the real sector, uplift of human resources and investment needs of the poor and their productive transformation by reinforcing specific forms of spending in real goods and services.

Zakat spending stabilizes prices, quite contrary to spending in the Keynesian model of income determination, which is known to inflate prices. According to the monetarist argument such fiscally induced prices increase at all levels of output, not simply at outputs higher than the full-employment level. On the other hand, *zakat* is a take on wealth and income that is specific to the eight categories of spending. There is no deficit financing involved and no excess expenditure by the government. The amount that is taken out of income cuts into the saving of the *zakat* payer. Hence, saving as financial withdrawal is reduced, while a part of it is converted into mandatory spending as *zakat*.

Hence in Malaysian development planning the role of *zakat* should be comprehended and applied into a general equilibrium form of relationship among money, real economic activity (output), prices, factor mobilization (human resource development). One such way would be to increase *zakat* payments to community level development centers to be mobilized into real economic projects operated by marginal labour, which can be paid *zakat*. A voucher as shareholding can be linked with *zakat* payment to promise future dividends to the holder upon increased production and human resource development. The voucher is like community money linked to the real economic activities for generating profitability and productivity. Its value depends upon the endogenous relationship of money to the real economy.

Since *zakat* is specifically meant for Muslims, therefore, in the context of Malaysia it can play a significant role for the uplift of Bumiputeras within the development plan. The circular flow of resources that links up the real goods with money at the grassroots where *zakat* becomes ameliorative, it necessarily becomes effective within the participatory framework of development. In this, the donors and recipients play a co-determining role on the allocation of resources in productive directions. While this is an empowering experience, the holding of vouchers along with this development would bring about enterprise expansion capability and entitlement generating possibilities over time. In all such linkages of an ethico-economic perspective of community economic development a perpetual evolutionary equilibrium on price level and output generation is maintained. This is a sure sign of human and economic sustainability. Sustainability is now determined by the attainment of social wellbeing simulated in the light of its interlinked relationships.

In the ethico-economic general equilibrium model of poverty alleviation and community economic development the instrument of business co-operation among government, large-scale enterprises and small-scale enterprises is endogenously interrelated with the phasing out of interest-based transactions and *zakat*. Each of these outlets causes mobilization of resources in the direction of higher output levels and price stability with perpetual evolutionary equilibrium. The result is factor mobilization and productivity. These result in entitlement and empowerment of the poor and bring them up to self-sufficiency.

Within the ethico-economic general equilibrium model it is necessary to establish effective organization of the participatory and conscious interrelationships. Without this central institutional factor much of the linkages among the variables and their relations would not be realized. *Zakat* and interest free transactions would ultimately devolve into mere charitable outcomes having no obvious productive consequences. For sometime now such a consequence was noted for Malaysia even with the use of *zakat* in one form of a general equilibrium systemic relationship (Choudhury & Malik, 1992).

CONCLUSION

In this paper we have introduced the concept of pervasive complementarities between economic efficiency and distributive equity in socio-economic development possibilities. This can be viewed as a substantively different socio-economic praxis than the pervasive nature of marginal substitution of neoclassical economics with at best a local nature of complementarities among alternatives.

Using such a conceptual background and analytical methods we conclude from the quantitative aspects of this paper that although HDI was introduced by UNDP to measure a social aspect of development beyond traditional macroeconomic reliance on real rates of growth, yet it remains a grossly macroeconomic measure. Real GDP measure fails to explain the social questions of tradeoff that remain embedded in an economic and social scenario under a neoclassical guise. There is need therefore, to extend the structure of HDI to incorporate such variables that look at the grassroots dynamics of participation, discourse and consensus formation. Instead, the existing HDI measure merely reflects market variables without having any policy, institutional, social contractarian and community-based dynamics reflected in its computation.

As the process of globalization proceeds, the development debate increasingly projects the direction of nations towards adopting a growth-led paradigm of change. In view of this it is difficult to expect the problems of empowerment, entitlement, community economic development and microenterprise development to be addressed by the existing nature of HDI (index). If the economic order of globalization is to be reconstructed on a complementary politico-economic front interconnecting the diverse possibilities through endogenous interrelationships, then HDI should be considered in the light of microeconomic variables and their interrelationships.

We suggest in this regard community-based surveys on a host of economic, social and institutional variables along with policy variables in them that can then be interrelated to form indexes. Such indexes will reflect meaningful visions of change and direction of community development in various nations through a mix of factors.

By our empirical results we conclude that the neoclassical economic model of economic growth is being thoroughly adopted by the medium HDI countries. This has caused major developmental tradeoffs or ineffectiveness of the growth paradigm in alleviating poverty and bringing about greater degree of equality. Growth and distributive justice have thus conflicted with each other. In this paper we have prescribed the circular causation model of pervasive complementarities among possibilities rather than the competing and individuating model of the neoclassical genre. Public policies and institutional reorganization are to be carried out according to this pervasively complementary worldview.

REFERENCES

Buchanan, J.M. (1954), "Social Choice, Democracy, and free Markets", *Journal of Political Economy,* Vol. 62: 114-23.

Buchanan, J. & Tullock, G. (1962), *The Calculus of Consent,* Ann Arbor, MI: Michigan University Press.

Choudhury, M.A. (1993), *Comparative Development Studies, In Search of the World View,* London, Eng: Macmillan & New York, NY: St. Martin's Press.

Choudhury, M.A. (1999), "A Critique of Econometric Modeling for Development Studies: A Political Economic Approach with Special Reference to Malaysia", in B.N. Ghosh ed. *Political Economy of Development in Malaysia,* Kuala Lumpur, Malaysia: Utusan, pp. 105-124.

Choudhury, M.A. (2000a), *The Islamic Worldview*, London, Eng: Kegan Paul International.

Choudhury, M.A. (2000b), "A Social Contractarian Theory of Markets: Neoclassicism, Rawls, Gauthier and the Alternative", *International Journal of Social Economics*, Vol. 27, No. 3, pp. 194-212.

Choudhury, M.A. (2002), "Human Development, Military Expenditure and Social Wellbeing, in B.N. Ghosh ed. *Contemporary Issues on Development Economics*, London, Eng: Routledge.

Choudhury, M.A. & Korvin, G. (2001), "Sustainability in knowledge-centered Socio-Scientific Systems", *International Journal of Sustainability in Higher Education*, Vol. 2, No. 1.

Choudhury, M.A. Korvin, G. & Seyyed, F. (2002), "Discovering micro-level Tradeoffs in Economic Development and Studying their Fractal Character", Indonesian Management and Accounting Research Journal, Vol. 1, No. 1.

Choudhury, M.A. & Malik, U.A. (1992), *The Foundations of Islamic Political Economy*, London, Eng: Macmillan & New York NY: St. Martin's.

Government of Malaysia (1991), *The Second Outline Perspective Plan, 1999-2000*, Kuala Lumpur, Malaysia: National Printing Department.

Government of Malaysia (1996), *Malaysian Seventh Development Plan 1996-2000*, Kuala Lumpur, Malaysia: Economic Planning Unit.

Holland, T.E. (1987), "On Parallelism in Neoclassical Economic Theory", *International Journal of Social Economics*, 14:3/4/5, pp. 191-98.

Johari, M.Y. Hj. (1991), "Poverty Profile in Sabah and Rural Development Strategies after 1990", in M.Y.Hj. Johari ed. Issues and Strategies in Rural Development, Sabah, Malaysia: Institute for Development Studies & Konrad Adenauer Foundation, pp. 3-49.

Korten, D.C. (1995), "Ecological Revolution", in his *When Corporations Rule the World*, London, Eng: Earthscan, pp. 261-76.

Mehmet, O. (1988), *Development in Malaysia, Poverty, Wealth and Trusteeship*, Petaling Jaya, Malaysia: Institute of Social Analysis.

North, D.C. (1981), "A Neoclassical Theory of State", in his *Structure and Change in Economic Theory*, New York, N.Y: W.W. Norton, pp. 26-30.

Okun, A.H. (1975), *Equality and Efficiency, the Big Trade-Off*, Washington, D.C: The Brookings Institute.

Phelps, E.S. (1989), "Distributive Justice", in J. Eatwell, P. Newman & M. Milgate eds. *New Palgrave: Social Economics*, New York, NY: W.W. Norton.

Rawls, J. (1971), *A Theory of Justice*, Cambridge, MA: Belknap Press of Harvard University Press.

Romer, P.M. (1986), "Increasing Returns and Long-run Growth", *Journal of Political Economy*, Vol. 94, pp. 1002-37.

Sen, A. (1986), *Poverty and Famines: an Essay on Entitlement and Deprivation*, Oxford, Eng: Clarendon Press.

Shackle, G.L.S. (1972), *Epistemics and Economics*, Cambridge, Eng: Cambridge University Press.

Tennyson, B. ed. (1999), "The Role of Micro-enterprise in Community Economic Development in Global Perspective, Special Issue of *Humanomics*, 15:2/3.

United Nations Development Program (2000), *Human Development Report 2000*, New York, N.Y: Oxford University Press.

Von-Mises, L. (1960), "The Science of Human Action", in his *Epistemological Problems of Economics*, Princeton New Jersey: University of Princeton Press.

World Bank (2000), *World Development Report 2000-2001*, New York, N.Y: Oxford University Press.

STATISTICAL APPENDIX
MEDIUM HUMAN DEVELOPMENT COUNTRY DATA

#	*Country*	*HDI Value 1998*	*HDI Rank*	*HPI Value 1998*	*GDI Value 1998*	*GDP Per Capita (US $)*
1.	Costa Rica	0.797	48	4.0	0.789	2800
2.	Trinidad	0.793	50	5.1	0.784	4618
3.	Mexico	0.784	55	10.4	0.775	4459
4.	Panama	0.776	59	8.9	0.770	3200
5.	Malaysia	0.772	61	14.0	0.762	4251
6.	Venezuela	0.770	65	12.4	0.763	3499
7.	Fiji	0.769	66	8.4	0.755	2416
8.	Colombia	0.764	68	10.4	0.760	2392
9.	Mauritius	0.761	71	11.6	0.750	4034
10.	Brazil	0.747	74	15.6	0.736	4509
11.	Thailand	0.745	76	18.7	0.741	2593
12.	Philippines	0.744	77	16.1	0.739	1092
13.	Peru	0.737	80	16.5	0.723	2611
14.	Paraguay	0.736	81	16.4	0.723	1781
15.	Lebanon	0.735	82	10.8	0.718	2999
16.	Jamaica	0.735	83	13.4	0.732	1559
17.	Sri Lanka	0.733	84	20.3	0.727	802
18.	Turkey	0.732	85	16.4	0.726	3167
19.	Oman	0.730	86	22.7	0.697	5581
20.	Dominican Rep.	0.729	87	15.4	0.720	1799
21.	Maldives	0.725	89	25.4	0.720	1247
22.	Ecuador	0.722	91	16.8	0.701	1562
23.	Guyana	0.709	96	10.0	0.698	825
24.	Iran	0.709	97	19.2	0.691	1275
25.	China	0.706	99	19.0	0.700	727
26.	Tunisia	0.703	101	21.9	0.688	2283
27.	South Africa	0.697	103	20.2	0.689	3918
28.	El Salvador	0.697	104	20.2	0.693	1716
29.	Cape Verde	0.688	105	22.0	0.675	1354
30.	Algeria	0.683	107	24.8	0.661	1521
31.	Viet Nam	0.671	108	28.2	0.668	331
32.	Indonesia	0.670	109	27.7	0.664	972
33.	Syria	0.660	111	19.3	0.636	1209
34.	Swaziland	0.655	112	27.4	0.646	1409
35.	Honduras	0.653	113	23.3	0.644	722
36.	Bolivia	0.643	114	17.4	0.631	964
37.	Namibia	0.632	115	26.6	0.624	2133
38.	Nicaragua	0.631	116	24.2	0.624	452
39.	Egypt	0.623	119	32.3	0.604	1146
40.	Guatemala	0.619	120	29.2	0.603	1533
41.	Botswana	0.593	122	28.3	0.584	3611
42.	Mexico	0.589	124	38.4	0.570	1388
43.	Lesotho	0.569	127	23.3	0.556	486
44.	India	0.563	128	34.6	0.545	444
45.	Ghana	0.556	129	35.4	0.552	399
46.	Zimbabwe	0.555	130	30.0	0.551	703
47.	Cameroon	0.528	134	38.5	0.518	646
48.	Pakistan	0.522	135	40.1	0.489	511
49.	Comoros	0.510	137	33.0	0.503	403
50.	kenya	0.508	138	29.5	0.503	334
51.	Congo	0.507	139	31.9	0.499	821

Source: Human Development Report 2000.

ENERGY CONSUMPTION IN INDIA AND CHINA: A COMPARATIVE REVIEW OF TRENDS AND CHALLENGES

Ashir Mehta

INTRODUCTION

India's ongoing population explosion has placed great strain on the country's environment. This rapidly growing population, along with a move toward urbanization and industrialization, has placed significant pressure on India's infrastructure and its natural resources. Deforestation, soil erosion, water pollution and land degradation continue to worsen and are hindering economic development in rural India, while the rapid industrialization and urbanization in India's booming metropolises are straining the limits of municipal services and causing serious air pollution problems.

Despite a greater commitment by the Indian government to protect public health, forests, and wildlife, policies geared to develop the country's economy have taken precedence in the last 20 years. While industrial development has contributed significantly to economic growth in India, it has done so at a price to the environment. Not only is industrial pollution increasing public health risks, but abatement efforts also are consuming a significant portion of India's gross domestic product (GDP). As such, one of the main responsibilities of the Ministry of Environment and Forests (MoEF) continues to be the reduction of industrial pollution.

China's gradual transition to a market economy, which has been proceeding for two decades, has put China among the world's fastest growing economies. While economic growth has increased incomes and improved health indicators, as well as reduced overall poverty levels, growth has not been totally benign. Environmental pollution from coal combustion is damaging human health, air and water quality, agriculture and ultimately the economy.

This chapter traces the energy 'culprit' in exacerbating environmental problems in two largest economies of the world, India and China, particularly in terms of air pollution and carbon emissions. In the process it reviews the trends in energy consumption, carbon intensity and carbon emissions in the two countries relative to some of the major developing and developed nations of the world. It concludes with the challenges that face the two countries as they enter the 21st century, with respect to mitigating their environmental problems through alternative use of renewable energy.

AIR POLLUTION–THE ENERGY 'CULPRIT'

India

Sources of air pollution, India's most severe environmental problem, come in several forms, including vehicular emissions and untreated industrial smoke. Continued urbanization has exacerbated the problem of rapid industrialization, as more and more people are adversely affected and cities are unable to implement adequate pollution control mechanisms.

India's reliance on coal-fired power plants for its electricity generation has undermined some of the vehicular-oriented air quality improvement initiatives. Despite the fact that India is a large coal consumer, its Central Pollution Control Board has been slow to set sulfur dioxide (SO_2) emissions limits for coal-fired power plants, mainly because most of the coal mined in India is low in sulfur content. Coal-fired power plants do not face any nitrogen oxide (NOx) emissions limits either, although thermal plants fueled by other fossil fuels are subject to particulate matter emission standards. Again, however, the government's support for air quality standards has been undermined by the lack of enforcement of these standards.

China

A report released in 1998 by the World Health Organization (WHO) noted that of the ten most polluted cities in the world, seven can be found in China. Sulfur dioxide and soot caused by coal combustion are two major air pollutants, resulting in the formation of acid rain, which now falls on about 30% of China's total land area. Industrial boilers and furnaces consume almost half of China's coal and are the largest single point sources of urban air pollution.

Energy Consumption in Selected Asian Countries, 1980-2001

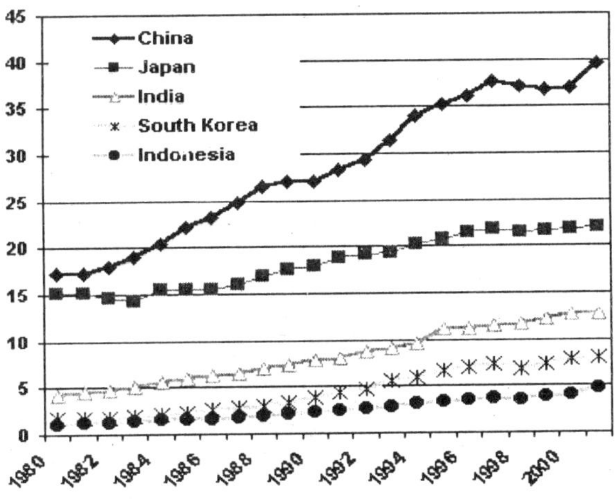

Energy Consumption

India

India's energy consumption is increasing rapidly, from 4.16 quadrillion Btu (quads) in 1980 to 12.8 quads in 2001. This 208% increase is largely the result of India's increasing population and the rapid urbanization of the country. Higher energy consumption in the industrial, transportation, and residential sectors continues to drive India's energy usage upwards at a faster rate even than China, which experienced a 130% increase in energy consumption from 1980 to 2001.

Despite the rapid growth between 1980 and 2001, India's energy consumption is still below that of Germany (14.35 quads), Japan (21.92 quads), China (39.67 quads), and the United States (97.05 quads). In addition, India's per capita energy consumption, which stood at 12.6 million Btu in 2001, is well below most of the rest of Asia and is one of the lowest in the world (although this may be more the result of India's large population rather than a low level of energy consumption). The 103% rise in India's per capita consumption between 1980, when per capita energy usage was just 6.2 million Btu, and 2001, is more problematic in the long-term, however.

Coal accounts for just over 50% (6.5 quads) of India's energy consumption. The power generation sector uses the majority of this coal, with heavy industry a distant second. Petroleum (4.4 quads) makes up 34.4% of India's energy consumption, while natural gas (6.5%) and hydroelectricity (6.3%) account for much of the remainder. Natural gas is growing in importance, as its share of India's energy consumption has risen from just 1.4% in 1980, while hydroelectricity-which made up 11.5% of the country's energy usage in 1980-has declined in relative importance. Nuclear (1.7%) and geothermal, wind, solar, and biomass (0.2%) made up a very small share of the country's energy consumption in 2001.

India's Fuel Share of Energy Consumption 2001 (Btu)

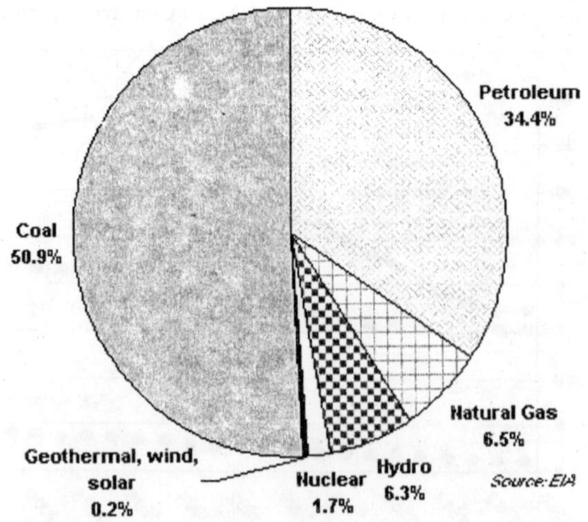

China

Outside of Japan, energy consumption in East Asia is dominated by one sector in one country-the industrial sector in China. Overall, China's energy consumption accounts for approximately 53% of East Asia's (excluding Japan) total energy consumption. In 2001, China accounted for 9.8% of world energy consumption. By 2025, projections indicate that China will be responsible for approximately 14.2% of world energy consumption.

Of the 39.7 quadrillion Btu of total primary energy consumed in China in 2001, 63.4% was coal, 25.8% was oil, 6.9% hydroelectricity, and 3.1% natural gas. While residential consumption has increased its share of China's energy demand over the last decade, the largest absolute gains in consumption were from the industrial sector.

While China ranks second in the world behind the United States in total energy consumption and carbon emissions, its per capita energy consumption and carbon emissions are much lower than the world average. In 2001, the United States had a per capita energy consumption of 341.8 million Btu, greater than 5.2 times the world's per capita energy consumption and slightly over 11 times China's per capita consumption. Per capita carbon emissions are similar to energy consumption patterns, with the United States emitting 5.5 metric tons of carbon per person, the world on average 1.1 metric tons, and China 0.6 metric tons of carbon per person. With a growing economy and increasing living standards, however, per capita energy use and carbon emissions are expected to rise. It is important to emphasize that while per capita energy use is relatively low, overall Chinese consumption of energy and the resultant carbon emissions are substantial, due to the country's large population and heavy use of coal.

Per Capita Energy Consumption of Selected Countries

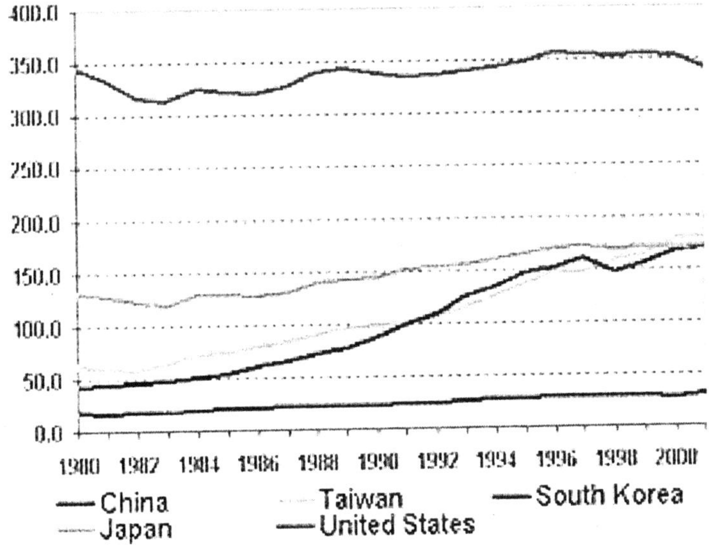

Carbon Emissions

India

In 1992, India signed the United Nations Framework Convention on Climate Change as a non-Annex I country, meaning it is not obligated to reduce its emissions of carbon and greenhouse gases (GHG). India ratified the agreement in 1993. While India recognizes the importance of reducing these harmful emissions, the Indian government also places a high priority on economic development. As such, India is not a signatory to the Kyoto Protocol that mandates specific commitments by countries to reduce their emissions of greenhouse gases by an average of 5.2% below 1990 levels by the agreed 2008-2012 time frame. Nevertheless, India accepted (ratification was unnecessary) the Kyoto Protocol on August 26, 2002.

India's non-participation in the Kyoto Protocol has been cited as a major reason behind the opposition to implementing the Protocol by several signatories, including the United States. In 2001, India, with 251 million metric tons of carbon equivalent emitted, ranked fifth in the world in carbon emissions, behind the United States, China, Russia and Japan. Although India's carbon emissions stood at only 80% of Japan's (316 million metric tons of carbon equivalent) total and less than one-sixth of the United States' (1,565 million metric tons) carbon emissions that same year, the rapid growth of India's carbon emissions - in combination with its exclusion from the Protocol - is the main point of controversy.

Between 1990 and 2001, India's carbon emissions increased by an astonishing 61%, a rate surpassed only by China's 111% increase during the same time period. India's carbon emissions are expected to continue to increase throughout the decade, offsetting the planned reduction in GHGs from the European Union and other countries that plan to implement the Protocol's emissions cut requirements. The rise in India's carbon emissions has been exacerbated by the low energy efficiency of coal-fired power plants in the country. With the high capital costs associated with replacing existing coal-fired plants, a scarcity of capital, and the long lead time required to introduce advanced coal technologies, it stands to reason that many of India's highly-polluting coal-fired power plants will have to remain in operation for the next couple of decades.

As such, India's contribution to world carbon emissions is expected to increase in coming years, with an estimated average annual growth rate between 2001 and 2025 of 3.0% in the EIA International Energy Outlook 2003 reference case (compared to 3.4% in China and 1.5% in the United States). The absolute increase in emissions will partially be a function of the degree to which coal is relied upon as a major energy source. If coal consumption is substituted by oil and natural gas consumption, India's overall carbon emissions would be reduced.

India's per capita carbon emissions are relatively low-at 0.25 metric tons of carbon per person in 2001, India's per capita carbon emissions were less than one-quarter of the world average and 22 times less than the United States.

However, the country's per capita carbon emissions are expected to increase in the coming years due to the rapid pace of urbanization, a conversion away from noncommercial towards commercial fuels, increased vehicular usage and the continued use of older and more inefficient coal-fired plants. In fact, due to fast-paced industrialization, per capita emissions are expected to triple by 2020.

India's Carbon Emissions, 1990-2001

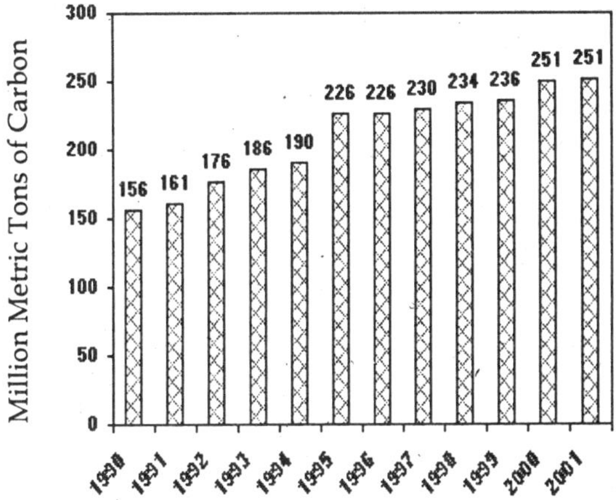

Source: EIA

2001 Energy-Related Carbon Emissions

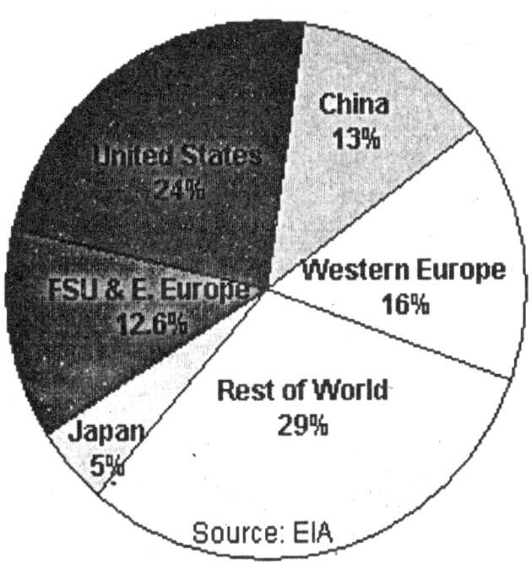

China

With 12.7% of the world's total, China is the second largest emitter of energy-related carbon dioxide emissions after the United States. China's share of world carbon emissions is expected to increase in coming years, reaching 17.8% by 2025. Carbon mitigation strategies are focusing on technologies to reduce emissions from industrial boilers and motors. Other mitigation efforts emphasize improving Chinese vehicles' efficiency. Estimates suggest that transportation sector energy consumption could grow by nearly 7% per year as the government pledges major investments in the country's transportation infrastructure. If this growth is not accompanied by improvements in vehicular fuel-efficiency standards and a replacement of outdated technology, carbon emissions from the transportation sector will grow significantly.

Overall, total Chinese energy-related carbon emissions more than doubled since 1980, when the government began implementing energy conservation laws. One study attempting to determine the causes of this increase concluded that China's decrease in energy intensity since 1980 has not been sufficient to counterbalance the large increase in emissions due to economic and population growth. Increased energy demand has encouraged China to accelerate the development of cleaner fuels such as natural gas, coalbed methane and hydropower. Current efforts by China to offset coal consumption include the development of natural gas and coalbed methane infrastructure, increasing the number of combined heat and power plants, adding approximately 3,000 megawatts (MW) of hydropower annually, and developing renewable energy resources such as wind and photovoltaic for electricity generation.

China is a non-Annex I country under the United Nations Framework Convention on Climate Change, meaning it has not agreed to binding emissions reductions in the Kyoto Protocol, which it ratified in August 2002. China's domestic greenhouse-gas reduction activities are based on "no-regrets" strategies in energy efficiency and conservation, clean energy supply and reforestation. In other words, policies are enacted to cut energy costs and reduce local pollution, while having the auxiliary benefit of reducing carbon emissions.

Energy and Carbon Intensity

India

In 2001, India's energy intensity (energy consumption per dollar of GDP) stood at 25,307 Btu per $1995. Although this figure is one of the highest in Asia, surpassed only by Pakistan (26,229 Btu per $1995) and China (35,619 Btu per $1995), India's carbon intensity has remained relatively flat over the past 20 years, even falling from a high in 1995 (30,459 Btu per $1995) back below 1980 level (25,861 Btu per $1995). By contrast, China's energy intensity level in 2001 was just one-third of its 1980 level of 105,632 Btu per $1995. India's still elevated energy intensity level is due in large part to the growth of energy-intensive industries that has taken place in the country during the course of its economic expansion, coupled with the virtual absence of energy efficiency and conservation measures in most industrial sectors.

Carbon intensity (carbon emissions per dollar of GDP) in India also is relatively high compared to its neighbors. In 2001, India's carbon intensity measured 0.5 metric tons of carbon per thousand $1995. In Asia, only China's carbon intensity (0.75 metric tons of carbon per thousand $1995) was higher than that of India, but whereas China has become less carbon intensive over the past 20 years, India's carbon intensity has remained at virtually the same level as in 1980.

India's heavy reliance on coal, much of it low-quality, goes a long way towards explaining the country's relatively high carbon intensity level. Indian economic policies such as high import tariffs on high-quality coal and subsidies on low-quality domestic coal also have contributed to increased use of low-quality coal, although initiatives to encourage the use of higher-quality coal, such as reducing the tariff on imported coal, may help in reducing the country's carbon intensity. The introduction and adoption of technologies to reduce coal consumption and/or improve the efficiency of the coal that is combusted is an important government priority, given that the majority of India's power generation is coal-fired.

China

Unlike other developing countries such as India, South Korea and Brazil, both the amount of energy and carbon consumed per dollar of GDP have decreased dramatically in China over the past two decades. With average annual GDP growth rates around 7-8% over the last decade and energy consumption growth rates somewhat lower, China has been reducing its energy intensity. This is in large part a result of efforts by the Chinese government to conserve energy, and the adoption of more modern industrial plant equipment. China's Energy Conservation Law entered into force on January 1, 1998. Further efforts by the government to increase overall energy efficiency have included the reduction of coal and petroleum subsidies. Coal consumption is again rising, however, after declining in the late 1990s, and China's energy intensity increased slightly in 2001. At the same time, the government has promoted a shift towards less energy intensive services and higher value-added products, as well as encouraged the import of energy intensive products.

Challenges Ahead–The Shift to Renewable Energy

India

Despite a trend towards urbanization, more than 70% of India's population still lives in rural areas. As the Indian economy develops, one of the greatest challenges that India's local and regional governments face is providing people in rural areas with access to energy. Renewable energy projects - in the form of solar-, wind-, and hydropower-generated electricity-are the key to providing rural areas with energy where power is in short supply. In addition, replacing coal- and other fossil fuel-generated electricity supplied to India's cities with energy from renewable energy sources could aid in reducing air pollution and help to meet the growing energy needs of the country's large metropolises as well.

India is the only country that has a separate government ministry exclusively for non-conventional energy sources, and India has one of the largest national programs to promote the use of solar energy. Whereas the majority of developed countries have turned to solar energy mainly out of

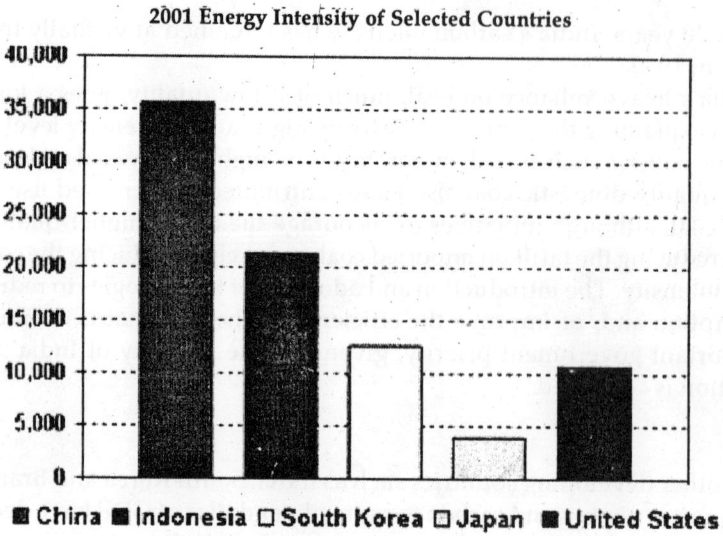

concern about the environment and energy security, the use of solar power in India is being advocated as a way to provide energy to regions where there is a shortage of electricity. Rather than build new, expensive generating capacity or connect rural areas to the existing power transmission infrastructure, India is turning to the use of solar energy. In many small villages and remote areas, solar photovoltaic systems are far more cost-effective than conventional energy.

Wind-generated energy is also an important component of India's strategy to boost the use of renewable energies. India is rich in wind energy potential, and the country has been adding installed wind power capacity at an impressive rate. According to the Ministry of Non-Conventional Energy Sources, India now expects to exceed its target of installing 1,500 MW of wind power in the 2002-2007 period. The improvement in grid connections, which have previously slowed the development of wind power in India, as well as an effort to provide incentives to wind-power producers, has spurred the growth of the wind energy industry in India.

Nevertheless, at the same time that small and micro-level wind and solar energy projects are taking shape, the Indian government is looking to large-scale hydroelectric plants to meet its future energy needs. India has an estimated hydropower potential of 150,000 MW, but hydropower's share of India's energy consumption and production has declined in the past 20 years. The share of hydropower in the country's total installed generating capacity, which was over 40% about 20 years back, has fallen to 25% and only about 23% of India's hydropower potential has been exploited. India's state-owned National Hydroelectric Power Corp. (NHPC) is planning to commission 1,090 MW of capacity by mid-2004, ending a protracted period of lackluster growth, and the government hopes that subsidies to support hydropower plant development will help it attain a goal of building 50,560 MW, almost tripling the country's current installed hydropower capacity.

China

After coal, renewables (including hydroelectricity) account for the second largest share, 18.6% in 2001, of China's electricity generation. With assistance from the United Nations and the United States, China hopes to embark on a multi-million dollar renewable energy strategy to combat pollution. Wind resources are concentrated in the northern and western regions of China, as well as along the coast, and are suitable for both rural village electrification and large-scale, grid-connected electricity production. The highest wind potential in China lies along the coast and the offshore islands, in or near many of the major population centers. The next highest wind potential region covers Inner Mongolia and the northern Gansu Province, both of which are home to numerous villages with no access at present to grid-based electricity.

Current utilization of solar energy includes small-scale uses, such as household consumption, television relays and communications. Solar energy consumption is, however, increasing steadily. Specifically, the number of solar kitchen ranges is climbing steadily, a significant fact when one considers that air pollution caused by indoor coal burning adversely affects the natural environment and detrimental to human health.

While solar and wind power provide significant renewable energy potential, China's growth in renewables will in the next decade will be dominated by hydropower, particularly with completion of the 18.2-gigawatt Three Gorges Dam project in 2009. Although the Three Gorges Dam is seen as both an important source of energy for China's growing electricity consumption needs and a means of taming the Yangtze River, notorious for its disastrous floods, the controversial dam also could prove to be an environmental disaster. Thus far, few attempts have been made to address concerns regarding the accumulation of toxic materials and other pollutants from industrial sites that will be inundated after construction of the dam.

By 2025, the share of nuclear power used for China's electricity generation is expected to increase to 4% from the little over than 1% currently.

CONCLUSIONS

There are many factors influencing future energy consumption and carbon emissions, including population growth, economic development, industrial structure changes, technological progress and a shift in the energy mix.

India faces significant challenges in balancing its increased demand for energy with the need to protect its environment from further damage. Sheer population growth and urbanization make the task all the more difficult for the Indian government, as increased vehicular ownership will contribute to existing air pollution problems and urbanization raises the health risks from that pollution. A rapidly increasing population will also lead to an increase in electricity demand, taxing the already straining power generation, transmission and distribution infrastructure and putting pressure on the power sector to add new capacity to the system. Already, shortages of electricity have hampered India's industrial growth.

As such, electricity is one of the keys to both India's economic development and its environmental protection efforts. The Indian government has introduced initiatives aimed to discourage firms from generating electricity using older, inefficient coal-fired plants, and it has reduced subsidies on low-quality coal. The government has used fiscal incentives, in the form of customs waivers and soft loans, to encourage the installation of pollution abatement equipment, and market mechanisms such as user charges, deposit refund systems, marketable permits and taxes for implementing pollution measures also are being contemplated.

China, like India, is a developing country in its industrialization stage. With economic development, population growth and higher living standards, the amount of primary energy consumed will almost undoubtedly increase in the future, as will the resultant carbon emissions. These absolute increases will occur despite continued technological improvements and reductions in energy intensity.

China has introduced bold initiatives to cut back on coal use. In an effort to encourage a switch to cleaner burning fuels, the government has introduced a tax on high-sulfur coals, and in Beijing, officials aiming to phase out coal from the city center have established 40 "coal-free zones," and have made plans to construct natural gas pipelines. Similar efforts are taking place in other major Chinese cities. A system of emissions trading for sulfur dioxide, similar to that used in the United States, is being tested in some cites with pilot projects, and may eventually be applied nationwide.

One of China's main priorities as it enters the 21st century is developing and utilizing technologies to solve the major environmental challenges it is currently facing and will face in the future. These efforts are focused on technologies that will treat wastewater, prevent air pollution and improve environmental monitoring systems. There are a number of policies that the State Environmental Protection Administration is considering. Adopting the "polluter pays" principle and allowing for accumulation of funds for pollution abatement are currently policies being enacted. Ensuring that fees charged on pollutants are higher than abatement costs and strengthening existing laws, which are not strongly enforced and impose only small fines on pollutant emissions exceeding the legal limit, also are being considered.

Future Chinese environmental initiatives also may include formulating a tax structure beneficial to environmental protection, and granting preferential loans and subsidies to enterprises that construct and operate pollution treatment facilities or produce environmentally friendly products.

GMS ECONOMIC INTEGRATION IN THE ESTABLISHMENT PROCESS OF ASEAN CHINA FREE TRADE AREA

Christopher Gan

INTRODUCTION

Nearly every developing country is in, or is discussing some form of regional cooperation as an important part of the development process linking development opportunities with international trade and economic cooperation. By the middle of the 1990s, most major economies were a member of at least one regional organisation attempting to promote economic integration and cooperation. Some are members of more than one regional group (see Table 1). It is almost certain that a country that is not a member of any form of regional cooperation or regional trade agreement will be adversely impacted in their terms of trade (Cai, 2003).

Supporters argue that regional cooperation help member countries gradually work towards global free trade by allowing countries to increase the level of competition slowly and give domestic industries time to adjust. In addition, it can be valuable arenas for tackling volatile trade issues such as agricultural subsidies, which have been a stumbling block in World Trade Organisation (WTO) multilateral negotiation. Political pressures and regional diplomacy can resolve issues that cause deadlock in multilateral negotiations. Katzenstien (1996) argued that neighbourhood geographical proximity, functional interdependence and transborder externalities provide favourable ground for regional economic cooperation. Regional cooperation also generates economies of scale and savings in transportation costs which can accelerate economic growth (Lorenz, 1991).

The intensifying regionalism in other areas has also raised concern among the Greater Mekong Subregion (GMS) economies over the diversion of trade and investment flows (Cai, 2003). For example, the European Union's (EU) expansion to include ten Eastern European countries and the enlargement of the North American Free Trade Agreement (NAFTA) to form a Free Trade Area of the Americas by 2005 can adversely position the GMS states in a vulnerable and weaker bargaining position in multilateral trade negotiations. Furthermore, EU and NAFTA have formed themselves into increasingly closed

Table 1
Recently Established or Proposed Free Trade Areas in the Asia-Pacific, 1999-2004

Country/Grouping	*Partners*	*Status of Agreement, 2004*	*Country/Grouping*	*Partners*	*Status of Agreement, 2004*
ASEAN	China	Framework Agreement signed	Malaysia	China	Under Negotiation
	India	Framework Agreement signed		Japan	Under Negotiation
	Japan	Framework Agreement signed		USA	Proposed
	Korea	Under Study			
	USA (TIFA)	Under Negotiation			
	CER	Under Study			
	ASEAN +3	Under Study			
	EU	Proposed			
China	ASEAN	Agreement signed	Philippines	China	Under Negotiation
	Australia	Proposed		Japan	Under Negotiation
	India	Under Study		USA	Proposed
	Hong Kong	Agreement signed			
	Macau	Proposed			
	Malaysia	Under Negotiation			
	New Zealand	Proposed			
	Philippines	Under Negotiation			
	Singapore	Proposed			
India	ASEAN	Framework Agreement signed	Singapore	Australia	Agreement in force
	China	Proposed		Canada	Under Negotiation
	Korea	Proposed		China	Proposed
	Singapore	Under Negotiation		Egypt	Proposed
	Sri Lanka	Agreement in force		EFTA	Agreement in force
	Thailand	Framework Agreement signed		EU	Proposed (rejected by EU)
	BIMSTEC	Framework Agreement signed		India	Under Negotiations
	SACU	Proposed		Japan	Agreement in force
	COMESA	Proposed		Jordan	Agreement in force
	MERCOSUR	Framework Agreement signed		Korea	Under Negotiations
	Mauritius	Under Negotiation		Mexico	Under Negotiations
				New Zealand	Agreement in force
				Sri Lanka	Under Negotiations

Country/Grouping	Partners	Status of Agreement, 2004	Country/Grouping	Partners	Status of Agreement, 2004
				Pakistan	Proposed
				Taiwan	Proposed
				USA	Agreement in force
Hong Kong	China	Agreement signed	Taiwan	Costa Rica	Proposed
	Macau	Agreement signed		Japan	Proposed
	New Zealand	Under Negotiation		New Zealand	NZ without from negotiation
				Panama	Under Negotiations
				Singapore	Proposed
				USA	Proposed
Japan	ASEAN	Framework Agreement signed	Thailand	Australia	Agreement signed
	Canada	Proposed		Bahrain	Agreement signed
	Chile	Under Study		China	Agreement signed
	Korea	Under Study		India	Agreement signed
	Malaysia	Under Negotiation		Japan	Under Negotiation
	Mexico	Under Negotiation		Korea	Under Study
	Philippines	Under Negotiation		New Zealand	Under Study
	Singapore	Agreement in force		Peru	Agreement signed
	Thailand	Under Negotiation		South Africa	Under Study
	Australia	Proposed		USA	Under Negotiation
				BIMSTEC	Agreement signed
Korea	Australia	Under Study		Vietnam	Sri Lanka
	China	Under Study			
	Chile	Agreement signed			
	Japan	Under Study			
	Mexico	Under Negotiation			
	New Zealand	Under Study			
	Peru	Proposed			
	Singapore	Under Negotiation			
	Thailand	Under Study			
	USA	Under Negotiation			

Source: Rajan, Ramkishen S. and Rahul Sen, "The New Wave of FTAs in Asia: With Particular Reference to ASEAN, China and India," Unpublished Paper, June 2004).

markets with substantial bargaining power in multilateral trade negotiations as blocs. This can create some resentment feeling of GMS being excluded and isolated in the global economic competition (Cai, 2003).

The Greater Mekong Subregion (GMS) Program which was started in 1992 is an informal framework for subregional economic cooperation in the GMS. The Program initially focused promoting economic and social development by strengthening economic linkages among Cambodia, Lao PDR, Myanmar, Thailand, Vietnam and Yunnan Province of the People's Republic of China. The GMS Program is guided by mutual principles and institutional agreements compared to the strict constitution or set of by laws of other regional cooperation program such as ASEAN and NAFTA (Asian Development Bank, 2002; 2004). The achievements of the last ten years and the remarkable goodwill and trust among member states have opened new opportunities for enhanced development and deeper integration. In addition, the Program provides a springboard to further integrate with other ASEAN members since five of the GMS countries are members of ASEAN.

Almost a decade has passed since the GMS Program was initiated. As the GMS economies increase their degree of openness to the world markets along with their comparative advantage in low-cost labour, they should develop short and long-term strategies to increase their domestic competitiveness and maintain their sustainable economic cooperation. The GMS countries needs to deepen its regional economic integration because the region have to keep up with competitor countries and groups of countries that are fast opening up their markets and using their natural and human resources to enhance their attractiveness to foreign investors. Thus an ASEAN-China Free Trade Agreement can increase intraregional trade and investment, improve efficiency and economies of scale and develop a larger market for capital and talent, thereby creating greater opportunities for businesses for GMS countries and ASEAN members.

The paper examines Chinese economic strategies towards an ASEAN-China Free Trade Agreement (FTA) within the GMS framework. An ASEAN China FTA will help GMS stabilise its economic relationships with ASEAN, which is China's fifth largest trading partner. Furthermore, it also assesses the impact of the ASEAN-China FTA on the process of GMS closer regional integration with ASEAN states.

THE GREATER MEKONG SUBREGION PROGRAM

The Greater Mekong Subregion (GMS) is made up of six countries: Thailand, Lao PDR, Vietnam, Cambodia, Myanmar and the Yunnan Province of the People's Republic of China. Home to 250 million people, the GMS countries are indelibly linked to both the global trade system of which they are a part, and to the different national systems which constitute each of them. The GMS has a total land area of 2.3 million square kilometres, is about the size of continental Europe, is rich in natural resources and diverse in language, ethic background and cultural heritage. After being mired in armed conflicts for decades, relative peace across the region in recent years has fostered economic liberalization, increasing intergovernmental cooperation, and freer cross border flows of labour, goods, and cultures. The average income is 20 per cent below the average income of developing Asia (Asian Development Bank, 2004).

The region is seen as an emerging trade bloc particularly with China as a major economic powerhouse. With these trends, the sub-region has come to be seen by investors as "a new frontier of Asian growth". Chinese Premier Zhu Rongji urged the GMS countries to commit themselves to continue pursuing their common vision of a subregion that is more integrated, prosperous and welcomes investment to bring out their respective advantages and accelerate their economic growth (Rajan and Sen, 2004).

The GMS Program was formed in 1992 to promote closer economic relationship among the six countries. The goals of the GMS Program since its establishment were to promote both economic and social development among member countries by strengthening economic linkages. Much has been accomplished in the development of economic cooperation and integration, including air linkages, broader area development (example the East-West Corridor) and triangle development initiatives, and now it seems that the time and circumstances call for increased formal attention to regionally address policies and programs vital to social development. For example, in the November 2002 Joint Summit Declaration, the GMS leaders strongly advocate for regional cooperation and policy making to combat illegal cross border trafficking of humans, trade of drugs and the spread of HIV/AID disease health hazard to the population of the region (Asian Development Bank, 2002).

Over the past 12 years, the GMS Program has served as a catalyst for GMS countries economic cooperation in development. The region is supported by sound macroeconomic and financial policies conducive for investment and development. In addition, former centrally planned economies have adopted market-oriented systems markedly increasing cross-border trade and investment. It has created new opportunities for further cooperation and partnership in the pursuit of economic growth and prosperity. More importantly, the Program includes initiatives for resolving policy, regulatory and other non-physical barriers to cross-border traffic, complementing investments in transportation infrastructure, human resource development and tourism (Asian Development Bank, 2002). The GMS Program also has a peace component fostering greater trust among member countries and creates an environment conducive to formal cooperation and integration, which would stimulate regional policy formulation for social development (Asian Development Bank, 2002). This includes several bilateral border development initiatives and cooperation on transport agreements including several new air linkages.

Unlike the ASEAN or other regional arrangement, the distinct feature of economic cooperation in GMS Program has been informal cooperation agreements over wide issues including trade, investment, technology transfer, infrastructure development and exchange of information. By and large these cooperation agreements have been soft and fragmented and depend on the degree of mutual cooperation and goodwill among the six countries through the removal of structural impediments (Asian Development Bank, 2002). The Program fosters closer cooperation among member countries through the removal of structural barriers rather than tariff reduction as common in ASEAN. The structural barriers include poor road and telecommunications linkages between member countries and lack of information about neighbouring markets. However, it is difficult to tell what is intraregional and interregional within the GMS countries because the region shows a low degree of regionness. The GMS Program lacks any kind of formal regionalist framework and thus a lack of policy makers with region wide authority, i.e. hegemony (Hettne, 1996).

In view of the Globalization trends, there is a need to review and reform the GMS Program to strengthen, streamline and make it more responsive to the rapidly changing global environment, the needs of its stakeholders, especially business and industry. For example, the GMS Economic Zone initiated by the Asian Development bank in 1992 was expected to play a significant role in subregional economic development in the region. However, over a decade since its inception, few GMS projects have been implemented and completed (Masviriyakul, 2004). The progress was further hampered by the 1997 Asian financial crisis.

The critical question is whether the GMS Program can foster deeper regional integration and create a dependable regional organisation commensurate with the GMS economic competitiveness and sustainability? Or, will the GMS Program remain a region of soft and fragmented markets? There is a growing need for GMS identity within and outside Asia through an affirmative identity of common culture as well as a defensive identity of a common race. The GMS Program "is not, and cannot be, the framework to deal with each and every issue associated with Globalization. It is critical for GMS to be deeply integrated, which allows free flow of new ideas and best endeavour implementation without fear of peer pressure and non-performance consequences. There is also concerned that current perception of widespread terrorist threats to global trade may lead economies to enforce and tighten safety measures beyond that which is necessary. This will inadvertently lead to new barriers and increase transaction costs. An ASEAN-China Free Trade Agreement will help to promote a more cordial atmosphere and cooperative relationship between GMS and ASEAN in economic, political and security sphere thus contributing to a more stable regional market. This reflects an active challenge and response by the GMS and ASEAN to the deepening and widening regionalism in the global economy (Cai, 2003).

CHINA-GREATER MEKONG SUBREGION STRATEGY

China's economic strategy towards the Mekong Subregion was formulated formally in 1984 when China allowed the 27 border districts of Yunnan Province to be trading posts with her neighbours before the GMS was established (Masviriyakul, 2004). In addition, China is a part owner of the section of the Mekong that is called "Lancang Jiang" in Chinese, which flow from Tibet to Yunnan some 2,160 kilometers (about half the length of the

Mekong). By joining the GMS Program in 1992, it provided China an opportunity to develop Yunnan Province, particularly the border towns. It also coincided with China's western regional development plan in 2000 aimed at narrowing the economic disparity between the people on its East Coast and hinterland provinces. Yunnan in the Southwest has been regarded as the gateway to Sichuan, Guizhou, Guanxi provinces and the Tibet Autonomous region, with great potential to further integrate with neighboring countries (Masviriyakul, 2004).

The Central Committee of the Communist Party of China, Yunnan Provincial Committee of the Communist Party of China, and Yunnan Provincial People's Government have promoted Yunnan as a competitive bio-resources province and rich in ethnic culture, and an international passageway linking China to South and Southeast Asia. This strategic outlook fits within the GMS and ASEAN-China Free Trade Area proposal, opening the doors to trade with ASEAN members (Masviriyakul, 2004; UNDP, 2002).

There is also a plan to construct a railway from Singapore to Kunming under the Trans-Asia railway project, which will facilitate greater trade transactions and the flow of peoples in the North-South economic corridor. Furthermore, Chinese Prime Minister Zhu Rongji proposed Chinese government support for the project during the China-ASEAN Senior Officials Meeting in Singapore in November 2000 (Masviriyakul, 2004). The Trans-Asia railway project will enhance greater economic integration among the GMS and ASEAN members within the GMS framework, Yunnan Province of China and Thailand have taken the lead role in pushing many GMS projects, especially economic cooperation in the North-South economic corridor linking Yunnan Province and northern Thailand via Laos or Myanmar. Furthermore, Myanmar, Laos, and Vietnam bordered Yunnan for some 4000 kilometers and played a significant role in border trade and foreign investment. There have been 17 border towns and 92 outlets established in Yunnan province since the 1984 decision to allow the 27 border districts to establish trade relationship with their neighbours (Masviriyakul, 2004).

China has developed international shipping route along the Lancang-Mekong River. It reflects China's desire to encourage exports to mainland Southeast Asia and beyond through Yunnan Province. Thailand is also linked with Yunnan Province via the Mekong River. Thus, Yunnan can potentially become the transport hub and investment center for the Mekong Subregion facilitating manufacturing and tourism development.

WHAT IS ASEAN CHINA FREE TRADE AGREEMENT (FTA)?

China and the 10-member Association of Southeast Asian Nations (ASEAN) – Brunei, Cambodia, Indonesia, Laos, Malaysia, Myanmar, the Philippines, Singapore, Thailand and Vietnam – recently signed an economic co-operation framework agreement in 2002 creating the world's biggest free trade zone of nearly two billion people with a combined gross domestic product of two trillion dollars by 2010. The Agreement similar to a European Union-style East Asian common market, would lead to the creation of an ASEAN-China FTA within ten years and pave the way towards closer cooperation in the elimination of tariffs and non-tariff barriers on trade in goods, create an open and competitive investment regime and encourage the simplification and standardization of Customs procedures. It also includes an "early harvest" clause that includes quick reduction of tariffs on a number of goods that will take effect within a targeted date of three years from July 1 next year when the Agreement comes into force. The newer ASEAN members like Cambodia, Laos, Myanmar and Viet Nam (who are also members of the GMS) will be offered special and differential treatment and flexibility in implementation (Goh, 2002) China's trade with ASEAN hit a record high 78.25 billion dollars in 2003, up 42.8 per cent from 2002, according to official statistics from the General Administration of Customs. China's imports from ASEAN jumped 51.7 per cent to 47.33 billion dollars last year while exports grew at a slower pace of 31.1 per cent to 30.93 billion dollars, leaving a trade deficit of 16.4 billion dollars. The ASEAN-China FTA will create a market of 1.7 billion consumers with a combined gross domestic product of 2.0 trillion dollars and total trade of 1.23 trillion dollars. It will be the biggest free trade zone of its kind in the world when it is realized in 2010 (Goh, 2002, Cai, 2003).

In 2001, ASEAN's trade with the rest of the world decreased due to the impact of the "September 11" terror attack on the United States and the ensuing global economic slowdown. However, ASEAN and China continued registered as much as 41.615 billion US dollars in trade volume in 2001, a rise of 5.3 per cent from the previous year (see Tables 2 and 3). Surveys released by China's Southwestern Yunnan Province, which borders ASEAN countries, further show that trade volume between China and ASEAN has risen by an average of over 15 per cent annually since 1995 (Beijing Time, 2002).

Table 2
China Imports from the Greater Mekong Subregion (in million U.S dollars)

Country	*Year*							
	1985	*1990*	*1995*	*1999*	*2000*	*2001*	*2002*	*2003*
Cambodia	0.6	0.2	5.2	8.9	23.8	16.7	22.3	23.6
Lao PDR	8.6	5.9	8.8	8.7	4.9	6.8	8.8	10.2
Myanmar	3.7	33.3	136.0	92.3	111.7	122.0	124.5	154.1
Thailand	271	269	1642	1861	2806.0	2863.0	3553.0	5710.0
Vietnam	-	7.8	361.9	746.4	1536.4	1417.4	1013.2	1323.5
Imports from GMS	283.9	316.2	2153.9	2717.3	4482.8	4425.9	4721.8	7221.4
Imports GMS 4	12.9	47.2	511.0	856.3	1676.8	1562.9	1168.8	1511.4
Total ASEAN	-	-	6200.9	9590.8	14178.9	14516.0	19547.5	26999.1
GMS trade as % of ASEAN Trade	-	-	34.7%	28.3%	31.6%	30.4%	24.1%	26.7%
Total Imports	42479	53809	132163	165718	224721	243567	295440	412836

Source: ADB Key Indicators 2004.

ASEAN is now the fifth largest trade partner for China, following Japan, the United States, the European Union and the Republic of Korea. At the same time, China has become ASEAN's sixth major trade partner. Over the next three years, China-ASEAN trade is expected to grow at an annual rate of 10 per cent and reach 63 billion US dollars in 2005. Thus both Chinese and ASEAN business communities had realized the bright prospects for the Free Trade Area proposal. Furthermore, with the establishment of ASEAN-China business networks, companies in the region can better exchange commercial information (Beijing Time, 2002). The FTA will 'create a large single production base for foreign direct investment to take advantage of the comparative advantages of ASEAN countries and China.

Table 3
China Exports to the Greater Mekong Subregion (in million U.S dollars)

Country	*Year*							
	1985	*1990*	*1995*	*1999*	*2000*	*2001*	*2002*	*2003*
Cambodia	0.6	3.3	56.8	85.9	112.9	86.9	276.8	324.1
Lao PDR	-	15.9	21.5	24.4	33.9	59.9	59.7	108.1
Myanmar	8.9	137.7	679.6	447.2	559.6	547.3	797.3	998.5
Thailand	223.0	1107.0	2096.0	2495.0	3377.0	3711	4928.0	6067.0
Vietnam	-	4.6	329.7	673.1	1401.1	1606.2	2364.9	3496.4
Exports to GMS	232.5	1268.5	3183.6	3725.6	5484.5	6011.3	8426.7	10994.1
Exports toGMS 4	9.5	161.0	1087.6	1230.6	2107.5	2300.3	3498.7	4927.1
Total Exportsto ASEAN	-	-	7129.7	12331.7	18137.0	17399.2	23212.2	28222.9
GMS trade as % of ASEAN Trade	-	-	44.6%	30.2%	30.2%	34.5%	36.3%	38.9%
Total Exports	27329	62760	148955	194931	272128	266698	325711	438129

Source: ADB Key Indicators 2004.

It will take six years to establish the FTA between China and ASEAN. This means by the end of 2009 under the FTA, tariffs will be lowered to 0-5 per cent in all commodities (with the exception on a few commodities) and all non-tariff barriers will be eliminated (Cai, 2003). Service trade and investment will also be liberalised and China has offered to unilaterally open its market to some ASEAN members five years ahead of the agreement.

According to the terms of the agreement, China and ASEAN countries will also strengthen economic ties by promoting co-operation in five major areas: IT, agriculture, investment, human resources and the development of the Mekong River. China will also provide financial support for infrastructure projects like the Kunming-Bangkok highway and the Trans-Asia railway.

The FTA is designed to attract investment in that it would not matter much if an investor locates his factory in China, or any other part of ASEAN (including the GMS). By having the FTA, investors can enter China without really having to locate to China, for example. This is really an effort to make ASEAN and GMS members much more attractive to foreign investments.

China's World Trade Organisation accession has added further momentum to a larger regional co-operation. In addition to increasing access to each other's markets and encouraging mutual investment, many Asian governments also believe that closer economic ties will help them to reap the benefits of China's membership, thereby reducing their dependence on US markets. What's more,

China's integration into the region will not only contribute to greater economic stability for ASEAN and the GMS region, but it may go some way towards allaying fears that China's economic growth might be achieved at the expense of its neighbours (Zhang, 2002).

Over the course of the last decade, the strongest rate of growth has been in the trade of manufactured products, with trade in computers/machinery and electrical equipment rising the most. The fact that these products were both the leading exports and imports of both ASEAN and China suggests the importance of intra-industry trade, brought about by product differentiation and economies of scale (see Tables 4 and 5)

The exports where ASEAN enjoys the greatest advantage are mineral products (including mineral fuels), plastics/rubber, wood and wood articles, pulp and paper and fats and oils. They account for 42 per cent of China's imports from ASEAN. But these commodities constitute only 11.6 per cent of China's exports to ASEAN in 2000. Other sectors where intra-industry trade is large include machinery and electrical appliances, chemicals, optical, and precision and musical instruments. Among them, machinery and electrical appliances account for 39 per cent of China's exports to ASEAN and 41 per cent of China's imports from ASEAN (ASEAN-China Expert Group, 2001).

Table 4
Structure of ASEAN Exports to China, 1993, 1999

1993			*1999*		
Product	*Exports (US $ Billion)*	*Share*	*Product*	*Exports (US $ Billion)*	*Share*
Lubricants/Fuels/Oil	1.46	32.3%	Computer/Machinery	1.94	20.3%
Wood	1.03	22.6%	Electrical Equipment	1.71	17.9%
Fats and Oils	0.38	8.4%	Lubricants/Fuels/Oil	1.09	11.4%
Computer/Machinery	0.29	6.4%	Fats and Oils	0.52	5.4%
Electrical Equipment	0.29	6.0%	Wood	0.51	5.1%
SUB-TOTAL	3.43	75.7%	SUB-TOTAL	5.77	60.3%

Source: ASEAN Secretariat; ASEAN-China Expert Group, 2001.

Table 5
Structure of ASEAN Import to China, 1993, 1999

1993			*1999*		
Product	*Exports (US $ Billion)*	*Share*	*Product*	*Exports (US $ Billion)*	*Share*
Electrical Equipment	0.48	11.1%	Computer/Machinery	3.24	26.63%
Computer/Machinery	0.42	9.7%	Electrical Equipment	2.44	20.0%
Lubricants/Fuels/Oil	0.39	9.0%	Lubricants/Fuels/Oil	0.52	4.3%
Cotton	0.24	5.6%	Fats and Oils	0.43	3.6%
Tobacco	0.18	4.2%	Wood	0.30	2.5%
SUB-TOTAL	1.72	39.6%	SUB-TOTAL	6.9	57.0%

Source: ASEAN Secretariat; ASEAN-China Expert Group, 2001.

A recent study undertaken by a task force of Thai economists demonstrated an ASEAN China FTA could potentially increase ASEAN's GDP by 0.38 per cent and China's by 3.6 per cent. It would increase ASEAN's export of rice, garments, sugar, paper, chemicals, rubber and steel to China and boost China's exports of food, beverage and tobacco, petroleum products and coal to ASEAN members (the Straits Times, 15 February 2002; Zhang, 2002).

The Rationale and Impact of the ASEAN China FTA on GMS and ASEAN Integration

Intra-regional trade, led by foreign direct investment, has developed rapidly in recent decades. Large companies and transnational corporations have established horizontal and vertical production linkages among the neighbouring Asian countries, in order to exploit scale economies and to enhance their value chain. This has resulted in increased production networks across the region improving production efficiency and costs. The economic success of other regional trading blocs, such as the EU and NAFTA, has convinced the Asian governments that they could achieve similar results by duplicating such organisations.

The collapse of the Seattle Round and the struggle of the Doha Round in multilateral trade negotiation have forced many countries to aggressively explore alternative trade arrangement as the primary means of hastening the liberalisation process and integration. Furthermore regional economic cooperation processes are not required to follow the reciprocity principle set by the WTO. Regional cooperation also generates economies of scale and savings in transportation costs which can accelerate economic growth (Lorenz, 1991). Thus there have been various proposals for a regional mechanism for economic cooperation in East Asia, among which the proposals for an ASEAN plus Three (APT), East Asian FTA and ASEAN Plus One (APO) trading blocs. The main objective is to explore practical ways and means to deepen and expand the existing cooperation between ASEAN and the three Northeast Asian countries.

Laos, Cambodia, Myanmar and Vietnam became members of ASEANS in the late 1990s. All transitional economies in mainland Southeast Asia decided to open up their economies in to compete in the global economy. Hence, the GMS have become the key player that fuels investment prospects in the subregion and East Asia (Masviriyakul, 2004). This includes private investment in trade, production (both agricultural and industrial), tourism and other services. Furthermore, the ASEAN-Mekong Basin Development Cooperation framework see the significance of the North-South Economic Corridor (Kunming-Chiang Rai), as Singapore and Malaysia are pushing the Singapore-Kunming road and railway projects (Masviriyakul, 2004). This shows that the GMS development programs are partly influenced by other ASEAN countries. This reflects the economic rationale for an ASEAN China FTA, which will economically benefit both regions.

The primary goal of the GMS Program is to create closer economic integration among the member states. Thus the ASEAN China FTA implications for GMS economic relationships are extensive. The ASEAN China FTA can be viewed as international trade and investment opportunities between GMS and ASEAN members. For example, Yunnan imports from Thailand grossed at US$6.8 million in 2001while exports to Thailand in the same year reached US$36.39 million. In addition, Thailand investment in Yunnan province ranked fifth among foreign investment worldwide (Masviriyakul, 2004).

The decision to form an ASEAN China FTA also reflects the bitter experience of the 1997 Asian financial crisis. The lack of a mechanism for closer policy coordination and cooperation among the region's governments led to rapid and unchecked contagion of the 1997 crisis. This painful experience revealed how much the GMS and ASEAN economies were closely interdependent and how each of them was fragile and vulnerable to any economic crisis. Thus there is an urgent need for the formation of a formal regional mechanism to deal with similar crisis in the future.

Deeper regional cooperation avoids any help from outside the region such as the International Monetary Fund (IMF) bailout of Thailand and Indonesia during the 1997 financial crisis. A deeper regional cooperation is required for harmonization of cross-border listing, trading, clearing and settlements, securities lending and borrowing, etc. More institutional efforts are needed to create a regional financial market infrastructure in the GMS region.

The crisis significantly transformed the political economy of the GMS and ASEAN, providing a new doormat for closer regional economic cooperation between the two regions. Furthermore, as a result of the crisis, China has been changing its perspective and becoming positive and active in promoting regional cooperation and institution buildings (Cai, 2003). The crisis indirectly fosters a GMS-ASEAN closer integration.

ASEAN is generally a well-organised regional institution, but it is far from representing the interests of ASEAN members as a whole, given the association's main objective in strengthening regional cooperation among its ten members five of whom are also members of the GMS (Cai, 2003). After achieving higher economic growth since its inception in 1967 than virtually any other part of the world, ASEAN's resilience was put under severe strain by a number of events. Its credibility as an international organisation suffered as a result of unanticipated events such as the 1997 financial crises, the SARS and bird flu outbreak, the hostage crises in the Philippines and the Bali and Jakarta bombing. The Jakarta bombing has raised the question as to how ASEAN would tackle the terrorism problem at the regional level (Pushpanathan, 2003). Conflicts within ASEAN reveal that richer members are busy focusing on domestic recovery from the 1997 financial crisis while delaying economic integration with their new, less-developed colleagues (Myanmar, Vietnam, Lao PDR and Cambodia).

ASEAN like the GMS is also not in a position to exert substantial influence on regional and global affairs, besides being unable to compete with EU and NAFTA. Furthermore, ASEAN members are basically competing with, rather than complementing one another and depend much more on regional or global economic markets, technology and capital (Cai, 2003). These inherent weaknesses reflect ASEAN's inability to provide strong leadership and assistance to crisis-ridden members during the 1997 Asian financial crisis. Thus, an effective strategy for ASEAN to rejuvenate and strengthen itself and to improve its influence in the regional and global market is to seek cooperation with GMS and China.

The gap and disparity in economic development levels among ASEAN and GMS members and between ASEAN and GMS prevent effective economic cooperation and the creation of a hegemonic state in the region. The GMS and ASEAN governments have varying policy priorities and pursue diverse economic and social policy given the diverse economic differences and background (Cai, 2003). For example, the Mekong River Commission (MRC), formed by Thailand, Vietnam, Laos and Cambodia in 1995 to ensure that the Mekong isn't ruined by development (Wain, 2004). However, efforts to coordinate the management and conservation of the Mekong basin have been hampered by the lack of an umbrella organisation with authority over the entire river. China and Myanmar are not members of the MRC and do not have to consult downstream countries about dam-building on the Mekong. In addition, some of the MRC members disregard the MRC directives in pursuit of national interests. For example, Vietnam failed to notify Cambodia that it was building a second dam on the Sesan, a Mekong tributary. Similarly Thailand proposed water-diversion schemes did not obtain approval from other MRC members (Wain, 2004). The GMS program itself does not treat the Mekong water resource management as a political or security issue. There are no international rules requiring a country to obtain opinions from its neighbours for every dam it builds (Asian Development Bank, 2002). Thus policy coordination and cooperation among such diverse members within a regional grouping could materialise with an ASEAN-China Free Trade Agreement.

Some analysts have questioned the effectiveness of ASEAN as an economic entity and its ability to act more cohesively to advance its own regional integration (Rajan and Sen, 2004). The growing income disparity between the richer and less well-off member countries may act as a stumbling block to deeper economic intra-ASEAN integration. This could further hinder the implementation of ASEAN-AFTA agreements. Furthermore some ASEAN countries have taken a non-conventional liberal approach in pursuit of their external economic interests. For example, Thailand and Singapore has recently formed a "Singapore-Thailand Enhanced Economic Relationship" to intensify bilateral economic trade across various sectors (Rajan and Sen, 2004). Furthermore bilateral arrangement has been negotiated with Australia and New Zealand and Singapore has plans for bilateral agreements with Canada and Mexico (Menon, 2000).

The new waves of bilateralism have tended to involve many middle and high income countries while lower income countries (such as Lao PDR, Cambodia, Vietnam and Myanmar) have been left out in the cold. This could exacerbate the gap between the richer ASEAN members and the less well off members and leading trade fragmentation and political tensions. There will be little incentive for expansion, coordination and consolidation within ASEAN since this would diminish the value of preferential access between partners. This bilateralism is a reflection of ASEAN internal weakness and it further erodes ASEAN credibility to act as a unified regional hub in Asia. Thus, an ASEAN China FTA could resolve some of the bilateralism confronting for Laos, Cambodia, Vietnam and Myanmar who are both members of the GMS and ASEAN. The FTA would accord these countries with better bargaining leverage and power.

Challenges Ahead for China and the GMS

Despite the desire for, and the benefits that would accrue from ASEAN and China integration, the road to a FTA is likely to confront uncertainties and challenges ahead. The difficulty lies in convincing how a FTA will benefit every member involved. The establishment of an ASEAN China FTA will reduce the amount of revenue derive from trade tariffs and severely impact Cambodia, Lao PDR, Myanmar and Vietnam (see Table 4) who relied heavily on international trade taxes as a source of government revenue (Lao-Araya, 2002). These governments will be force either to reduce expenditure, borrow to finance increased deficit, or compensate for revenue loss. Furthermore, this will reduce poverty reduction and social protection programs.

The wide divergence among GMS and ASEAN countries—in terms of standards of living, political system and cultural heritage—may prove something of a stumbling block to the success formation of the FTA. GDP per capita, for instance, ranges from US$30,000 for Singapore to US$370 for Vietnam, while populations vary from China's 1.26 billion to a mere 320,000 in Brunei (Zhang, 2002).

A free-trade agreement would expose a number of domestic industries to vulnerable unfettered foreign competition. Chinese rice farmers, for example, may lose out to those in Vietnam and Thailand, while Filipino household electronic manufactures may find it hard to compete with their Chinese counterparts. Inevitably, these industries will lobby for protection. This would be yet another test for the Chinese government, which is already wrestling with the challenges of having to open its markets after its accession to the WTO (Zhang, 2002) Both the GMS and ASEAN members may also find themselves in conflict, since many of their major exporting industries such as textile, shoe and information technology are in direct competition. What's more, when it comes to attracting foreign direct investment (FDI), the ASEAN countries are likely to be in direct competition with China. In 2001, while China received record level of FDI in 2001—about 80% of the total FDI flowing into Asia—there were some FDI declines in some major ASEAN countries (Zhang, 2002).

The creation of an ASEAN China FTA would be an ambitious undertaking at a time when ASEAN-Free Trade Area (AFTA) initiated in 1991, still faces many problems. Disagreements over issues such as exceptional treatment for Malaysian automobiles and Thai petrochemicals have put the achievement of its free trade objectives by 2003 into doubt. Adding powerful new members could add to frictions in the liberalisation process (Zhang, 2002). The GMS and ASEAN governments will also face the difficulty of removing all the barriers that currently prevent the trading bloc from functioning effectively and efficiently. For example, current strict controls on capital flows and cross-border labour movement make the efficient allocation of resources and labour virtually impossible. It is also unlikely that ASEAN countries will allow the huge numbers of Chinese (who, observers claim, are poised to flood the ASEAN labour markets) the similar cross-border access permitted workers in the EU (Zhang, 2002). Furthermore, many doubt that the AFTA will be a success given ASEAN countries are direct competitors in many areas, which will take a long time for them to develop into a complementary economies (Hettne, 1996).

An interesting question is why China proposed the ASEAN China FTA now? What could she gain from such a proposal? The ASEAN economies cannot provide China with its most needed commodities, i.e., foreign investment, international markets, cutting-edge technologies and management skills (Zhang, 2002). In addition, under the "early harvest" clause agreement, China would have to offer unilateral, preferential treatment for ASEAN exports years ahead of the other ASEAN countries.

China sees long-term geopolitical advantages to an ASEAN China FTA process. The ASEAN countries are strategically significant to China, since they are a key source of rubber, timber, petroleum, natural gas and palm oil—materials that China imports in large quantities More importantly, the sea route via the Malacca Strait provides is a lifeline for the Chinese economy (which has become increasingly dependent, of late, on foreign oil supplies) (Zhang, 2002).

CONCLUSIONS

The last decade has seen the rise of globalization and regional trading arrangements, China's emergence as a global economic power house and the growing interdependence between ASEAN and China. Furthermore, China's WTO accession will create market opportunities and challenges for the GMS, ASEAN and China. All sides should now build on the important changes that will take place in China and the momentum of their fast growing economic linkage. Thus the establishment of an ASEAN-China FTA will create a sense of community between the GMS, ASEAN members and China. Their geographic closeness, long historical ties and shared culture provides a good framework for further cooperation. The sense of community engendered by an ASEAN-China FTA will contribute immensely to peace and stability in the Asia Pacific region.

ASEAN and China have important and rapidly growing trade and investment relations. The importance of trade with China is particularly true for ASEAN countries with common borders with China–Laos, Myanmar and Vietnam. Thus the adoption of this framework of economic cooperation between ASEAN and China will catapult ASEAN-China relations forward and establish a solid foundation for GMS-ASEAN growth and stability over the years.

The removal of trade barriers between the GMS, ASEAN and China will lower costs, increase intra-regional trade and increase economic efficiency. The FTA will lead to greater specialization in production based on comparative advantage. Trade creation occurs when some domestic production in one FTA member is replaced by lower-cost imports from another member. This will boost real income for the lower income group member as resources flow to sectors where they can be more efficiently and productively utilized. The proposal could build synergies between ASEAN and GMS members by allowing cooperation to expand to include areas of common interest such as agriculture, energy, finance, HRD, etc. It could also create the necessary institutional mechanisms to ensure effective implementation of the proposal (ASEAN-China Expert Group, 2001).

In addition, the GMS, ASEAN and China are major destinations for foreign direct investments rather than significant investors in each other's economy. If all sides could agree on a program of further trade and investment liberalization and facilitation measures, the prospects for ASEAN-GMS economic relations could be further bolstered. The formation of an ASEAN-China FTA should also attract US, European and Japanese companies, which are interested in making inroads into the Asian market, will also be attracted to invest in the integrated market. The integration of ASEAN with GMS can entice more foreign corporations, which each market alone cannot otherwise attract. With a larger market, more intense competition, increased investment and economies of scale, enterprises will invest more in research and development, hence promoting technological innovation (ASEAN-China Expert Group, 2001).

However, the framework of cooperation must recognize the differences in levels of development among the members. The GMS and ASEAN includes some of the least developed countries in the world. A move towards an FTA between ASEAN and China must be sensitive to and attempt to address the concerns of other trading partners. Capacity building programs to enhance the capacities of the least developed countries to export their products should also be part of the proposal and should contain measures intended to enhance trade and investment flows in the short, medium and long-term.

REFERENCES

ASEAN-China Expert Group, "Forging Closer ASEAN-China Economic Relations in the Twenty-First Century," ASEAN-China Expert Group on Economic Cooperation October 2001.

Asian Development Bank, "The GMS Beyond Borders: Regional Cooperation Strategy and Program 2004-2008," March 2004.

Asian Development Bank, "Economic Cooperation in the Greater Mekong Subregion: An Overview," Asian Development Bank, September 2002.

Cai, Kevin G. (2003), "The ASEAN-China Free Trade Agreement and East Asian Regional Grouping," *Contemporary Southeast Asia* 25, No. 3, pp. 387-404.

"China, ASEAN Economic, Trade Ties Speed Up," *Beijing Time*, December 18, 2002.

Goh, Geraldine, ASEAN-China Free Trade Area Negotiations to Start Next Year, "ASEAN Secretariat, Jakarta, Indonesia, October 30, 2002.

Hettne, Bjorn (1996), "Globalization: the New Regionalism and East Asia," in Toshiro Tanaka and Takashi Inoguchi (eds), Selected Papers Delivered at the United Nations University Global Seminar 1996, Shonan Session, Hayama, Japan, September 2-6.

Katzenstein, Peter J. (1996), "Regionalism in Comparative Perspective," ARENA Working Paper.

Lao-Araya, Kanokpan (2002), "How can Cambodia, Lao PDR, Myanmar, and Vietnam Cope with Revenue Lost due to AFTA Tariff Reductions?" ERD Working Paper Series No. 29, Asian Development Bank, November.

Lozenz, Detlev (1991), "Regionalisation versus Regionalism–Problems of Change in the World Economy," *Intereconomics*, January-February, pp. 3-10.

Masviriyakul, Siriluck (2004), "Sino-Thai Strategic Economic Development in the Greater Mekong Subregion (1992–2003)," *Contemporary Southeast Asia 26*, No. 2, pp. 302–19.

Menon, Jayant, "The Evolving ASEAN Free Trade Area: Widening and Deepening," *Asian Development Review*, Vol. 18, No. 1, pp. 49-72.

Pushpanathan, S. (2003), "Appreciating, Understanding the ASEAN Concept," The Jakarta Post, 9 August.

Rajan, Ramkishen S. and Rahul Sen (2004), "The New Wave of FTAs in Asia: With Particular Reference to ASEAN, China and India," Unpublished Paper, June.

United Nations Development Program (UNDP), "Economic Cooperation Among Developing Countries in the Lancang-Mekong Subregion: An Introduction", paper presented in the seminar on Lancang-Mekong Subregional Free Trade Experiment and Demonstration zone, held in Kunming, Yunnan China, 5 April 2002, p. 19.

Zhang, Allan, "Is An Asian Trading Bloc Feasible?" Pricewaterhouse Coopers, 2002.

CHINA'S ECONOMIC GROWTH AND FOREIGN TRADE REFORMS

Asli Karasu and Ozlem Ozdemir

INTRODUCTION

Among all the Asian countries, China has been the country, whose economic achievement has been discussed the most in the academic literature the most lately. Many researchers have investigated the possible reasons behind China's enormous economic growth. This chapter aims to assess the excess economic growth in China especially focusing on the foreign trade reforms as the main factor.

Since the beginning of the 1980s, China has achieved the highest economic growth in the world, that averaged between 9.3% as demonstrated in Table 1. No other national economy has displayed such a high economic growth since the last twenty-five years. Producing 4% of the world's total Gross Domestic Product (GDP), China has been among the first six economic powers of the world like the U.S., Germany and Japan in year 2003 (Hongli, 2003/A). All these facts point out the Chinese miracle. What is interesting is that China accomplished to be among the world's biggest economic powers although it is still a developing country.

Table 1
China's GDP Growth Rates between 1979 and 2004 (%)

Year	*Growth Rate (%)*
1979-1992	9.3
1993	13.5
1994	12.7
1995	10.5
1996	9.7
1997	8.8
1998	7.8
1999	7.1
2000	8
2001	7.3
2002	8
2003	9.1
2004	9.5

Sources: Years 1979-2002: Morrison, 2003, p. 4.
Years 2003 and 2004: www.uschina.org/statististic/economy.html.

Moreover, China achieved to be among the world's leading economies in only twenty-five years, which is considered a very short time for a state to maintain such a high economic growth. After the Communist government was established in 1949 by the leadership of Mao Zedong, China was ruled by a very strict communist regime that left no place to capital ownership. It is only after Deng Xiaoping came to power in 1978 and announced economic development as China's priority that the country met the rules of capitalist economic system, and began to be governed accordingly. Under Deng Xiaoping's governance, China's economic take-off started.

Table 2 demonstrates China's leading role in the growth of the world economy. The table presents the findings of *Bank Credit Analysis,* a Canadian research firm. According to Bank Credit Analysis, between 1995 and 2002, the U.S. accounted for only 20% of global GDP growth while China accounted for 25%. The other Asian countries follow China with having share of 18% in the global GDP growth. Thus, China has accounted for a quarter of the global GDP growth between 1995 and 2002, and has surely been the locomotive of the world economy.

Table 2
Countries' Share of Global GDP Growth Between 1995 and 2002

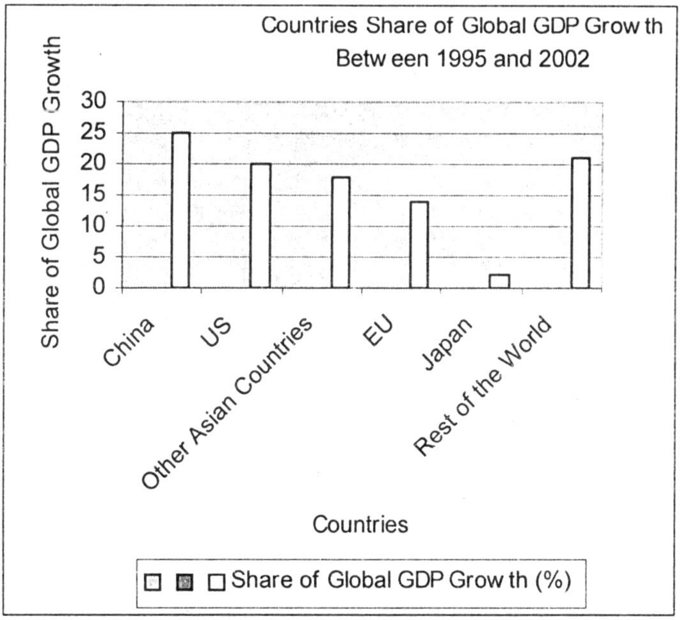

Source: The Economist, ISSN: 9770013061145, p.71.

In assessing China's economic growth, we especially focus on the role of its foreign trade, because based on statistical data, we consider foreign trade as the major factor of its economic development. In year 1980, China's Gross Domestic Product (GDP) was US$ 245 billion, and its volume of foreign trade was US$38.1 billion, making up merely 15% of its GDP as shown in Table 3.

However, starting by year 1980 and especially accelerating in the 1990s, China's Trade/GDP ratio has increased from 9% to 30-%40%, and its exports/GDP ratio has increased from 4% to around 20%. In Table 3, we see that by year 2002, China owed 50% (half of its GDP) to foreign trade. In year 2004, China's GDP was US $ 1 trillion 472 billion while its volume of foreign trade was US$ 1 trillion 127 billion making up 76% of its GDP, and its exports was US$ 591 billion, making up 40% of its GDP. Thus, from 1980 to 2004, China foreign trade to GDP ratio had increased from 13% to 76%, which is a very dramatic high surge. This signifies that foreign trade (especially the volume of its exports) is the leading contributor of China's Gross Domestic Product.

Table 3
China's Foreign Trade Between 1978 and 2004

Year	*Exports ($ billion)*	*Imports ($ billion)*	*Total Trade ($ billion)*	*Exports/GDP (%)*	*Trade/GDP (%)*
1978	9.8	10.9	20.7	4	9
1980	18.1	20.0	38.1	7	15
1985	27.4	42.3	69.7	9	24
1990	62.1	53.4	115.5	17	31
1993	91.8	103.6	195.4	21	40
1995	148.8	132.1	280.9	22	41
1997	182.7	142.4	325.1	20	36
2001	266.1	243.6	509.7	23	43
2002	325.6	295.2	620.8	26	50
2003	438.4	412.8	851.2	32	63
2004	591.0	536.0	1127.0	40	76

Sources: Exports, Imports, Total Trade Volume, Export/GDP, Trade/GDP Between 1978 and 1997: Jun, 1999, p.119.
Exports, Imports, Total Trade Volume Between 2001 and 2002: http://www.uschina.org/statistics/2003 tradeper formance. html
Exports, Imports, Total Trade Volume Year 2003: http://news.ft.com/servlet/2004jan9/China
Year 2004: www.dbresearch.com/servlet/reweb2.ReWEB?rwkey=u793

Note: Exports/GDP and Trade/GDP ratios after year 1997 are authors' calculations.

China's high ranking and its percentage in the overall world foreign trade also demonstrates its success as a foreign trader. As shown in Table 4, in year 2003, China has been the world's top third player after U.S. and Germany, which are its leading rivals.

Table 4
The World's Top Traders in 2003

Country	*Volume of Exports (US $ billion)*	*Volume of Imports (US $ billion)*	*Volume of Total Trade (US $ billion)*
U.S.	713.76	1263.37	1976.93
Germany	748.42	601.76	1350.18
China	438.37	412.84	851.21
Japan	469.98	381.2	851.17

Kwan, 2004/A, p. 2.

Today, China stands out as such a big economic power that is considered as the most challenging rival of the world's super power- the United States, and it is perceived as one of the greatest phobias of the other nation states. How China-once a very poor socialist country has succeeded to become the world's most vigorous economy- has been an intriguing research topic in economic literature. Based on the tables and the data presented, we consider foreign trade as the major factor accounting for China's economic growth. Thereon, we believe that the foreign trade reforms initiated under the leadership of Deng Xiaoping have sustained the boom of foreign trade in China. Thus, in this paper, we investigate the foreign trade reforms accomplished in China, and elaborate on how China, under those reforms, has succeeded to be the world's most vigorous foreign trader in the world. The chapter is organized as follows: First, a general background is presented about the foreign trade reforms initiated by Deng Xiaoping. Then, these reforms are analyzed under the headings of decentralization of the trade management system, the regional targeting policy, sectoral targeting policy, incentives for exporting enterprises and foreign direct investment (FDI) reforms. Finally, the impacts of foreign trade reforms on China's foreign trade and the boom of its economy are discussed as final remarks in the conclusion of the chapter.

THE FOREIGN TRADE REFORMS IN CHINA

Deng Xiaoping is the architect of the foreign trade reforms in China. After Deng came to power, he initiated his "open door policy", which basically opened the doors of China to foreign investment and capital. Deng and his cadre set it as their mission to take China out of poverty, and bring it to a certain state of prosperity in order to make the country stronger.

After China initiated the "open door policy" under the leadership of Deng Xiaoping, it achieved a great success in expanding its foreign trade and especially its exports. It is because of the huge increase of its exports that China is able to lead a favorable balance of trade with most of its trade partners. Therefore, it is vital to analyze the reforms and factors that have actualized China's "export miracle." Those reforms are analyzed under five categories: These are mainly the decentralization of its trade management system, the regional targeting policy, the sectoral targeting policy, incentives for exporting enterprises and foreign direct investment reforms.

Deng Xiaoping began to implement the trade reforms first by dismantling the state monopoly on foreign trade and decentralizing China's trade management system. Thus, we should first analyze how China's foreign trade went through a process of decentralization.

DECENTRALIZATION OF THE TRADE MANAGEMENT SYSTEM

China's trade management system went through a significant decentralization process since the late 1980s. During Mao's era, foreign trade in China was carried out by special corporations, called specialized foreign trade corporations (FTCs). Only the FTCs had the right to carry out the foreign trade in China. On the export side, the FTCs had the role of buying commodities from domestic producers, and selling them on international markets at the offered prices. The central government attained the foreign exchange earnings of the FTCs. On the import side, the domestic importers were not allowed to import directly, but to apply to the FTCs (Chan, Tracy and Wenhui, 1999). There were only 13 FTCs operating in the country. Thus, both the scope and the volume of the foreign trade taking place in China were limited. In this highly centralized system, there was a lack of information of international market demand and supply, and thus foreign trade in China was conducted in very inefficient terms.

In order to encourage competition among the FTCs and the expansion of foreign trade, Deng ordered the establishment of more FTCs at both the central and the provincial level. By 1988, there were about 5000 FTCs operating in the country, and by 1996, they had exceeded 7000. The FTCs were mostly state-owned, and supervised by the Ministry of Trade and Economic Cooperation (MOFTEC). Although they were state-owned and supervised by MOFTEC, the government decreased its dominance on the operations of FTCs significantly. Apart from very special commodities, the government no longer has control on the exportation of commodities. However, before the reforms have started, the government was closely supervising which products to export.

The government also liberalized the trading system by granting the domestic manufacturing companies "trading rights". In this way, the manufacturing companied did not have to go to FTCs, and this naturally spurred the export activities in the country. All these measures relaxed the government's monopoly on foreign trade (Jun, 1999).

Decentralization also occurred among the local governance. This led to competition among the localities, which were trying to serve better both to their own citizens and to the foreigners. Thus, after the 1980s each locality pursued to attract more foreign investment, the establishment of new exporting enterprises and FTCs. This fierce competition among the localities acted as an important factor in China's export boom (Chan, et al., 1999).

THE REGIONAL TARGETING POLICY

In 1979, Deng decided to initiate some experimental measures to promote exports. In order to achieve this, the government selected two coastal regions-Guangdong and Fuijan, and began to implement some policies to expand the exports and FDI in those two regions. The first measure was to open four "special economic zones" (SEZs) in Guangdong and Fuijan. The three SEZs are located in Guangdong's cities-Shenzhen, Shekou and Zhuhai while the last one is located in Fuijan's city-Xiamen. Both Fuijan and Guangdong are neighboring regions, and Guangdong province is geographically adjacent to Hong Kong and Macao. Before 1979, Fuijan and Guangdong were one of the poorest regions in China (Chan et al., 1999).

Deng had a certain motive in establishing the SEZs in Guangdong and Fuijan, and that was to make those two provinces China's export and FDI centers. Thus, he especially had focused on the two provinces, and he accomplished his objective of transforming Guangdong and Fuijan, which were once China's poorest provinces, into the country's most prosperous regions. Especially region Guangdong's success of attracting FDI and exports is stunning, because its economic development led to the emergence of a very prosperous region called Pearl River Delta (PRD), that is nearby Guangdong (Chan et al., 1999). Thus, it is necessary to explain the export and FDI boom in Guangdong and Pearl River Delta fully.

Guangdong and Pearl River Delta (PRD) are the best examples of China's regional targeting policy. Having a very strategic location near to Hong Kong and Taiwan, Guangdong is located in a region called Pearl River Delta, which is the area covering 47,000 square kilometers containing highly strategic cities and regions like Macau, Guangzhou-Guangdong's capital city- and Hong Kong. Since the open door policy, both Pearl River Delta and Guangdong have been the centers of exports and FDI in China (Kemenade, 1997).

During the era of Mao, Guangdong was a neglected province, because it was near Taiwan, and due to security concerns, Mao did not want this province to develop. Guangdong received almost no money from the central government. It is Deng Xiaoping, who transformed the neglected Guangdong, into China's tiger province with the establishment of the special economic zones (SEZs) in the province. For Deng, political issues had minor importance, and he envisioned that China could benefit from Guangdong's geographical proximity to Hong Kong and Taiwan. Deng's strategy worked out well. With the establishment of the SEZs in Guangdong, the region became attractive for the exporters and investors in Hong Kong and Taiwan, who wanted to benefit from the rich yet inexpensive land and labor resources in the region. Deng not only established SEZs in Guangdong, he also implemented major FDI liberalization policies in the region. (FDI reforms will be fully analyzed in the next section). But to give an example of the FDI liberalization policy, in 1988, in order to encourage the inflow of FDI to Guangdong, Deng raised the ceiling to $30 million for the amount of foreign investment allowed to enter the province without the government's approval. Thus, complicated procedures of application processes for investments up to US$30 million were not necessary, and this incentive became a major motivation for the foreign investors coming to Guangdong (Kemenade, 1997).

The establishment of the SEZs and the liberalized FDI implementations in Guangdong expanded the region's exports. From 1978 to 1996, while China's exports grew at an annual average rate of 16%, Guangdong's exports grew at an 23%. Moreover, while China's national export-to-GDP ratio was 19% in 1996, Guangdong's export-to-GDP ratio was 76%. In 1978, when the reforms had not started yet, the export/GDP ratio was barely 13% in Guangdong (Chan, et al.,1999). Thus, it can be seen that compared to China as a whole, Guangdong's export rates had seen a dramatic increase. This is mainly because most of the products produced by the Hong Kong firms in Guangdong were sent to Hong Kong, and then re-exported to all around the world. In a way, Guangdong was "Hong Konginized" (Thompson, 1998, p. 74).

Another factor, which enabled Guangdong in being China's pivotal center of exports and FDI was its successful de-centralization process, in which the counties and township had considerable autonomy. This de-centralization encouraged many exporting enterprises to be established at the local level. Whereas the localities of Guangdong enjoyed great autonomy, another region-Shanghai-imposed considerable control over its localities. These two different practices produced stunning results, because in 1978, Shanghai was the leading exporter in China. However, since the early 1990s, Guangdong's exports have long surpassed Shanghai's. Thus, de-centralization has led to competition among the enterprises, and this in the long run has increased the region's exports (Chan, et al., 1999). Since the 1990s, Guangdong has kept its leadership as an exporter in China. In 2003, as well, Guangdong's most developed city-Shenzhen- became China's leading exporter city, achieving 14.2% of the overall exports in China Thus, Guangdong maintains its predominant position as the leading exporter region of China, and today it is such a region that it exports more than many of the nations in the world (http://english.mofcom.gov.cn/article/200312/20031200158295_1xml). Generating 11% of China's GDP, one-third of its foreign trade and one quarter of all China's FDI in year 2002, it is no doubt that Guangdong has been the "dragon economy" of China (htttp://www.cbbc.org/ezine/feauture.html).

It is also with the development of Guangdong that the emergence of Pearl River Delta took place. The growth of Guangdong in the mid-1990s has spurred the economic growth in its nearby regions extending from Hong Kong through Shenzhen, Dongguan, Guangzhou, Foshan, Shunde to Jiangmen. With the emergence of such a highly developed region, this area began to be called the Pearl River Delta. Now, Pearl River delta is considered to be the richest region of China having the most exports and the FDI. Bearing less than 3% of China's population, it contributes almost 7% of its GDP. Excluding Hong Kong and Macao, the PRD economy (measures in purchasing power parity terms-PPP-) is larger than the national economies of Malaysia, Portugal and Greece. Including Hong Kong and Taiwan, the PRD economy (again in PPP term) is 45% of Canada's economy, which is among the G-8 (Leman, 2003). Thus, the economy of Pearl River Delta is even stronger than a medium sized national economy, and this has been achieved by Deng's regional differentiation policy.

Today, the PRD is where most of the "Made in China" products in light-manufacturing industry-ranging from toys and electronics to textiles-are produced and exported to all around the world. Thus, it is called "the workshop of the world" (Kwan, 2003/B). Although since the late 1990s, PRD is being challenged by another region called Yangtze River Delta, which is around Shanghai, the Pearl River delta still continues being the leader of China's exports and FDI in the 2000s (Leman, 2003). In the twenty-first century, the PRC government also wants to welcome more value-added, high-technology investments to China (*http://www.cbbc.org/ezine/feature.html*). Since the last few years, this has been began to be achieved as well. For example, many Japanese automobile firms-like Nissan and Toyota-have based their factories and operations in the PRD. Thus, besides being export and FDI center, PRD has also assumed the role of being China's "high-tech industrial base." Since 2002, the PRC government is also leading the project of constructing a 30-km. bridge linking Hong Kong with Guangdong and Macao (Kwan, 2003/B). In this way, the Pearl River Delta will be more integrated. Such an integration will surely spur the foreign trade and investment among the cities and regions in the Pearl River Delta. Thus, the PRD's economic strength in China seems unshakable, even more enhancing in the twenty-first century.

Special Economic Zones (SEZs) are other form of proof of success behind Deng Xiaoping's regional targeting policy. The establishment of the SEZs in China began to take place in 1979 experimentally in two provinces-Guangdong and Fuijan. Deng's intention in establishing these SEZs was to provide certain privileges to the firms wanting to do foreign trade in these areas and to attract foreign direct investment (FDI) to the regions by giving more autonomy. The government wanted to test if such benefits given to the SEZs would really escalate the foreign trade and foreign direct investment. By establishing the SEZs, Deng wanted to prove to the international community that the Chinese Communist Party had the vision and skills to make trade reforms and catch up with Taiwan and Korea (Chan, et al.1999).

When the export and FDI volumes increased in the four SEZs, the State Council opened fourteen more coastal cities in 1985 and in 1988 Hainan Island to foreign trade and FDI incentives (Gamer, 1999). Thereon, the coastal provinces of China became the center of China's exports and FDI. Moreover-the high export success of the Pearl River Delta in the 1990s prompted the Chinese government to open more free trade zones in the 1990s.

At the state, provincial, city and district level, there are many different special economic zones (SEZs) now. These are mainly:

1. ***Free-trade zones (FTZs):*** They give incentives for international trade and export processing.
2. ***Export-processing Zones (EPZs):*** They are specialized zones devoted to the development of export processing.
3. ***Border and Economic Cooperation Zones:*** They aim to improve frontier trade and export processing with neighboring countries.
4. ***Economic and Technological Development Zones:*** Zones that offer technological facilities and services.
5. ***High technology Industrial Development Zones:*** They encourage the production of high-tech products (Walton, 2004).

Especially Free-trade zones (FTZs) and export-processing zones (EPZs) are the most effective SEZs in China. As the kinds of the zones increased, the number of cities becoming free-trade zones increased as well. After the four special economic zones, 15 new free trade zones were established in the 1990s.

Most of the free-trade zones are located in the Guangdong province. The FTZs cover areas ranging from 6 to 10 km2. Activities such as warehousing, foreign exchange transactions, marketing, trading and export promotion are being carried out in the free-trade zones. The Chinese government provides many incentives the firms operating in the FTZs. These incentives are mainly exemption from customs duty and value-added tax (VAT) and the maintenance of liberal exchange rules. During the first and second years of their operations, the companies in the FTZs do not give tax to the government. During the third, fourth and fifth years of their operations, they give 50% of the tax rate of the foreign invested enterprises (FIESs), which is around 15% of the income earned. After they complete the five years of operation, the companies at the FTZs are taxed according to the general taxing regulations of the FIEs. Not only exports, but also imports entering the FTZs are exempt from the customs duties and VAT (Walton, 2003).

Export processing zones (EPZs) are the other zones that carry importance for the expansion of China's exports. Compared to the FTZs, export-processing zones are recently established in year 2000. While 15 EPZs were established in year 2000, now this number has grown to 38. Most of the EPZs are located in central and western China, especially in province Jiangsu as result of the government's policy to strengthen the interior regions of China, and mitigate the provincial income differences in this way. There are differences between the scope of the activities of the FTZs and the EPZs. First of all, compared to free-trade zones, the activities permitted in the export-processing zones are limited. In the EPZs, only export processing, warehousing and freight transport are allowed. Another major difference is the export rebate policy in the FTZs and the EPZs. Because the EPZs are specialized zones only for export processing, if a company operating in an EPZ purchases goods from a firm in China, the company in the EPZ will receive an export rebate. Thereon, the firm, which buys the product, will be exempt from the value-added tax (VAT). However, companies in the free-trade zones will have to pay the VAT and can apply for the export rebate only after the good is exported. In this respect, companies in the export-processing zones have more advantages. Moreover, there are no VAT charges on public utilities in export-processing zones unlike in FTZs. What is common between the two zones is that imports are tax-exempt. Thus, although export-processing activities are allowed in the FTZs as well, companies, that solely lead export activities, choose to operate in the EPZs because of the more wide range of incentives they offer. This leads many analysts to argue that EPZs will overtake FTZs in the near future (*Walton, 2003*).

The establishment of SEZs not only increased exports, but also attracted FDI, new technology and know-how, which were transferred to the domestic firms through joint ventures and other kinds of partnership. This has strengthened the domestic industry as well.

The establishment of the special economic zones (SEZs) has taken place as an experimental policy of the government to increase China's exports. When it proved to be successful, different kinds of zones followed the SEZs. The SEZs surely transformed Guangdong and Pearl River Delta to the centers of the foreign trade in China. Targeting Guangdong and Pearl River Delta as the main centers of foreign trade in China, and basing most of the SEZs in those regions surely has been a wise tactic considering their volume of export and overall foreign trade performances. Today, it can be said that China owes its outstanding foreign trade performance to a great extent to the regional targeting policy initiated in the 1980s.

SECTORAL TARGETING POLICY

Other than regional targeting, Deng applied sectoral targeting policy to encourage the growth of exports beginning by the 1980s. Sectoral targeting policy basically emphasized providing specific incentives for the export of certain products, which were basically light industrial products, textiles, machinery and electronics. Mao Zedong had given more importance to the production of heavy industrial goods. Deng, on the other hand, was aware that China could not achieve a high growth based on inefficient, heavy industry, and thus he shifted the importance to the production of light industrial products. Thereon, Deng began to implement policies that not only encouraged the production but also the export of light industrial products, and it can be said that today China owes its leadership of world's leading exporter country in textiles and machinery to the sectoral targeting policies initiated under Deng's leadership.

The government used many methods, such as "foreign exchange retention system" and tax reductions in the application of its sectoral targeting policy. Exchange retention rate is "the percentage of foreign exchange earnings that an exporting enterprise is allowed to retain" (Jun., 1999, p. 123). Previously, the Bank of China allocated almost all the foreign exchange earnings. The exporters were allowed to retain very low percentage, which was around 10% of their foreign exchange earnings for most of the products. After the system was introduced, the exporters were given the chance to retain a higher percentage of their foreign exchange earnings. While in the 1980s, the rate that could be retained was 50% for the machinery and electronic goods, in the 1990s, it increased to 70%. Such a high increase of retention rate naturally expanded the number of people wanting to export. In 1994, when the government unified its multiple exchange rates, it abolished its foreign exchange retention policy altogether, but since that time, the policy motivated many Chinese firms to export light industry goods (Jun., 1999).

In the 1990s, the government especially focused its attention on the encouragement of the export of electronical goods. For this purpose, the government provided incentives such as electrical power, tax reduction on inputs to the exporting firms. The government also established special funds for technological improvements. In this way, many technological exporting firms were established. (Jun., 1999).

To sum up, beginning by the 1980s with the application of sectoral targeting policy, China's growth of light industrial products expanded. It is by the sectoral targeting strategy that today China is among the world's leading exporter countries of products such as electrical machinery and textiles.

INCENTIVES FOR EXPORTING ENTERPRISES

China's growth of exports has been sustained by two sources: domestic firms and foreign-invested exporting enterprises (FIEs). As China's exports began to increase during the 1980s, the Chinese government began to give many incentives to both the domestic and FIEs. The FIEs were established especially on the coastal cities of China. The government decided that the profits of such enterprises would be exempt from income tax. Moreover, had the enterprise re-invested in China, the scope of such tax exemptions and additional incentives would be enlarged. These incentives increased the number of FIEs operating in China. Moreover, when the Pearl River Delta and 14 Open Coastal Cities were established in 1985, the number of FIEs increased even more. Thereon, the domestic firms began to lose their share in China's overall exports (Chan, et al.,1999). Table 5 demonstrates how China's domestic exporting firms lost their share after 1980 and how FIEs increased their share in China's exports.

Table 5
Share of Domestic Firms and Foreign-invested Enterprises (FIEs) in Exports between years 1980 and 1997 and in year 2002

Year	*Share of Domestic Firms*	*Share of FIEs (%)*
1980	99.95	0.04
1981	99.85	0.15
1982	99.76	0.24
1983	98.52	1.48
1984	99.73	0.26
1985	98.91	1.09
1986	98.07	1.93
1987	96.93	3.06
1988	94.83	5.17
1989	90.65	9.35
1990	87.42	12.58
1991	83.23	16.77
1992	79.56	20.43
1993	72.49	27.50
1994	71.32	28.68
1995	69.30	31.70
1996	59.30	40.70
1997	59.00	41.00
2002	48.00	52.00

Sources: Years 1980-1997 Chan, Tracy and Wenhui, 1999, p. 25.
Year 2002: (http://www.uschina.org/statistics/2003tradeperformance.html).

Table 5 shows that especially after year 1992, the share of domestic enterprises fell significantly, and the FIEs rose. In year 2002, the FIEs had the majority of share (52%) in the overall exports of China. In year 2004, the FIEs accomplished 2/3-more than 60% of all the exports of China (www.kobifinans.com.tr). This has close relation with the foreign direct investment (FDI) that expanded greatly in China in the mid-1990s. As the amount of FDI increased in the country, more FIEs became established, and the exporting performance of the FIEs increased accordingly. Especially the regions-Guangdong, Fuijan in the Pearl Delta River the Yangtze Delta River are the ones, which attracted the most FDI, and the most exports accordingly. Thus, "there is a close correlation between the influx of foreign capital and export growth" (Chan, et al.,1999, p. 26). Moreover, compared to other regions, the FIEs constitute the major share in the exports in the Yangtze Delta and the Pearl River Delta. Thus, the presence of foreign capital and know-how in those regions reduce the operations of domestic exporting enterprises. FIEs especially excelled in the operations of high-tech and export-oriented industries, because China's Ministry of Foreign Trade and Economic Cooperation (MOFTEC) encouraged the FIEs to operate in those sectors. "In industries, where China is self-sufficient (such as green tea processing) or which are politically or culturally sensitive (such as media), MOFTEC prohibited the FIEs to operate" (*http://www.cbbc.org/ezine/archive/business-guides/guides9.html*) However, those restrictions will no longer be applied to the FIEs according to the WTO regulations.

Another result of the opening of such regions to foreign investment has been the promotion of labor-intensive manufacturing scheme, that is still predominant in China. China has attained a comparative advantage in labor-intensive manufacturing, because when foreign investment came to the coastal provinces, China had a huge unemployed population, which was once engaged in agriculture. This population had a strict labor discipline, attained from the collectivization days in the 1950s. Moreover, the people had a high literacy rate. When those people with high labor discipline and literacy rate began to work for very low wages, China took a leap in manufacturing (Chan, et al.,1999). China still has this comparative advantage of huge and skilled labor force, working for very low wages, compared to many countries in the world. Thereon, since the 1990s, China has profoundly incorporated its huge labor force into international economy.

The Chinese government supported its domestic exporting enterprises as well. First of all, it provided the exemption of custom duties. Moreover, the Bank of China offered trade credits to exporting enterprises in domestic currency. Between 1985 and 1991, the volume of trade loans almost quadrupled. The Bank especially provided loans to textile and electronic & machinery equipment exporters.

However, in 1996, the government removed almost all of the incentives, and even imposed value-added on all exports. It is no doubt that the advantages and incentives offered to exporters played a critical role in expanding China's exports. However, the removal of the incentives and yet the growth of exports proves that China's "export miracle" did not solely depended on incentives. The reforms had been established well, and even without the incentives, the Chinese did and still are successful exporters.

As a result of China's export reforms, not only its GDP increased dramatically, but also advanced technologies and managerial know-how entered China (Jun, 1999).

The devaluation of the renminbi expanded China's exports further. Thereon, China began to use this devaluation as a policy to increase its exports (Chan, et al.,1999). Even today, China is being criticized harshly by the international community, (especially by the U.S.) which claims that China is artificially devaluing its currency, and thus using it in an unjust way to promote its exports.

It must be noted that while the government is the key actor in the success of export boom, the Chinese people must be credited for their ability to benefit from the incentives provided to them and contribute to the promotion of exports. Thus, both the government and the public have played a good tennis match-the government has served well, and the Chinese public, with their entrepreneurial spirit- has responded to the serves very successfully. Combined with the sound polices of the government, the entrepreneurial spirit of the Chinese people have actualized the "export miracle" of China.

FOREIGN DIRECT INVESTMENT (FDI) REFORMS

"The essence of socialism is liberating and developing productive forces."

Deng Xiaoping

Foreign direct investment has played a crucial role in the expansion of China's foreign trade and thereby in the growth of its economy for almost twenty-five years. China has proved that foreign trade and FDI complement each other. Since the initiation of Deng Xiaoping's open door policy, China has made great achievements in expanding its FDI inflows by improving its FDI policy framework. Deng Xiaoping's intention in liberalizing China's FDI framework and attracting more FDI in this way was to expand the Chinese exports. Thus, China's export promotion aim was the underlying theme of its will to expand the FDI.

Table 6 proves the success of China in attracting huge amounts of FDI between 1979 and 2004.

As seen in Table 6, between 1979 and 1990, FDI inflows to China had increased at reasonable rates. It is in the 1990s that FDI inflows to China had expanded. In 1990, China received almost US$4 billion FDI. In 1999-only 9 years later- China's FDI amount had increased to US$40 billion. This stark volume of 10 multiplence is one of the best proves of FDI expansion in China. In year 2002, China surpassed the United States and became the top country in the world in terms of inflow of FDI (Kwan, 2003/C, p.1). China has preserved its leadership in receiving the most FDI in the world in the years 2003 and 2004 as well. Figure 1 also proves that China has attracted the FDI in the world steadily despite crises.

As Figure 1 demonstrates as well, the FDI flow to China has not been affected by the regional and global economic crises. While the FDI inflows to countries in Southeast Asia have decreased as a result of the Asian Financial crisis in 1997, the dotcom bubble bursts in 2000 and the September 11 incident, the FDI inflows to China have not decreased as a consequence of those three major crisis at all as seen in the figure. Not only in Southeast Asia, but globally the foreign direct investment have been staggering since 2000, and China still manages to attract FDI (Öðütçü, 2003). Thus, such as a continuous of China in receiving FDI from the world is worth praise.

China owes its success in being the world's largest FDI recipient to the FDI reforms initiated by Deng Xiaoping. We will give brief information about the FDI reforms by categorizing them under three periods: The 1980s, the 1990s and the 2000s.

Table 6
Utilized FDI Inflows into China Between Years 1979 and 2003

Year 1979-1982	Volume (US $ billion)
(cumulative)	1.77
1983	0.64
1984	1.26
1985	1.66
1986	1.88
1987	2.31
1988	3.19
1989	3.39
1990	3.49
1991	4.37
1992	11.20
1993	25.76
1994	33.79
1995	35.80
1996	40.20
1997	44.20
1998	45.60
1999	40.40
2000	40.70
2001	46.90
2002	52.70
2003	53.51
2004	61.00

Sources: Years 1979-1994: Chai, Kueh and Tisdell, 1997, p. 147.
Years 1995-1997: Stiglitz and Yusuf, 2001, p. 414.
Years 1998-2002: European Union Commission, 2003.
Years 2003 and 2004: http://www.uschina.org/statistics/fdi1979-03.html.

Figure 1: The Flow of FDI to China and the Southeast Asian Countries

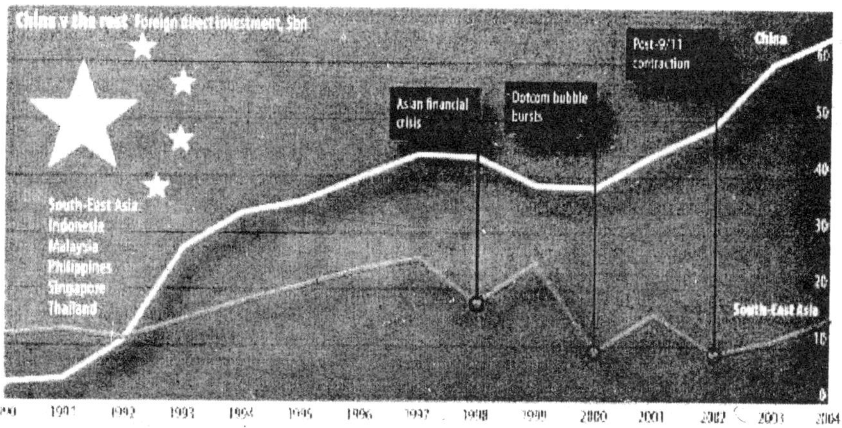

Source: Lockwood, 2003, p.74.

The 1980s

FDI was banned in China during Mao Zedong's era. It is with Deng Xiaoping s open door policy that China allowed the flow of FDI (Zhang, 1998). The passing of the "Chinese-Foreign Equity Joint Ventures" law in 1979 has started China's FDI reforms. Under this law, the Chinese government accepted the utilization of foreign capital (http://english.mofcom.gov.cn/article/200406/20040600233643_1.xml).

The opening of the four special economic zones in 1980 and of the 14 coastal cities to investment in 1984 were the other major steps that the PRC government took to encourage the FDI. Still, these were experimental policies for the Chinese government. There was not an absolute freedom in the FDI implementations, and the regulations were still strict. For example, the foreigners were not let to have the majority shares in the joint ventures (Zhang, 1998). Moreover, in the 1980s, foreigners were allowed only to establish export-oriented joint ventures with the Chinese companies (http://www.fdimagazine.com/news/printpage.php/aid/554/China.html). Thus, from the foreigners' point of view, China lacked credibility and commitment to the liberalization of the FDI regulations. Nevertheless, as seen in Table 1.7, the steps that the Chinese government took increased the FDI inflow to the country in the 1980s.

In the 1980s, the first investors in China were small export-oriented Hong Kong firms. The government opened foreign exchange swap centers in Shenzhen in 1986, and then in Shanghai in order to encourage the foreign investors to invest their money in China. This increased the foreign exchange coming to China, and motivated other states-especially China's neighbors such as Japan and Taiwan- to come. Although the foreign investors were panicked by the Tiananmen Incidents in 1989, this did not reduce the inflow of FDI as seen in Table 1.6. This is because the government, especially Deng Xiaoping successfully assured the global community that China had no intention to close in itself (Zhang, 1998). With all the experimental policies, the 1980s can be considered as "Feeling the stones phase in China" (Chen and Shanberge, 2004).

The 1990s

In order to ease the tension of the Tiananmen Square Incident, Deng Xiaoping toured around China's southern coastal areas and SEZs in 1992. The purpose of Deng's visit was to reassure the global community that China was determined to progress the open door policy, and was willing to liberalize more of its trade and FDI regulations (OECD, 2000).

After Deng's tour, the PRC government began to prove their commitment to FDI reforms by taking major liberalization measures. First, the government, let foreigners to manufacture goods for sale in the domestic Chinese market (*http://www.fdimagazine.com/news/printpage.php/aid/554/China.html*). Secondly, almost all sectors of the economy-from real estate, banking, services to retail, infrastructure, telecommunications and energy- were let to foreign investment though with varying degrees. These policies spurred the inflow of FDI to China, and in 1993, by attracting US$25.76 million investment, China became the world's second largest investment destination after the United States (Zhang, 1998). This was a great success for a country, which allowed the presence of FDI only 14 years ago.

In the mid-1990s, the PRC government allowed the establishment of wholly foreign-owned enterprises, and this has been a milestone on China's FDI liberalization process. The establishment of the wholly foreign-owned spurred the inflow of FDI to China. Today, the wholly foreign-owned enterprises are the leading FDI form that is being utilized in China. (http://www.fdimagazine.com/news/printpage.php/aid/554/China.html). As stated in the section about regional differentiation, especially Guangdong province has been the major recipient of China's FDI inflows in the 1990s, and this especially due to the establishment of the wholly foreign-owned enterprises in Guangdong.

China made especially two very important changes in its finance system, which attracted more FDI to the country. The first change was that in 1994, the government unified its exchange rate system, and the second one was that in 1996, the government maintained the current account convertibility. These two changes meant that exporters and importers could make their transactions and get foreign exchange (IMF, 2002). Such a financial liberalization naturally motivated more foreign enterprises to invest in China.

In the 1990s, the foreign investors believed in the PRC's commitment to increase the share of FDI in China. Coupled with the successful reforms actualized, the 1990s can be considered as the period of expansion of FDI in China.

The 2000s

As seen in Table 6 and Figure 1, the inflows to China have been increasing in the 2000s as well making China the world's largest FDI recipient since the last two years.

In the 2000s, one of the major factors, which spurred FDI to China, has been the competition among the provinces and cities to attract the most FDI. Cities, especially like Shanghai, Shenzhen and Guangzhou, have applied various liberalizing measures to enable the setting up of the investments, and be among the top preferential regions of FDI in China. For example, in 2002, Shenzhen issued new regulations such as reducing the time period for a business license from 10 days to five days and providing business guidebooks for foreign-invested enterprises (FIEs). Likewise, Shanghai has offered incentives to firms, which have the intention of setting up their critical units- such as headquarters and research and development (R&D) centers- in Shanghai. Beijing-another competitive city of FDI- has implemented new regulations, which made easier getting the work permits and residency. Therefore, just like special economic zones have been competing with each other, the cities and provinces in China have been in a similar competition for attracting the most FDI. Both the foreign companies, the cities and the country benefit from this rivalry (*http://www.uschina.org/statistics/2003 foreigninvestment.html*).

China's WTO membership has liberalized its FDI environment and contributed to its promotion as well. Especially in the services sector, China has liberalized many of its commitments based on its WTO commitments. First of all, it let foreigners to participate in securities brokerage and the legal services, which had been protected by the Chinese government to a great extent. Since China's accession to WTO, the number foreign firms operating in the legal and securities sectors saw a rapid increase. Environmental and engineering services besides printing and publications distribution are the other sectors, in which more FDI projects began to be implemented since China's WTO accession. Finally, in the banking sector, which was highly protected by the PRC government before the WTO membership, many leading banking and investment firms entered or extended their operations in China. For example, in 2004, the PRC government gave permition to Goldman Sachs to enter the domestic investment banking market, and this prompted Goldman Sachs to establish joint ventures with two Chinese securities firms. Moreover, in August 2004, HSBC obtained 20% stake on the Bank of Communications. Coupled with the FDI reforms accomplished in the 1990s, the WTO regulations made the investment environment in China more transparent (www.uschina.org/statistics/2005 foreigninvestment.html).

China has four classification categories in the legal framework of its FDI projects. These categories of industries are "encouraged, restricted, permitted and prohibited" (OECD, 2003, p. 5). After its accession to WTO, China reduced the restricted and prohibited projects types. As stated, these are mainly in the services sector. However, China still prohibits some sectors, which it considers traditional-such as the production of green tea, traditional Chinese medicine, rice, paper and ink tablets. Another prohibited category of FDI is the futures companies. While the global community may show some understanding to China protecting its own traditional industries, the prohibition of the establishment of the futures companies is not anticipated at all. Thus, both the WTO and the foreign companies are expecting China to liberalize the futures sector (OECD, 2003).

Since 2000, more firms from Japan, Taiwan and South Korea especially in sectors- such as clothing, furniture and light electronics- have relocated their production facilities to China. This is a great advantage for the China, because in this way, the foreign investments of those firms, became more stable. The foreign enterprises have preferred to locate their production facilities to China in order to enjoy abundant and cheap land and labor force, and increase their competitiveness in this way. Not only the production facilities, but also headquarters of the many Multinational Companies (MNCs) are being transferred to China's major cities, such as Beijing and Shanghai. In 2002, there were 70 regional headquarters and 37 international purchasing centers of foreign companies in Shanghai (*http://www.uschina.org/statistics2003 foreigninvestment.html*). This signifies that China is now the center of world's leading MNCs, and it is where major and key business decisions are taken and being implemented. Thus, the presence of headquarters, production facilities and research & development centers have all given China "A Strategic Global Business Role."

There are now 420,000 foreign companies operating in China, and they are actualizing more than 60% of all China's exports (Lardy, 2004). Thus, foreign enterprises in China are the major actors of China's exports. We can say that as a result of the 25 years of the process of China's FDI liberalization, Deng Xiaoping's objective-expanding FDI in order to promote China's exports-has been fulfilled.

CONCLUSION

While China was one of the poorest countries devastated by Mao Zedong's harsh communist policies, it became one of the world's most dynamic traders after the 1990s. It alone accounted for one fifth of global trade expansion between 2000 and 2003 (Goldstein and Lardy, 2004). In this chapter, we argued that the foreign trade reforms initiated in the 1980s have enabled China to accomplish scoring such a high trade volume.

As elaborated in the chapter, the PRC government first decentralized the trade management system by allowing the establishment of the foreign trade corporations (FTCs), then applied the regional targeting policies by establishing special economic zones (SEZs), targeted light industry sectors for development, provided incentives for exporting enterprises and finally gave access to foreign investment to the county and encouraged their utilization.

Although China is being governed in a communist political system, the PRC government had led very strategic capitalist economic policies, which utilized the country's high population and expanded the potential of the country. Many critics are arguing that China will not be able to sustain this high economic and foreign trade growth in the coming years. We will not make such an assumption of whether or not the Chinese economy is going to expand more. However, we certainly argue that foreign trade is underlying basis of the growth of Chinese economy, and it is one of the major determinants of China's economic growth.

REFERENCES

BOOKS and ARTICLES

Chai, J.C.H., Kueh, Y.Y. and Tisdell, C.A. (Ed.). (1997), *China and the Asia-Pacific Economy*. Commack, NY: Nova Science Publishers.

Chan, T., Tracy, N. and Wenhui, Z. (1999), *China's Export Miracle: Origins, Results and Prospects*. New York: St. Martin's Press.

Chen, H. and Shanberge, J. (2004, April), The Future of the Joint Venture. *Journal of the European Union Chamber of Commerce in China*.

Available on site *http://www.sinomedia.net/eurobiz/v200404/story0404.html.*

European Union Commission Policy Paper for Transmission to the Council and the European Parliament (2003, September 10). "A Maturing Partnership-Shared Interests and Challenges in EU-China Relations".

Available on site *http://europa.eu.int/comm/external_relations/china/com_03_533_en.pdf.*

Gamer, R.E. (Ed.) (1999), *Understanding contemporary China*. Boulder: Lynne Rienner Publishers.

Goldstein, M. and Lardy, N. (2004), 'What Kind of Landing for the Chinese Economy *Institute for International Economics* Washington D.C. *Available on site http://www.iie.com/publications/pb/pb04-7.pdf*

Hongli, A.Z. (2003, August 4), China Opportunities for ST. *Embassy of the People's Republic of China.* Available on site *http://www.bizcn-sg.org.sg/China/%20Opportunuties%20%20for%20ST.ppt.*

Jun, M. (1999), *The Chinese Economy in the 1990s.* New York: St. Martin's Press.

Kemenade, W. (1997), *China, Hong Kong, Taiwan Inc.* New York : Knopf.

Kwan, C.H. (2003/B), Pearl River Delta to Remain the Engine of the Workshop of the World-Factors Providing Industrial Upgrading Firmly in Place. *Research Institute of Economy, Trade and Industry (RIETI).*
Available on site: *http://www.rieti.go.jp/en/china/03121201.html.*

Kwan, C.H. (2003/C), The Complementary Relationship Between Japan and China-An Update. *Research Institute of Economy, Trade and Industry (RIETI).*
Available on site: *http://www.rieti.go.jp/en/china/03091201.html*

Kwan, C.H. (2004/A), China surpasses Japan to Become the World's Third Largest Trader-But the "Workshop of the World" is still Fragile. *Research Institute of Economy, Trade and Industry (RIETI).*
Available on site *http: rieti.go.jp/en/china/04032301.html.*

Leman, E. (2003), Can the Pearl River Delta Region Still Compete? *US-China Business Council The China Business Review 2003.*
Available on site *http://www.chinabusinessreview.com/public/0305.html.*

Lockwood, C. (2003), Cheer up, South-East Asia. *The Economist: The World in 2004.*

Organization for Economic Cooperation and Development (OECD) Policy Brief (September 2003), "Attracting to Investment to China ".
Available on site *http://www.oecd.org/dataoecd/14/30/11724736.pdf.*

Morrison, W.M. (2003), *Congressional Research Service Issue Brief for Congress.*

Organization for Economic Cooperation and Development (OECD) Working Papers on International Investment (December 2000), "Main Determinants and Impacts of Foreign Direct Investment on China's Economy".
Available on site *http://www.oecd.org/dataoecd/11/45/1902798.pdf.*

Organization for Economic Cooperation and Development (OECD) Policy Brief (September 2003), "Attracting to Investment to China ".
Available on site *http://www.oecd.org/dataoecd/14/30/11724736.pdf.*

Öðütçü, M. (2003), "Galiba Çin Treni de Kaçýyor".
Available on author's site *http://www.megmetogutcu.com/cin_treni.pdf.*

Stiglitz, J.E. and Yusuf, S. (Ed.) (2001), *Rethinking the East Asian Miracle.* Washington D.C. World Bank; New York: Oxford University Press. *The Economist.* p. 71 ISSN: 9770013061145.

Thompson, K.W. (Ed.) (1998), *China, Taiwan, Japan, the United States and the World.* Lanham, MD: University Press of America.

Walton, J. (2003), Zoning In. *US-China Business Council The China Business Review.*
Available on site: *http://www.chinabusinessreview.com/public/0309.walton.html.*

Walton, J. (2004), WTO: China Enters Year Three. *US-China Business Council The China Business Review.*
Available on site *http://www.chinabusinessreview.com/public/0401/01.html.*

Zhang, D.D. (1998), *China's relations with Japan in an era of economic liberalism.* Commack, NY: Nova Science Publishers.

INTERNET SOURCES

http://www.fdimagazine.com/news/printpage.php/aid/554/China.html.
http://www.uschina.org/statistics/2003foreigninvestment.html.
www.uschina.org/statistics/2005foreigninvestment.html.
www.uschina.org/statististic/economy.html.
http://www.uschina.org/statistics/2003tradeperformance.html.
http://news.ft.com/servlet/2004jan9/China.
www.dbresearch.com/servlet/reweb2.ReWEB?rwkey=u793.
http://english.mofcom.gov.cn/article/200312/20031200158295_1xml.
htttp://www.cbbc.org/ezine/feauture.html.
http://www.uschina.org/statistics/fdi1979-03.html.
http://www.fdimagazine.com/news/printpage.php/aid/554/China.html.
www.kobifinans.com.tr
http://www.cbbc.org/ezine/archive/business-guides/guides9.html
http://www.uschina.org/statistics/2003tradeperformance.html
http://english.mofcom.gov.cn/article/200406/20040600233643_1.xml

INDO-ASEAN ECONOMIC RELATIONS: SOME DIMENSIONS

Sandeep Kumar

Cooperation and rising regionalism is a global phenomenon because countries-big and small alike-have used this to respond to global challenges and developments. They integrate because they do not want to lose out in the global competition for export markets and foreign direct investment. Due to dynamics in multilateral trade negotiations, small nations resort to regionalism influence. Emergence of regional trading blocks like EC, NAFTA, SAARC, etc. and the density of relations between India and 10-member Association of South-East Asian Nations (ASEAN) has resulted in strengthening of trade relations between the nations in particular and world at large.

India's economic structure is largely complementary to ASEAN economies with significant area of mutual gains; therefore, India greatly values its ASEAN relationship that is rooted in the deep social, cultural and economic ties that India has enjoyed with South East Asia throughout history. For centuries, Indian people have interacted with others, having been in each other's extended neighborhood. And with ASEAN westward enlargement, common ASEAN and India are now immediate neighbors, sharing a land boundary. These linkages, with the passage of time, have created a natural sense of affinity and empathy.

In the last decade, India has pursued its relationship with ASEAN with renewed vigour, under our "Look East Policy". This, coupled with a decade of economic reforms and liberalization in India, has contributed significantly towards the strengthening of our relations with the ASEAN countries. India became a Sectoral Dialogue Partner in 1992 and subsequently a Full Dialogue Partner in 1996. The institution of Dialogue Partnership is a very important component of India's relationship with ASEAN. India shares ASEAN's vision of property through cooperation. There is no gainsaying that India remains keen to exploit this Dialogue Partnership for mutual benefit. India's emerging relationship with ASEAN is based on real-time complementarities in fields as diverse as trade, investment, infrastructure, human resources development, science and technology, tourism and culture. The focus of ASEAN-India current cooperative activities is significantly technology-based whether they relate to advanced materials, bio-technology, space technology or information technology.

With the signing of the framework agreement on Free Trade Agreement (FTA) between India and ASEAN, there is now a clear institutional framework for operationalising economic cooperation between them. Once established, this agreement is expected to link India more closely with the south East Asian economies. The aim is to increase bilateral trade between ASEAN and India.

With this backdrop the objectives of this paper is to study different dimensions of economic cooperation between India and ASEAN countries. The study is based on secondary data published by CMIE and other sources. Present study is divided into five sections. Sections (i) presents analysis of merchandise trade between ASEAN and India. It includes issues and challenges, growth and instability of India's trade with ASEAN. Section (ii) includes investment relation between ASEAN and India in the liberalized regime. Section (iii) presents Indian industrial joint ventures in ASEAN countries because joint ventures serves many purposes like direct increase in export of capital goods, machinery and other component. Section (iv) presents areas of Mutual cooperation between India & ASEAN counties. Analysis shows that there are significant potentials for expanding beneficial economic relation between ASEAN & India. Last Section (v) presents conclusions of the study and policy implication and future prospects for strengthening and increasing economic relations between India and ASEAN countries.

SECTION-I: MERCHANDISE TRADE BETWEEN INDIA & ASEAN COUNTRIES

Selected statistics of merchandise trade shows the studies trends in India's merchandise exports to ASEAN and Input form ASEAN, their growth and instability are given in Table 1, 2 & 3.

Table 1
Selected Statistics of Merchandise Trade between ASEAN Countries & India

Countries	*Arithmetic Average (X)*		*Standard Deviation (s)*		*Coefficient of Variation (C.V.)*		*Growth Rates*	
	India's Exports in mn US$	*India's Imports in mn US$*	*India's Exports in mn US$*	*India's Imports in mn US$*	*India's Exports in mn US$*	*India's Imports in mn US$*	*India's Exports in mn US$*	*India's Imports in mn US$*
Indonesia	358.05	554.11	182.48	369.36	50.97	66.66	25.77	0.96
Malaysia	407.89	962.69	182.24	551.60	44.68	57.30	0.41	4.58
Philippines	141.49	33.91	69.94	26.54	49.43	78.26	0.15	0.25
Singapore	743.93	1080.73	187.87	328.18	25.26	30.37	0.04	0.54
Thailand	401.53	207.08	124.26	122.88	30.95	59.34	3.10	0.78
ASEAN-6	2162.79	2860.33	743.63	1327.50	34.38	46.41	0.05	1.05
World	31209.29	36757.35	9047.31	11752.38	28.99	31.97	-	1.27

The compound growth rates have been worked out by an exponential function of the form:

Table 2
Trends in India's Merchandise Exports to ASEAN, 1991-92 to 2001-02 ($ Billion)

India's Exports to	*1991-92*	*1992-93*	*1993-94*	*1994-95*	*1995-96*	*1996-97*	*1997-98*	*1998-99*	*1999 2000*	*2000-01*	*2001-02*	*Growth (%)*	*Insta-bility*
World	17.9	18.5	22.2	26.3	31.8	33.4	35.0	33.2	36.7	44.1	43.7	23.02	9.11
ASEAN-6	1.02	1.24	1.67	1.90	2.70	2.85	2.42	1.59	2.19	2.81	3.39	20.22	15.08
Indonesia	0.15	0.14	0.23	0.28	0.66	0.59	0.44	0.18	0.32	0.39	0.54	23.02	29.26
Malaysia	0.20	0.19	0.25	0.29	0.39	0.53	0.49	0.32	0.45	0.60	0.77	31.82	23.25
Philippines	0.06	0.05	0.06	0.09	0.14	0.18	0.24	0.12	0.14	0.20	0.25	38.03	34.81
Singapore	0.39	0.59	0.75	0.77	0.90	0.98	0.76	0.52	0.67	0.86	0.97	9.64	13.46
Thailand	0.20	0.25	0.36	0.41	0.47	0.45	0.34	0.32	0.45	0.53	0.63	14.81	16.99
Vietnam	0.01	0.02	0.03	0.06	0.12	0.12	0.13	0.12	0.15	0.22	0.22	90.54	69.30

Source: Calculated from CMIE, Foreign Trade and Balance of Payment, Centre for Monitoring India Economy, September, 2003.

Table 3
Trends in India's Merchandise Imports to ASEAN, 1991-92 to 2001-025 ($Billion)

India's Exports to	*1991-92*	*1992-93*	*1993-94*	*1994-95*	*1995-96*	*1996-97*	*1997-98*	*1998-99*	*1999 2000*	*2000-01*	*2001-02*	*Growth (%)*	*Insta-bility*
World	19.5	21.9	28.7	23.3	36.7	39.2	41.5	42.4	49.87	50.1	51.3	25.89	10.09
ASEAN-6	1.27	1.23	1.94	1.10	2.69	2.92	3.38	4.41	4.92	3.88	3.99	41.22	20.82
Indonesia	0.07	0.06	0.32	0.12	0.46	0.60	0.73	0.83	0.96	0.90	1.04	99.52	54.72
Malaysia	0.39	0.40	0.49	0.25	0.90	1.04	1.18	1.61	2.03	1.15	1.14	47.91	30.15
Philippines	0.03	0.005	0.01	0.006	0.02	0.02	0.03	0.04	0.06	0.06	0.09	58.48	79.95
Singapore	0.69	0.63	0.90	0.63	1.12	1.06	1.20	1.38	1..54	1.44	1.30	23.00	14.39
Thailand	0.05	0.06	0.17	0.06	0.17	0.20	0.23	0.27	0.33	0.32	0.42	65.95	45.00
Vietnam	0.04	0.06	0.04	0.04	0.15	0.002	.009	0.009	0.01	0.06	-	81.97	65.33

Source: Calculated from CMIE, Foreign Trade and Balance of Payment, Centre for Monitoring India Economy, September, 2003.

$\text{Log } Y_1 = a + b_1 + u_1$

The export/import instability measure is based on residuals

The export/import instability measure

$= 100/\text{Log } \overline{Y}\ \Sigma (\log Y_t - \log \hat{y})^2/n\text{-}2]^{1/2}$

1. The coefficients of variation in Table 1 show that our exports and imports to ASEAN countries are consistent with Singapore, but more variable with Veitnam. Consistency of exports to ASEAN countries by India are in array of Singapore (25.26), Thailand (30.95), Malaysia (44.68), Philippines (44.43) Indonesia (50.97) and Vietnam. Imports from ASEAN to India are in array of Singapore (30.37) Malaysia (57.30), Thailand (59.34), Indonesia (66.66), Philippines (78.26) and Vietnam (81.46).
2. Table 1 reveals that India's exports and imports are more consistent with the world but more variable with ASEAN-6 countries.
3. The growth rates or trend values of exports and imports with ASEAN-6 countries shows positive except imports from Vietnam.
4. Average exports of India to ASEAN-6 is 2162.79 Million US$ and imports from ASEAN are to the tune of 2860.33 US$.
5. Trade of India either with the World or with ASEAN has to led flowing out rather than flowing in of funds.

The estimation of growth and instability in the trade flows is an issue of special significance in the analysis of trade behavior. The trade sector has very crucial linkages with other sectors of the economy in the process of development and structural transformation. The export activity provides the foreign exchange earnings, which are badly needed to purchase the imports that, in turn constitute the crucial inputs for development. These imports may be of capital goods, raw materials and consumer goods, each of which has a supporting role in the process of development. The following observation emerge form the merchandise trade between India and ASEAN during (1991-92 to 2001-02) as shown in the table 2 and table 3.

One, India's exports to world have more than doubled form about US $ 17.99 billion in 1991-92 to US $ 43.70 billion in 2001-2002. India's exports to world are growing at a compound rate of 23.02 per cent. India's exports to ASEAN have gone up form 5.7 per cent of its world exports in 1991-92 to 7.7 per cent in 2004-02. The overall trend has been upward, except for the period of 1997-99 when East Asian crisis occurred. The increasing trend of India's exports to ASEAN has been accompanied by a shift in the share of individual countries in India's total exports to ASEAN during this period. With the exception of Singapore, which recorded growth of 9.64 per cent, all other ASEAN member countries registered double-digit growth in India's exports. India's exports to Vietnam registered a growth rate of 90.54 per cent during the period. However, Singapore has continued to remain the biggest market in ASEAN for India's merchandise exports, followed by Malaysia, Thailand, Indonesia, and the Philippines. The maximum variability in India's exports to ASEAN has been registered (69.30 per cent) in the case of Vietnam followed by Philippines. India's exports to World and to Singapore were comparatively less volatile.

India's imports from ASEAN registered an increase of more than three times, from US $ 1.3 billion in 1992 to about US $ 4.65 billion in 2002-03. ASEAN accounted for 8 per cent of India's imports from the world in2001-02. Thus, ASEAN countries have a greater significance for India as imports sources than as export markets. India played a significant role by positively contributing to ASEAN-export led recovery from the crisis (Asher *et al.*, 2003).

India-ASEAN merchandise trade was worth more than US $ 9.5 billion in 2002-03. Since India's imports from ASEAN have outpaced those of its exports, the balance of trade has been mainly in favour of ASEAN during 1991-92 to 2002-03. India registered bilateral trade surpluses with Thailand and Philippines, whereas converse was true in the case of Indonesia, Malaysia and Singapore.

SECTION-II: INVESTMENT RELATION IN LIBERALIZED REGIME

Investment relation between ASEAN and India has until now remained rather limited. This is due to the fact that only Singapore and to some extent, Malaysia has significant investment in India and due to the limited capacity of Indian companies to invest abroad until recently. The trends in Foreign Direct Investment (FDI) inflows from ASEAN Countries (Indonesia, Malaysia, Philippines, Singapore, Thailand and Veitnam) to India over the period 1996-2001 has been presented in Table 4 & 5. During this period, large companies from ASEAN countries made occasional investments in India. The share of ASEAN in India's total FDI increased nearly fourfold form 2 per cent to about 8 per cent between 1996 and 1998. However, after the economic crisis in ASEAN in 1997-98, there was a decline in the flow of FDI from ASEAN economics into India.

Table 4

Trend of India's Approved FDI Inflows by Countries

(Account in US $ million)

Countries	*1998*	*1999*	*2000*	*2001*
Indonesia	7.13	0.00	0.02	0.01
Malaysia	437.01	26.97	3.53	2242
Philippines	0.00	0.00	0.15	0.41
Singapore	185.98	191.80	71.93	80.50
Thailand	0.08	1.63	0.08	0.26
Vietnam	0.00	0.20	0.00	0.00
ASEAN-6	630.20	220.60	75.71	103.60
Total FDI in India	7800.89	6753.94	8613.83	6249.00
Share of ASEAN-6 (%)	8.08	3.27	0.88	1.66

Source: ASEAN FDI Statistics Database 2003.

Among the ASEAN countries, Malaysia, Singapore have been the major investors in India. Malaysia has made substantial investments in expanding capacities in selected infrastructural areas. It has also been cooperating to assist

India in providing infrastructure expertise and investments in the energy sector, particularly for oil and gas exploration and in downstream processing activities. ASEAN investors developed relatively more positive attitude towards investing in India in the mid 1990. There has been high level of satisfaction among those firms that decided to invest in India. This emphasizes the point that those who are able to change the mindset and overcome their negative bias towards India has a positive experience and more importantly of profitability of their Indian operations.

Table 5
FDI in ASEAN from India, 1998-2001

S. No.	*Particulars*	*1998*	*1999*	*2000*	*2001*
1.	Inflows from India (US $ million)	55.19	16.58	40.27	6.12
2.	Total FDI Inflows (US $ million)	21,899.25	22,313.33	8,625.29	10,352.17
3.	Share of India total Extra-ASEAN FDI inflows (%)	0.28	0.08	0.51	*0.66*
4.	Share of India in ASEAN's total FDI inflows (%)	0.25	0.07	0.47	0.06

Source: ASEAN FDI Statistics Database, 2003.

India policy makers, however, are well aware that the existing volume of trade with ASEAN is relatively low and needs to be increased. They are therefore pursuing a policy of speedy alignment of the country's tariff levels with the ASEAN countries. In January 2004, India announced wide-ranging reduction in tariffs, with peak tariff falling to 20 per cent in addition, customs procedures have also been simplified to further reduce cross-border transaction costs. Both these will have a positive impact in facilitating trade.

The impending trade agreement with the individual ASEAN countries like Thailand and Singapore are also expected to help in this process, as will eventual ASEAN-India FTA. In 2000, India's average tariff rate was about 29 per cent as compared to an average of 10-12 per cent for ASEAN. However, India has already committed itself to progressively making tariff levels comparable with those in ASEAN by 2007. Indeed, the January 2004 export-import policy has reduced the maximum tariff on non-farm goods to 20 per cent. In India's import revenue to total imports is taken as an indicator of the effective rate, the tariff levels are already in single digit.

SECTION-III: INDIAN INDUSTRIAL JOINT VENTURES IN ASEAN COUNTRIES

India's industrial development has reached such a stage that it can assist development in a number of countries, which are developed more or less on its pattern. Here lies the scope for India's participation in joint ventures in specific countries of the ASEAN. In Malaysia for example, the establishment of the Federal Industrial Development Authority (FIDA), determined on speedy industrialization widened the scope for joint ventures. Right from the late 1950's as an incentive to industrialization, industries declared as having a pioneer status were exempted from company taxation to the extent of 4 per cent of the profits for the first two years of commercial production, and this period was subject to further extension also if circumstances demanded. Earlier additional benefits were given and the whole legislation was codified which accorded various concessions like a tax holiday on capital investments, FIDA has, thus become a clearing house for joint ventures or a contact center for local and foreign entrepreneurs. This has facilitated operations in recent years.

In Thailand, the promotion of Industrial Development Act of 1963 guaranteed freedom from taxation, remittance and tariff concessions to foreigners on their investments to specific industries including iron and steel, tin, oil refining, glass, cement, rubber, paints, paper, textile and sugar. Thailand's liberal investment policy, political cum economic stability industrial credit arrangements and rising domestic per capita incomes presented attractive conditions for a steady inflow of official and private investment from abroad.

In Singapore, joint ventures have been quite favourable. The political, economic and monetary stability with unique facilities for repatriation of capital and profit entering, coupled with a skilled and disciplined local labor force enhance chances of foreign participation in internal industrial development. Many foreign countries such as the U.K. the U.S.A., Japan, Hong Kong, Taiwan and Malaysia have participated in joint Ventures with Singapore.

The Philippines, because of her expanding industrial structures, holds out a promising scope for establishment of joint industrial venture, particularly in engineering fields. There are a number of good facilities and concessions to foreign investors, Foreign collaborations being freely allowed at the ratio of 60 per cent indigenous and 40 per cent foreign.

It is remarkable that Indian entrepreneurs have set up joint industrial ventures abroad (especially in ASEAN countries) not only in the lines of products in which they have successfully been operating in India for a long time but also diversified into new lines of products. At the end of 2001, Indian joint ventures were in production/operation in 12 major industry groupings, with substantial degree of concentration in the following industries: (1) Engineering and Electrical (2) Chemicals including dyestuffs; (3) Textiels (4) Vegetable oil Refining etc. (5)Hotels Restaurants and Confectioneries; and (6) Services like construction, Consultancy, Leasing Trading and Banking etc.

SECTION-IV: AREAS OF MUTUAL ECONOMIC COOPERATION:

There is significant potential for expanding mutually beneficial economic relations between ASEAN and India. This requires a systematic exploration of emerging economic opportunities between ASEAN and India-both by ASEAN as an organization as well as by individual ASEAN countries. Table 6 indicates some possible area of mutual economic cooperation that each ASEAN country may consider exploring with India. These areas span a wide range of areas from food and energy, security to infrastructure and Human Resource Development (HRD). India is seeking to diversify its conventional energy sources and significantly increase exploration of oil and gas in its territory. ASEAN countries, viz. Indonesia, Malaysia and Brunei possess enough expertise in this area, which can provide considerable scope for energy cooperation. The energy sector companies from ASEAN and India could cooperate with each other in oil and gas exploration and in downstream processing activities.

Table 6
ASEAN and India: Areas of Mutual Economic Cooperation

Countries	*Important area of mutual economic cooperation with India*
Indonesia	Food and energy security, oil exploration, health care, infrastructural development, ICT cooperation in IT related services and sourcing of manpower.
Malaysia	Infrastructural development, ICT cooperation in IT related services and sourcing of manpower, health care, oil exploration, education services.
Philippines	Health care, ICT cooperation in IT related services and sourcing of manpower, education services.
Thailand	ICT cooperation in IT related services and sourcing of manpower, gems and jewellery, food processing, heritage tourism.
Singapore	ICT cooperation in IT related services and sourcing of manpower, financial services, logistics and infrastructure development, tourism, education services.
Myanmar	Food security, technical assistance, development of infrastructural links, agriculture and natural resource monitoring, establish institutional linkages in financial sector.
Vietnam	Food security, technical assistance, development of infrastructural links, ICT cooperation in IT related services and sourcing of manpower, health care, oil and mineral exploration, education services
Combodia and Laos	Food security, technical assistance, development of infrastructural links, ICT cooperation in IT related services and sourcing of manpower, health care, oil exploration, education services.
Brunei	Energy security, oil exploration.

Cooperation in the Civilian nuclear power sector for energy is also feasible and desirable, Mineral exploration and processing is another area that could be actively explored by India and some countries in ASEAN.

For India as well as most ASEAN countries, food security is an important area of concern. There is scope for cooperation in improving productivity and in reducing wastage through application of knowledge, including bio-technology, to various components of agricultural and agro-processing value chain.

More specifically, India faces persistent shortage of cooking oil, while Malaysia and Indonesia are major palm oil producers, creating opportunities for mutually beneficial major exporters of these products. This indicates another potential area of expansion of bilateral trade. Thailand's expertise in food processing industry, particularly in deep sea fishing and other marine related activities represents another area wherein cooperation is likely to be fruitful. Singapore's largest super market operator, NTUC Fairprice could consider using India as a procurement base for variety of food related and other products. This may assist in Singapore's goal of food security.

Among the lower income transition ASEAN countries such as Vietnam there are several other areas particularly those related to agricultural research and biotechnology, where the consider facilitating trade and investments in agro-chemicals and fertilizers.

Given the emerging expertise of India in I & T services, ASEAN countries are likely to significantly benefit from cooperating in the area of information and communication technology, particularly in the development of human resources and on software programs in the local languages of the respective ASEAN countries.

India has expressed its willingness to asset less developed ASEAN countries in enhancing their capacity in application of information technology (IT). Government organizations and companies in Malaysia, Indonesia and Singapore have an opportunity to gain form outsourcing IT work to Indian companies. They may also consider using of IT manpower from India.

A related area of cooperation is that of entertainment and multimedia sector. Firms from ASEAN and India could consider joint production of film, television programme and internet content for both domestic and international audiences. Bollywood movies and some Indian T.V. channels and serials currently do enjoy some popularity and so restrictive practices in this area among ASEAN countries need to be reviewed.

Indian could also cooperate with ASEAN in pharmaceutical and health care service sector. Most of the ASEAN countries are heavily dependent ton imported drugs and health care equipments, Indian pharmaceutical companies are internationally competitive in certain area particularly in generic drugs that are much cheaper than branded drugs. Given the rapidly rising health care costs in many ASEAN countries due to populating and individual ageing and sexually transmitted diseases, opportunities exist in health care activities and generic and other drugs including sourcing for HIV-AIDS drugs.

SECTION-V: CONCLUSIONS

India's merchandise exports are less than merchandise imports form ASEAN-6 countries. Trade shows advantage with Philippines, Thailand, and Vietnam. But we are depending more on Vietnam, Malaysia and Singapore. Hence, there is a need to improve exports to Vietnam, Malaysia and Singapore. It is also necessary to reduce merchandise imports from Vietnam, Malaysia, and Singapore by producing import substituting commodities. On the whole it may be suggested that India has to take necessary steps to improve export goods production while producing import substitution goods that are being to improve export goods production while producing import substitution goods that are being imported from ASEAN-6 countries for a favorable trade relations.

India has to strengthen in the areas of computer software, light engineering and pharmaceuticals, process and development, well developed RD infrastructure and manpower.

India-ASEAN trade now exceeds US $ 9 billion but has rarely scratched the surface of its potential. Indian's exports to the ASEAN have recorded a compounds annual growth rate of 20.22 per cent between 1991-92 to 2001-02, which is lower than the growth rate of India's exports to the world, which registered a rise of 23.02 per cent per annum during the same period. There has been a remarkable growth in India's exports to Malaysia, Indonesia, and Philippines. The distribution of India's imports from ASEAN region shows a compound annual growth rate of 41.25 per cent, which exceeds the imports from the rest of the world. It is found that India's exports to ASEAN countries are lower than imports form the region resulting n trade balance in favour of ASEAN. The analysis of export instability revealed that exports to Vietnam are more volatile than the import from Vietnam. The import instability index at 79.95 per cent was the highest for Philippines followed by Vietnam (65.33 per cent).

India needs to review its regulatory policies and gradually dismantle the protective barriers in the conduct of external trade. This would ensure the profitability of exports and encourage exporters to probe the possibility of penetrating into the new markets of the region. India should also harmonize and standardize its trade facilitations and investment procedures and standards.

Indian remains very keen to join hands with ASEAN to work for a better future for all of us. There is much scope for expanding and deepening our cooperative agenda, for there is much that is common between India's goals for economic development and those of ASEAN. The possibilities fro functional cooperation between us are limitless. India is hopeful that our enthusiasm and our efforts will result in tangible gains for all of us.

India's relations with ASEAN have grown considerably over the last decade, but a vast potential still remains untapped. ASEAN has considerable strengths in the old economy and ambitions in the new economy. India has needs in the old economy and competence in the new economy. India's economic structure is highly complementary to that of East Asia's as evidenced by the strength of East Asian countries that lies in IT Hardware and electronic equipment, heavy engineering product development and marketing, underutilized capacity in construction and need and ability to invest in R&D, compared to India's potential for computer software, light engineering and pharmaceuticals, process development, huge potential demand for infrastructure and well developed R&D, infrastructure and manpower.

REFERENCES

Asher, M.G., R. Sen and S. Srivastava (2003), "ASEAN-India: Emerging Economic Opportunities" in *Beyond the Rhetoric: The Economics of India's Look East Policy*, edited by F. Grare and A. Matoo, Manohar Publications, New Delhi, India.

Asher, M.G., and S. Srivastava (2003), "Indian and Asia Economic Community", *Discussion paper No. 53*, RIS, New Delhi.

Centre for Monitoring Indian economy (CMIE), (2203), Foreign Trade and Balance of Payment, Mumbai, September.

I.I.F.T., *Indian Joint Ventures Abroad, A Report* 2003, p. 61.

I.I.F.T., *ibid*, p. 69.

I.I.F.T., *ibid*, p. 77.

K.K. Kaushik and Sanju Karol (2004), ASEAN-India Trade Relations Issues and Challenges: Source Conference Volume 87th IEA Conference.

M.V. Narasimha Sarma, G.B. Franklin and D. Kailasa Roa (2004), Merchandise Trade between ASEAN and India An Empirical Evaluation Source Conference Volume 87th IEA Conference.

Prakash Chandra Deogharia (2004), Indo-ASEAN Economic Cooperation Source Conference Volume 87th IEA Conference.

P.L. Sablok and Sandeepa Malhotra (2004), India's Role in the Asean Economic Community: Source Conference Volume 87th IEA Conference.

Suman Pamecha and Geetanjali Sharma (2004), ASEAN-India Economic Relations: Future Prospects Indo-ASEAN Joint Ventures: Source Conference Volume 87th IEA Conference.

Sharma and Mehta (2004), Exploring India-ASEAN Economics Partnership in Globalisation World, Borkewell, New Delhi.

"India's Economy at the Midnight Hour: Australia's India Strategy", East Asia Analytical Unit, Department of Foreign Affairs and Trade.

Prime Minister Sri A.B. Vajpayee's Speech at ASEAN Business and Investment Summit October 7, 2003 Bali, Indonesia.

Rahul Sen, Mukul G. Asher, Ramkishen S. Rajan, "ASEAN-India Economic Relations-Current Status and Future Prospects".

Singh, K. and R. Kumar (1996), *India's Trade with ASEAN*, Chugh Publications, p, 91.

Wadhwa C.D. (1993), *Regional Economic Co-operation in Asia*, p. 155.

IMPORTS AND EXPORTS BETWEEN ASEAN AND INDIA

Geetanjali Sharma

INTRODUCTION

The Association of South East Asian Nations looked towards India with which these countries had economic and cultural relations since time immemorial. Among the developing countries, India was the first country with which the ASEAN nations were keen on broad basing the economic relations in view of their weariness of the Japanese aggressive economic policy. India went in for the co-operations in three broad areas namely trade, industry and technical know-how.

Trade between India and the countries of the ASEAN grouping, individually as well as collectively has grown at a high rate. But in the later period of this decade imports from the ASEAN have been much more than the exports to the ASEAN from India. It caused imbalance in the balance of trade[1].

India has economic ties with the South-east ASEAN Countries since time immemorial, and it is an established fact 'that intimate trading connections existed from B.C. times between Indian ports of the Bay of Bengal and leading peoples like Mons living on the opposite shores[2].

"Indian attention shifted meanwhile to the Malay Peninsula as a source of gold."[3]

"It contributed substantially to the early phases of India's cultural influence on South-east Asia. The characteristic are forms of Amaravati (The Pallavan capital), both Budhist and Hindu, have been found at widely dispersed points in Southeast Asia."[4]

"One leading South Indian historian argues that substantial colonies of resident Indian merchants, intermarrying locally, became the basic transmitters of India's culture."[5]

"The basic political classics of Hindu literature transmitted to South East Asia, including the Code of Manu, the Santiparvan from Mahabharata and the Arthashastra were masterpieces of political realism."[6]

It is now an acknowledged fact that India has economic relations with the countries belonging to Southeast ASEAN region. The commodities traded were of high value in small bulk. They were mostly textiles, gold, precious stones, corals, pearls and spices, etc.

BASIC FACTORS INFLUENCING THE INDO-ASEAN TRADE RELATIONS

First, there is the capacity to adapt technology to the conditions obtaining in the host country because these are often similar to the ones obtaining at home. For example, Indian firms can set up textile plants in Indonesia drawing on their skills at designing plants in roughly similar circumstances. India is now capable of offering fertilizer-manufacturing technology on the basic of turnkey projects for setting plants based on varied feedstock. Nearly 80 per cent of the equipment for any plant is now made in India.

The second factor is the specialisation in product suitable for Third World Market as plastic goods, aluminum utensils and umbrellas in which investors from developed countries have no interest.

Third, in order to promote appropriate products at lower cost for price-sensitive low income markets. Indian multinationals have often modified their technology usually in a more labour-intensive direction since quality and uniformity were not as important as keeping costs low.

Fourth, Indian firms are not only least expensive to their hosts but also more co-operative. The lower cost results from technical fees and royalty kept deliberately low for competitive reasons and the generally lower cost of expatriate staff.

Lack of working capital with Indian joint ventures, however, has acted as a major bottleneck to take full advantage of the positive factors mentioned earlier. This may have the consequences of confining Indian firms to low technology and low -cost fields. Only in exceptional cases will they be able to get a chance to enter more sophisticated areas unless they join forces with partners from industrial countries.[7]

MOTIVATING FACTORS

Factors in general influencing the Indo-ASEAN economic ties in regard to joint ventures and trade may be given as below : (i) The desire to protect the export markets for their products which have been threatened by import substitution measures under the policy of industrialisation of the host countries; (ii) The attractive package of incentives offered by the host countries for foreign investors; (iii) Geographical proximity of ASEAN countries of India; (iv) Relatively stable and favourable investment climate in the host countries; (v) The search for more profitable avenues of business in more prosperous and faster growing ASEAN markets; (vi) The desire to maintain some control on foreign exchange in their own hands; and (vii) Last, but not the least, the encouragement given by the Government of India to Indian entrepreneurs to set up joint ventures abroad (generally under minority equity participation) as a part of its export promotion policy by allowing the cash participation to some extent in the equity to be held abroad.[8]

FORMATION OF ASEAN

The Association of South East ASIAN Nations (ASEAN) was founded on August 8, 1967[9] when the foreign ministers of Indonesia, Malaysia, Philippines, Singapore, and Thailand signed the ASEAN Declaration in Bangkok. This declaration was based on the promised that regional co-operation would foster peace, freedom, social justice and economic well-being amongst its members. Co-operation during the formative years was limited mainly to the economic and cultural fields.

AIMS AND PURPOSES

The Aims and purposes of the ASEAN as embodied in the ASEAN declaration, are as follows:

1. To accelerate economic growth, social progress and cultural development in the region;
2. To promote regional peace and stability;
3. To promote active collaboration and mutual assistance on matters of common interest in the economic, social, cultural, technical, scientific and administrative fields;
4. To provide assistance to each other in the educational, professional, technical and administrative spheres;
5. To collaborate more effectively for the greater utilisation of their agriculture and industries, the expansion of their trade including the study of the problems of international commodity trade, the improvement of their transportation and communication facilities and the raising of the living standards of their people;
6. To promote South East ASIAN Studies; and
7. To maintain close and beneficial co-operation with existing international and regional organisations with similar aims and purposes and to explore all avenues for even closer co-operation among themselves.

ORGANISATIONAL STRUCTURE

In order to carry out these objectives, an organisational structure was set up. The highest policy making body of the ASEAN is the meeting of foreign ministers commonly known as the Ministerial Meeting. The ASEAN Economic Ministers constituted by far the most important group and are responsible for live permanent ASEAN Committees, viz.: Committee on Industry, Minerals and Energy (COIME); Committee on Trade and Tourism (COTT); Committee on Food, Agriculture and Forestry (COFAF); Committee on Finance and Banking (COFAB); Committee on Transport and Communication (COTAC).

INDIA'S IMPORTS FROM THE ASEAN

India's imports from ASEAN countries consisted mainly rubber, vegetable oils, copra, mineral fuels, tin, rice, hide, skins, lac, gums, spices, chemicals and related products. The commodity composition of imports is being taken up on individual basis of the members of the ASEAN.

Imports from Indonesia

India's imports from Indonesia have consisted mainly of mineral fuels as other items like spices and skins are of negligible importance. Since the middle of the nineties, imports of mineral fuels from Indonesia have gone down considerably and overall imports also have reduced (see Table 1).

Table 1*
India's Imports From ASEAN Countries (U.S. Million Dollars)

S. No.	*Countries*	*2000*	*2001*	*2002*
1.	Indonesia	09.11	14.73	19.35
2.	Malaysia	18.70	22.15	25.76
3.	Philippines	08.66	11.93	13.17
4.	Singapore	31.53	36.91	44.26
5.	Thailand	10.51	14.67	18.06
6.	Brunei	00.61	01.93	02.73
	ASEAN	79.12	102.32	123.33

Source: *Directorate General Commercial Intelligence and Statistics, Calcutta, 2003.

Imports from Malaysia

As regards non-traditional items, vegetable oils, copra, rubber and betelnuts are the principal items. Although imports of most of these items have declined in absolute terms (in tune with the overall import trend), tin imports are still maintained due to absence of workable tin deposits in India.

Imports from Philippines

India's imports from the Philippines were heavily concentrated in the category of "Crude materials except fuels" which has been changed in favour of the categories "Manufactured Goods" specially "Chemicals and related Products "and" Non-Ferrous metallic based manufactured goods." Table 1 highlights the pattern of India's major imports from Philippines in recent years.

Imports from Singapore

Rubbers, vegetable oils, copra, mineral fuels, tin and raw jute and cuttings have been our principal imports from Singapore.

Imports from Thailand

So far as the composition of the import trade from Thailand is concerned, items like rice, vegetables, textiles, hides and skins are important items while lac, gums and resin are of occasional significance.

Imports from Brunei

Brunei exports lac, gums, hides and kins to India.

INDIA'S EXPORT TRADE WITH THE ASEAN

India's exports to ASEAN countries consist mainly of traditional items like cotton textiles, sugar, jute, and non-traditional items like paper, rubber and metal manufactures, electric and non-electric machinery, transports equipments, pharmas, and cinefilms, fish & fish preparations, vegetables and fruits, etc. The salient features of the composition of major products of India's exports to ASEAN countries are presented in Table 2.

Indo-Indonesian Export Trade

India's exports to Indonesia which consisted mainly of traditional items like cotton textiles and non-traditional items like paper manufactures, rubber manufactures, metal manufactures, electric and non-electric machinery transport equipments, pharmaceuticals and cinema to graphic films etc. are presented in Table 2.

Table 2*
India's Exports From ASEAN Countries (U.S. Million Dollars)

S. No.	Countries	2000	2001	2002
1.	Indonesia	37.01	44.94	65.36
2.	Malaysia	195.63	218.25	237.44
3.	Philippines	35.44	45.73	59.07
4.	Singapore	310.55	328.43	336.27
5.	Thailand	115.77	119.22	136.55
6.	Brunei	06.39	12.39	13.71
	ASEAN	720.79	763.50	848.30

Source: *Directorate General Commercial Intelligence and Statistics, Calcutta, 2003.

Indo-Malaysian Export Trade

Traditional items like cotton textiles, sugar and jute and non-traditional items like medicinal and pharma products, paper, rubber and metal manufactures and electric and non-electric machinery and transport equipments are being exported from India to Malaysia.

Indo-Philippine Export Trade

India's exports to Philippines consisted mainly of traditional items like jute manufactures, maga score, hides and skins and non-traditional items like pharma products, rubber and metal manufactures, electric machinery and transport equipments.

Indo-Singapore Export Trade

Singapore has been a very important trading partner for India in South East Asia. Important export items of the traditional category are mainly cotton textile, jute products, fish and fish preparations, fruits and vegetables, sugar spices, lac, hides, skin and manganese etc.

Indo-Thailand Export

Jute manufactures, cotton textiles as traditional items and cine films, metal manufactures, paper, pharma products, electric and non-electric machinery, transport equipments and rubber manufactures as non-traditional items are being exported from India to Thailand.

Indo-Brunei Export Trade

Brunei imports, jute, cotton textile, metal manufactures and electric and non-electric machinery.

PROSPECTS FOR FUTURE CO-OPERATION BETWEEN INDIA AND ASEAN

This current state of India's economic relations with selected countries and country grouping in the ASEAN region has indicated complementarities in some of the areas relating to investment in the results of all countries of the ASEAN region. It is possible to indicate some of the selected areas where economic co-operation can be further strengthened on regional and sub regional (and even bilateral) basis in the near future.

These is considerable scope for investment co-operation through joint ventures in several areas. Once again India can take the initiative in several areas. The emphasis should be on trade creating joint ventures in industries and services which will either increase the level of mutual trade or increase export earnings of the concerned, or both. Appropriate measures like buy back guarantees, preferential buying and tariff concessions can be devised to improve the chances of success of such trade creating joint ventures. Besides joints investments can be made in several infrastructural services which will be trade supporting in nature. Some of the areas in which such ventures could be set up in South-East Asia are.[10] (1) Iron and Steel; (2) Power generation and distribution; (3) Ready-made garments; (4) Shipping services linking major ports of South ASIAN countries (5) Communication services among these countries; (6) Banking; (7) Insurance; and (8) Tourism.

Yet another step in promoting mutual trade among South Asian Countries would be the establishment of Regional (South Asian) Centre for the Trade Information. This will enable business units in the ASEAN countries to get all basic and required information quickly on the business environment and business opportunities.

Greater scope for mutual economic co-operation between India and ASEAN countries exists through investments in joints ventures in industrial and services sectors. The appropriate technology argument is still largely valid for exports of technology from India in a few selected areas, atleast in Indonesia, Malaysia and Thailand. It should, however, be noted that the degree of appeal of the "appropriate technology" argument is gradually fading away on account of large balance of payments surpluses usually enjoyed by most of the ASEAN countries. India and Singapore can invest in each other's market for producing goods in high technology area. These can be trade creating in nature. There is need to carefully identify new areas of such investment, especially if they are of trade creating nature.

The ASEAN policy makers preference for relatively "open economy" be encouraging competition among foreign investors and the "look east" (towards Japan) direction for trading and investing partners would place limits on the scope for new joint industrial ventures from India. Indian entrepreneurs and technicians will increasingly find their comparative advantage shifting away from "turnkey projects", which are based largely on Indian machinery, equipment and materials, to providing consultancy services for projects using more and more of machinery, equipment and materials from Japan, Australia and other developed countries of Western Europe, USA and Canada. There will be greater scope for export to ASEAN countries of other services from India like management services (to revive "sick" industrial units) and for offshore banking. India and ASEAN countries can also mutually benefit by the expansion of tourism. India can attract more investment from ASEAN countries, especially from persons of Indian origin. It can also learn from countries like Singapore the importance of providing efficient infrastructure. Infrastructural services like shipping and communications have to be improved to support schemes for expansion of trade and for setting up trade creating joint ventures. Finally, it needs to be said that economic co-operation among any group of countries depends on their political relationship. India's efforts to build up and strengthen business ventures will have to be conducted against the backdrop of its political relationship with the countries concerned.

NOTES AND REFERENCES

1. Singh, K. and R. Kumar (1996), India's Trade with ASEAN, Chugh Publications, p. 91.
2. John F. Cady: South East Asia-Its Historical Development, McGraw Hill, p. 25.
3. Ibid., p. 27.
4. Ibid., p. 27.
5. K.A. Nilakanta Sastri (1999), South Indian Influences in the Far East, p. 122.
6. Ibid., p. 35.
7. I.I.F.T., Prospects and Procedure of Selling in Governmental Markets-A Study on Indonesia and Philippines, January, 1999.
8. Wadhva, Charan D. Indo-ASEAN Motivating Factors, p. 188.
9. Singh, K. and R. Kumar, op. cit., 1996, p. 69.
10. Directorate General Commercial Intelligence and Statistics, Cacutta, Report, 2003, p. 67.

FORMATION OF CURRENCY UNION IN SAARC COUNTRIES-ISSUES AND PROSPECTS

S.M. Jawed Akhtar

INTRODUCTION

There has been a great deal of interest in the formation of a currency union since the countries of the European Union decided to introduce a single currency for Europe. This includes the South Asia and the regional organization known as the South Asian Association for Regional Cooperation (SAARC), which has announced the goal of attaining an economic union and expressed the desire for a common currency. A currency union is usually defined as an area through out which a single currency circulates. An economic think tank has presented a compelling case for the South Asian region to form an economic and monetary union, ultimately moving towards a single currency. This can be effected in a phased manner, beginning with a parallel currency to be known as the South Asian Rupia or SAR as a unit of account backed by a SAARC reserve fund. The proposal has been mooted in the report on South Asian Development and Cooperation (2004) prepared by the Research and Information System (RIS), a think tank attached to the External Affairs Ministry. It suggests that the transition to the European Union style economic and monetary union can be made gradually by implementing the South Asian Free Trade Area (SAFTA), forming a SAARC Customs Union and then going for a parallel currency as an intermediate step to a single currency. This is expected to not only facilitate intra-regional trade, but also create a mechanism for funding joint infrastructural development projects. Eventually, it is envisaged SAR could replace national currencies much in the same way as the euro has replaced currencies in Europe.

SOME FACTS ABOUT SAARC COUNTRIES

South Asian Association for Regional Cooperation (SAARC) is a fairly recent organization, established in 1985 by the seven member states of Bangladesh, Bhutan, India, Maldives, Nepal, Pakistan and Sri Lanka. It is an association based on the consciousness that in an increasingly interdependent world, the objectives of peace, freedom, social justice and economic prosperity are best achieved in the South Asian region by fostering mutual understanding, good neighbourly relations and meaningful cooperation among the Member States which are bound by ties of history and culture. In fact, it is a manifestation of the people of South Asia to cooperate regionally and to work together towards finding solutions to their common problems in a spirit of friendship, trust and understanding based on mutual respect, equity and shared benefits.

The economies of SAARC region are challenged by basic economic problems like vast population, huge unemployment, high rate of inflation, acute adverse balance of payment situation etc. They differ greatly in land area, GDP and population, although they have similar levels of human and economic development. They also share unusual feature of having a common border with only one other member country. The SAARC countries account about 25 per cent of world population and only 3.5 per cent of total land area. However, their share in world output is a mere 2 per cent. Further, their share in world merchandise trade is about 1.0 per cent. Barring Maldives, all the SAARC countries are low-income economies. Their per capita income ranges from 230 (Nepal) US $ to 2090 (Maldives) US $. Their average per capita GNP taken together was 714 $ in 2002. Table 1 shows some basic facts about SAARC countries.

It is clear from Table 1 that India has the largest area, population, real GDP growth rate during 1991-01, highest FDI inflows and lowest per capita foreign aid, while Maldives has the smallest area, lowest population, HPI value, and average annual change in CPI during 1990-01, but highest per capita GDP and HDI value during the same period. On the other hand, Sri Lanka is having highest life expectancy and literacy rate, while lowest population growth rate and infant mortality rate.

REVIEW OF LITERATURE

The first theoretical framework for optimum currency area was provided by R. Mundell in 1961. In his analysis he assumes that wages and prices are sticky in the short-run. This means that changes in real exchange rates have to be achieved through the use of nominal exchange rates. Mundell then proceeds to weigh the costs and benefits of a group of countries coming together to form a currency union. The cost of forming a currency union is the loss of the nominal exchanger rate as an economic instrument for macroeconomic adjustment. The countries in the currency union also lose the ability to carry out independent monetary policy. The benefits of joining a currency union are the exchange rate stability leading to lower transaction costs and increased trade and investment. Mundell argues that countries that experience positively correlated shocks are more suitable candidates for a monetary union. McKinnon (1963) in his study argues that economies with large tradeable sectors are better suited for currency union because the loss of the exchange rate as an independent policy instrument is a smaller concern for these countries. This is because of open economies, the use of the exchange rate to correct imbalances is less effective than domestic policy. In McKinnon's model, the exchange rate is used to maintain the external balance and the price of non-tradeable goods is assumed to be stable in domestic currency terms. Barro

Table 1
Some Facts About SAARC Countries

	Regional Performance Figure	*Bangladesh*	*Bhutan*	*India*	*Maldives*	*Nepal*	*Pakistan*	*Sri Lanka*
1.	Population (2001, million)	140.9	2.1	1033.4	0.3	24.1	146.3	18.8
2.	Area (000 KM Sq.)	144	47	3287	0.3	147	796	66
3.	Life Expectancy (2001)	60.5	62.5	63.3	66.8	59.1	60.4	72.3
4.	Literacy Rate (2001)	40.6	47.0	58.0	97.0	42.9	44.0	91.9
5.	GDP Per Capita (PPP US $, 2002)	1720	1833	2570	4798	1350	1949	3390
6.	Infant Mortality Rate (Per 1000 live birth, 2001)	51	74	67	58	66	84	17
7.	HPI-I Value (%)	42.6	–	33.1	14.8	41.9	40.2	18.3
8.	Real GDP Growth Rate (1991-2001)	5.0	–	6.1	–	4.9	3.5	2.9
9.	Average Annual Change in CPI (1990-2001)	5.1	9.6	8.7	6.3	8.1	9.1	9.9
10.	AnnualPopulation Growth Rate (1975-2001)	2.4	2.3	2	3	2.3	2.8	1.3
11.	FDI Inflows (million $)	45	–	3449	12	10	823	242
12.	Per Capita Foreign Aid ($, 2001)	28	–	2	–	16	14	18
13.	GDP Per Capita Income ($, 2002)	360	590	480	2090	230	410	840
14.	HDI Value (2001)	0.50	0.51	0.59	0.75	0.49	0.49	0.73

Source: World Development Report-2003, Human Development Report-2003 World Investment Report-2003.

and Tenreyro (2002) in their work on currency union found that sharing a common currency enhances trade, increases price co-movements and decreases the co-movement of shocks to real GDP. Thiam NG (2002) in his study on the formation of currency union in the Southeast Asian countries observed that the pattern of shocks across Southeast Asia suggests that Singapore, Malaysia and Indonesia would be a good partners of a currency union. These three countries experience highly correlated supply, demand, and external shocks compared with the EU and NAFTA. Further he found that the average correlations of shocks across the ASEAN countries are also higher than those of EU countries, and hence the ASEAN countries are good candidates for a monetary union. Maskay N.M. (2003) in his study pointed out that members of SAARC countries are not suitable candidates for a currency union, since they are prone to asymmetrical economic disturbances with large adjustment costs and exhibited low economic integration. The sequence of monetary cooperation in South Asia should be structured and harmonized with the level of regional integration.

OBJECTIVE AND SOURCES OF DATA

In this paper entitled "Formation of Currency Union in SAARC Countries-Issues and Prospects" an attempt has been made to analyse the different aspects of forming a currency union in SAARC countries. For this purpose, following three parameters have been selected. On the basis of these parameters we can analyse the feasibility of formation of currency union in the SAARC region.

- Intra-regional trade among SAARC countries;
- Pattern of economic imbalances in SAARC countries; and
- Exchange rate policy of SAARC countries.

The study is exclusively based on secondary data. Relevant data for the study have been collected from World Development Reports (World Bank), Human Development Report (UNDP), International Financial Statistics (IMF), World Investment Report (UNCTAD), Economic Survey (Ministry of Finance, Govt. of India) and South Asian Development and Cooperation Report.

DISCUSSION

Intra-regional Trade among SAARC Countries

One common features of the SAARC region regarding trade is that intra-regional trade among SAARC countries is not significant in total trade of this region. By the end of 2000 intra-regional trade among SAARC countries did not accelerate and was only 3.8 per cent of the region's total trade reflecting limited inter-regional factor mobility. Rather it is extra-regional trade, which plays dominant role in total trade of the region. European Community (EC), Japan and USA are the major markets of the SAARC region. In general EC has been found to be largest market of the SAARC region except Sri Lanka, for which USA has occupied the largest market for exports. Table 2 shows the level of exports within various blocs.

Table 2
Exports within Bloc

(Per cent of total exports)

Year	*SAARC*	*EU*	*NAFTA*
1970	3.2	59.5	36.0
1980	5.2	60.8	33.6
1985	4.8	59.2	43.9
1990	3.2	65.9	41.4
1995	4.4	62.4	46.2
1996	4.3	61.4	47.6
1997	4.0	53.8	49.1
1998	5.3	55.2	51.7

Source: World Development Report-2000/2001.

Table 2 clearly depicts that intra-regional trade among SAARC countries remained low of mere 3-5 per cent, while on the other hand intra-regional trade among EC and NAFTA has been very much significant. For example, among EC it varied between 53 to 66 per cent, while for NAFTA it is 33 to 52 per cent during 1970-98. The reasons of insignificant intra-regional trade among SAARC countries are the existence of high tariffs on a variety of goods, non-tariff barriers such as quantitative restrictions, fiscal charges and discriminatory practices and ban on imports. On the other hand, the extra-regional trade among SAARC countries plays dominant role in total trade of the region (Table 3).

Table 3
Direction of Trade of SAARC Countries

(Per cent)

Country	*Exports*						*Imports*					
	USA		*EU*		*Japan*		*USA*		*EU*		*Japan*	
	1991	*1999*	*1991*	*1999*	*1991*	*1999*	*1991*	*1999*	*1991*	*1999*	*1991*	*1999*
Bangladesh	26.6	31.2	41.3	40.3	3.1	1.6	5.1	5.3	14.3	10.1	9.0	6.7
India	16.3	22.2	28.3	25.1	9.3	5.2	9.7	9.0	29.9	26.6	7.0	5.9
Maldives	22.2	17.0	37.0	36.6	3.7	1.3	0.6	1.1	9.9	51.4	4.3	1.3
Nepal	23.7	30.8	58.0	24.6	0.8	0.9	1.4	1.6	12.2	5.1	21.6	1.9
Pakistan	11.4	22.9	32.4	29.2	8.0	3.6	11.2	6.4	27.0	17.3	14.8	7.7
Sri Lanka	28.1	39.9	28.4	29.3	5.1	3.6	5.7	2.8	15.7	21.9	11.7	7.2

Source: South Asian Development and Cooperation Report-2001-02.

Pattern of Economic Imbalances Among SAARC Countries

The correlation of economic imbalances is one important criterion for a country deciding to join a currency union. Countries facing positively correlated economic imbalances will be better suited for a currency union because it allows the use of union-wide policy to correct imbalances. When forming a currency union, each country losses the monetary policy as a policy instrument. Hence, if imbalances are uncorrelated, the countries will not be able to use monetary policy to facilitate adjustment to them. However, if imbalances are positively correlated a union-wide policy can be used to facilitate adjustment. However, economic imbalances may be analysed on the basis of economic parameters such as:

- GDP growth rate,
- Import and export growth rate,
- Rate of inflation,
- Population growth rate,
- Amount of foreign aid,
- FDI inflows, and
- GDP per capita.

Table 4 gives the details of above parameters for the SAARC countries. It is clear that India has registered higher real GDP growth rate i.e. 6.1 per cent during 1990-01 among the SAARC countries, while Sri Lanka achieved a growth rate of just 2.9 per cent during the same period. In case of trade, Maldives has high levels of both export as well import, while India has low levels of both exports and imports among the SAARC countries. Annual average change in CPI is highest in Sri Lanka and lowest in Bangladesh. Bangladesh is more dependent on foreign aid while India is least dependent among SAARC countries. GDP per capita is highest in Maldives and lowest in Nepal among SAARC countries. In short, the above economic indicators do not reflect uniformity among these countries. There exists large degree of economic imbalances among SAARC countries.

Table 4
Macroeconomic Indicators of SAARC Countries

Economic Indicators	*Bangla-desh*	*Bhutan*	*India*	*Mal-dives*	*Nepal*	*Pakis-tan*	*Sri Lanka*
1. Real GDP Growth Rate (1991-01)	5.0	–	6.1	–	4.9	3.5	2.9
2. Export (% of GDP)	15	30	14	93	22	18	37
3. Import (% of GDP)	22	60	15	76	32	19	44
4. Average Annual Change in CPI (1990-01)	5.1	9.6	8.7	6.3	8.1	9.1	9.9
5. Per Capita Foreign Aid ($, 2001)	28	–	2	–	16	14	18
6. Total Debt Service (% of GDP)	1.4	1.2	1.9	3.7	1.6	5.0	4.5
7. Net FDI Inflows (% of GDP, 2001)	0.2	0.0	0.7	2.0	0.3	0.7	1.1
8. Annual Population Growth Rate (1975-01)	2.4	2.3	2	3	2.3	2.8	1.3
9. GDP per capita (PPP, US $, 2002)	1720	1833	2570	4798	1350	1949	3390
10. Inflation (% of GDP, 1980-00)	6.8	8.3	8.2	6.7	9.4	8.1	9.9

Source: Human Development Report-2003, World Development Report - 2004 World Investment Report-2003.

Exchange Rate Policy of SAARC Countries

There also exists diversity in the exchange rate system of the SAARC countries. India, Sri Lanka and Pakistan all have a managed float, while Bangladesh,

Bhutan, Maldives and Nepal have a pegged exchange rate (IMF, IFS 2002). The peg of the Bhutan and Nepalese currencies to the Indian rupee is fairly rigid. Exchange rate data also suggest that Maldives has a form of pegged arrangement to the U.S. dollars. Countries that join the currency union lose their individual currencies and along with it the ability to use the exchange rate as a buffer against domestic and foreign disturbances. Economic shocks will affect each member of the currency union differently. However, each member of the currency union no longer has the ability to take an individual policy response to economic disturbances.

The creation of free trade area in SAARC countries could help set the stage for the creation of a currency union among the member countries. This is because a currency union eliminates exchange rate fluctuations among the countries involved and the transaction costs associated with them. This tends to promote increased trade and investment among the countries in union. In fact, one of the main aims of the introduction of the euro was to enhance the gains from the creation of a single European market (Emerson et.al. 1992).

CONCLUSION

A currency union requires fundamental conditions to be met before it can come into existence. Europe can be treated as an exception. The EU represents 6.3 per cent of world's population, 20 per cent of global GDP, and over 40 per cent of world exports. South Asia has 25 per cent of world 's population, 2 per cent of global GDP and less than 1 per cent of global trade. In comparison to the Indian economy, all other countries have very weak formal financial systems so that the claim of mutual benefits is more fictitious than real. Product output is lopsided in India's favour, since GDP is almost 75 per cent of the combined output of the entire region and its export trade is over 60 per cent of the SAARC total. Intra-SAARC trade is in the vicinity of 5 per cent of the global trade of its member countries.

The other major economic blocs have not been particularly energetic about introducing a common currency. The NAFTA is by default dominated by the dollar, but that doesn't make it a currency union. While many of the economies, owing to the pressure of the dollarisation of transaction, considered switching over to the dollar, this was not the outcome of a managed and negotiated process of creating a union. A union, after all, is an entity that benefits all its constituent members. ASEAN offers possibly the most proximate point of comparison for South Asia. It is among the most well integrated economic blocs and which is 18 years older than SAARC, is still at the stage of implementing the Asian Free Trade Area and the Asian Investment Area. But despite the presence of certain favourable conditions ASEAN's difficulty lies in the high level of economic disparities within the region. However, if this is the real constraints that have barred the immediate possibility of common currency in ASEAN, the South Asian condition is even more pitiable.

Economic, financial and political convergence is necessary to ensure the symmetry that is required for a currency union. Currency union is a technically complicated matter that traditionally involves the concept of optimum currency areas. It prescribes the economic circumstances, which make a currency union beneficial to the countries involved. Important criteria to identify an optimum currency area include high intra-regional trade, uniformity in exchange rate policy, possibility of high labour mobility, flexibility in real wages and the low incidence of asymmetric shocks i.e all countries in the proposed union must be similarly affected by external developments, as this indicates higher prospects for integration. However, the conditions prevailing in the SAARC countries do not support our criteria of forming a currency union. Hence, this suggests that the members of the SAARC countries are not good candidates for a monetary union.

Despite the above situations the members of SAARC countries have expressed a desire for higher levels of economic cooperation, as stated in the declaration at the 11th SAARC Summit, held in Kathmandu in Jan. 2002, for a South Asian Economic Union (SAEU). The SAARC group of eminent persons (GEP) report have in turn provided a roadmap toward economic integration, a South Asian Free Trade Area, a South Asian Custom Union in 2015 and SAEU by 2020. However, explicit condition for each stage of integration have not been specified, but the broad roadmap and milestones have been suggested. It is hoped that closer economic integration and SAEU will accelerate economic growth, promote the welfare of South Asian citizens and improve their quality of life.

REFERENCES

Alesina, Alberto and Barro (2002), "*Currency Unions,* Quarterly Journal of Economics, pp. 409-36.

De Grauwe, Paul (1994), "*The Economics of Monetary Integration*", 2nd Revised Edition, Oxford University Press, New York.

Frankel, Jeffrey and Rose (2002), "*An Estimate of the Effect of Currency Unions on Trade and Income*", Quarterly Journal of Economics (Forthcoming).

Frankel, Jeffrey and Rose (1998), "*The Endogeneity of the Optimum Currency Area Criteria*", Economic Journal, pp. 1009-25.

Govt. of India (2002-03), "*Economic Survey*", Ministry of Finance and Co. Affairs, Economic Division, New Delhi.

IMF (2003), "*International Financial Statistics Year Book*".

Khan, S. and Z.S. Khan (2003), "*Asian Economic Integration: A Perspective on South Asia*" Journal of Asian Economics, 13, pp. 767-85.

Mundell, R.A. (1961), "*A Study of Optimum Currency Areas*", American Economic Review, 51, No. 4: pp. 657-65.

McKinnon, R.I. (1963), "*Optimum Currency Areas*", American Economic Review 53, No. 4, pp. 717-25.

Maskay, N.M. (2003), "*Patterns of Shocks and Regional Monetary Cooperation in South Asia*", IMF Working Paper, Washington.

Maskay, N.M. (2001), "*South Asian Monetary Integration in Light of the Optimum Currency Area Criteria Patterns of Shocks*", South Asia Economic Journal, 2:2, pp. 203-19.

Rose A. (2000), "*One Money One Market: Estimating the Effect of Common Currencies on Trade*", Economic Policy.

Rose, A. (2000), "*Currency Unions: Their Dramatic Effect on International Trade*", Economic Policy, pp. 8-45.

SAARC (1997/98) "*SAARC Vision Beyond the 2000: Report of the SAARC Group of Eminent Persons*".

—— (2002) "*Declaration of the 11th Summit in Kathmandu*", Nepal, Jan. 6.

Sachdeva S.D. (2004), "*Unification*", Sunday Times of India, Special Report, Jan. 4, New Delhi.

Sarkar, A. (2003/04), "*An Econometric Modeling of Trade Flows between SAARC and ASEAN*", Foreign Trade Review, Vol. XXXVIII, No. 3 & 4.

Thiam, N.G. (2002), "*Should the Southeast Asian Countries Form a Currency?*", The Developing Countries, XL-2, pp. 113-34.

UNDP (2003), "*Human Development Report*", Oxford University Press, New Delhi.

UNCTAD (2003), "*World Investment Report*", Bookwell, Delhi.

World Bank (2004), "*World Development Report*", Washington, D.C.

REEXAMINING THE ROLE OF SMALL AND MEDIUM-SIZED ENTERPRISES IN THE MALAYSIAN ECONOMY

Mohd. Khairuddin Hashim

INTRODUCTION

Businesses in most countries are being conducted by small, medium and large enterprises. As far as Malaysia is concerned, small and medium-sized enterprises (SMEs) plays an important role in its business system. Apart from their significant numbers, SMEs contributions to the nation's economy are significant in terms of employment opportunities, goods and services produced, innovation, and new business ventures (Hashim and Wafa, 2002).

In recent years, there has been a growing interest in the role that SMEs can play in economic development among policy makers, consultants and academics. Despite this growth, SMEs has not attracted much research efforts. Their role and contributions to the national economy, for instance, have not attracted much research attention and also not being emphasized. More studies are therefore needed to examine this important aspect of SMEs. Such studies, while contributing to the small business literature, would also be very useful to small business owners and managers, policy-makers, academics, and consultants. Moreover, understanding their role and contributions would also help us to explain why they are considered important in the Malaysian economy.

The purpose of this paper is to examine the important role that SMEs play in the Malaysian economy. For this purpose, the paper is presented in six sections. The paper begins in Section two by reviewing the new definitions of SMEs in Malaysia. Following this, Section Three presents the economic segments where SMEs are found. Accordingly, Section Four highlights the different types of SMEs. Section Five of the paper explains the important contributions of SMEs to the Malaysian economy. Finally, the paper is concluded in Section Six.

NEW DEFINITIONS OF SMES

In Malaysia, it appears that different people tend to have their own perceptions and interpretations of small and medium-sized enterprises (SMEs) Given this, over the years, SMEs have been defined in many different ways. In general, however, small and medium-sized enterprises in Malaysia are commonly been classified by using fixed quantitative criteria such as the number of employees, amount of capital, amount of assets and sales turnover.

Earlier on, in 1996, the Small and Medium-Sized Industry Development Corporation (SMIDEC) which officially replaced the former Small-Scale Industry Division in the Ministry of International Trade and Industry (MITI) developed newer definitions of SMEs in Malaysia. The Small and Medium-Sized Industry Development Corporation characterized SMEs as:

- Small-sized business enterprise is "an enterprise with a paid-up capital of less than RM500,000 and employs full time employees not exceeding 50 persons."
- Medium-sized business is "an enterprise with a paid-up capital of RM500,001 to RM2.5 million and employs full time employees of between 51 to 75 persons."

Realizing the unsuitability of the earlier definitions of SMEs, in January 1998 [as reported in the *New Straits Times*, January 19, 1998] the Ministry of International Trade and Industry (MITI) reclassified SMEs in the manufacturing sector to include larger firms. By this time, MITI redefined SMEs as follows:

- A small-scale firm is a company "with less than 50 full time employees, and with an annual turnover of not more than RM10 million."
- A medium-scale enterprise is a company "with between 51 and 150 employees, and with an annual turnover of between RM10 million and RM25 million."

Table 1
Definitions of SMEs Offered by the National SME Council

Industry	*Micro*	*Small*	*Medium*
Manufacturing, manufacturing-related services, and agro-based industries	Sales turnover of less than RM 250,000 or 5 full time employees.	Sales turnover of between RM 250,000 and less than RM 10 million or 5 to 50 full time employees	Sales turnover of Sales turnover of between RM10 to RM25 million or 51 to 150 full time employees
Services, primary agriculture, and information and communication technology	Sales turnover of less than RM 200,000 or less than 5 full time employees	Sales turnover of between RM200,000 and RM 1 million or 5 to 19 full time employees	Sales turnover of between RM 1 million to RM5 million or 20 to 50 full time employees.

However, more recently, in further recognizing the importance of the SMEs sector in the national economy, the Malaysian Government in 2004 established the National SME Development Council. The Council which is headed by the Honorable Prime Minister to oversee the healthy growth and development of the SMEs sector in Malaysia redefined SMEs into three broad categories based on different industries. The newly revised definitions of SMEs offered by the National SME Council are summarized in Table 1 below.

SMEs ECONOMIC SEGMENTS

For a very long time, small and medium-sized enterprises (SMEs) accounted for a large portion of the total number of businesses in the Malaysian economy. Like in many other countries, small businesses in Malaysia also operate in various industries in different economic segments. Although SMEs operate in almost all industries, they differ in their scope and importance. Their nature and importance vary not only from industry to industry, but also from country to country. However, as a whole, the Malaysian SMEs are largely found in the following four broad economic segments; services, manufacturing, basic raw materials producers and agriculture.

Services

Small and medium-sized enterprises that operate in this area of business comprise those involve with construction, wholesale and retail trade, transport and storage, business services (such as accounting firms, advertising agencies, private employment agencies, secretarial, tax and management consultants), personal services (such as barber and beauty shops, laundries, photographic studio, insurance agencies, and travel agencies) automobile and repair, and maintenance services (such as automobile and motorcycle repair, computers, electrical and electronics repair, upholstery and furniture repair, cleaning) entertainment and recreation services (bowling alleys, cinemas, amusement park, cyber cafe), and providing services such as in hotel and restaurant businesses.

Manufacturing

In this business segment, small and medium-sized enterprises involve in the activities of converting of basic raw materials into useful products such as such as bakeries, sawmills, toy factories, shoe factories, clothing manufacturing factory, furniture manufacturing plants, job printing shops, wood processing, soft drink bottling, food processing, small machine shops, ironworks, ready-mixed concrete plants, fertilizer plants, rubber gloves plant, plastic bags and paper boxes manufacturing plant, and more recently, electrical and electronics appliances and components.

Raw Materials Producers

Small and medium-sized enterprises in this business area include activities such as processing and production of basic raw materials such as raw food, textile, chemicals, rubber, plastic, metallic and non-metallic materials. Some quarries and sand and gravel companies might be classified in this category.

Agriculture

In the field of agriculture, small and medium-sized enterprises are involve as agricultural producers and natural-product producers of rubber, rice, oil palm, coconuts, cocoa, pepper, tobacco, fish, prawn, oyster, clam, cockles, sea weed, fruits, tapioca, sweet potatoes, yam, sugar cane, flowers, herbs and vegetables.

Chicken, duck, quail, ostrich and turkey hatcheries, bird nest, and small-scale cattle, deer, goat and sheep ranches are also examples of original, agricultural producers.

Out of the four business areas mentioned above, small and medium-sized enterprises appears to be relatively most important in manufacturing. Collectively, the SMEs involve in manufacturing activities contribute significantly not only in terms of their numbers, but also in terms of their economic outputs and other contributions.

TYPES OF SMEs

Besides knowing how small and medium-sized enterprises (SMEs) are being defined, it is equally essential to understand that they are heterogeneous. Small and medium-sized enterprises have different structures and they develop different patterns of behaviour, particularly when adapting to their business environment. These firms vary from each other in many ways. SMEs differ in type of founders, in management style and sophistication, in stage of development, technological advancement, firm characteristics, capabilities, resources, business requirements, as well as in their general performance.

The review of the small business literature indicates prior studies have attempted to catalogue the different types of SMEs. According to these studies, the variety of SMEs evolved from the imperfections in the economy that may have resulted from different phases of economic growth and development, changes in consumer demand, levels of technology and infrastructure, as well as the personal characteristics of owners/entrepreneurs (ESCAP, 1992; Rizzoni, 1990; Hosmer, Cooper and Vesper, 1977).

From their studies, researchers have been able to not only identify, but also to classify the SMEs into different categories based on their various features such as the personal characteristics of the owners/entrepreneurs, characteristics of the sector where the small firm operates, the stages of the firms' life cycle, the characteristics of the firms' technology, their levels of economic activities, and their different patterns of behaviour.

The Economic and Social Commission for Asia and the Pacific (ESCAP) managed to identify three types of SMEs. According to the ESCAP (1992), SMEs in the Asia and Pacific regions consist of a broad range of plant sizes and technologies, both across and within these developing countries. The SMEs in this region covered three broad levels of business activities. On the basis of these three broad levels of business activities, ESCAP categorized the SMEs into the following types.

The Modern SMEs

The modern SMEs are found at the top of the three broad levels of business activities. These modern SMEs often worked closely with large firms as subcontractors, vendors, and producing products such as metal goods, paints, processed foods, plastic goods and wood products. This type of enterprises generally use more advanced technology and normally locate their operations closer to cities and ports that have well developed infrastructure facilities.

Furthermore, factors such as urbanisation and localisation tend to influence the growth and development of these SMEs.

The Traditional SMEs

Contrarily to the modern SMEs, the traditional SMEs are made up artisans, workshops, household units and crafts. Specifically, this particular type of small businesses normally depended heavily on domestic markets for supply of raw materials as well as for sales of their final products. This variety of SMEs, however, operate with low technology, in fragmented markets and are usually labour-intensive.

The Agro-based SMEs

The agro-based SMEs are commonly located between the modern and the traditional SMEs. In general, this group of small businesses are often found in semi-urban areas. They cluster around towns and populated areas. The agro-based small businesses utilise agricultural raw materials as major production inputs and may also depend on other outside markets for selling their products. This type of SMEs are also seen to have potential to assist underdeveloped economies in their development process.

According to the ESCAP (1992), of these three groups of SMEs, the modern SMEs are considered to be the most important. The modern SMEs are viewed as significant because they emphasized on skill and knowledge-based activities. Additionally, these SMEs are found to be more adaptable to their existing business environment.

SMES' CONTRIBUTIONS TO THE MALAYSIAN ECONOMY

Today, more and more countries are realizing that collectively SMEs' economic contributions are almost as significant as those of the larger enterprises. Although SMEs may not match the resources and capabilities of larger companies, they are viewed as important sources of new jobs, innovation and growth.

The following section examines their contributions in terms of their numbers, economic output, job opportunities, export potential, savings, training, stimulating competition, assisting large companies, innovation, as a seed-bed for big companies to grow, and also as a breeding ground for new business ventures and entrepreneurs.

Number of Business

In terms of their numbers, the data indicate that SMEs represent a major portion of the total number of firms in the Malaysian manufacturing sector. The figures showed that in the 1960s, 1970s, and 1980s, SMEs constituted more than 90 per cent of the total number of manufacturing firms in the country. However, more recently, in the year 2003, the figure indicate that SMEs accounted for more 80 per cent of the total number of manufacturing firms in the Malaysian economy.

Economic Output

The value-added output from SMEs was worth about RM4.3 billion or about 20 per cent of the total production in the manufacturing sector in 1991. From 1991 to 1995, the average annual growth of SMEs in total output was 7.8 per cent and added-value 9.8 per cent, respectively.

In 1995, they accounted for 14.7 per cent of the total economic output and 17. 6 per cent of the added value output. Nevertheless, by the year 2003, SMEs contributed 29.1 per cent of the total manufacturing output and 26.1 per cent of the total manufacturing added value. More significantly, the Malaysian Government projected that by the year 2020, the value-added products from SMEs would be worth about RM120 billion or 50 per cent of the total production in the manufacturing sector.

JOB OPPORTUNITIES

The smaller initial investment of establishing a small business would not only be able to provide an enterprising person a means of livelihood, but also to offer employment opportunities to others. In 1981, SMEs accounted for 41.2 per cent of the total employment opportunities in the manufacturing sector in Malaysia. From 1991 to 1995, the average growth of employment in SMEs amounted to 4.7 per cent per annum. In 1994, SMEs accounted for 18.5 per cent of the total employment in the manufacturing sector. As of 1995, the SMEs accounted for 17.9 per cent of the total employment opportunities in the manufacturing sector. By the 2003, it was reported that SMEs generated 32.5 per cent of the total employment opportunities in the area of manufacturing.

EXPORT POTENTIAL

External markets represent an important mechanism for generating income that allows an economy to grow. As such, the long term growth prospects of an economy depend on the ability of its business enterprises to exploit international markets. With regard to this, the figures indicated that the manufacturing firms contributed significantly to the total manufactured exports of Malaysia.

In 1992, the amount was 69.0 per cent in 1993, 74.3 per cent in 1994, 75.2 per cent in 1995, 82.1.4 per cent in 2002, and 79.4 per cent in 2003 (MITI Report 2003). Since SMEs consist of more than 80 per cent of the total manufacturing firms in Malaysia, they have indeed contributed to generating income through exporting. The figure indicates that at present SMEs account for about 26 per cent of the total manufactured products in the country. The following Table 2 presents the contributions of the manufacturing sector to the total Malaysian manufactured exports.

At the present moment, the Malaysian government is encouraging more manufacturing firms, particularly the SMEs to shift their dependence on the domestic market to the production for export markets. The emphasis on external sales can be seen from the increased government efforts to assist SMEs to identify export markets since the 1990s. The government is aggressively helping SMEs to venture into more international markets by providing various exporting incentives, identifying potential gateways, and establishing offshore distribution centers.

Table 2
Manufacturing Sector Contributions to Total Manufactured Exports

Year	*Contributions to Total Manufactured Exports (%)*
1992	69.0
1993	74.3
1994	75.2
1995	75.4
2002	82.1
2003	79.4

In addition, the government is also stressing on SMEs to contribute to external income through import substitution, that is by replacing goods or services which were previously imported. As examples, the government is presently encouraging more SMEs to venture into the production of food products as well as the reduction of the import contents of local production.

SAVINGS

Small businesses help to increase savings in two ways. First, the initial financing for SMEs in most cases comes from their own sources. Second, given the limited amount of their initial financing, SMEs are most often likely to save by spending less on fixed assets such as building, machinery and equipment when operating their businesses. Although they may spend less, SMEs tend to maximize the utilization of these assets.

In the United States of America, for instance, Hodgetts and Kuratko (1995) revealed that small firms purchased, used, and often revitalized used capital equipment to reduce the risks and long run costs of entry and expansion of their businesses. More significantly, the use of capital equipment that might otherwise lie idle helps to maintain higher output levels which in turn adds jobs to the economy.

TRAINING

Previous studies have shown that SMEs act as a useful training ground for the less-skilled workers and individuals with no prior work experience. According to Megginson, Scott and Megginson (1991), SMEs trained their employees by enabling them to handle different activities simultaneously. As a result, their employees have more varied learning experience than they could have in larger organizations. Furthermore, the freedom to make decisions and the varieties of functions lend zest and interest to employees work experience. In this way, SMEs would be able to train people to become better leaders, and at the same time help to develop their talents and energies more effectively.

Concurrently, employees of small businesses also act as a source of good applicants for big firms. It has often been reported that experienced workers in SMEs have the tendency to quit and work for higher salaries with larger businesses. With their comprehensive learning experience, their emphasis on risk taking, and exposure to innovation and flexibility, these workers become valued employees of the larger companies.

The study by Gaedeke and Tootelian (1991) pointed out that although workers in SMEs may receive less formal on-the-job training than those in larger firms, they are more likely to obtain training from other sources such as vocational, apprenticeship programmes or university-sponsored programmes. An earlier study by Pickle and Abrahamson (1990) also provided evidence of the influence of SMEs on training. According to these authors, SMEs provide about 67 per cent of initial job opportunities and are responsible for most of the initial on-the-job training in basic skills to young people.

STIMULATE COMPETITION

Evidence from developed countries suggest that SMEs can help to stimulate competition in an industry. According to Smallbone (1994), on the basis that SMEs are more flexible, more dynamic, and more sensitive to shifts in demand than larger firms, they can stimulate competition among themselves as well as larger firms.

Small companies can keep larger companies on their toes through competition since competition acts as the regulator that transforms the selfishness of firms into providing better service to customers. Longenecker, Moore and Petty (1994) indicated that in the United States of America, the existence of many healthy small businesses in an industry are viewed as a desirable bulwark of the capitalistic system.

Megginson, Scot and Megginson (1991) further revealed that SMEs have become a controlling factor in the American economy by keeping the bigger companies on their toes. According to these authors, the smaller businesses help to check the development of monopolies and encourage competition in price, design and efficiency by introducing new innovative products and services.

AS SUPPLIERS TO LARGE COMPANIES

Increasing numbers of SMEs are performing various functions for large companies in Malaysia. Over the years, they have played a significant role as supporting firms to large manufacturers in industries such as automotive, wood, engineering, electrical and electronics. Since the Fourth Malaysia Plan (1981 to 1985), the government has made various attempts to link SMEs with the large firms. At the moment, under the Entrepreneur and Co-operatives Development Ministry and the Ministry of International Trade and Industry, the government is increasingly promoting the linkages between SMEs and large firms through programmes such as the Franchise Development Programme, The Vendor Development Programme, the Industrial Linkage Programme, and the Global Supplier Programme.

Under the Vendor Development Programme, many small businesses have been developed as vendors in various industries in the manufacturing sector. For instance, in the year 2000, more 250 SMEs were converted into vendors in at least 10 different industries in the manufacturing sector. Over the years, the total number of vendors under the Programme have been increasing steadily. At the same time, growing numbers of large local corporations, as well as multinational companies are participating as anchor companies under this programme.

As suppliers to large companies, small firms helps to contribute to local and regional economic development through their complementary supplier and customer relationships with other businesses. By becoming the suppliers, they not only help the large companies, but they also increase the external competitiveness of these firms (Smallbone, 1994).

In Malaysia, more and more small firms are becoming specialist suppliers to large firms. This can be seen from the increasing number of small firms becoming vendors through the various Industrial Linkage Programmme. As vendors, the small firms are able to produce parts and components at a lower cost than the large companies could achieve in-house.

For example, in Malaysia, the nation's largest carmaker, PROTON Holdings Berhad presently has a total of 287 vendors and 3,000 sub-vendors to assist the company to produce 80 per cent of the total of 20,000 to 30,000 parts and components that are required to make a Proton car (as reported in the *New Straits Times*, April 21, 2005).

Similarly, in the United States of America, small businesses provide big companies with various types of services, supplies, and raw materials. In the study by Siropolis (1992), it was reported that General Motors used to buy its various parts and components from 37,000 suppliers who were mostly small.

Additionally, Ismail (1992) showed that the linkages between transnational corporations (TNCs) and local SMEs provide more business for local firms through TNCs local sourcing of their components parts, tools, equipment, and sub-contracts jobs of general services, as well as assisting in the upgrading of the technical capabilities of the local SMEs.

In fact, over the years, many large firms rely extensively on SMEs to provide many of their needs in the form of components parts and auxiliary services. Meredith (1982) in his study noted earlier that it is more economical for large firms to subcontract with smaller suppliers than to undertake production of certain component parts themselves. Furthermore, large firms also often rely on SMEs (wholesalers and retailers) for the distribution of their products to consumers.

INNOVATION

Past studies in developed countries indicate that SMEs do contribute as a source of innovation at an aggregate level. On the basis that they are more flexible, more dynamic, and more sensitive to shifts in demand than larger firms, SMEs tend to be more innovative (Smallbone, 1994).

According to Megginson, Scott and Megginson (1991), besides being sources of new ideas, materials, processes, and services, SMEs tend to be more flexible in their operations. They tend to be able to switch their production readily in the face of changing demands within their field and capacity.

In their study, Pickle and Abrahamson (1990) also found that workers in small businesses make a significant contribution to innovation in United States of America USA). Findings of the study indicated that the incidence of innovation among small business workers was substantially higher than among workers in large corporation. More specifically, the study discovered that small firms produce two and half times as many innovations large firms relative to the number of persons employed. Furthermore, Pickle and Abrahamson reported that since the World War II, small businesses have been responsible for developing more than half of the new products and service innovations in the USA.

ACT AS A SEED-BED

Small business also serve as a seed-bed from which larger companies can grow. This seems to be the case in developed countries such as in the United States of America, Japan and United Kingdom. In Malaysia, although limited studies have examined SMEs as a seed-bed where larger companies grow, the evidence indicate many of the large public listed companies in Malaysia grew from smaller companies.

Evidence from the print media suggested that over the years, there are quite a number of Malaysian small private enterprises that managed to grow big and were able to be listed on the Kuala Lumpur Stock Exchange as public companies. The information on these companies indicated that most of them started from very small, some by only one person, but they managed to survive and grow big. The following Table 4 presents 13 public listed companies that started as small companies. All of these companies began their operation in the manufacturing sector. Nevertheless, to date, some of them have successfully diversified into various other business areas.

Table 4
SMEs that Became Public Listed Companies

	Name of Company	*Year Established*	*Industry*
1.	Thong Guan Industries Berhad	1942	Plastic products
2.	Audrey International (M) Berhad	1950	Garments
3.	Yung Kong Galvanising Industries Berhad	1960	Iron and Steel
4.	Pensonic Berhad	1965	Electrical products
5.	Woodlander Holdings Berhad	1967	Wood products
6.	Elba Holdings Berhad	1969	Garments
7.	Komarcorp Berhad	1975	Labels
8.	Rhythm Consolidated Berhad	1976	Paper products
9.	Changhuat Corporation Berhad	1978	Plastic
10.	Zaitun Berhad	1978	Consumer products
11.	Caelygirl Berhad	1986	Garments/Textiles
12.	Autoair Holdings Berhad	1989	Air conditioners
13.	Serisar Industries Berhad	-	Furniture
14.	Mitrajaya Group	1985	Construction
15.	Eurospan Holdings Berhad	1972	Furniture
16.	Tat Sang	1980	Furniture

In the USA, many of the companies on the Fortune's list of 500 largest corporations also grew from small businesses. Wal-Mart Stores Inc., Dell Computer Corporation, IBM Corporation, Ford Motor Company, Chrysler, Sears Roebuck, Hewlett-Packard, Procter & Gamble Company, Walt Disney Company, McDonald's Corporation, Microsoft Corporation, Intel Corporation, J.C. Penny, Inc., Amway, and Mcdonnell Douglas are some examples of the large American corporations started by entrepreneurs with very limited capital. Likewise, in Japan, large corporations such as Sony, Mazda, Masushita Electric, Honda Motor Company, Ltd, Nippon Chisso Hiryo, and Toyota also started from small businesses.

BREEDING GROUND FOR NEW BUSINESS VENTURES AND ENTREPRENEURS

Small business represents an opportunity to encourage new business ventures as well as attracts more entrepreneurs. In Malaysia, SMEs are known to be a means of entry for new entrepreneurs. An earlier study by Weston (1967) indicated that industries with the following characteristics will attract new SMEs:

(a) technology requirements are easily met.

(b) managerial experience requirements are not significant.

(c) funding or capital requirements are relatively low.

(d) the market for goods produced or resold is local.

Besides serving as a breeding ground for new business ventures, there is increasing evidence that suggests SMEs, which are traditionally dominated by male entrepreneurs are now attracting more female entrepreneurs. Although the actual numbers are not known, there are studies indicating the numbers of women entrepreneurs in Malaysia are increasing steadily. Due to their increasingly important role in the Malaysian economy, women are increasing their participation in the creation of new enterprises.

The trend is however, more evidence in developed nation such as the USA. Studies in the USA have showed that the number of women becoming entrepreneurs has risen dramatically during the last few decades. From 1980 to 1985, the number of women-owned proprietorships increased by 47.4 per cent, to a total of 3.7 million (Longenecker and Moore, 1991). Further observation by Hodgetts and Kuratko (1995) indicated that the women-owned businesses are growing at an incredible rate. By 1990, nearly five million sole proprietorships in United States were owned by women. Including partnerships and corporations, women-owned businesses accounted for 31 per cent of all small businesses. Presently, it has been reported that the figure has come close to 50 per cent.

CONCLUSION

Given their important role in the Malaysian economy, it is fair to assume that the volume of small business activities will increase in absolute terms if the SMEs are willing to position themselves to take advantage of the new reality in the global business environment. The global business system provides all sorts of opportunities for businesses to increase their revenues, cut down their costs, and boost their profits. SMEs will apparently grow in number and size, and at the same time will continue to take a somewhat larger proportion of the total volume from the larger firms. It is well to recall that the small business share of the total is still large and that SMEs are in no immediate danger of extinction.

Preservation of a strong SMEs sector in Malaysia, however, should still require a lot in the way of government support. However, superiority in the production and marketing of goods and services constitutes the greatest guarantee of continued life for SMEs. The primary justification for the government's involvement and commitment is to provide freedom of opportunity for the sector.

Apart from the other SMEs supporting agencies, the Malaysian government established the Ministry of Entrepreneur Development in 1995 to: (1) provide guidance for owners of small businesses; (2) advice them in solution of management and production problems; (3) assist small firms with adequate training in various areas; and (4) provide sponsorship to entrepreneurs.

The creation of the Ministry of Entrepreneur Development (today known as the Entrepreneur and Co-operatives Development Ministry) represents a positive attempt by the government to strengthen the SMEs sector in Malaysia. This approach is infinitely preferable to the occasional governmental intervention introduced to assist small businesses. Nevertheless, SMEs would do well not to consider themselves as a "privileged" group dependent upon government assistance and preferential intervention.

In preparing the SMEs to cope with the new challenges, the government has already began accelerating the growth of the SMEs sector through various steps such as focusing on quality, encouraging more high technology ventures, introducing further tax cuts, developing efficient operations and upgrading the standards of health and safety. Furthermore, the government will continue to transform the manufacturing industry into a more dynamic sector with high value added, capital intensive, high technology as well as skill and knowledge intensive industries.

REFERENCES

BauMack, C.M. (1988), *How to Organize and Operate a Small Business* (8th ed). Prentice Hall: New Jersey.

Broom, H. N. & Longenecker, J.G. (1975), *Small Business Management* (4th ed). South-Western Publishing Company (4th ed.): Cincinnati.

Chee P.L. (1986), *Small industry in Malaysia.* Berita Publishing Sdn Bhd: Kuala Lumpur.

Diah, M. (1985), The Development of Small Scale Industry in Malaysia. Text of Address to Malaysian Institute of Management, Kuala Lumpur.

Ghazali, M.M. & Shaari, A.H. (1988), *Small and Medium Scale Enterprises in Malaysia: Technological and Managerial Capacity.* Universiti Putra Malaysia: Kuala Lumpur.

Hassan, H. (1992), The Competitiveness of Malaysia's Small Business. *Public Enterprise*, Vol. 12, Nos. 1-2, pp. 49-62.

Longenecker, J.G., Moore, C.W., & Petty, W.J. (1994), *Small Business Management* (9th ed). Southern Western Publishing Company: Ohio.

Megginson, L.C., Scott, C.R. and Megginson, W.L. (1991), *Successful Small Business Management* (6th ed). Richard P. Irwin: Boston.

Meredith, G.G. (1982), *Small Business Management in Australia* (2nd ed.) McGraw-Hill: London.

Mohd J., Nawawi, Jamaluddin C.S. & Johari S. (1990), Strategies Toward Improving SMIs in Malaysia: With a Particular Reference to the Manufacturing Sector. *Proceedings of the International Conference on Small and Medium Scale Enterprises*, Universiti Utara Malaysia, Langkawi Island.

Pickle, H.B. & Abrahamson, R.L. (1990), *Small Business Management*, John Wiley and Sons: New York.

Shahadan, F., Mat Zin, M.B.R, & Mahbar, Z. (1990), Growth Constraints of SMEs in Malaysia: Myth or Reality? *Proceedings of the International Conference on Small and Medium Scale Enterprises*, Universiti Utara Malaysia, Langkawi Island.

Tate, E.T., Megginson, L.C., Scott, C.R. & Trueblood, L.R. (1982), *Successful Small Business Management* (3rd ed.). Business Publications, Inc: Texas.

ROLE OF BANGLADESH SMALL INDUSTRIES AND COMMERCE BANK IN PROMOTING SMALL SCALE ENTERPRISE: A CRITICAL ASSESSMENT

Md. Saiful Islam

INTRODUCTION

With human civilization, people have flourished their economic activities to attain better lives. In the early days they had to depend just on agriculture and even during the 1970s almost of 60 per cent country's value added accrued from agriculture sector (World Bank 2003). However, with faster growth of population and fragmentation of land, they are to opt for different non-farm activities to meet the increasing needs of growing population. Therefore, soon after independence Bangladesh adopted for massive nationalization of industry and opted for controlled development strategy, during the late seventies it moved towards the strategy of mixed economic development, and during the eighties it followed an open economic system with greater emphasis on private sector development. Thus throughout the decades of planned development it exerted huge efforts to manage the changing economy and achieve industrial development.

However after more than 30 years of planned development efforts, it remained one of the least developed countries among the developing ones of the world, with agriculture as a dominant sector of the economy. For example, Bangladesh with a per capita income of US$ 386 is positioned in the low human development group of HDI and the value of its index was only 0.478 in 2000 (UNDP 2003), and agriculture still remains the dominant sector of the economy where 80 per cent of its total population directly depends on it (Ministry of Finance 2002). Therefore, the industrial base and share of industry in overall economic activities remained very small, e.g., 17 per cent of GDP (World Bank 1998). Moreover, agriculture cannot employ the growing population, and thus a significant proportion (34%) of the population in Bangladesh live in abject poverty with low productivity (World Bank 2003). Therefore, to raise productivity of farm laborer, to employ the workless population, and to enhance the standard of living of the mass, it is urgent to promote small scale enterprises in the country.

The Small scale enterprises (SSEs) are considered to be the most important for growth and development of such a developing economy as Bangladesh, which has abundant of surplus labor. To achieve economic development, this surplus labor should be shifted to industry that calls for the development of SSEs, as the SSEs require low capital and low level of technology. Besides promotion of small industries has direct impact on balanced growth for a developing country as it forms the base of industrial structure and accelerates the process of industrialization in most of the countries in the world. The relative share of SSEs in total employment and total output seem to be about 80 per cent and 50 per cent respectively in many of the Asian, African and Latin American countries (Khan, 1993). In Bangladesh, for example, SSEs provided nearly 82 per cent of industrial employment and 43 per cent of industrial output during the eighties (GOB 1990).

Thus, the contribution of SSEs in the process of economic development is paramount, and in spite of this fact, this sector is facing a number of problems mainly inadequacy of supply of capital. Therefore in 1989, the Bank of Small Industries and Commerce (BASIC) was established with a view to supply adequate capital and unhindered financial services to the SSEs. It has a statutory obligation to deploy at least 50 per cent of its advances to the SSEs and to ensure timely credit facilities to them.

Thus, BASIC bank provides a variety of services that include full fledge commercial banking services such as collection of deposit, short term trade financing, and working capital finance, and micro credit to the urban poor through linkage with NGOs. Its services are specially directed towards the promotion and development of the entrepreneurs in the small industries sector. The importance of SSEs is mainly because of labor intensity, use of indigenous raw materials and easily adaptable technology, and local skill-entrepreneurship. The present study aims to uncover the role of BASIC bank in the promotion of SSEs in the process of economic development of a country like Bangladesh.

METHODOLOGY

This study is mainly based on primary data. A detailed survey was made to collect primary data through the schedule approach with two separate questionnaires; one for the BASIC bank personnel and the second one to gather information and opinions of the clients of this institution (SSEs) as to the difficulties and problems encountered by them while seeking assistance from the BASIC bank. To uncover the views of the clients of the bank, a random sample of 41 SSEs in the south-western region of Bangladesh namely Khulna city and its suburbs, and Jessore is carried out[2]. Data have been processed by using computer packages and appropriate statistical tools such as SSPS is applied to analyze the collected data and verify the validity of the hypotheses.

Besides, secondary data from different annual reports of the BASIC bank and unpublished official records of the bank are also used. Unpublished information has been collected from official files and records to have a comprehensive picture of the role (policies and operations) of BASIC bank in the development of the SSEs in this region.

Objectives of the Study: The main objectives of this study are as follows:

- To evaluate the role of BASIC bank in the promotion of SSEs in Khulna region.
- To identify the status in terms of problems faced by the SSEs in Khulna region.
- To suggest policy options addressing the role of BASIC bank and the SSEs.

AN OVERVIEW OF THE BASIC BANK: BACKGROUND INFORMATION

BASIC bank is as a scheduled bank and a blending of development banking and commercial banking. Bank of Small Industries and Commerce (BASIC) was established as a banking company under the Companies Act 1913. It was incorporated under this Act on the 2nd of August 1988 and lunched its operations from the 21st January 1989 with a single branch. The Bank was established as the policy makers of the country felt the urgency for a bank in the private sector for financing Small Scale Industries. The bank started as a joint venture enterprise of the BCC Foundation with 70 per cent shares and the remaining 30 per cent shares with the Bangladesh Government. However, when the BCC Foundation became nonfunctional following the closure of the BCCI, the Government of Bangladesh took over 100 per cent ownership of BASIC on 4th June 1992. Thus the bank became a state owned enterprise. In 2001, however, the official name of the bank was changed to BASIC (Bangladesh Small Industries and Commerce) Bank Limited. At present it has 26 branches operating over the major industrial hubs of the country.

ROLE OF BASIC BANK IN PROMOTION OF THE SSES

Bangladesh, the world's highest densely populated country with 1020 people per square kilometer (World Bank 2003) widely differs in inter-regional development. Majority of its population (nearly 80 per cent) live in rural areas, with low level of living, and mainly rely upon farm activities. The industrial sector accounts for only 15 per cent of GDP (Ministry of Finance 2003) and the industrial base of the country is clustered around the capital city Dhaka and port city Chittagong only. Therefore there is an urgent need for variety of promotional activities such as entrepreneurial development, regional dispersion of industry and coordination of the activities among regional level financial institutions and other operational agencies, training of personnel, availability of relatively inexpensive consultancy services to entrepreneurs particularly of the SSEs. Hence the BASIC bank is targeted to fulfill this role, and as a financial intermediary it plays the following functions:

MOBILIZATION OF DEPOSITS

Deposit mobilization in Bangladesh in general remained quite small (Islam and Moniruzzaman 2000, and Khalily et. al 1987). One of the most important macro economic problems in Bangladesh is the vast gap between saving and investment. For example, gross domestic saving as the per centage GDP in 2001 was only 16.07, while that of gross investment was 23.08 per cent, led to a gap of 6.89 per cent of GDP (World Bank 2003). Therefore mobilization of deposits remained the primary function of the banking sector. Thus, as a part of banking system, the BASIC bank is to play a paramount role in mobilization of deposits, which constitutes the core of its fund generating activities. For example during 1999, the amount of fixed and saving deposit grew from Tk. 2615 million to Tk. 3727 million and from Tk. 280 million to Tk. 293 respectively. The volume of deposit mobilization in this region by the two branches of BASIC bank is summarized in table 1.

Table 1
Deposit Mobilization of BASIC Bank in Khulna Region (Million Tk.)

Year	*Jessore branch*	*Khulna branch*	*Total*	*Growth Rate (%)*
1998	51.32	231.70	283.02	–
1999	63.59	209.01	272.60	-3.68
2000	67.86	271.98	339.84	24.67
2001	103.41	247.21	350.62	3.17
2002	150.90	269.24	420.14	19.83
2003	165.20	280.91*	446.11	6.18

Source: Field Survey, May, 2004. *Up to September.

Data in table 1 capture the actual scenario of deposit mobilization by the BASIC bank in Khulna region. It shows that the growth of deposits is not promising at all. Except two years particularly 2000 and 2003 growth of deposits was either very low or negative. Thus, the surveyed data reveal that the bank failed to maintain a sustained growth in deposit mobilization during the period under study.

LOANS AND ADVANCES

The foremost role of any bank is to intermediate between the savers and borrowing investors. That is, it mobilizes savings from savers in the form of bank deposits, which it uses as bases to extend credits in the form of loans and advances to investors of various categories. However, in spite of the fact that the volume and growth of deposit mobilization by BASIC bank has been very poor (table 1), the growth of loans and advances extended by the two branches in the region to various kinds of investors marked a significant increase over the years except year 2000 (table 2) due to the bank's smooth linkage to several banking institutions to raise funds to finance development-banking activities[3].

BASIC BANK AND SMALL INDUSTRIES DEVELOPMENT

The state of the industrial development in this region is not promising at all, and the contribution of industry in the region's GDP is even less than 10 per cent (table 3). Moreover, of this meager contribution of industry, the share of the SSEs was only 2.43 per cent in 2000 that shows the insignificant contribution and poor status of small scale industries in Khulna area.

Table 2
Loan and Advances by BASIC Bank in Khulna Region (Million Tk)

Year	*Khulna branch*	*Jessore branch*	*Total*	*Growth rate (%)*
1998	124.33	31.30	155.63	–
1999	155.50	35.40	190.04	22.11
2000	139.13	46.20	185.33	-2.48
2001	188.89	113.30	302.19	63.06
2002	278.94	133.80	412.74	36.58
2003	372.93*	190.00	562.93	36.39

Source: Field Survey, April-May 2004, *Up to September.

Table 3
Industrial Value Added in the Khulna Region (per centage)

	1992-93	*93-94*	*94-95*	*95-96*	*96-97*	*97-98*	*98-99*	*99-2000*
Share of Industry in Khulna's GDP	9.27	9.37	9.61	9.64	14.03	9.69	9.19	8.69
Large Scale	97.04	97.21	97.39	97.43	97.41	97.52	97.60	97.57
Small scale	2.96	2.79	2.61	2.57	2.59	2.48	2.40	2.43

Source: BBS (2002).

Therefore promoting and financing small scale industries remained the urgent and the foremost job that shoulders on the BASIC bank in this region. The bank was mainly launched to meet the financial requirements of the SSEs, and it has a statutory obligation to extend at least 50 per cent of its total loans and advances to this sector. With this end, industrial loan to the SSEs have increased over the recent years both in terms of volume and growth rate, but remained insignificant as a percentage of total loans and advances. Thus the statutory obligation of extending at least 50 per cent of its advances to the SSEs remained simply a dream, and the sector is therefore badly affected. Data on table 4 capture these facts.

Table 4
Industrial Credit by BASIC Bank in Khulna Region (Million Taka)

Year	*Khulna branch*	*Jessore branch*	*Total*	*Growth rate (%)*	*As % of total Advances*
1998	20.51	11.90	32.41	–	20.83
1999	34.30	11.20	45.50	40.39	23.94
2000	46.50	12.20	58.70	29.01	31.67
2001	74.84	17.90	92.74	57.99	30.69
2002	119.73	44.00	163.73	76.55	39.67
2003	170.48	74.30	244.78	49.50	43.48

Source: Field Survey, April-May, 2004, *Up to September.

Major Findings: The major findings of this study are summarized in the following table 5.1 and 5.2.

Table 5.1
A Summary of Survey Findings

		No of SSEs	*Percentage*
Types of advances	Short term	37	90.24
	of which working capital	10	24.39
	Long term	04	9.76
Education	Undergraduate	13	31.70
	HSC	24	58.54
	SSC	4	9.76
Management Training	Yes	02	4.88
	No	39	95.12
Separate Marketing Division	Available	14	34.15
	Not available	27	65.85
Research & Development	Available	11	26.83
	Not available	30	73.17

Table 5.2
A Summary of Survey Findings: Customers Perspective

Interest rate	High	26	63.41
	Moderate	06	14.63
	Low	09	21.95
Obstacle to get loan	Yes	03	7.32
	No	38	92.68
Obstacle to pay back loan	Yes	21	51.22
	No	20	48.78
Support Services	Available	02	4.88
	Not available	39	95.12
Amount of Loan	Sufficient	33	80.49
	Insufficient	08	19.51

PROBLEMS OF THE SSEs

Although the SSEs are playing paramount role in the process of economic development of Bangladesh economy by providing employment to bulk of the labor forces and also significantly adding to industrial output, this sector is facing a number of problems including inadequacy of capital supply. The problems often faced by the SSEs are presented below in terms of two categories:

Internal Constraints

Inadequacy of Capital Supply: Capital supply to the SSEs in comparison with that to large scale enterprises historically remained quite small due to several reasons[4]. The banking sector exclusively favored the large and medium scale enterprises and neglected the small-scale industrial units in extending credits. For example during 1991-97 a total of 711.71 billion Taka was extended as industrial finance, of which almost 93 per cent was channeled to large and medium scale enterprises, while that of only 7 per cent was extended to the SSEs including the cottage industry (Islam 2003). Therefore, BASIC bank was lunched to look after the financial needs especially of the SSEs. However, after 15 years of operation of this bank, inadequacy of capital remained the main problem for the SSEs.

Inadequately Trained Workforce: As the SSEs faces short supply of capital, their capital bases are quite low in comparison to those of large enterprises. Therefore, low capital base inhibit the ability to train up their workforce adequately.

Lack of Specialized Education and Management Skills: Our survey data reveal that only 31.7 per cent of the entrepreneurs have only undergraduate education (Bachelor degree). None of them have any graduate education, and most of them have little educational qualification (table 5.1). Similarly data on Table 5.1 also highlights the fact that only 4.88 per cent of the entrepreneurs have management training, and rest of the 95.12 per cent of the entrepreneurs have no specialized training in industrial organization and no skill in management.

Difficulty in Separating Household Finance from Business Finance: As the entrepreneurs of the SSEs have no specialized education in industrial organizational and no skill in management, they are hardly capable enough to separate household finance from business finance.

Lack of Information Processing Ability: Lack of proper education among the entrepreneurs invariably affects the information processing ability of the SSEs. They suffer from inadequacy of data and information. They have little or no knowledge about dynamic role of entrepreneurship, little ability to analyze public policy, information, and secondary data.

Outdated Technology and Low Productivity: As the capital bases of the SSEs are quite narrow, with untrained workforce, having lack in information processing ability, they mainly opt for outdated and own techniques. These eventually affect the productivity the SSEs.

External Constraints

Besides the internal problems, the SSEs face many external problems which are equally important. They include low purchasing power of the customer, unstable political condition, regional/local administration that is more of an obstacle than a source of support owing to prejudice, inefficiency, and/or incompetence; limited access to raw materials and intermediate products and markets, difficulty in getting access to information e.g. technology, know-how, and markets, limited access to formal credit and financial services, and lack of adequate organizations that provide effective services.

However, in a business environment with many internal as well as external problems as discussed above, a small scale entrepreneur succeeds in his business due to efficiency, not because of his ability to conceptualize market opportunities or plan ahead in strategic terms. In contrast, large companies, which can usually afford specialist staff, the small entrepreneur is a relatively isolated individual trying to deal with day-to-day operational problems. He often operates without adequate quantitative data or other information, and follows the strategy of other successful entrepreneurs. Due to low wages, limited job security and a low status in a small-scale enterprise, he cannot easily recruit and keep qualified employees.

Problems of Market and Market Development

Market and Marketing Environment

Markets in our country are characterized by the very limited purchasing power of the average consumers. In recent years the small firm has to contend with the shift from import controls to import liberalization. These factors bring about intense competition resulting in price cutting. A variety of laws at the national and local levels also constrict the operations of the SSEs. These laws range from price control to regulatory measures that prescribe mandatory registration and payment of fees. These factors intensify the pains and problems of the SSEs operating in this region.

Entrepreneur

An entrepreneur needs to know how to sell, how to design products, how to compute costs and how to undertake market research to run any business successfully. Data in table 5.2 captures that more than 95 per cent of the entrepreneurs had no educational background in entrepreneurship and management training. However, the entrepreneurs of the SSEs in this region gain knowledge and management skills through experience rather than education.

Marketing Organization

It is clear that market development cannot proceed without the appropriate marketing organization. The survey reveals that only 34.15 per cent of the enterprises have separate marketing division to deal with their products, and the majority (65.85 per cent) of the entrepreneurs does not have any marketing section.

Marketing Arrangements

There are instances when middlemen provide the SSEs with their input requirements but arrange to pay with their production at an agreed price. This usually results in a lower profit margin for the entrepreneurs of the SSEs. The issue arises whether government either directly or through the banking system can provide financing for working capital which would allow them to get credit and increase sales. This calls for the enhanced financing to the SSEs including the working capital finance. However, our survey revealed that the BASIC bank even failed to supply the stipulated amount of credit (at least 50 per cent of total advances) to them. Here it is to be mentioned that here the obligation is at least 50 per cent, that is, the bank is designed and therefore desired to raise its financing the SSEs even more than 50 per cent of its total advances so as to facilitate growth and development.

ASSESSMENT OF THE ROLE OF BASIC BANK: ECONOMETRIC EXERCISE

Amount of Loan and Employment-A Linear Relation

We try to test whether level of financing and volume of capital has any impact on the employment level created by the SSEs. Number of persons employed by the SSEs is recorded as employment data, while amount of credit (lac taka) taken by the SSEs from the BASIC bank is recorded as loan amount. We assume that greater the amount of loan available for financing, the greater will be the level of employment in the SSEs. This hypothesis is summarized in the following equation:

$$X = \alpha + \beta Y + U \qquad ...(1.1)$$

Here, X stands for employment level, Y for volume of loan, U for disturbance term. The letter α refers that even the firm does not borrow still it has some positive level of employment. The regression analysis produces the following results that are summarized in the table 6 below. The estimated equation is expressed in terms of equation 1.2.

$$X = 5.79 + 1.32\,Y \qquad ...(1.2)$$

Table 6

Variable	*Estimated Coefficient*	*Standard Error*	*t-statistic*	*R-squared*	*Signi.*
	5.79	1.23	4.72	0.46	0.00
Loan	1.32	0.26	5.01		0.00

Dependent variable: Employment

Estimated equation ⟹ Employment = 5.79 + 1.32 Loan

The estimation of above equation tells us that there is a strong and positive relation between loan and employment. The greater the volume of loan available for industrial investment, the larger will be volume of employment in the economy. However, the volume of loan extended to the SSEs by the BASIC bank has been significantly limited and the statutory obligation of extending at least 50 per cent of its advances to the SSEs remained a dream. Besides, the interest rate charged to entrepreneurs of SSEs also remained quite higher (in a range of 12 to 14 per cent). Thus of the surveyed entrepreneurs, 63.41 per cent considers this range of interest as high. Accordingly, 51.22 per cent of borrowing entrepreneurs face problems in paying back the high interest burden (table 5.2).

Redistribution of Income and Source of Economic Growth

The BASIC bank works as a financial intermediary and source of economic growth through mobilization of deposits and advancing loan to the SSEs that increases the capital stock in the process of investment. The following table captures these facts.

Table 7
The Size of Deposits and Loan and Profit in Khulna Region (Million Tk)

Year	*Deposits*	*Advances*	*Industrial Credit*	*Profit*
1998	283.02	155.63	32.41	17.93
1999	272.6	190.04	45.5	16.75
2000	339.84	185.33	58.7	15.61
2001	350.62	302.19	92.74	21.88
2002	420.14	412.74	163.73	24.81
2003	446.11	562.93	244.78	26.52

Source: Field Survey, April-May, 2004.

Deposits and Disbursement of Loan

The main task of any financial intermediary is to bridge up the financing gap by mobilizing savings from surplus units and extending credits to deficit units. Thus, BASIC bank mobilizes deposits and extends financial assistance to the industrial units in order to play a positive role in the promotion of SSEs. Here an attempt has been made to examine any possible relationship between these three variables viz. deposits, disbursement of loan and profit. With this end, we formulate the following two separate equations to estimate possible relationships among them.

$$\text{Advance} = \alpha_0 + \alpha_1 \text{ Deposit} + U \qquad ...(2.1)$$

$$\text{Profit} = \beta_0 + \beta_1 \text{ Advance} + U \qquad ...(3.1)$$

The equations 2.1 and 3.1 have usual meaning and interpretations as the equation 1.1 have. The findings of the regression analysis are summarized in the table 8, and table 9 below. The estimated equations are of the following types.

$$\text{Advance} = -446.59 + 2.13 \text{ Deposit} \qquad ...(2.2)$$

$$\text{Profit} = 12.53 + 0.026 \text{ Advance} \qquad ...(3.2)$$

The equation 2.2 reveals that there is a positive and strong relationship between disbursement of loans and volume of deposits. Greater the volume of deposits mobilized, the larger amount of loan disbursement will take place.

Table 8

Variable	*Estimated Coefficient*	*Standard Error*	*t-statistic*	*R-squared*	*Signi.*
Constant	-446.55	145.56	-3.07	0.88	0.04
Deposit	2.13	0.41	5.22		0.01
Dependent Variable: Advances	Estimated Equation: Advances = -446.59 + 2.13 Deposit.				

Disbursement of Loan and Trend of Profit

Profit accrues from the difference between lending rate of interest and the interest rate bank pays against deposits and is termed as interest rate spread. Thus larger the interest rate spread, the greater will be the level of profit. Given the interest rate spread, the volume of profit will depend on the amount of loan disbursement. Therefore, an attempt is made, to test whether there is any significant relationship between these two variables. Table 9 and equation 3.2 summarizes the test results that reveal that there is a strong, positive, and statistically significant relationship between these two variables.

Table 9

Variable	*Estimated Coefficient*	*Standard Error*	*t-statistic*	*R-squared*	*Signi.*
Constant	12.53	1.49	8.43	0.88	0.00
Advances	0.026	0.004	6.02		0.00
Dependent Variable: Profit	Estimated Equation: Profit = 12.53 + 0.026 Advances				

Thus, surveyed data reveal that BASIC bank appears as a successful financial intermediary in terms of deposit mobilization, loan disbursement with a view to profiteering. Data on the following table 10, further acknowledge these facts that the bank maintained a good recovery of its disbursed loans, measured in terms of low percentage of classified loans that enabled the bank as a high profit making one.

Table 10
Classified Loan as % of Total Loan

Year	*Khulna Branch*	*Jessore Branch*
1998	1.00	Not found
1999	0.46	Not found
2000	0.50	Not found
2001	0.73	0.12
2002	0.49	0.46
2003	1.16	0.31

Source: Field survey, April-May, 2004.

However it remained unsuccessful to meet its legal obligations as already mentioned. Besides, it has no commitment to meet the long term credit requirement of the industrial sector in this region. Surveyed data show that, of the loans and advances less than 10 per cent was long term; rest of the extended credit in the region was short term in nature that also includes working capital. High rate of lending rate again was the important factor that prevented many borrowers to opt for long term credit that is likely to impose greater interest burden on the entrepreneurs of the SSEs. Thus, high lending rate affected the safer borrowers adversely. That is, as the lending rate remained high, many safer borrowers dropped out of the loan market.

CRITICAL EVALUATION OF BASIC BANK'S PROMOTIONAL ROLE

BASIC bank is not a simply a commercial bank, but it is a blending with development banking. Therefore, as a specialized financial institution, the bank is expected to look after the SSEs, it was originally established for. Thus, a careful evaluation of its performance shows that it failed to address the following issues:

- Identifying the prospective entrepreneurs and motivating them.
- Identifying new areas of investment where opportunities exist and prospective entrepreneurs can enter, and thus accelerate industrialization.
- Counseling and suggesting the small entrepreneurs regarding improvements and expansion of their business.
- Providing technical and managerial advice to the entrepreneurs of the SSEs so that they can materialize the floated prospects.
- To carry market research and survey for specific products and to identify potential industrial regions.
- To conduct project supervision where necessary, and render technical and administrative facilities.
- To set up information cells and data banks relating to industrial and economic activities.
- Training of new entrepreneur, and rehabilitation management consultancy.
- Creation of and strengthening institutional infrastructure, identification of industrial promotion needs of deserving segment of the industrial sector and evolving measure for their growth and development with appropriate support services.
- Support for industrial potential surveys, particularly in the 'no industry region.

LACKING OF PROVISION OF TECHNICAL ASSISTANCE AND GENERAL ADVISORY SERVICES

Our survey also reveals that available services of BASIC bank by and large go those SSEs, which are situated in urban areas and use modern mechanized techniques. The bank does not play any role regarding:

- Coordination and promotion of small and tiny industries;
- The branches at Khulna region do not facilitate the tasks of economic investigation, credit, marketing, training information, infrastructure etc. depending on the local need. As a result in one hand the efficient use of local resources has been tapped and on the other hand the further developments of small scale industries have not been accelerated.
- No special assistance is provided to encourage location of industry in backward areas. Assistance in term of low rate of interest has not been charged and other incentives include preferential treatment in the grant of industrial licenses and outright subsidy on fixed capital investment. Besides, they do not play any role regarding development of industrial estates/areas and preliminary feasibility studies.

FAILURE TO PROVIDE LOAN ACCORDING TO MEMORANDUM STIPULATED

It is well defined that the objective of the BASIC bank is unique in blending development financing and commercial banking. The memorandum of BASIC bank stipulates that at least 50 per cent of its loanable funds shall be extended for financing small scale industries, but the survey and collected data reveal that it completely failed to comply with this stipulated legal obligation as already discussed.

LIMITED BRANCH

The SSEs are scattered throughout the country not necessarily always in urban areas. In Bangladesh nearly 75 per cent of its total population lives in rural areas. But all the branches of BASIC bank are located in the urban areas. Therefore, a major portion of the deserving SSEs is deprived from the services of the bank.

Thus we find that most of the functions performed by BASIC bank are financial in nature and not promotional as desired. If any bank is able to comply with the desired, above mentioned role and functions, it can be said to have made a reasonably good contribution towards fulfilling its role as a promotional agency. However in this process, the bank cannot be said to have made reasonable contribution in the promotion of the SSEs in Khulna region.

SUMMARY AND CONCLUSIONS

The foregoing analysis suggests that the role and importance of the SSEs in the economic development of developing economies such as Bangladesh is well recognized and inevitable. Therefore, the government of Bangladesh like other developing countries have introduced special support program to encourage the growth and development of the SSEs. This resulted in the establishment of BASIC bank to ensure timely credit to the SSEs at concessionary rates. But credit is not the only element in the myriad of factors of business environment in which the SSEs operate, and it alone cannot be expected to induce the type and level of responses desired for healthy promotion of the SSEs. Therefore government policies on pricing, agricultural development, industrial incentives and law and order situation all determine the vigor with which the small industries will develop.

The access of the SSEs to institutional credit remained limited and highly competitive even when credit programs are designed specifically for them. The BASIC bank even failed to extend its stipulated minimum amount of loan to the SSEs. The bank also failed to foster any comprehensive support services to the SSEs operating in this region. Improving their access to credit requires improvement of overall functioning of the urban financial market in general and in particular, the BASIC bank needs to adopt some of the positive features of the informal finance such as low transaction costs, limited collateral requirements, and easy procedures.

Technical assistance, both as part of the loan appraisal and supervision is an essential element in financing the SSEs. The way in which the technical assistance is provided, needs to be carefully worked out to avoid conflict and to ensure effectiveness. The cost of the assistance also needs to be clearly separated from the cost of financing. Thus we find that although the BASIC bank has a number of promotional activities to produce industrial development in the country, its contribution is not significant. The study indicates that it is yet to start working on all the facets of its scope. Thus it has played only a limited promotional role in the development of the SSEs in the region.

RECOMMENDATIONS

The foregoing analysis suggests that the SSEs generate more direct jobs per dollar of investment than do the large enterprises. They can serve as training grounds for developing technical and entrepreneurial skills and by virtue of their greater use of indigenous technological capabilities; they promote local inter-sectoral linkages and contribute to the dynamism and competitiveness of the economy. Therefore with the existing services by the BASIC bank the following issues should be addressed to achieve the targeted objectives.

Markets: There seems to be a need for some government or private organizations in terms of supplying market information, giving publicity to their products and consolidation of production either through cooperative associations of small firms.

Support Infrastructure: Support of infrastructure in terms of training, information, technical consultancy, marketing and financial assistance, as well as hard infrastructure in terms of roads, bridges, and ports should be facilitated to enhance the development of the SSEs in the region.

Law and Policy: Laws and regulations at the national and local levels should be facilitative of the development of these enterprises rather than be restrictive. The taxes and other fees should be kept at a minimum to encourage the setting up and formal registration of different small scale enterprises.

Product Design: The entrepreneurs should be guided for product design by making available copies of such specifications by yielding design specialists.

Entrepreneurship Development: There is a need to set up an appropriate training program in all enterprise facets, including marketing, managing, and financing and so on. This will call for the continuous training of the entrepreneur in managerial skills and the provision of financing and other functional assistance and will facilitate firm development.

Expanded Government Assistance: In general, government efforts to extend marketing assistance should be maintained and expanded. In this respect a network of government assistance units at the lowest political level may be more relevant than one at a regional or national level.

Services by the BASIC Bank: We have already mentioned that the operation of BASIC bank is concentrated to provision of different financial services. But there are several factors, on which the success of the SSEs depends; therefore the BASIC bank should add the following services.

Consultancy Fee Subsidy Scheme: Consultancy fee subsidy is needed to the SSEs for consultancy to small enterprises related to agriculture, horticulture, sericulture, and pisciculture, to subsidy to new entrepreneurs to meet cost of market research, to provide marketing assistance, for consultancy on use of non-conventional sources of energy and conservation measures and to control of pollution

Interest Subsidy Scheme: Interest subsidy is needed for self-development and self-employment of unemployed persons, for socio-economically backward section of people, for encouraging quality control measures in the small enterprises, and for encouraging the adaptation of indigenous technology.

Entrepreneurship Development Scheme: Entrepreneurship development program should be started that requires identifying persons with entrepreneurial urge, who are confident in what they are doing or want to do. Efforts should be made to select those people likely to succeed in business ideas. The selection process of clients should reveal the applicant's background, age, and earlier working experience, the realism of his business idea, motivation, entrepreneurial attitudes, and other relevant information. Then training to the selected persons is needed so their infantile business ideas are converted into realities. The training component should cover all major areas of business.

Market Encounter Program: Market encounter programs aims at bringing the producers and potential customers together. The program essentially includes occasional such as monthly and quarterly sales fair for the SSEs products for high-potential producers.

Enlargement of branch offices: BASIC Bank is the only financial institution aimed at the promotion of the SSEs, and unfortunately all of its branches are located in either metropolitan cities or in district headquarters. Therefore to reach its benefits to nationwide scattered SSEs, extension, and expansion of branches into urban and sub-urban areas is desired in the promotion of the SSEs.

NOTES

1. The paper is the product of a research project titled "The Role of Bangladesh Small Industries and Commerce Bank in the Promotion of Small Scale Enterprises: Problems and Prospects-A Case Study in Khulna Region", and financed by the Research Cell, Khulna University, Bangladesh. Therefore, the authors acknowledge the financial support extended by the Khulna University authority. Authors are also grateful to the staffs of the BASIC Bank Limited for extending their coordinal and all out cooperation.
2. In Bangladesh, BASIC bank has 26 branches of which two are located in the southwestern region i.e., Khulna region, one in Khulna city and an other is at Jessore.
3. For example, BASIC bank has linkages with Kreditanstalt fur Wiederaufbau- a German bank, and Asian Development Bank, where the first one is financing for micro credit scheme and small-scale industries. Total outstanding amount of fund from the above sources in 1999 increased to Tk. 369 million from Tk. 345 million in 1998 representing a 7 per cent growth (Annual Report, 1999).
4. It is not our intention to discuss those reasons here; rather we simply want to state the comparative financial services available to the SSEs.

REFERENCES

BASIC Bank, Annual Report 1996, 1997, 1998, 1999, 2000, and 2002.

Barrow, B. (1993), *The Essence of Small Business,* Prentice Hall International (UK) Ltd.

Chopra, C. (1888), *Managerial Business and Finance,* Deep and Deep Publications, New Delhi, India.

Gupta, R.K. (1993), *Development Banks and Industrial Development,* Deep & Deep Publications, New Delhi., India.

Islam M.S. (2003), Industrial Credit Allocation: The Role of Banking Sector in Bangladesh, *Business Review,* Khulna University, Vol. 3, No. 2, , July-December.

Islam, M.S. and Aktaruzzaman K. (2001), 'The Problems of Rural Women Entrepreneurs in Bangladesh: A Case Study of Jhenaidah District', *Islamic University Studies (PART-C),* Vol. 4: No. 1, June.

Islam M.S. and Moniruzzaman A.K.M. (2000), 'Domestic Saving Mobilization in Bangladesh: The Role of Scheduled Banks', *Islamic University Studies (PART-C),* Vol. 3, No. 2, December.

Khalily M.A.B., Meyer R.L. and Husak L.J. (1987), Deposit Mobilization in Bangladesh: Implications for Rural Financial Institutions and Financial Policies, *Bangladesh Development Studies,* Vol. 15, No. 4.

Khan, A.R. (1991), *Entrepreneurship Small Business and Lives of successful Entrepreneur,* Abul Printing Press, Dhaka, Bangladesh.

Khan, M.A. (1992), *Entrepreneurship Development in India,* Kanishka Publishing House, New Delhi, India.

Miya, S. (1997), *Business Finance and Financial Management,* the Eagle Publication, Dhaka, Bangladesh.

Ministry of Planning (2002), Statistical Year Book of Bangladesh 2000, Bangladesh Bureau of Statistics, June.

Ministry of Finance (2001), Bangladesh Population Census Report, Bangladesh Bureau of Statistics.

Ministry of Finance (2002), Government of Bangladesh, Economic Review, June.

Ministry of Finance (2003), Government of Bangladesh, Economic Review, June.

Ministry of Planning (1990), The Fourth Five Year Plan (1990-95), June.

UNDP (2003), Human Development Report, Deepening Democracy in a Fragmented World.

World Bank (1998), The World Development Report, Washington D.C.

World Bank (2003), *The World Development Report,* Sustainable Development in a Dynamic World: Transforming Institutions, Growth, and Quality of Life, Washington D.C.

World Bank (2003), *The World Development Indicators,* C.D. Version.

REFORMS IN DISSEMINATION OF TECHNOLOGY IN AGRICULTURE: A STUDY OF NATIONAL AGRICULTURAL TECHNOLOGY PROJECT IN INDIA

Aditya Keshari Mishra

PROLOGUE

Agriculture in India, since its inception, has been witnessing a perpetual change. One of the prime factors that have revolutionized India's agriculture–both in terms of its practices and productivity–is Green Revolution (GR), an outcome of training and visit system (during mid-1970s). It has succeeded in bringing a dynamic shift in agriculture. This can rightly be considered as the 'first generation technology', which includes high yielding varieties such as hybrids, chemical fertilizers, pesticides, intensive irrigation etc. (Jha 2001). Such achievement of GR has largely been due to 'public research and extension' that too because of the efforts of the Department of Agriculture (DoA). However, by the early 1990s it was realized that extension should broad base its programmes. Thus, the whole framework of research and extension has been changed in the post-green revolution (PGR) era, owing to the challenges, demands and technological gap of the GR (Sharma 2002). As a result, the research and extension has adopted to disseminate technology through the prism of 'participatory-cum-interactive model'. In this context, the National Agricultural Technology Project (NATP), a recent innovation in the field of agricultural research and extension, financed by the World Bank, has emerged to undertake efforts to enhance agricultural productivity and sustainability by mobilizing farmers and farmwomen into groups. Operationalizing its determined objectives, NATP implements a multi-agential approach by establishing a network between the public and private agencies and also farmers' organizations along with the involvement of the third sector, the NGOs. The present study seeks to emphasize a critical understanding of the functioning of NATP with special emphasis to its technological dissemination component. The empirical insight has been gained from Khurda district of Orissa, India.

A BRIEF HISTORY OF AGRICULTURAL EXTENSION IN INDIA

Agricultural extension relates to the process of carrying out the technology of scientific agriculture to the farmers so as to enable them to utilize the knowledge for better agriculture and thereby better socio-economic development. At the outset, the agricultural research and extension in India is initiated by the public sector. However, public sector extension has undergone several changes since the early 1950s, beginning with the Community Development Programme (CDP) in 1952 through the National Extension Service in 1953. The focus of extension has been on community development, but there has been a steady progression towards transfer of technology (ToT), with the Intensive Agriculture District Programme (IADP), which started in 1961-62, followed by the Intensive Agriculture Area Programme (IAAP) in 1964-65, the High Yielding Varieties Programme (HYVP) in 1966-67, and the Small and Marginal Farmers Development Programme (SMFDP) in 1969-70. As a product of public sector, the emergence of Training and Visit (T&V) system has led to the triumphant conglomeration of GR.

The invention of the T&V extension management system, funded by the World Bank, started in the mid-1970s was an important step towards the emergence of the GR (1966-80) in India. It is considered as the cornerstone of India's agricultural achievement that has transformed the country from "abject food deficiency to self-sufficiency" (Sharma 2002). But, the revolution was confined only to the irrigated areas of the country, and at the same time, it was selectively implemented in some specific crops. The extension service was largely carried out by the State Department of Agriculture (DoA). However, the allied departments such as Animal Husbandry, Soil Conservation, Horticulture, Fisheries were not able to focus on extension due to lack of infrastructure, trained personnel and resources. According to Rita Sharma (2002):

> *... The T&V system operated with low level of involvement of farmers. The 'top-down' approach generated uniformity rather than specificity and lacked focus on location specific needs of regions, disadvantaged areas, target group requirements, etc. the linkages between research-extension and farmer remained weak or nonexistent.*

In the post-green revolution (PGR) era, the focus of research and extension has been redirected towards developing agricultural practices, diversification of farming systems for employment and income generation, intensive agriculture with biotechnology, and nonetheless, providing farmers with latest technologies and provision of location-specific technologies (Sharma1999). Furthermore, the changing economic scenario in India and the need for appropriate agricultural technologies and agro-management practices to respond food and nutritional security, poverty alleviation, diversifying market demands, export opportunities, and environmental concerns reflect new challenges to the technology dissemination system in PGR era (Sharma 2002). As a result, there has been an increasing demand towards the invitation to the 'second generation technology' in the field of agricultural research and extension. In this context, the Xth Five-Year Plan (2002-2007) approach Paper[2] has highlighted the following options:

> *... Strengthening of our agricultural research and development system and a significant improvement in the sophistication of the technology dissemination methodologies are essential to achieving rapid and sustained growth in agriculture productivity.*

DISSEMINATION OF TECHNOLOGY (DOT): LINEAR TO INTERACTIVE MODEL

As mentioned earlier, agricultural research and extension in pre PGR phase was confined to transfer of technologies generated by the public agency through appropriate dissemination techniques such as field visits, farmers' meetings, demonstrations etc. (Sulaiman and Hall 2002). This type of process of dissemination can be equated to the Rogers model of 'diffusion of innovation' (1962). This model of dissemination is referred to as the linear model of technology dissemination because it demonstrates a linear relationship between research, extension and farmer. The linear model of dissemination of technology focuses on "generation of technology", which is developed by scientists, disseminated by extension agents and finally adopted by the farmers. The T&V system is regarded as one of such innovation. In this process, farmers do not hold any 'say' over the process of 'technology' development and its dissemination. Hence, the model was criticized (Sulaiman and Hall 2002) by the practitioners.

A participatory form of dissemination of technology (DoT) in agriculture, which is considered as second generation technology has emerged as a response to the linear model in the literature of transfer of agricultural technologies. This "participatory innovation" entails an integration of different actors. It operates through the process of social interaction between different actors starting from grassroots level to the central level. In fact, the interactive model of DoT in agriculture refers to *the integration of different agents in a common platform where the scientists, extension agents and the farmers' are interdependent on each other towards the process of development and dissemination of technologies.* Hence, this participatory rhetoric adopts multi-agential/departmental, in contrast to, mono-agential/departmental approach. Coming to its target individual the approach gives central focus on 'groups' rather than an individual. It is because the mere vulnerable individual farmers find themselves difficult to face the local situation due to the increasing nature of risk and insecurity arising out of the insecure global market competition. Hence, it acts as a defense and also a viable strategy to strengthen the bargaining power. Furthermore, the 'group' model is considered as an alternative viable to achieve a close contact with the public extension agents, community participation, resources mobilization etc.

One such major experiment in India in recent years is National Agricultural Technology Project (NATP). It is designed to facilitate the generation of location-specific agricultural technologies through new institutional arrangements by bringing about the farmers and scientists together and simultaneously, to disseminate such technological innovations to farmers through new institutions with the central focus on SHGs of farmers, both men and women.

NATIONAL AGRICULTURAL TECHNOLOGY PROJECT

The National Agricultural Technology Project (NATP), a recent intervention in agricultural research and extension, is an instrument that aims at introducing and disseminating technologies in the field of agriculture. The project has been initiated by the Ministry of Agriculture, Government of India with the financial assistance from the World Bank and is running with the assistance of the National Institute of Agricultural Research Extension Management (MANAGE) in 28 districts covering seven States of India: Andhra Pradesh, Bihar, Jharkhand, Himachal Pradesh, Maharashtra, Orissa and Punjab over a period of five years (1998-2003)[3]. Khurda, Koraput, Ganjam and Sambalpur are the project districts of NATP in Orissa unit. The Indian Council of Agricultural Research is mandated to accelerate research and to improve the dissemination of location-specific and sustainability enhancing technologies. The MANAGE, Hyderabad, is responsible for its institutional set up. As a facilitating agency, operating in the seven States of the country, the MANAGE plays an instrumental role in the innovations in technology dissemination (ITD). The NATP in India has adopted new approaches towards the process of generation and dissemination of agricultural technologies. The viable approaches of NATP are: interactive bottom-up model; diversified and location-specific technology; multi-agential-cum-multi-departmental approach; target group oriented; and nonetheless, is decentralized in nature (Mishra 2004b).

As an initiative in the field of agricultural research and extension, the NATP is multi-departmental in nature, which consists of departments like Agriculture, Animal Husbandry, Fishery, Horticulture and Soil Conservation. Like panchayati raj institutions, the NATP follows a three-tier structure forming an organic whole; at the village level, it is farmers'/women's interest groups (FIGs/WIGs); at the block level, it is Farm Information and Advisory Centre (FIAC) that deals with two organs namely, Block Technology Team (BTT) and Farmers Advisory Committee (FAC); and at the district level, it is Agricultural Technology Management Agency (ATMA), which consists of ATMA Governing Board (AGB) and ATMA Management Committee (AMC). However, the individual farmers'/women's interest groups constitute the central focus in this three-tier structure. In terms of emphasis, this project reflects a shift in agricultural extension. It manifests a shift from "top-down" approach to a "bottom-up" approach through its technological dissemination unit (TDU), thereby taking into consideration the agro-ecological situation of the farming system. NATP is based on three metamorphic objectives: (i) to develop an effective public extension system, which is demand driven in nature; (ii) to involve efficient NGOs to help different categories of farmers by organizing them into groups and thereby increasing access to new technology and strengthening their voice in providing feedback to research and extension;

and (iii) to focus on public agricultural extension system with an emphasis on location-specific and sustainable technologies.

METHODOLOGY

The present study seeks to explore an empirical insight gained from Khurda district of Orissa, India. It operates in a socio-cultural context. Khurda district of Orissa was selected for its empirical site; because it has been projected by the MANAGE as the most successful district of all the NATP pilot districts. Chilika and Tangi, two blocks of Khurda were selected for the study. The fieldwork was carried out over a total duration of six months. In these two blocks, almost all the FIGs/WIGs either formed by or functioning under ATMA have been studied. 121 out of a total number of 127 groups were interviewed. The remaining six groups were difficult to be traced out. 15 SHGs have collapsed (nine groups in Chilika and six in Tangi). Therefore, the study is based upon the remaining 106 groups. The groups interviewed were spread over 54 villages. Though the interview basically focused on the FIGs and WIGs, members of the block level agencies like BTT and FAC were also interviewed. Several long informal discussions were held with the State Consultant, Orissa unit of NATP. An interview guide was used to collect data from various groups and sources. Apart from these primary sources, data have also been collected from ATMA/FIAC documents.

ATMA'S ENDEAVOUR TOWARDS "GROUP FORMATION"

The Agricultural Technology Management Agency (ATMA), Khurda, which came into existence in April 1999, has registered four hundred sixty three (463) FIGs/WIGs in ten blocks. The Farmers' Advisory Committee and the Governing Board of ATMA are in charge of registering these groups at the village level. At the initial stage of the project, the non-governmental organizations (NGOs) extended their hands to some extent in order to establish/form such groups. However, groups formed in these two selected blocks are totally by the efforts of AGB and FAC members. There has not been a single instance in the two blocks, where a group (FIG/WIG) was formed by the effort of any NGO. It is also mentioned in ATMA guideline that there is a provision of Rs. 2000/- of "cash incentives" towards each member who successfully forms a group[4].

After completion of three months, fifty per cent i.e. Rs. 1000/- will be given to the organizer of the group through the consent of BTT. Another fifty per cent will be paid to the organizer of that particular group only through the recommendation of BTT subject to the group's continuation, at least, for a period of six months.

The groups formed in these two blocks are quite interesting. It is seen that there are 44 groups in Chilika block, out of which the FIGs and WIGs are 11 (25%) and 33 (75%) respectively. There are 77 groups in Tangi in which the number of FIGs is only 14 (18.19%) in comparison to 63 (81.81%) of WIGs. Thus, there is high concentration of WIGs than FIGs in both the blocks. Interrogating towards the reason behind such a high proportion of WIGs, the

Convenor of BTT, Chilika replies "it is easier to motivate/form groups by women than men because the later are always 'profit-oriented'".

The FIGs/WIGs, developed by ATMA, are self-help groups (SHGs). These are supposed to be homogeneous groups based on social interaction, comprising of 10-20 members, formed by men/women farmers from same economic level where every member saves his/her money that is deposited partly in 'formal saving unit (FSU)' as well as in 'informal saving unit (ISU)' that operates at the village level[5]. In fact, the groups save their money in formal saving unit (FSU) i.e. bank account and informal saving unit (ISU) i.e. common fund, which operates at grassroots level. However, it is seen that the groups are more interested to save in ISU because they use to receive more profits from ISU than FSU. By taking into account the total amount saved in both the units, groups can be divided into three categories, namely, minor (below Rs. 30,000), medium (Rs.30,000 - Rs. 50,000) and major (Rs. 50,000 onwards).

It is seen that 82.87 per cent of FIGs/WIGs (74.29% WIGs) in Chilika block, and 87.32 per cent of FIGs/WIGs (67.6% WIGs) in Tangi block belong to the minor category. While on the other hand, only one FIG out of 35 FIGs/WIGs (less than 3%) in Chilika and two WIGs out of 71 FIGs/WIGs (less than 3%) in Tangi belong to the major category. Thus, the empirical observation reveals that out of 106 FIGs and WIGs in both the blocks, the category of minor constitutes 85.85 per cent, followed by the category of medium and then followed by the category of major. What is more interesting to look at is; the economic capital of FIGs/WIGs through saving and non-refundable bank-loan has touched an amount of Rs. 7, 85,567/- and Rs. 8, 90,184/- in FIAC, Chilika and Tangi respectively by the time of interview, which is nothing but an indication towards an inauguration of microfinance agenda.

However, one needs to analyze whether members are from different households or from a particular or selected privileged household. Although the members are supposed to be drawn from different families in the village, information gathered from the fieldwork suggests that the mobilization of membership is confined to closely related families or inter-generational families, which give them the required number for the formation of a group. The idea is to achieve and share socio-economic profits among the members of the family. Thus, the groups formed in both the blocks are family-centric in nature.

Caste and land-ownership are the key axes of stratification in the village society of India. In the coastal tract of Orissa, including Khurda district, Khandayats constitute the dominant land-owning caste (Mohapatra 1997). To understand the nature of caste composition of SHGs, one must make note of three broad social divisions. These are general, schedule castes (SCs)and scheduled tribes (STs)[6].

Table 1 shows that 90 per cent of all farmers in the district belong to the categories of Marginal and Small farmers. Large farmers are small in number in the district, and most of them belong to the general caste category. A large number of SC households are landless in the district.

Table 1
Caste wise Operational Holding-and Category wise (Nos.)
(Khurda District)

Category	*S.C.*	*S.T.*	*General*	*Total*
Marginal (Below 1.00)	11051 (9.01)	4847 (3.95)	66821 (54.49)	82719 (67.46)
Small (1.00-1.99)	2993 (2.44)	1435 (1.17)	23515 (19.18)	27943 (22.79)
Semi-medium (2.00-3.99)	669 (0.54)	621 (0.51)	8696 (7.09)	9986 (8.14)
Medium (4.00-9.99)	97 (0.08)	77 (0.06)	1704 (1.39)	1878 (1.53)
Large (10.00-Above)	-	12 (.009)	83 (0.06)	95 (0.08)
Total	14810 (12.08)	6992 (5.7)	100819 (82.22)	122621 (100.00)

Source: District Statistical Handbook, Khurda, 1999.

The SHGs in Khurda district may be mono-caste or multi-caste types. In our selected blocks of Chilika and Tangi, there are sixty-five mono-caste groups (may be general or SC or ST), and forty-one multi-caste groups (may be a combination of GC or GT or GTC)[7]. In both the blocks together, the SHGs of mono-caste category includes 61.32 per cent comprising general castes (46.06%), SC (8.49%) ST (3.77%) whereas multi-caste category accounts 38.68 per cent composing GC (29.35%), GT (3.77%), and GTC (5.67%). A majority in the category of general caste are from the dominant caste of Khandayats.

DISSEMINATION OF TECHNOLOGY: AN INTERROGATION

The ATMA, a distinct level structural mechanism, is engaged in implementing and disseminating technology among the farmers and farmwomen. For this purpose, the FIAC, an institution having BTT and FAC, is a block level extension mechanism for transferring technology to FIGs/WIGs. This alternative model of extension has developed a triadic relationship among BTT, which constitutes extension functionaries, FAC and the individual farmer/ farmwoman groups. The following model represents this relationship:

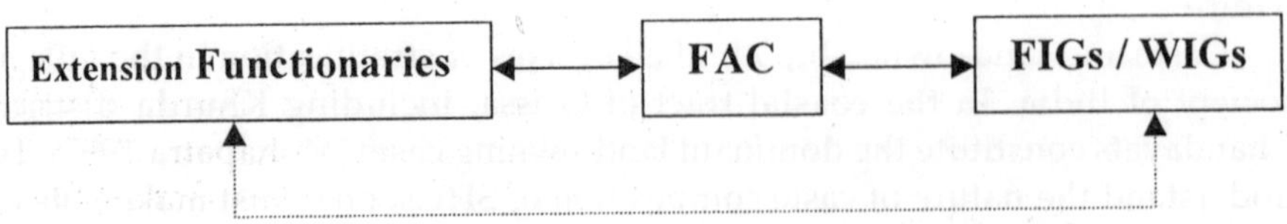

The BTT imparts agro-technologies and other allied technologies through training programmes, exposure visits and demonstrations by consulting the FAC members. The FAC acts as an intermediating link between the extension functionaries and the FIGs/WIGs. It takes an account of the needs, problems, requirements of the group and reports to the extension functionaries. That means, the extension functionaries get hold of all information concerning the group through FAC. However, the extension agency i.e. the BTT directly imparts the actual training programmes to the groups.

TRAINING PROGRAMME: A UNIQUE FEATURE OF NATP

Training programme is a characteristic feature of NATP. Training programme constitutes the central medium of transfer of technology. The ATMA's total endeavour of transfer of technology rests on the "training programme". As stated earlier, this project aims to enhance the skill of the farming community through its multi-departmental approach. As the Secretary of Mahalaxmi Mahila Samiti, Kuhuri, Tangi, explains: "training programmes give us an exposure to new ideas". Institute on Management of Agricultural Extension (IMAGE), a state level mechanism at Bhubaneswar, Orissa acts as a mini-MANAGE at the state level. It organizes training programmes for the grassroots level extension functionaries. It conducts different training programmes and workshops for block and village level extension agents and also for a small number of FIGs/WIGs representatives. The IMAGE has offered sixty-three (63) courses for NATP through training programmes and workshops till the time of interview. However, the BTT plays a crucial role in disseminating technologies to the target groups.

ROLE OF BTT

The BTT, a team of specialists of the Department of Agriculture and allied departments, is in charge of providing technical services to the individual FIGs and WIGs. Annually, it prepares block action plan (BAP) in consultation with the FAC. Accordingly, they conduct the activities mainly through training programmes, exposure visits and demonstrations. The number of training programmes, exposure visits and demonstrations, arranged by BTT, Chilika, is 188, 18 and 230 respectively till the time of the interview. However, the study did not get any data for Tangi block.

TRAINING PROGRAMME: ISSUES, DILEMMAS AND CONTRADICTIONS

Certain queries that automatically emerge from the understanding of ATMA's endeavour are: What is meant by the technological training by ATMA? Does it seek to replace the indigenous techniques of the farming community? What is the degree of its acceptance by the village farmers? In other words, is such technological package accepted by the FIGs/WIGs? If yes, to what extent? The best way to seek answers to the above queries is to learn from the groups who are directly associated with the technological package of ATMA at grassroots level.

The Chairman, FAC, Tangi, mentions about these queries very boldly:

> *Any sort of agricultural technology should follow three things namely, material transfer, design transfer and capacity transfer; but ATMA is engaged in disseminating only the design transfer. In Orissa, where maximum numbers of individuals live below poverty line, mere dissemination of design will be fruitless*

> *without facilitating it with material/infrastructure and capacity transfer wherever necessary. This training programme is only giving the ideas without looking at the capacity of the FIGs/WIGs. Hence, appropriate technologies should be disseminated by taking into consideration the energy, infrastructure, location and socio-economic conditions of the preponderant sections of the farming community.*

The above assertion is explanatory towards the very nature of training programme that is resorted to by ATMA functionaries to impart it among the farmers. The training programme must not remain insouciant to existential factors like infrastructural support and socio-economic conditions of the farmers. It can really be farmer-oriented only when ATMA begins, at the outset, to make a sense of the overall conditions/needs of the farming community before attempting any actual training endeavor. Otherwise, the effort for realizing a holistic goal of an all round agricultural development would remain partial, selective, incomplete and fragmented.

Secondly, has this process of dissemination of technology through training programmes, demonstrations and exposure visits been able to replace the traditional one? The response that emerges from the study is mostly negative. Not surprisingly, despite several organizational, bureaucratic campaigns and counseling, people still resort to traditional mode of pursuing their agriculture.

Case 1

The experience of Maa Ramachandi Sugarcane Sangha, Harichandanpur, an FIG of Tangi, is a case in point. In this case, the BTT functionaries prompted and, in fact, exhorted the group to grow sugarcane in accordance with the new techniques suggested by them. The group started the cultivation accordingly. But to its utter misfortune, the BTT officials vanished and absconded after two initial visits. Without being disheartened, the group members carried on the sugarcane cultivation without any outside technical assistance from ATMA. They grew sugarcane according to their own indigenous/local knowledge systems[8] and got maximum profit in the harvest. According to one of the members of the group:

> *We have mastered our own skill relating to our style of production. Adoption of ATMA's new technique implies total rejection of our continuing practice, which has hitherto been proving itself beneficial to the masses. It also implies to believe in men (officials) who are non-committal and absconding in nature. Moreover, it means developing a dependency habit upon these officials. Our indigenous practices need not be evaluated as inferior to the so-called modern ones. Traditional Technology (TT) refers to the unique, traditional, local knowledge, existing within and developed around the specific conditions of women and men indigenous to a particular geographic area. It has two powerful advantages over outside knowledge-it has little cost and is readily available. TT is found to be socially desirable, economically affordable, and sustainable and involves minimum risk and widely believed to conserve resources. For a development project, however, it does not matter whether the technique is really indigenous or foreign or is a mixture of both. What is important is that instead of looking only for techniques and solutions from outside the community, it is very rational to first look at what is in the community and then use knowledge, which is found to be more effective (not necessarily exclusively foreign*

> *or exclusively indigenous). Hence any development project should focus on bottom to top approach rather than the reverse.*

Case 2

The experience of Mahavir Krushi Vikash Parisada, an FIG, Tangi, is another case in point. According to the Secretary of the group, the ATMA training programme is a weak mechanism. Expressing his voice of utter disappointment mixed with optimism, he says:

> *The group engaged itself in groundnut cultivation in a large barren land in accordance with the advice of the BTT officials. However, at the end of the cultivation, they did not find any groundnut from the soil. In fact, the technical assistance did not result in any return except losses. Thus, this training programme proves to be barren. Hence, the entire expense of the training programme made by ATMA, Khurda, should rather be distributed in cash among the group members in equal share and thus, farmers be encouraged with such financial boost to rise at their own capacity.*

Although the training programme has been successful in creating total beneficiaries (TB), yet they constitute only 11.32 per cent of the total target groups formed, which has been explained in the next section. The rest constitutes the category of partial beneficiaries (PB) and non-beneficiaries (NB). The category of PB and NB constitutes 88.68 per cent. The above peculiar example of 11.32 per cent is just 'a tip of the iceberg'.

TECHNOLOGY DISSEMINATION AND FARMERS' INVOLVEMENT

It is said that technology innovation, technology diffusion and technology acceptance are the three pillars of technology promotion. Thus, in case of ATMA, one has to assess how far the technology/training package proposed by the extension functionaries is received, adopted and adapted by the FIGs/WIGs, who are the target groups of the package. The technology package under the ATMA is basically endowed with training programmes, exposure visits and demonstrations. So, one can make an attempt while conceptualizing the type of beneficiaries, with reference to these three categories. Thus, under the technology dissemination component, the type of beneficiaries can be seen in terms of their level of involvement in training programmes, exposure visits and demonstrations, not only in terms of technology designs but also its practicability, actual adoption and marketability.

Thus, in this process of evaluation of the types of beneficiaries, the study has focused on three aspects: 'know how (technology)', 'application' and 'outcome'. Based on these three aspects, the study visualizes three types of beneficiaries: total beneficiaries, partial beneficiaries and non-beneficiaries. First, total beneficiaries (TB) are defined as those groups who receive the 'know-how' (technology) and are able to adopt it to put into practice and the outcome of the practice is positive i.e. increase in production and marketability. Second, partial beneficiaries (PB) are defined as those groups who receive the 'know-how' (technology), may or may not be able to adopt it to put into practice and the outcome of the practice is negative i.e. neither increase in production nor marketability. Third, non-beneficiaries (NB) are defined as those groups who may or may not receive the 'know-how' (technology), are not able to adopt it to put into practice and the outcome is negative i.e. neither increase in production nor marketability. This has been shown in table 2.

Table 2
Beneficiaries in Chilika and Tangi Blocks

Categories	*Chilika*		*Tangi*		*Total*
	FIG	*WIG*	*FIG*	*WIG*	
Total Beneficiaries	3 (2.83)	1 (0.94)	3 (2.83)	5 (4.72)	12 (11.32)
Partial Beneficiaries	1 (0.94)	11 (10.34)	6 (5.67)	20 (18.87)	38 (35.85)
Non-Beneficiaries	2 (1.89)	17 (16.03)	5 (4.72)	32 (30.19)	56 (52.83)
Grand Total	35 (33.02)	71 (66.98)	106 (100)		

*N.B. The figures in bracket indicate the percentage of the concerned figures.

Table 2 indicates that there are 11.32 per cent of TB FIGs and WIGs in both the blocks. In case of PB and NB, the WIGs are the highest number (75.43%) in both the blocks. Together, the PB and NB categories in both the blocks constitute 88.68%. It is also seen that more than half of the groups (52.83%) are in NB category.

Table 3
Caste and Nature of Beneficiaries

Categories	*Chilika (N=35)*			*Tangi (N=71)*			*Total*
	TB	*PB*	*NB*	*TB*	*PB*	*NB*	(N=106)
General	3 (8.57)	7 (20.00)	8 (22.86)	5 (7.04)	16 (22.53)	13 (18.31	52 (49.06)
GC	1 (2.86)	4 (11.43)	6 (17.14)	2 (2.82)	5 (7.04)	13 (18.31)	31 (29.24)
GT	0 (0)	0 (0)	2 (5.71)	0 (0)	1 (1.41)	1 (1.41)	4 (3.77)
ST	0 (0)	0 (0)	0 (0)	0 (0)	0 (0)	4 (5.63)	4 (3.77)
SC	0 (0)	1 (2.86)	3 (8.57)	0 (0)	1 (1.41)	4 (5.63)	9 (8.49)
GTC	0 (0)	0 (0)	0 (0)	1 (1.41)	3 (4.22)	2 (2.82)	6 (5.67)

Table 3 shows that 8 numbers of TB groups are from general caste, followed by GC (3) and then GTC (1). Both these general and GC categories are dominated by Khandayats. It shows that general caste is a necessary condition for achieving the status of TB. Among this general category, the Khandayats are the dominant caste. The SC groups and ST groups do not have any share in TB. Even in the PB and NB categories, groups from general category are dominant, along with GC category. The ST groups do not have any share in any categories except NB.

TOTAL BENEFICIARIES

Total beneficiaries refer to the target groups, which have accepted the total package as proposed by the extension agency. Under this "beneficiary" category, the FIGs/WIGs have not only accepted the newly proposed training but they also keep on converting it into actual practice, thereby increasing the production and marketability. Hence, in this category, the inculcation of training and the acceptance/translation/utilization/sustenance/production/marketability of the technology are positively correlated.

The percentage of TB in both the blocks is 11.32 in relation to the total number of groups formed in both the blocks. But, there are more of TB-FIGs in Chilika where as there are more number of TB-WIGs in Tangi. Coming to the category of Caste categorization, there are 8 FIGs from general, 3 from GC and 1 from GTC category respectively in both the blocks. The study unearths that Khandayats are the major shareholders in the category of TB. Members from category of GT, SC, ST in both the blocks do not have any share in TB.

A Case

Maa Mahamangala ATMA Sahayak Gosthi (FIG), Tarapi, Chilika, is a case in point. This group consists of eleven members. This is a mono-caste group in which all the members are from Khandayat category only. Out of these eleven members, three are landless, another is having below one acre and rest of the members are having one acre of land each. This group is regarded as one of the most successful groups in FAC Chilika. The Secretary of the group is the member in FAC, Chilika. The group has received training programmes on Diary Farm, Poultry, Fishery, Sunflower and Groundnut cultivation. The members have activated all the training programmes in accordance with the technical assistance of the BTT, Chilika from the beginning to the end of all the activities that they have performed well, till today. According to the members of the group:

> *The first and foremost thing behind our success is the 'we-feeling' among the members. We are sharing all the investments and profits among ourselves. So far, we have not received any loss. Our credit goes to our group leader, the Secretary who has been showing incentives by screening out various training programmes in consultation with the BTT, Chilika. In fact, ATMA has led us from "darkness to light" through various training programmes and demonstrations.*

In fact, it can be stated that because of his membership in FAC, Chilika, the Secretary of the group has been able to transform this group into a successful one. Thus, the case shows that the achievement of the group depends on two factors; firstly, the nature of group solidarity through cooperation and good leadership quality and secondly, its synergy with technical personnel (BTT). Therefore, the achievement is the result of the solidarity between group and public agency.

Partial Beneficiaries

Partial Beneficiaries are those target groups who accept the technology as recommended by extension agents, but are unable to continue the practice due to some constraints like lack of financial assistance, lack of infrastructural assistance, marketability etc. In this category, the inculcation of training/ technology and the acceptance/utilization/sustenance are partially correlated. Here, the category of 'application' is undertaken but the 'outcome' does not necessarily give positive results.

The percentage of PB in Chilika and Tangi blocks is 35.85 in relation to the total number of target groups. There are 31 PB-WIGs and 7 PB-FIGs in relation to total numbers of PBs. The general mono-caste group has the maximum number of PB as compared to the rest. Among the general category, Khandayats are the major share holders and followed by GC in two blocks.

A Case

The example of Jayaguru Mahila ATMA Sahayak Gosthi, Begunia, (WIG), which has been developed by FAC, Chilika, is illustrative. The group comprises twenty members. It is a mono-caste group where all the members belong to the Khandayat category. As far as their landholding is concerned, six members have 1 acre, four members have 1.5 acres and other members have 2 acres of land each. The group has saved an amount of Rs. 14,292/- both in FSU and ISU. This group engaged itself in mushroom cultivation in a large part of land in accordance with the technical advice of BTT, Chilika. Although it reaped rich harvest, it faced severe loss due to marketing problem. The extension mechanism did not cooperate in this regard to assist in arranging marketing facility for the group. Ultimately, the group had to bear the entire loss. The Secretary and the President of the group had to pay the entire amount of loss to the rest of the group members. After that, the members did not show any incentive to work together due to the severe loss of the group. Thus, the group stands nominally without any activity. The technical persons do not visit to this group any more. As a result, there is no more cooperation and coordination among the members and also no trust towards the technical personnel due to their negligence on the group.

In fact, the partial beneficiaries can be referred to as the beneficiaries in terms of skill. They are one step ahead of the non-beneficiaries (discussed below) in the sense that they have got the experience of experimenting the techniques, which are recommended by the BTT. Owing to lack of trust in BTT officials, infrastructural support and marketing facility, the PB is unable to perform any activity in both the blocks.

NON-BENEFICIARIES

The target groups in this category may or may not accept the technical assistance, but they are unable to practise the prescribed techniques in ground reality. The inculcation of technology and the practice of such inculcation are negatively correlated. Here, there is no case for application and outcome. There could be several reasons for such negative correlation, such as lack of infrastructure, poor surveillance, lack of group coordination and support by public extension agencies (like BTT) and so on. The percentage of NBs in both the blocks is 52.83 in relation to the total number of groups in both the blocks.

Like PB, there are maximum number of NB-WIGs (49) in comparison to NB-FIGs (7) in Tangi and Chilika. So far as the caste component is concerned, it is observed that the entire caste categories have independent share, although the general category has a larger share occupying 21 target groups out of total NB-FIGs/WIGs. Then follows GC (19) category in both the blocks.

A Case

Maa Tarini Mahila ATMA Sahayaka Gosthi (WIG), Nimikheta, Chilika is a case in point. The group comprises of ten members. It comes under GC category where one member is from Tanti (SC), one from Badhei and remaining eight are from Khandayat category. The former two individuals do not occupy any land. Among Khandayats, three persons having 3 acres of land, another 3 below one acre and remaining three are landless. The BTT and FAC, Chilika, have disappeared after opening up of the group. It shows that they had a malafide intension in terms of attaining some financial gain. The group has not received any training from the extension agents. The group exists without any function. They just collect monthly fees from the members. There is no coordination and cooperation among the members. The members act according to their own ways.

Such high percentage of NB is symbolic as well as symptomatic of poor achievement of ATMA in these two blocks. On the whole, the number and percentage of NBs in both the blocks are the highest as compared to the total percentage of PB and TB. Moreover, the percentage of NB crosses the 50% mark in the total number of target groups in both the blocks. This implies that ATMA has not been successful to promote more number of TBs under its initiatives: it has witnessed a sharp rise in NBs, which is some thing to worry about and which urges that there is a need for ATMA to rethink its approach, if it is interested to create beneficiary farmers' groups under the category of TB only and if it is really committed to make the programme of NATP a grand success.

EPILOGUE

The NATP, an innovation in agricultural extension tries to highlight its role in dissemination of technologies in the field of agriculture as well as in allied sectors. However, the result of the dissemination at ground level shows a different picture altogether. Only a small minority of about 11.32 per cent of the FIGs/WIGs is considered as the total beneficiary of the project. Out of the total TBs, the percentage of TB-FIGs is more in number in Chilika than Tangi (50% in Chilika and 21.43% in Tangi), although majority of the groups formed in two blocks of Khurda district under NATP are WIGs. It is important to recognize the rate of reception and utilization of disseminated technologies in the ground reality of women in agriculture. Hence, it is a major flaw in the process of group formation to focus primarily on women in an agricultural technology dissemination project. Almost all of these WIGs are in fact excluded from the process of technology transfer. Most of the FIGs under TBs are successful as a result of their network with the 'political elites (Sarapanchas at

Gram Panchayat level)' and 'bureaucratic elites (officials at the grassroots, block and district levels)'. However, the most vulnerable groups, SCs, STs and women are almost excluded. Thus, quantitative measures such as number of groups formed are misleading. As a result, the basic approach of NATP i.e. "groups as partners than mere agents in the process of DoT" has to be reinvented if such technological package is serious to achieve its objectives.

The innovation in dissemination of technology as projected by NATP in the context of agricultural research and extension reveals a process of 'hierarchy' among the farming groups. It is seen that the actual beneficiaries are only 11.32 per cent whereas a large majority (88.68%) is deprived of the benefits of its package. Thus, it raises the question: how democratic is NATP in its approach? It has contributed to the phenomenon of "polarization" between the actual beneficiary and the deprived one. The study demonstrates that a particular caste 'Khandayat', the dominant caste of the region is in advantage position to avail maximum benefits from the project, which is possible because of its networking with the 'political elites' as well as 'bureaucratic elites'.

It is methodologically imperative here to visualize the role of NATP at the grassroots level, which came as a facilitator of DoT. The DoT under NATP has made a clear distinction between traditional technology and 'alternative technology (as developed and suggested by NATP)', which is considered as the 'modern technology' by NATP officials. This alternative technology tends to be hegemonic in nature. Hegemony in the sense, NATP sanctions a particular technological package as the only valid, useful and trustworthy form of practice and it de-recognizes the traditional technology of farmers (as observed from the case of Mahavir Krushi Vikash Parisad (FIG), Kuhuri, Tangi). It insists the farmers to follow one particular technology that it considers to be superior and therefore it believes in the slogan - "follow it or get lost". But, it has to be remembered that the worth/ trustworthiness of a particular technology has to be gauged in terms of its utility, predictability, service and location, not solely in terms of the stamp of 'only valid-cum- universal technology'. It is almost irrational and unethical to discourage the traditional technology, which has been beneficial to the farmers. Rather, it is also possible to impart any alternative technology through the prism of traditional technology that is hitherto rendering benefits to the farming groups.

Moreover, there is nothing wrong in conducting scientific research on traditional technology, which has been persisting perennially being farmer-friendly. Thus, the current innovation in DoT in agriculture is marked by inequality (between beneficiary and non-beneficiary farmers), discrimination (between modern technology and traditional technology) and hegemony (of modern technology over traditional technology). Furthermore, the DoT, although emerged with basketful of integrated technological options, has remained stuck at the institutional level, especially at the stage of "design" of DoT.

Thus, while interrogating the process of DoT through NATP, a meticulous understanding espouses that although NATP tries to bring about the long-persisting distinctions between innovation, implementation and application relating to "DoT" through its participatory-cum-interactive model; it fails to achieve its objectives at ground reality. What is interesting to observe is that although the project was primarily an initiative for the development and dissemination of agricultural technologies, it has successfully paved the way for the initiation and mushrooming of microfinance agenda. Thus, NATP has proved itself as a blessing in disguise for the success and wide acceptance of microfinance in the field of agriculture (Mishra 2005).

Thus, any innovation in DoT should deal with a wide range of issues faced not only by the farmers but also the farming system as a whole, which includes infrastructure, research, input, 'local situation', credit and access to market and, nonetheless an integration of different actors into a common platform.

NOTES

1. I would like to thank all of the resource persons at the December, 2004 the XXX All India Sociological Conference on National Policy on Social Sciences at DDU Gorakhpur, Gorakhpur, Uttar Pradesh, India for their extremely useful feedback on an earlier version of this paper. I would also like to express my deep sense of appreciation to Dr. Vinod Kumar Jairath for his painstaking patience and intellectual comments. Lastly, I would convey my in-depth gratitude to Prof. E. Haribabu whose comments were exceptionally significant in reshaping my thinking.
2. Government of India, Planning Commission, X Plan Approach Paper, September 2001.
3. Initially the project was sanctioned for a period of five years from 1998-2003. Later on it was extended to one more year.
4. Mentioned in "Guideline for Group Formation by FAC or Non-Govt. Organizations (NGOs)", ATMA, Khurda.
5. The study takes into account formal saving unit as the running of a 'bank account' whereas the informal saving unit refers to the common fund, which generates through thrift and credit system at the grassroots level.
6. By taking into account different local castes, the study undertakes the caste structure of the study area into three categories like general, schedule caste and schedule tribe. The general caste consists of the local castes, such as, Brahmin, Karana, Khandayat, Badhei, Bhandari, Bania, Gauda and Gudia. The Schedule caste comprises the castes like Bauri, Betara, Dhoba, Keuta and Tanti. The schedule tribe constitutes only the Nodhas.
7. General = General Caste, GC = General and Schedule Caste, GT = General and Schedule Tribe, ST = Schedule Tribe, SC = Schedule Caste, GTC = General + SC + ST.
8. Indigenous knowledge system refers to a cumulative body of knowledge and beliefs handed down through generations by cultural transmission about the relationship of living being, (including human) with their environment.

SELECTED READINGS

Jha, P.N. (2001), 'Indian Agriculture at the Crossroads and the Strategies for Technology Development and Technology Dissemination for Meeting the

Challenges in 21st Century', B. S. Hansra (*etal.) Modernizing Indian Agriculture in 21st Century: Challenges, Opportunities and Strategies.* New Delhi: Concept Publishing Company.

Melkote, S. (1991), *Communication for Development in the Third World.* New Delhi: Sage Publications.

Melkote, S. and Vallath, C. (1992), *Communication Gap in Development.* Jaipur: Rawat Publications.

Mishra, A.K. (2004a). *Globalization and Agricultural Extension Reforms: A Study of National Agricultural Technology Project in Orissa.* Unpublished M.Phil dissertation submitted at University of Hyderabad, Hyderabad, Andhra Pradesh, India.

—— (2004b), 'National Agricultural Technology Project: Transcending Technological Gap'. *The Kurukshetra.* Vol. 52 (07).

—— (2005), "Microfinance through self-help Groups: An Interpretative Understanding through NATP". *Small Enterprises Development, Management, Extension (SEDME).* Hyderabad: National Institute of Small Industry Extension Training.

Mohapatra, L.K. (1997), "Society in Orissa", P.K. Mishra (ed.) *Comprehensive History and Culture of Orissa.* New Delhi: Kaveri Books.

Paroda, R.S. (1999), 'Green Revolution: For a Food Secure Future', *The Hindu Survey of Indian Agriculture.*

Rogers, E. (1962), *Diffusion of Innovations.* New York: The Free Press.

Samanta, R.K. (1997), 'Reorienting Extension in Changing Global Agricultural Perspective', R.K. Samanta and K.K. Arora (ed.) *Management of Agricultural Extension in Global Perspective.* Delhi: B.R. Publishing Corporation.

Sharma, R. (1999), 'Agricultural Research and Extension Interface-Indian Experience', *Agricultural Research and Extension Interface in Asia.* Tokyo: Asian Productivity Organisation.

—— (2002), 'Reforms in Agricultural Extension: New Policy Framework', *The Economic and Political Weekly.* Vol. 37 (30).

Sing, A.K. (2000), *Agricultural Extension: Impact and Assessment.* India: Published by AGROBIOS.

Sulaiman, V.R. and A. Hall (2002), "Beyond Technology Dissemination: Reinventing Agricultural Extension". *Outlook on Agriculture,* Vol. 31(4).

REFERRED DOCUMENTS

- Agricultural Technology Management Agency (ATMA), MANAGE-NATP Series-2, 1999.
- Certificate of Farmers and Farm Women Federation, FIAC, Chilika.
- Detail Information of the Group List of ATMA, Khurda.
- District Statistical Hand Book, Khurda, 1999.
- Guideline for Group Formation by FAC and NGOs, ATMA, Khurda.
- Implementation of G.B. Discussion, ATMA, Khurda.
- Innovation in Technology Dissemination, NATP Series-1, 1999.
- List of FIGs/WIGs, FIAC, Chilika.
- List of FIGs/WIGs, FIAC, Tangi.
- List of Seminars and Workshops as developed by IMAGE, Bhubaneswar.

- Pani Panchayat in Orissa, Department of Water resources, Government of Orissa, 2001.
- Role and Responsibilities of FAC members, ATMA, Khurda.
- State Agricultural Policy, Government of Orissa, 1996.
- Strategic Research and Extension Plan (SREP) Guidelines, MANAGE-SREP Series-3, 1999.
- Strategic Research and Extension Plan of Khurda District, MANAGE-SREP Series-6, 2001.

FOREST DEVELOPMENT IN INDIA: AN INTER-STATE ANALYSIS

I. Sundar

INTRODUCTION

There is a growing concern throughout India that environmental problems resulting from human activities pose a threat to sustainability of life support system. Due to deforestation, over grazing and population growth, the sustainability of the ecosystem is very much affected. Hence, the preservation and conservation of forest resource is an essential aspect of sustainable development. In order to protect forest resources much legislation has been enacted in India from time to time. The history of the formulation of forest policy in India recent past may be traced back to the creation of the Imperial forest department in 1864 under the colonial rule.

The main objective for setting up the forest department was to ensure sustained availability of large number of sleepers required for the railways. The establishment of this department marked a beginning of the shift in the management of forests in India from community to the state. The first forest act was enacted in India in 1865 mainly to facilitate the acquisition of forest areas that could supply timber to the railways without abridging the existing rights of the people. The forest in this act was defined as land covered with trees, brushwood and jungle (Guha 1983).

The next forest act was enacted in 1878 after realizing that many of the provisions made in the previous act were not adequate for an effective control implied by the state. The definition of forest itself inhibited rising of plantations by the state on barren lands. The forest act of 1878 therefore reversed almost all provisions of the forest act of 1865 except the provisions of arrest without warrant. Some of the important provisions of the new act were as follows (i) any land whatsoever could be designated as forest (ii) treatment of customary rights of Indian villagers as based on privilege and not on right (iii) a bar to accrual of any further rights of people on reserved forests (iv) conservation of projected forests into reserved forests when required and (v) constitution of a third category of forests as village forests. This act provided a great deal of flexibility to the forest settlement officers of forest dwellers (Guha 1983).

A regulation on forest policy was made for the first time in 1894. The salient features of the policy were as followers: the sole object with state forests is administered for public benefit. In general, the constitution and preservation of a forest involve the regulation of rights and the restriction of privilege of use of the forest by the neighbouring population; forest situated on hill slopes should be maintained as protection forests to preserve the climate and physical conditions of the country and to protect the cultivated plains that lie below them from the devasting action of hill torrents; forests which are the reservoirs of valuable timbers should be managed on commercial lines as a source of revenue of the states; wherever an effective demand for cultivable land exists and can only be supplied from forest area, the land should ordinarily be relinquished without hesitation, subject to the following conditions: Honeycombing of a valuable forest by patches of cultivation should not be allowed. Cultivation must be permanent and must not be allowed to an extent as to encroach upon minimum area of forest that is needed to meet the reasonable forest requirements.

The Indian forest act of 1927 is largely involved redrafting of some clauses of the forest act of 1878. One major change is stated to be its reference to individuals and not individuals or communities which referring to rights on forests. A resolution on the first post independence forest policy was issued in 1952. While this policy retained the basic thrust of the earlier policy, it emphasized a balance across economic, ecological and social benefits from the forest on a functional basis into protection forests, national forests, village forests and tree lands. While the functions of protection forests and village forests were the same as laid down in the earlier policy, the national forests were meant for meeting the requirements of defence, communications and industries with a progressively increasing sustainable yield and the tree lands were proposed for improving physical and climatic conditions and for promoting the general well being of people. The provision of centralized management was considered even in this policy.

It was only about 25 years later that the forest policy of 1988 underscored community participation in protection and development of forests. The objectives of the forest policy of 1988 were stated as follows. (i) maintenance of environmental stability through preservation and restoration of ecological balance (ii) conservation of natural heritage (iii) check on soil erosion and denudation in catchment's areas of rivers, lakes and reservoirs (iv) check on extension of sand dunes in desert areas of Rajasthan and along coastal tracts (v) sustainable increase in forest tree cover through massive afforestation and social forestry programme (vi) step to meet requirement of fuel wood, fodder, minor forest produce and timber of rural and tribal population (vii) increase in productivity of forests to meet the national needs (viii) encouragement to efficient utilization of forest produce and optimum substitution of wood and (ix) steps to create massive people's movement with involvement of women to achieve the objectives and minimize pressure on existing forests. Thus forest preservation and conservation have been initiated in India two centuries ago. Despite seven efforts, forest coverage, degradation and regional variation in distribution of forest resources are common problems of forest management. This paper makes an attempt to analyze the same.

Data presented in table 1 indicate the distribution of forest coverage and regional variation in distribution of forest area in India. The total area under forest coverage is 3287263 sq km area in India. However wide spread regional variation is observed in area under forest coverage. The per cent of area under forest coverage is highest in Andaman and Nicobar Islands (92.29%)More than 50 per cent of the area under forest coverage is observed in Tripura (52.89%), Nagaland (85.78%), Mizoram (89.06%), Meghalaya (69.81%), Manipur (78.01%) and Arunachal Pradesh (81.92%).

The national average area under forest cover is 19.27 per cent of the geographical area. The states such as West Bengal (9.41%), Uttarpradesh (11.55%), Tamilnadu (13.12%), Rajasthan (3.90%), Punjab (2.75%), Maharashtra (15%), Jammu and Kashmir (9.20%), Haryana (1.37%), Gujarat (6.42%) and Andhrapradesh (15.74%) have below national average area under forest coverage. At the national level recorded area under forest cover was 765204 hectares and it declined to 633397 hectares showing 82.77 per cnet of shortfall in forest area in India. Among the states in India, the area under forest coverage has increased in six stats viz., Arunachalpradesh (133.105). More than 70 per cent in decline in forest area coverage has been noticed in the states like West Bengal (70.28%), Tripura (88.14%), Tamilnadu (75.41%), Sikkim (118.08%), Kerala (92.10%), Karnataka (83.68%), Bihar (90.7%%) and Assam (77.58%). The major reasons for decline in area under forest coverage is due to deforestation in terms of forest fire, illicit felling of trees, mono cultivation practice, shifting cultivation practice, over grazing, forest land diversion for development work and so on.

The area under shifting cultivation is quite common in Andhrapradesh. In general, forestland cultivation for development works is quite common in India. It could be noted that in Maharashtra 103283 hectares of forestlands were converted to development work during 1989-90 and 1994-95. In Madhyapradesh in the same period 147068.29 hectares of forestlands were converted into non-forest use. In general land conversion for development work is quite low in Northeastern hill states. The major reason for land area conversion to non-forest use area power line, transmission, renewal of mining, construction of road, irrigation project and other development works. Hence, deforestation is a major threat to sustainability of life support system in India.

The per capita forest cover at the national level is 0.078 hectares, which is quite low. The per capita forest cover is quite remarkable in Arunachalpradesh, Mizoram, Nagaland and Andaman Nicobar Island. The per capita forest coverage is quite discouraging in West Bengal, Uttarpradesh, Tamilnadu, Punjab, Haryana, Gujarat, Bihar and Andhrapradesh as they have below 0.50 hectares. Out of total forest area the area under dense forest is worked out to 367260 hectares, open forest 261310 hectares and mangroves 4827 hectares.

The mangrove forest is located in 8 states in India. This type of forest coverage is highest in West Bengal and its coverage is considerable in Andaman Nicobar Island, Gujarat, Andhrapradesh and Orissa since they have more than 200 hectares of mangrove forest coverage. The mangrove forest coverage is

Table 1
State Wise Distribution Forest Area In India

State	*Geographical Area sq km*	*Recorded Forest Area*	*Actual Cover*	*Per cent of Forest Area Cover*	*Percentage Change (sq km)*	*Per capita Forest Cover (ha)*	*Dense Forest*	*Open Forest*	*Mangrove*
Andhra Pradesh	215068	63814	43290	15.74	67.84-	0.065	23048	19859	383
Arunachal Pradesh	83743	51540	68602	81.92	133.10+	7.931	54155	14447	-
Assam	78438	30708	23824	30.37	77.58-	0.106	15548	8276	-
Bihar	173877	29226	26524	15.25	90.75-	0.031	13300	13224	-
Gujarat	196024	19393	12578	6.42	64.86-	0.030	6337	5250	991
Haryana	44212	1673	604	1.37	36.10-	0.004	370	234	-
Himachal Pradesh	55673	35407	12521	22.49	35.36-	0.242	9560	2961	-
Jammu & Kashmir	222235	20182	20440	9.20	101.28+	0.265	11020	9420	-
Karnataka	191791	38724	32403	16,89	83.68-	0.072	24854	7546	3
Kerala	38863	11221	10334	26.59	92.10-	0.036	8454	1880	-
Madhya Pradesh	443446	154497	131195	29.59	84.92-	0.198	82745	48450	-
Maharashtra	307690	63842	46143	29.59	72.28-	0.058	23622	22397	124
Manipur	22327	15154	17418	15.00	114.94+	0.948	4937	12481	-
Meghalaya	22429	94.96	15657	78.01	164.88+	0.882	4044	11631	-
Mizoram	21081	15935	18775	69.81	117.82+	2.721	4348	14427	-
Nagaland	16579	8629	14221	89.06	164.80+	1.175	3487	10734	-
Orissa	155707	57184	46941	85.78	82.90-	0.148	26101	20629	211
Punjab	50362	2901	1387	30.15	47.81-	0.007	511	876	-
Rajasthan	342239	31700	13353	2.75	42.12-	-	3690	9663	-
Sikkim	7096	2650	3129	3.90	118.08-	0.771	2423	706	-
Tamilnadu	130058	22628	17064	44.10	75.41-	0.0931	8676	8367	21
Tripura	10486	6292	5546	13.12	88.14-	0.201	1819	3727	-
Uttar Pradesh	294411	51663	33994	52.89	65.80-	0.024	22958	11036	-
West Bengal	88752	11879	8349	11.55	70.28-	0.012	3557	2669	2123
A&N Islands	8249	7171	7613	9.41	106.16+	2.709	6520	127	966
Others	66427	11101	1492	92.29	13.44	-	1176	311	5
India	3287263	765209	633397	2.24	82.77	0.075	367260	261310	4827

Source: India Forestry Statistics, 2000.

lowest in Karnataka. The dense forest coverage is quite high in Arunachal Pradesh, Assam ad Andaman and Nicobar Islands.

Table 2 presents data on the state wise distribution of wastelands. The total lands in India is 1295.80 lakh hectares as per the survey made in 2000. Out of total wastelands, non-forest degradated area is 936.91 hectares and forest degraded area 358.89 hectares. At the national level 19.42 per cent of the area is under wasteland category. The area under wastelands is quite high in Sikkim state (50.30%), Nagaland (50.69%) and Manipur (58%). More than 20 per cent of the total land area under wasteland category in some states such as Assam (25.52%), Gujarat (21.95%), Jammu and Kashmir (29.45%), Meghalaya (44.16%) and Rajasthan (30.87%). The presence of wastelands indicates the growing potential to develop forest areas through massive level of implementation of afforestation and social forestry programmes.

Table 2
State Wise Distribution of Waste Lands in India

State	*Geographical Area sq km*	*Recorded Forest Area*	*Actual Cover*	*Per cent of Forest Area Cover*
Andhra Pradesh	76.82	37.34	114.16	18.81
Assam	9.35	7.95	17.3	25.52
Bihar	38.96	15.62	54.58	12.08
Gujarat	71.53	6.83	78.36	21.95
Haryana	24.04	0.74	24.78	8.45
Himachal Pradesh	14.24	5.34	19.58	56.87
Jammu & Kashmir	5.31	10.34	15.65	29.45
Karnataka	71.22	20.43	91.65	10.87
Kerala	10.53	2.26	12.79	3.73
Madhya Pradesh	129.47	71.95	201.42	15.72
Maharashtra	115.6	28.41	144.01	17.38
Manipur	0.14	14.24	14.38	58
Meghalaya	8.15	11.03	19.18	44.16
Nagaland	5.08	8.78	13.86	50.69
Orissa	31.57	32.27	63.84	13.71
Punjab	11.51	0.79	12.3	4.42
Rajasthan	180.01	19.33	199.34	30.87
Sikkim	1.31	1.5	2.81	50.3
Tamilnadu	33.92	10.04	44.01	17.7
Tripura	1.08	8.65	9.73	12.17
Uttar Pradesh	66.35	14.26	80.61	13.17
West Bengal	21.77	3.59	25.36	6.44
UTS	8.89	27.15	36.04	-
India	936.91	358.89	1295.8	19.42

Source: India Forestry Statistics, 2000.

Data presented in table 3 indicate the state-wise distribution of protected area. At the national level 525 wild life protected area recorded. The number of protected area is highest in Andaman and Nicobar Islands (106) and its number is considerable in Himachalpradesh (35), Madhyapradesh (43),

Table 3
State Wise Distribution of Wild Life Protected Areas

State	*No. of Wild Life*	*Area*	*No. of National Park*	*Area*	*No. of Protected Area*	*Percentage*
Andhra Pradesh	20	12084.59 (4.39)	1	352.62 (0.13)	21	12437.21 (4.52)
Arunachal Pradesh	9	6777.75 (8.09)	2	2468.23 (2.95)	11	9245.98 (11.04)
Assam	9	1381.58 (1.76)	2	930.00 (1.19)	11	2311.58 (2.95)
Bihar	19	4624.30 (2.66)	2	567.32 (0.33)	21	5191.62 (2.99)
Gujarat	21	16744.27 (8.54)	4	479.67 (0.24)	25	17223.94 (8.79)
Haryana	9	229.18 (0.52)	1	1.43 (0.00)	10	230.61 (0.52)
Himachal Pradesh	33	6315.92 (11.34)	2	1440.00 (2.59)	35	7755.92 (13.93)
Jammu & Kashmir	16	10163.67 (4.57)	4	3810.07 (1.71)	20	13973.74 (6.29)
Karnataka	20	4229.21 (2.21)	5	2472.18 (1.29)	25	6701.39 (3.49)
Kerala	12	1810.36 (4.66)	2	536.52 (1.38)	43	16990.41 (3.83)
Madhya Pradesh	32	10847.29 (2.45)	11	6143.12 (1.39)	43	16990.41 (3.83)
Maharashtra	24	14309.51 (4.65)	5	956.45 (0.31)	29	15265.96 (4.96)
Manipur	1	184.85 (0.83)	2	81.80 (0.37)	3	266.65 (1.19)
Meghalaya	3	34.21 (0.15)	2	250.00 (1.19)	5	970.00 (4.60)
Mizoram	3	720.00 (3.42)	2	250.00 (1.19)	5	970.00 (4.60)
Nagaland	3	34.35 (0.21)	1	202.02	4	236.37 (1.43)
Orissa	17	6175.49 (3.97)	2	1212.70 (0.78)	19	7388.19 (4.74)
Punjab	6	294.82 (0.59)	-	-	6	294.82 (0.59)
Rajasthan	22	5694.02 (1.66)	4	3856.53 (1.13)	26	9550.55 (2.79)
Sikkim	4	161.10 (2.27)	1	850.00 (11.98)	5	1011.10 (14.25)
Tamilnadu	13	2527.29 (1.94)	5	307.86 (0.24)	18	2835.15 (2.18)
Tripura	4	603.62 (5.76)	-	-	4	603.62 (5.76)
Uttar Pradesh	28	8078.52 (2.74)	7	5409.05 (1.84)	35	13487.57 (4.58)
West Bengal	16	1064.29 (1.20)	5	1692.65 (1.84)	21	2756.94 (3.11)
A&N Lands	94	437.16 (5.30)	6	315.61 (3.83)	100	752.77 (9.13)
India	445	115903.58 (3.53)	80	34829.53	525	150733.11 (4.59)

Source: India Forestry Statistics. 2000, Figures in parentheses denote percentages.

Uttarpradesh (35), Rajasthan (26), Maharashtra (29) and Andhrapradesh (21). Nearly 10 per cent of the protected area has been observed in Arunachalpradesh, Himachalpradesh, Sikkim and Andaman and Nicobar Islands. The proportion of protected area is quite low in Punjab, Nagaland, Manipur and Haryana. The presence of protected area indicates the positive move towards bio-diversity conservation.

Table 4
Prospects of Forest Growth

State	*Growing Stock Million cubic meter*	*Volume Per Hectare in cubic meter*	*Annual Increment in 000 cubic meter*
Andhra Pradesh	291.394	61.66	5929
Arunachal Pradesh	775.125	112.8	15243
Assam	304.423	124.2	6061
Bihar	96.72	36.38	1715
Gujarat	63.921	53.07	1459
Haryana	1.432	27.92	27
Himachal Pradesh	254.41	203.5	1603
Jammu & Kashmir	458.929	224.49	6402
Karnataka	272.411	84.23	5574
Kerala	98.883	95.67	1983
Madhya Pradesh	698.182	51.56	14122
Maharashtra	225.554	51.43	5008
Manipur	95.452	54.1	1889
Meghalaya	104.14	66	2150
Mizoram	66.012	35.3	1332
Nagaland	94.887	66.1	1903
Orissa	246.15	52.21	4432
Punjab	0.95	7.07	23
Rajasthan	12.892	9.84	292
Sikkim	13.286	125.9	767
Tamilnadu	69.602	39.31	1394
Tripura	15.452	27.9	316
Uttar Pradesh	338.633	99.71	5818
West Bengal	22.859	37.68	433
A&N Lands	79.644	119.62	1494
UTS	13.515	143.36	253
India	4740	74.42	87622

Source: India Forestry Statistics, 2000.

A study of data in table 4 indicates the state wise prospects of forest growth in India. At the national level, 4740 million cubic meter growth of forest coverage is estimated. The expected growing stock is quite high in Arunachalpradesh and Madhyapradesh, as their estimated level is beyond 500 million cubic metre. More than 200 million cubic metre of growing stock of forest is observed in Andhrapradesh, Assam, Himachalpradesh, Jammu and Kashmir, Karnataka, Maharashtra and Uttarpradesh. At the national level, volume per hectare cubic metre of forest growth is estimated as 74.42. This trend is above national average in the states of Andaman and Nicobar Islands, Uttarpradesh, Sikkim, Kerala, Karnataka, Jammu and Kashmir, Himachalpradesh and Arunachalpradesh. A similar situation has been observed with respect to the estimated annual increment in forest growth in terms of thousand cubic metre.

Table 5
Forest Afforestation

State	*Forest Area to be Regenerated Million Hectare*	*Proposed Investment in 20 years Rs. million*	*Area to be Planted Million Hectares*	*Proposed Investment 20 years Rs. million*
Andhra Pradesh	2.65	29400	2.280	14700
Arunachal Pradesh	0.10	1310	0.050	3007.12
Assam	0.92	5790.75	0.180	3816.50
Bihar	1.50	16965.74	2.710	31589.80
Gujarat	0.74	14195.59	1.880	890.77
Haryana	0.17	2384.56	0.700	11565.73
Himachal Pradesh	0.49	12777.40	0.410	14402
Jammu & Kashmir	2.05	22552.35	4.220	25597.27
Karnataka	3.09	41130.50	0.120	30632
Kerala	0.14	1329.60	0.120	10927.08
Madhya Pradesh	6.01	87138.16	1.380	102582.08
Maharashtra	2.68	151513.66	0.680	13390.79
Manipur	0.77	13058.26	0.310	419.70
Meghalaya	-	233.60	0	340
Mizoram	0.60	9669.70	0.020	100
Nagaland	-	401.50	-	396.30
Orissa	0.16	12480	0.280	4029.20
Punjab	0.31	8610.80	0.350	5300
Rajasthan	0.80	19840	4.340	108252
Sikkim	0.20	2240.74	0.080	3256.10
Tamilnadu	0.33	3642.40	0.380	3256.10
Tripura	0.04	401.50	0.040	396.30
Uttar Pradesh	2.28	18629.01	0.960	9479.61
West Bengal	0.30	10497.66	0.310	9205.40
A&N Lands	0.07	5534.89	-	-
UTS	0.03	355.50	0.003	420
India	26.43	391479.89	21.80	405605.45

Source: India Forestry Statistics, 2000.

A keen observation of data in table 5 indicates the targeted level of afforestation in India. At the national level 26.43 million hectares of forest area could be regenerated with the proposed investment of Rs. 391479.89 million for a period of 20 years. The targeted forest area regeneration is more than 2 million hectares in Andhrapradesh, Jammu and Kashmir, Karnataka, Madhyapradesh, Maharashtra and Uttarpradesh states. It is proposed to plant tree in 21.80 million hectares of degraded forest area with the proposed investment of Rs. 405605.4 million for a period of 20 years. The area under proposed tree plantation is more than one million hectare in states such as Andhrapradesh, Bihar, Gujarat, Jammu and Kashmir, Madhyapradesh and Rajasthan.

CONCLUSIONS AND POLICY SUGGESTIONS

It could be seen clearly from the above discussion that deforestation, a common phenomenon in India is due to population dependency on forest resources, overgrazing, forest fire, shifting cultivation, mono-cultivation. Diversion of forestland and so on. There is a marked variation in distribution of area under forest coverage in India. In some states the proportion of area under forest coverage is quite low indicating over exploitation of natural resources. States such as Arunachal Pradesh, Andaman and Nicobar Islands, Tripura, Sikkim, Orissa, Nagaland, Mizoram, Meghalaya and Manipur have larger area under forest cover. The area under forest cover is quite low in Haryana, Gujarat, Punjab and Rajasthan. Further wide variation is observed among states in India with respect to destruction of wastelands, protected area, targeted growth of forest area and proposed investment in afforestation. In order to bring about a balanced forest development in India, the following policy measures can be considered.

1. The actual forest cover has declined significantly in Orissa, Sikkim, Tamilnadu, Tripura and West Bengal with respect to recorded forest cover. Hence, there is a need to enhance the area under reforestation.
2. Efforts should be made to protect the mangrove forest since it is concentrated in certain pockets of the country.
3. Wasteland constitute about a half of the geographical area in Himachalpradesh, Manipur, Nagaland and Sikkim. This shows under utilization of land resources. Hence, there is a need to utilize the wastelands in the form of developing bio-diversity and life support system. In this context a massive level of implementation of joint forest management is desired.
4. Efforts should be made to increase the area under wild life protection particularly in states such as Nagaland, Manipur, Punjab and Haryana.
5. The area under forest cover is quite low in Haryana, Gujarat, Punjab and Rajasthan. Hence, a massive level of afforestation programme should be implemented.
6. Massive effort should be made to revegetate the forest-degraded areas particularly in states such as Andhrapradesh, Karnataka, Madhyapradesh, Maharashtra and Orissa, since they have more area under forest degradation.
7. An integrated wasteland development rational planning is essential to ensure the prospects of forest regeneration in different parts of the country.

8. More central assistance should be allocated to states where deforestation is rampant.
9. Proper steps could be made to accelerate the process of growing stock of forest resources in different parts of the country.
10. A proper planning could be followed for sustainable utilization of forest resources.
11. Stringent wild life protection act and proper action against culprits who are involved themselves in deforestation should be enforced.
12. Forestland diversion and forest area encroachment should be stopped with a view to ensure sustainability of forest resources.
13. The government should discourage the practice of mono-cultivation and shifting cultivation as they lead to bio-diversity loss and ultimately environmental degradation.

REFERENCES

Government of India (2002), Tenth Five-Year Plan (2002-2007), Vol. 1: Dimensions and Strategies. Planning Commission, New Delhi.

Government of India (2003), Forest Resources in India: An Overview.

Guha, Ramchandra (1983a), Forestry in British and Post-British India: A Historical Analysis (Part I & II), Economic and Political Weekly, 18 (43), October 22, 1882-1896.

Guha, Ramchandra (1983b), Forestry in British and Post-British India: A Historical Analysis (Part III & IV), Economic and Political Weekly, 18 (45 & 46), November 5-12, 1940-1947.

Saxena, N.C. (199%), Forests, People and Profit: New Equations for Sustainability. Natraj Publishers, Dehradun.

Saxena, Rakesh (1996), "The Vatra Tree Growers' Co-operative Society" in Katar Singh and V. Ballabh (ed.), *Co-operative Management of Natural Resources*. Sage Publications, New Delhi.

Saxena, Rakesh (2000), Joint Forest Management in Gujarat: *Policy and Managerial Issues*, Working Paper 149, August, Institute of Rural Management, Anand.

Singh, Satyajit (1999), Collective Dilemmas and Collective Pursuits: Community Management of Van Panchayats in the UP Hills, *Wastelands News*, May-July, 29.45.

IMPACT OF AOA ON AGRICULTURE OF THE SOUTH ASIAN COUNTRIES WITH SPECIAL REFERENCE TO INDIA

J. Cyril Kanmony

Agriculture was never under the purview of GATT. It was the group of developed countries, primarily the U.S. who sought in favour of non-inclusion of agriculture under the purview of GATT. But, due to substantial progress experienced in agriculture by developed countries like the U.S. and countries of the European Union in the eighties, they felt the need to find markets for their agricultural surplus. Accordingly agriculture was introduced as a new agenda in the Uruguay Round Negotiations in 1986. India signed the GATT agreement in 1994. Thereby it has put her agriculture into the framework of global competition and the rule of global market from the 1st January 1995. Agreement on Agriculture (AoA) is the major agreement carried out in the agricultural sector. Now, about 95 per cent of the global trade is governed by the rules and regulations of WTO. According to WTO, the developed member countries agreed to reduce their tariff bindings by 36 per cent with a minimum cut of 15 per cent for each tariff line over a period of six years from 1995. Developing countries agreed to reduce their tariff bindings by 24 per cent with a minimum of 10 per cent for each tariff line over a period of 10 years. The least developed countries are exempted from tariff reduction.

The second element of AoA is related to the setting up of a minimum level for imports of agricultural products by member countries as a share of domestic consumption. In other words, every country has to export a minimum amount of agricultural goods at preferential tariff rates to compete in other markets. If there are no current access provisions, a minimum access of 3 per cent of 1986-88 T.E base level consumption should be maintained. It is only one per cent to developing countries and the provisions do not apply to the commodities which are traditional staple diet of a developing county. The next provision of AoA is domestic support or domestic subsidy or export subsidy. It is agreed that subsidies to domestic producers should be cut down but it allows farm export subsidies. If Aggregate Measurement of Support (AMS) exceeds 5 per cent of the total value of agricultural production, it has to be reduced by 20 per cent over six years in the case of developed countries. But for developing countries if AMS exceeds 10 per cent, it has to be reduced by 13.3 per cent over ten years. Here also, the least developed countries are not subjected to any reduction commitments.

As a result of these agreements, the South Asian countries-Bangladesh, India, Nepal, Pakistan and Srilanka liberalised trade by considerably lowering their applied tariffs. In Bangladesh, the average applied tariff has been brought down to 21.1 per cent in 1999 from 79.9 per cent in 1989, though a slight increase was effected in 2002. In India also the tariff was reduced from 69.6 per cent in 1990 to 25.7 per cent in 1997 and then increased to 32.8 per cent in 2001. But, the average applied tariff was reduced from 46.3 per cent in 1995 to 17.9 per cent in 2002 in Pakistan. In Srilanka the tariff was 24.2 per cent in 1993, 24.0 per cent in 1997 and 13.9 per cent in 2001. On the other hand, in Nepal, the tariff was increased from 15.7 per cent in 1993 to 16.2 per cent in 1998 and then decreased to 16.0 per cent in 2002. All these are clearly depicted in the table given below.

Table 1
Changes in Tariff Basics on Primary Products in South Asian Countries with WTO

Country	*Year*	*Simple mean (%)*
Bangladesh	1989	79.9
	1999	21.1
	2002	22.4
India	1990	69.6
	1997	25.7
	2001	32.8
Nepal	1993	15.7
	1998	16.2
	2002	16.0
Pakistan	1995	46.3
	1998	42.7
	2002	17.9
Sri Lanka	1993	24.2
	1997	24.0
	2001	13.9

Source: World Bank Reports in Ramesh Chand and Seema Bathla.

These South Asian countries expected large benefits from the liberalised world trade. But, contrary to expectation, international agricultural prices declined very much. Developed countries protected their farmers by giving huge monetary support. But, developing countries neither had the mechanism nor resources to give subsidy. Hence, the export of agricultural products from these countries either declined or increased at a slower rate in comparison with import. The extent to which the net trade was affected in South Asian countries is illustrated in table 2 by taking four yearly averages of trade data, terming 1991-94 as pre-WTO period, 1995-98 as the launching years of WTO and 1999-2002 as post-WTO period.

Table 2
Agriculture Trade of South Asian Countries Before and After WTO
(US $ million)

Country	*1991-94*	*1995-98*	*1999-2002*
Bangladesh			
Export	128	139	105
Import	663	1,248	1,623
Net Trade	-535	-1,109	-1,518
India			
Export	3,085	5,557	5,087
Import	1,336	2,711	3,699
Net Trade	1,749	2,846	1,388
Nepal			
Export	49	48	58
Import	141	217	194
Net Trade	-92	-169	-136
Pakistan			
Export	956	1,101	1,067
Import	1,405	2,135	1,814
Net Trade	-448	-1,034	-747
Srilanka			
Export	528	923	969
Import	500	779	766
Net Trade	29	144	202

Source: FAOSTAT database in Ramesh Chand and Seema Bathla.

It is obvious from the above table that the export of agricultural products from Bangladesh increased from $128 million in the pre-WTO period to $139 million in the launching years. But, there was a sharp fall in the export of agricultural products in the post-WTO period. On the other hand, the import increased from $663 million in the pre-WTO period to $1248 million in the launching years and to $1623 million in the post-WTO period. Due to this disparity between export and import, the net trade deficit increased from $535 million to $1109 and then to $1518 respectively. In India also because of this tendency, the net trade shows a decline from $2846 million in the launching years to $1388 million in the post-WTO period. In Nepal, though the trade deficit increased from $92 in the pre-WTO period to $169 million in 1995-98 period, a slight decrease in trade deficit of $136 million was effected in the post-WTO period. On the other hand, in Pakistan the trade deficit increased from $448 million in the pre-WTO period to $1034 million in the launching years. But, during the post-WTO period it came down to $747 million. The only South Asian country which is benefited is Srilanka. The net trade has increased from $29 million to $144 million and then to $202 million in the corresponding period.

From these, it is very clear that South Asian countries except Sri Lanka have not benefited anything from the implementation of AoA, because developing countries failed to bargain properly in the UR and developed countries succeeded in securing the balance of AoA in their favour.

Now let us discuss in detail what happened to Indian agriculture because of the implementation of agreements on agriculture by analyzing some important aspects of Indian Agriculture.

WTO AND EXPORT OF INDIAN AGRICULTURAL PRODUCTS

Our performance on export front is very poor because of low level of output and tough market conditions added by the policy of protectionism adopted by developed countries (K. Ramachandran, 2005). The prices of agricultural commodities in the international market show a declining trend, while the costs of primary commodity move up due to various reasons like rising price of seeds, fertilisers etc. The following table gives a detailed view about the price movement of primary commodities in the global market between 1980 and 1998.

Table 3
Trend of Primary Commodity Prices in the Global Market (US $/MT)

Year	*Commodities*				
	Wheat	*Rice*	*Sugar*	*Cotton*	*Tea*
1980	240	571	877	2843	2305
1990	136	271	277	1819	2058
1995	149	269	246	1785	1249
1998	121	293	189	1389	1968

Source: World Bank Report in Ranjit Singh Ghuman P. 186.

It is very clear from table 1 that the price of wheat has decreased from $240 per metric tonne in 1980 to $121 per metric tonne in 1998. The price of rice has declined from $571 to $293, sugar from $877 to $819, cotton from $2843 to $389 and tea from $2305 to $1968 between these two periods. Certainly, it is highly disadvantageous to Indian agriculture.

The fall in the international price is mainly due to heavy domestic subsidy given by developed countries. In developed countries, the subsidies given are more than what the farmers produced. For example in the USA in 2001-02, some 25,000 cotton farmers received $4 billion of aid to produce a crop valued at only $3 billion (The Hindu, 30.4.2004). The annual agricultural subsidies in OECD countries have increased from US $246.2 billion during 1986-88 to 282.78 billion in 1999 against the Indian subsidy of $1.06 billion. The per farmer subsidy in the USA has increased from $17,000 in 1986-88 to $ 21,000 in 1999 while in India the subsidy rates are only $11 and $66 respectively. The per hectare subsidy in Japan was $10,048 in 1986-88 and in India it was only $8 but it increased to $11,792 in Japan against $53 in India in 1999. In Illinois, the average income of a farmer in 2002 was $37,000, out of which $16,000 came from government farm subsidies. In France, a subsidy rate of $ 23,000 is given for each acre where the farmers grow beet root in. In short, in India agricultural subsidies just stood about 3 to 6 per cent of the total output as compared to 72 per cent in Japan, 27 per cent in the USA, and 37 per cent in EU. While the farmers in the developed countries are insured against any uncertainty in the price fall, in India the farmers are unable to get any assured reasonable price for their commodities. The procurement price of rice is frozen at the 2002 level of Rs. 6.10 for a kg. It means that each dollar could buy more than 7 kg of rice (Devinder Sharma, 2004) Domestic prices of many crops in comparison to cost is very low and the magnitude and severity of the crisis created by the fall in the price due to indiscriminate import of agricultural products has been direct, unbearable, debilitating and fatal. Thousands of farmers in India lost their livelihoods as a result of increased unfair competition caused by dumped products in their markets in the post WTO period.

Further, the export competitiveness of Indian agricultural products especially wheat is not in favour of India. The increasing cost structure of wheat affect the viability of wheat exports. The competitiveness of Indian wheat in the international market has been worked out and given in the following table.

Table 4
Export Competitioners of Indian Wheat during 1991–1999

Year	*Ratio of Indian Wheat cost to US Wheat Price*
1991 – 92	1.11
1992 – 93	1.22
1993 – 94	1.32
1994 – 95	1.25
1995 – 96	0.90
1996 – 97	1.19
1997 – 98	1.64
1998 – 99	1.71

Source: Amar S.Guleria and Nagesh Singh p.155.

Table 5
Export of major Agricultural Commodities during 1993–94 to 1999–2000
(In Tonnes)

Year	*Wheat*	*Ground-nut*	*Raw Cotton & Waste*	*Basmati rice*	*Cashew*	*Spice*	*Non-Basmati rice*	*Pulses*
1993 – 94	390	254207	312558	527227	74842	18233	565187	43601
1994 – 95	86628	51123	70753	442125	76897	154954	448495	50507
1995 – 96	632468	117933	33281	373314	70068	203729	540699	61355
1996 – 97	1145898	148780	269584	523157	6885	222086	198904	55216
1997 – 98	1517	245401	157534	593323	76902	230531	1795743	168052
1998 – 99	1763	58326	41960	597793	77277	209828	4365888	104096
1999 - 00	20	73244	16750	606468	92461	195793	1216681	182228

Source: Ajit Kumar Sinha p. 348.

The above table clearly indicates that the competitiveness of Indian wheat is not in favour of Indian agriculture except only in 1995–96. It is significant to observe that the competitiveness after WTO is more disadvantageous than pre WTO period. Because of these incompetitiveness, the export of Indian agricultural commodities like wheat, groundnuts and raw cotton declines, the export of commodities like Basmati rice, Cashew, non- Basmati rice and spices stagnates and the export of commodities like pulses shows an increase. These can be understood from table 5.

From table 3 it is clear that export of wheat has decreased from 632468 tonnes in 1995-96 to 20 tonnes in 1999-2000. The same is observed in groundnuts and raw cotton. This declining tendency in export is reflected in the share of agro-exports in India's total exports which is illustrated in table 6.

Table 6
Share of Agro -Exports in India's Total Exports and Annual Percentage Charge

Year	*Percentage Share*	*Annual Percentage*
1990 - 91	19.40	29.47
1991 - 92	18.68	30.25
1992 - 93	17.61	14.93
1993 - 94	18.66	37.68
1994 - 95	16.57	5.30
1995 - 96	19.87	34.15
1996 - 97	20.40	14.67
1997 - 98	19.53	4.8
1998 - 99	18.47	2.93
1999 - 00	15.08	-6.06
2000 - 01	-	-
2001 - 02	13.4	-

Source: Economic Surveys of India in MD. Abdus Salam & K. Ramachandran.

The share of India's agro-exports in her global exports has declined from 19.2 per cent in 1995-96 to 13.4 per cent in 2001-02. It is also observed that the annual growth of agro-export has declined from 54.15 per cent in 1995-96 to 14.67 per cent in 1996-97, 2.93 in 1998-99 and -6.06 per cent in 1999-00. It is very clear that in export, Indian agriculture is negatively affected rather than positively.

GROWTH OF AGRICULTURAL PRODUCTION AND PRODUCTIVITY

Because of free import in the WTO regime, agricultural goods are available at a cheaper rate. It affects domestic farmers adversely in the form of fall in the growth of production and productivity of principal crops and thereby fall in the income of farmers. The growth of agricultural production experienced a fall in the nineties when compared with the eighties. The rate of growth of crop agriculture per annum was 3.4 per cent in the eighties. But it decreased to 2.2 per cent in the nineties. Food grains production has declined from 2.9 per cent to 2.0 between the two periods. In the same way cereals, rice, pulses etc declined while the production of wheat shows a stagnation. The rate of growth of productivity is also not favourable. The productivity of principal crops has fallen down from 2.56 per cent per annum in the eighties to 1.31 in the nineties. The rates are 2.74 per cent and 1.52 for grains, 3.19 and 1.27 for rice, 3.10 and 2.11 for wheat, and 4.10 and 0.61 for cotton. The productivity per worker in the agro based industries grew at the rate of 6.2 per cent during the pre WTO period (1984–85 to 1994–95) but it was only 1.5 per cent during the post WTO period (1994-95–2000–01) (Sekhar, 2003). From these, it is very clear that Indian agriculture in terms of production and productivity is not performing satisfactorily in the post WTO period.

Table 7
Capital Formation in Agriculture (at 1993–94 Prices)

Year	*Total Investment (Rs. In Crore)*	*Public Investment Rs in Crore*	*Per cent*
1993 – 94	13,523	4467	33.0
1994 – 95	14,969	4947	33.0
1995 – 96	15,690	4849	30.9
1996 – 97	16,176	4668	28.9
1997 – 98	15,942	3979	25.0
1998 – 99	14,895	3869	26.9
1999 – 00	16,582	4112	24.8
2000 – 01	16,545	4007	24.2

Source: Statistical Outline of India (2000-03) in Baij Nath Singh.

PUBLIC SECTOR INVESTMENT IN AGRICULTURE

Investment in agriculture by public sector shows a declining trend though the total investment increased slightly. In absolute term the total investment in agriculture has increased from Rs. 15,690 crore in 1995–96 to Rs. 16545 crore in 2000–01 after a fall in 1998–99. While the public investment in agriculture has decreased from Rs. 4849 crore in 1995–96 to Rs. 4007 crores in 2000-01. In percentage term it has decreased from 30.9 per cent to 24.2 per cent between these two periods. (K. Ramachandran, 2005). The table given above clearly explains the real facts about capital formation in agriculture during 1993–94 & 2000–01.

It is very clear from the above table that the public sector investment has fallen very sharply during the post WTO period though there was a slight increase during 1999–00. It is also observed that the share of public sector Gross Fixed Capital Formation in agriculture has come down to 5.8 per cent in 2000–01 from 7 per cent in 1995–96. The rate of growth of investment in agriculture and its allied sub sectors fell steeply from 3.19 per cent per annum from 1991-92 to 1995-96 to a very low level of 1.13 per cent during the post WTO period.

Because of the serious challenges faced by the Indian farmers from both within and outside, they are forced either to shift from their traditional farming activity or to end their lives. Many farmers are seeking jobs either in other rural areas or in cities. Many others starved and some others committed suicide. The areca farmers in Karnataka now receive less than half of the income in comparison with what they received in 1999 when the quantitative restriction on import of areca nut was lifted. Tea plantation workers in Kerala starved and committed suicide due to closure of estates (Sree Devi Jacob, 2003). In Andhra Pradesh nearly 3000 farmers committed suicide due to poverty and indebtedness (W. Chandrakanth 2004).

Unless proper steps are taken to divert Indian agriculture in the proper direction, Indian farmers will not be relieved of their sufferings. It is worthwhile to consider the following suggestions to ameliorate the sufferings of the poor farmers.

1. The Productivity in India which is only half of Chinese productivity, should be increased at least to the world level of 2.8 tonnes per hectare from the present level of 1.9 tonnes per hectare. For that India requires huge investment and so the public investment should be increased considerably.
2. Steps should be taken to remove or at least to reduce the subsidy given by developed countries to their farmers. At the same time proper subsidy and insurance protection must be given to Indian farmers who suffer a lot due to very low procurement prices.
3. Emphasis must be given to products of agro processing industries whose products have very good demand in the international market.
4. If necessary product wise policy must be formulated and implemented. An effective system of market intelligence and research on agricultural exports should also be developed.
5. Quality maintenance or standardisation of Indian agricultural commodities is a prerequisite for export promotion under Agreement on Sanitary and Phytosanitary Measures. Hence measures should be taken to standardise Indian agricultural products especially products having good scope in the foreign market.

BIBILIOGRAPHY

Chadha G.K. (Ed.) (2003), WTO & The Indian Economy, Deep & Deep, New Delhi.

Chand, Ramesh & Bathla, Seema (2003), 'WTO, Agriculture Negotiations and South Asian countries" South Asia Economic Journal, 6,1 January-July.

Chandra Kanth W., "Farmers Reeling under Free Market Forces", The Hindu 11.6.2004, p. 12.

Jaiswal, A.K. (2003), "WTO Agreement on SPS, "Economic and Political Weekly, November 8.

Kumarsingh, Ravishankar (Ed.) (2004), Economic Reforms in India, Abhijeet Publishers, Delhi.

Madaan, Devinder Kumar (2003), "WTO and Indian Agricultural Development: A case study of Punjab", The Indian Economic Journal January-March. 50, 3 & 4.

Mathur, Vibha (2002), Indian Economy and the WTO New Challenges and Strategies, New Century Publication, New Delhi.

Misra, S.K. & Puri V.K. (2002), Indian Economy Himalaya Publishing House, New Delhi.

Narasaiah, M.L. (2001), World Trade Organisation and the Developing Countries, Discovery Publishing House, New Delhi.

Raghavan, Chakravarthi "A fresh Trade In Security at WTO" The Hindu, 3.5.2004.

Ramachandran, Sushma "WTO meet/Three Pillars of Negotiations, Progress on Agriculture Agreement", the Hindu, 22.06.2004.

Rao C.H. Hanumantha, "Saving small farmers", The Hindu 11.06.2004. p. 10.

Rao, M.B. and Guru Manjula, WTO and International Trade, Vikas Publishing House, New Delhi 2003.

Reddy P. Indrasena and Reddy K. Krishna (2003), "WTO and competitiveness of Indian Agricultural Exports - A study" Indian Journal of Marketing, November.

Reddy V. Ratna & Reddy P. Prudhvikar (2003), "Domestic Policies in the Context of Trade Liberlisation" Indian Journal of Agricultural Economics, July-September, 58, 3.

Sharma, P.V. (2001), Emerging Issues of Indian Economic Development, Kanishka Publishers, New Delhi.

Sharma Devinder (2004), "WTO and Agriculture" Economic and Political Weekly, May 15.

Sekhar, C.S.C. (2003), "Agricultural Trade Liberlisation: Likely Implications for Rice Sector in India". Indian Journal of Agricultural Economics, October-December, 58, 4.

Venkatramani, G., "Diet Transition may hit Small Farmers", The Hindu, 07.05.2004, p. 14.

"WTO Strike Against Farm Subsidies" The Hindu, April 30, 2004, p. 10.

ESTIMATION OF SOME DEMOGRAPHIC PARAMETERS OF BANGLADESH USING 1991 CENSUS

Md. Rafiqul Islam & M. Korban Ali

INTRODUCTION

In a country, the success of a national plan and researches depend on the correct information about the population parameters based on national data. There are several agencies, organizations and researchers who have been providing the information about the population parameters of Bangladesh. But, few of them give information on national based. Since in a developing country like Bangladesh, vital registration system has not been started yet. So, most of the sources have been providing indirect techniques. Consequently, indirect techniques have been increasing demand to estimate population parameters from very few limited and defected data. There have been developed several indirect techniques in the last few decades. Widowhood Method is one of them. Hill (1975, 1977) has devised Widowhood Method to estimate adult mortality from widowhood information. Using the marital status data of Bangladesh Census 1974, estimation of male adult mortality from female widowhood information have been estimated by Widowhood Method (Kabir and Mosleh, 1989). Demographic parameters of Bangladesh have also been estimated by Widowhood Method based on the marital status from 1981 Census (Ali, 1990). In this study, using this method, an effort has been made to estimate some demographic parameters of Bangladesh only for both sexes using 1991 Census (BBS, 1994). So, the main objectives of the present study are:

(i) to estimate life expectancy at birth, ASDRs, CDR and CBR for both sexes,

(ii) to fit some mathematical models to age structure and ASDR for both sexes of Bangladesh in 1991.

METHODS AND MATERIALS

Sources of Data

To fulfill the above objectives of this study, age structure for both sexes, male and female marital status of 1991 census (BBS, 1994) has been used as raw data in this study. For linking infant mortality, child mortality and adult mortality at the time of life table construction, l_2 values have been borrowed from Vital Registration System (VRS) data (BBS, 1993).

Construction of Life Table

It is to be noted that for the estimation of ASDRs and life expectancy at birth for both sexes, male and female life tables are to be needed. So, the observed data of male and female marital status have been used to construct life tables.

Male and female adult mortality has been estimated by Widowhood Method (Hill, 1977) using 1991 census data of female and male marital status composition, respectively. For this view, proportion not widowed π_x has been corrected from the proportion not widowed π_x data as $\hat{\pi}_x = \frac{\pi_x}{1+p}$, where p is the proportion of remarriage.

According to (BFS, 1978) widow (female) remarriage in Bangladesh was around 3.8 per cent which is negligible. So, according to the suggestion of Brass (1978) male adult mortality has been estimated without adjusting for widow (female) remarriage. But in Bangladesh widower (male) remarriage was about 11.2 per cent. So, according to the suggestion of Brass (1978) female adult mortality has been estimated after adjusting for widower (male) remarriage. Therefore, proportion not widowed π_x has been converted to the probability of survival ratio using some weighting factors that are given by Hill (1977) corresponding to singulate mean age at marriage (SMAM) for one sex and weighted singulate mean age at marriage (WSMAM) for the other sex. Ultimately these probabilities of survival ratios have been converted to the l_x values for the adult ages corresponding to the representative model life tables in the adult ages.

Infant and child mortality l_2 values for male and female have been taken from BBS data. The l_x values for male and female have been estimated by linking these l_2 values with the adult mortality. For this purpose, a linear function $Y_x = a + b Y_x^s$ is fitted by trial and error method according to Sivamurthy and Sitharam (1980), where Y_x is equal to the logit of l_x and Y_x^s is equal to the logit survival function of l_x^s of standard life table (UN, 1982). Then, Y_x values have been converted to l_x values which is known as the number of persons surviving at an exact age x. The l_x values have been used to construct life tables. These life tables have been constructed and presented in Table 2.

Evaluation and Smoothing of Age Data

To evaluate the secondary data of 1991 Census population U. N. age sex accuracy index, Whipple's index and Myer's index have been calculated and these are found to be 70.41, 317.98 and 36.56 for both sexes. These indices indicate that age distribution for both sexes of 1991 census data is highly inaccurate. For this reason these data need to be adjusted. In this study age structure for both sexes of 1991 census population adjusted for undercount has been smoothed by latest smoothing method named 4253H, twice (Velleman, 1980). Smoothing method has been accomplished using the package Minitab Release 12.1. The adjusted age structure for undercount and smoothed age structure for both sexes of Bangladesh have been presented in Table 1 and depicted in Fig. 1.

Table 1
Observed and Smoothed Population by Age and Their Percentage Distribution of Census Population of Bangladesh for Both Sexes in 1991

Age Group in Years	*Observed Population (000)* *	*Smoothed Population (000)*	*Observed Per cent*	*Smoothed Per cent*
0-4	18695	18695	16.77	16.95
5-9	18391	16660	16.5	15.10
10-14	13442	13618	12.06	12.34
15-19	9500	10818	8.52	9.81
20-24	9365	9333	8.40	8.46
25-29	9471	8393	8.50	7.61
30-34	6797	7199	6.10	6.53
35-39	6149	5904	5.52	5.35
40-44	4734	4749	4.25	4.30
45-49	3627	3786	3.25	3.43
50-54	3224	3037	2.89	2.75
55-59	2015	2414	1.81	2.19
60-64	2379	1844	2.13	1.67
65-69	1168	1370	1.05	1.24
70-74	1242	1013	1.11	0.92
75-79	463	787	0.42	0.71
80+	795	707	0.71	0.64

Source: * [BBS, 1994]

Fig. 1
Observed and Smoothed Percentage Distribution of Population by Age for Both Sexes of Bangladesh in 1991. X: Age Group in Years and Y: Percent Population.

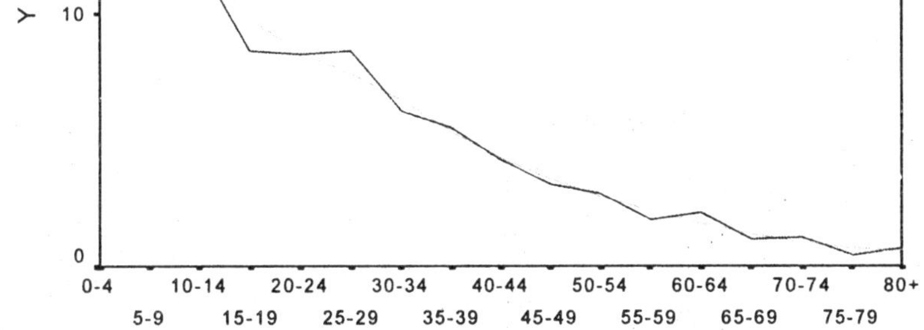

Table 2
An Abridged Life Table for Male and Female of Bangladesh in 1991

Age Group x	Male				Female			
	l_x	$_nd_x$	$_nL_x$	e_x	l_x	$_nd_x$	$_nL_x$	e_x
0	100000	9097	93632	55.13	100000	10493	92655	55.83656
1	90903	2904	89161	59.62	89507	3168	87606	61.34717
2	87999	1476	87261	60.57	86339	1583	85548	62.58348
3	86523	897	86075	60.6	84756	943	84285	62.74302
4	85626	600	85326	59.65	83813	618	83504	62.44332
5	85026	1312	421850	59.06	83195	1299	412728	61.90346
10	83714	575	417133	54.95	81896	553	408098	57.84568
15	83139	691	413968	50.31	81343	771	404788	53.22194
20	82448	819	410193	45.71	80572	927	400543	48.70729
25	81629	1005	405633	41.15	79645	1018	395680	44.2451
30	80624	1243	400013	36.63	78627	1218	390090	39.78558
35	79381	1717	392613	32.16	77409	1460	383395	35.37226
40	77664	2507	382053	27.82	75949	1845	375133	31.00417
45	75157	3718	366490	23.66	74104	2457	364378	26.71385
50	71439	5663	343038	19.77	71647	3724	348925	22.54421
55	65776	7885	309168	16.25	67923	5567	325698	18.64317
60	57891	10787	262488	13.12	62356	8088	291560	15.08439
65	47104	12636	203930	10.56	54268	10499	245093	11.95994
70	34468	12804	140330	8.51	43769	12491	187618	9.229112
75	21664	1886	103605	7.06	31278	3651	147263	6.916395
80+	19778	19778	49445	2.5	27627	27627	69068	2.500018

Note: $L_0 = .3\, l_0 + .7\, l_1$, $L_1 = .4\, l_1 + .6\, l_2$.

Estimation of Mortality Parameters

Various continuous functions of a life table are as follows:

$_nd_x = l_x - l_{x+n}$, $_nq_x = \frac{_nd_x}{l_x}$, $l_{x+n} = l_x\, {_nP_x}$, $_nL_x = \int_0^n l(x+t)$ which can be approximated as $_nL_x = \frac{n(l_x + l_{x+n})}{2}$ $(x \geq 2)$, $T_x = \int_0^\infty l(x+t)\,dt$ which can be approximated as $T_x = \sum_{t=0}^{\infty} L_{x+t}$, $e_x = \frac{T_x}{l_x}$ and ASDR $= \frac{_nd_x}{_nL_x}$ (Barclay, 1958). Two life tables have been briefly constructed and presented in Table 2.

The expectation of life at birth for both sexes has been estimated using the formula $_0^0 = \frac{e_0^f + s\, e_0^m}{1+s}$; e_0^m where, is the expectation of life at birth for male, e_0^f is the expectation of life at birth for female and s is the sex ratio at birth.

The life expectancy at birth for both sexes has been estimated and it is found to be 55.48.

Moreover, ASDRs for both sexes have been estimated using the formula

$$\text{ASDR} = \frac{{}_nd_x^m + {}_nd_x^f}{{}_nL_x^m + {}_nL_x^f}$$

from the constructed life tables and presented in Table 3 and depicted in Fig. 2.

Table 3
Age Specific Death Rates (ASDRs) for Both Sexes of Bangladesh in 1981 and1991

Age Group	*ASDR1991*	*Smoothed ASDR1991*	*ASDR1981**	*Smoothed ASDR1981*
0	0.10516	0.10040	0.14824	0.14392
1	0.03435	0.05183	0.05254	0.075647
2	0.01770	0.02195	0.02761	0.033358
3	0.0108	0.01004	0.01689	0.015873
4	0.00721	0.00575	0.01122	0.00903
5-9	0.00313	0.00323	0.00475	0.004927
10-14	0.00137	0.00186	0.00201	0.00274
15-19	0.00179	0.0017	0.00263	0.002495
20-24	0.00215	0.002	0.00316	0.002939
25-29	0.00252	0.00241	0.00362	0.003463
30-34	0.00311	0.00305	0.0044	0.004252
35-39	0.00409	0.00403	0.00553	0.005442
40-44	0.00575	0.00567	0.00736	0.007276
45-49	0.00845	0.0087	0.01027	0.010484
50-54	0.01357	0.01403	0.01567	0.016022
55-59	0.02119	0.02314	0.02346	0.025177
60-64	0.03407	0.03446	0.03643	0.036699
65-69	0.05152	0.04503	0.0539	0.047827
70-74	0.07713	0.07417	0.07995	0.077779
75-79	0.02207	0.1614	0.04226	0.167331
80+	0.4	0.30861	0.4	0.31875

Source: *[Ali, 1990]

Fig. 2
Age Specific Death Rates (ASDRs) for Both Sexes of Bangladesh in 1981 and1991.

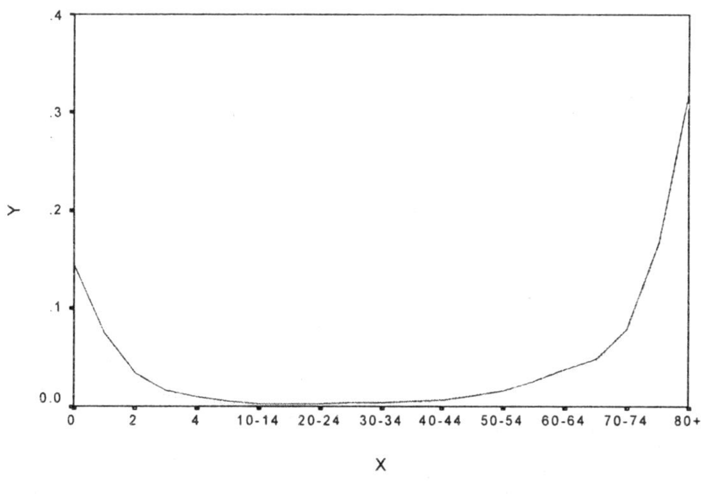

The CDR for both sexes has been estimated using the estimated ASDRs and smoothed age structure for both sexes applying the formula CDR-Σ $ASDR_x C_x$, where C_x is the age structure for both sexes. It is to be found that CDR for both sexes is 14.18.

Mathematical Modeling

Using the scattered plot of ages and population for both sexes (Fig. 3), it is observed that population is modified negative exponentially distributed with respect to ages. Therefore, a modified negative exponential model is considered. The from of the model is

$$y = c + e^{-(a x + b)} + u \text{ (Montgomery, 1982)}$$

where, x represents the age group; y represent population for both sexes; a, b, c are unknown parameters and u is the disturbance term of the model.

Fig. 3

Observed and Fitted Model for Age Distribution of Both Sexes of Bangladesh in 1991. X: Age Group in Years and Y: Population for Both Sexes.

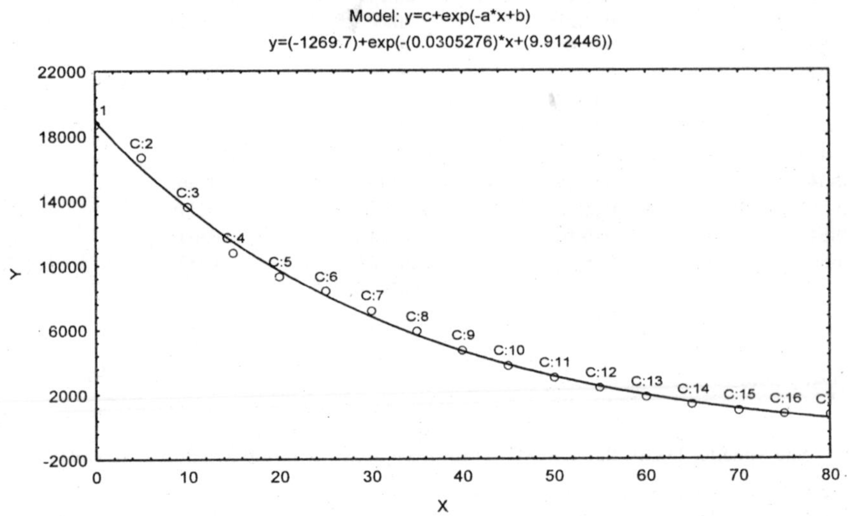

From the dotted plot of ages and ASDRs for both sexes (Fig. 4), it has been seen that ASDRs can be fitted by polynomial for different ages. In this case, an nth degree polynomial model is treated and the model of the nth degree polynomial is

$$y = a_0 + \sum_{i-1}^{n} a_i x^i + u$$

where, x is age group; y is ASDRs for both sexes; a_0 is the constant; a_i is the coefficient of x^i (i =1, 2, 3, ..., n) and u is the disturbance term of the model. Here we have to choose a suitable n for which the error sum of square is minimum.

Using the software STATISTICA, all these models have been estimated.

Fig. 4
Observed and Fitted Model for ASDRs for Both Sexes of Bangladesh in 1991. X: Age Group in Years and Y: ASDRs

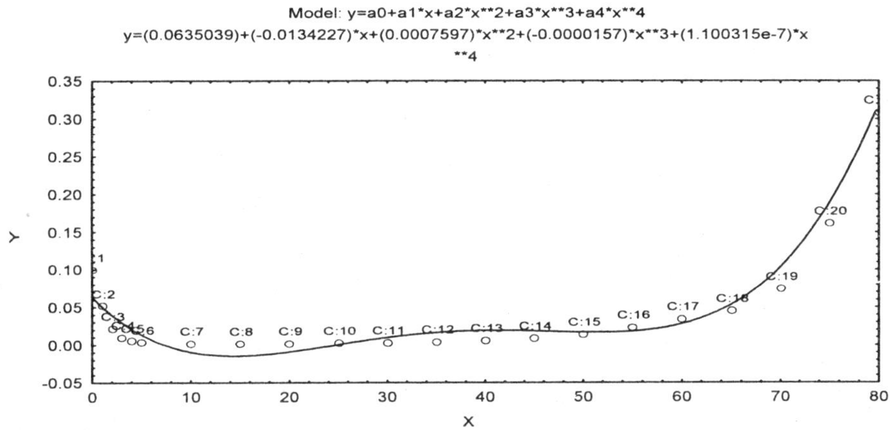

Model Validation

To check how much those models are stable over the population, the cross validity prediction power (CVPT), ρ^2_{cv}, is applied. Here

$\rho^2_{cv} = 1 - \frac{(n-1)(n-2)(n+1)}{n(n-k-1)(n-k-2)}(1-R^2)$; where, n is the sample size or number of cases, k is the number of predictor in the model and the cross-validated R is the correlation between observed and predicted values of the dependent variable (Stevens, 1996).

F-test

To clarify the measure of the overall significance of the model as well as the significance of R^2, the F-test is applied to the model. The F-test is as follows:

$$F = \frac{R^2/(k-1)}{(1-R^2)/(n-k)}$$ with (k-1, n-k) degrees of freedom (d.f.)

where k is the number of parameters to be estimated, n is the number of cases and R^2 is the coefficient of determination in the model (Gujarati, 1998).

Crude Birth Rate (CBR) for Both Sexes

There are various types of measures in fertility. But, in this study, we estimate CBR for both sexes only. Assuming intercensal growth rate between the intercensal period from 1981 to 1991 is equal to the growth rate (r) as in 1991. Now CBR for both sexes has been estimated from the balancing equation CBR = CDR + r assuming the net migration rate is zero. Intercensal growth rate has been estimated using the exponential growth rate formula $P_{t_2} = P_{t_1}$. Since the intercensal growth rate during 1981 to 1991 for both sexes is 24.6 per thousand. So, in 1991 the CBR for both sexes has been estimated as 38.78 per thousand.

RESULTS AND DISCUSSION

The life expectancy at birth for both sexes in 1991 is 55.48. In 1981 the life expectancy at birth for both sexes was 49.08 (Ali, 1990). From the above statistics the present estimates seems to be reasonable, as the developing country like Bangladesh is gaining life expectancy at birth at the rate 0.5 in an year (UN, 1956). Again it is also found that the life expectancy at birth for both sexes in 1991 was 56.1 (BBS, 1993) which is also close to our estimate. Therefore the expectancy at birth for both sexes around 55 or 56 is quite reasonable.

Again the ASDRs for both sexes of Bangladesh in 1991 presented in Table 3 and also in Fig. 2 shows the traditional U shaped pattern. We have compared the ASDRs for both sexes of Bangladesh in 1991 to the ASDRs for both sexes of Bangladesh in 1981 presented also in Table 3 and Fig. 2. From the Fig. 2, ASDRs for both sexes of Bangladesh in 1991 is lower than that of ASDRs for both sexes of Bangladesh in 1981 in each age group. It is found that the lowest ASDR for both sexes are 0.002495 in 1981 and 0.0017 in 1991 in the same age group 15-19. Also two curves are gradually decreasing in the age interval [0,20) and gradually increasing in the age interval [20,50) but rapidly increase in the age interval [50, 80+].

The CDR for both sexes of Bangladesh in 1991 is to be found in the present study as 14.18 but that in 1981 it was 18.01 (Ali, 1990). The rate of decrement of CDR during 1981-1991 is 21.27%.

In our estimate the CBR for both sexes of Bangladesh is 38.78 in 1991 but it was 46.21 for1981 (Ali 1990). The rate of decrement of CBR during 1981-1991 is 16.08%.

Thus the present study conclude that estimates are quite reasonable and the trend of fertility as well as mortality have been indicating a declining pattern.

The fitted equations of this study are as follows:

$$y = -1269.7 + \exp(-0.0305276x + 9.912446) \qquad \text{(i)}$$

$$y = (0.0635039)+(-0.0134227)x+(0.0007597)x^2+(-0.0000157)x^3 +(1.100315e\text{-}7)x^4 \qquad \text{(ii)}$$

It should be noted that the usual models i. e. Gompertz, Makeham and logistic were also applied but seem to be worse fitted with respect to their shrinkages. Therefore, the result of these model were not shown here.

The estimated CVPP, ρ^2_{cv}, corresponding to their R^2 is shown in Table 4. From this table we see that all the fitted models in equations (i) and (ii) are highly cross- validated and their shrinkages are 0.000565, and 0.02459, respectively. These imply that more than 99 % the fitted model (i) will be stable and 93% the fitted model (ii) will be stable. The information on model fitting has been presented in Table 5. From Table 5, it is shown that all the parameters of the fitted models are highly statistically significant with more than 96% of variance explained.

The calculated values of F-test of the models (i) and (ii) are 2585 with (2, 14) d.f. and 103.24 with (4, 16) d.f. respectively where as the corresponding tabulated values are only 6.51 and 4.77 at 1% level of significance, respectively. Therefore, from these statistics it is concluded these models and their corresponding R^2 are highly statistically significance. As a result, these models are good fit.

Table 4
Estimated Cross-Validity Prediction Power, of the Predicted Equations of Age Distribution and ASDR for Sexes of Bangladesh in 1991

Models	*n*	*k*	R^2	r^2_{cv}
Equation (iii)	17	1	0.99731	0.996745
Equation (iv)	21	4	0.96267	0.93808

Table 5
Results on Model Fitting

Models	*Percentage of Variance Explained*	*Parameters*	*Significant Probability (p)*
Model 1	99.73	a	0.000
		b	0.000
		c	0.000
Model 2	96.27	a_0	0.00003
		a_1	0.00002
		a_2	0.0002
		a_3	0.00001
		a_4	0.000003

CONCLUSION

The CBR, CDR, ASDRs and life expectancy at birth for both sexes of Bangladesh have also been estimated from the same source of data. It is to be noted that the method of estimation of the population parameters (e_0^0, ASDRs, CBR, CDR) for very few limited and defective data is likely to be fitted for developing countries like Bangladesh. Age structure and ASDRs for both sexes follow modified negative exponential model and 4th degree polynomial model respectively.

REFERENCES

Ali, K. (1990), Construction of Life Tables and Estimation of Demographic Parameters of Bangladesh, The Rajshahi University Studies Part-B, Vol. 18.

Barclay, G.W. (1958), Techniques of Population Analysis, John Wiley and Sons, Inc.

BBS (1994), Bangladesh Population Census 19991, Vol.1, National Series, Analytical Report, Government of the People's Republic of Bangladesh, Dhaka.

BBS (1993), Statistical Yearbook of Bangladesh of 1992; Government of the Peoples Republic of Bangladesh, Dhaka.

Brass, W. (1978), Indirect Method of Estimating Mortality: Illustrated by the Application to Middle East and North African Data, In ECWA. The Population

Frame Work, Data Collection, Demographic Analysis, Population Development, United Nations.

BFS (1978), First Report on Bangladesh Fertility Survey1975, Ministry of Planning. Government of Bangladesh.

Gujarati, Damodar N. (1998), "Basic Econometric", Third Edition, McGraw Hill, Inc., New York.

Hill, K. (1975), Estimation of Adult Mortality by Indirect Means, Unpublished Ph.D. Thesis, University of London, London.

Hill, K. (1977), Estimation Adult Mortality Levels From the Information on Widowhood, Population Studies. Vol. 31 (i).

Kabir, M. and Mosleh, Uddin M. (1989), Techniques of Demographic Analysis, Society for Project Implementation Research Evaluation and Training, Dhaka.

Montgomery, Douglas C. and Peck, Elizabeth A. (1982), "Introduction to Linear Regression Analysis", John Wiley and Sons, New York.

Velleman, P. F. (1980), Definition and Comparison of Robust Nonlinear Data Smoothing Algorithms, Journal of the American Statistical Association, Volume 75. Number 371, Page 609-615.

Sivamurthy, M. and Sitharam, K. S. (1980), Handbook of Indirect Methods for Mortality Estimation, CDC Occasional Paper, Cairo Demographic Centre, Egypt.

Stevens, J. (1996), Applied Multivariate Statistics for the Social Sciences, Third Edition, Lawrence Erlbaum Associates, Inc., Publishers, New Jersey.

United Nations (1956), Methods for Population Projections by Sex and Age, Department of Economic and Social Affairs, Manual-III, New York.

United Nations (1982), Model Life Tables for Developing Countries, Department of International Economic and Social Affairs, Population Studies, No. 77.

ASIAN URBANIZATION: CERTAIN PUBLIC HEALTH CONSEQUENCES OF URBAN SOCIAL STRESS

M. Asif and Tariq Wali

INTRODUCTION

Given the current wide-scale increasing urbanization the world over, more than half the world's population is projected to live in urban areas by 2008 and more than 60 per cent of it will start living in cities by 2030, up from almost half now and just a third in 1950. As cities boom, natural resources, energy production, land, water, coasts and seas shall, inter alia, face serious risks from this high-paced urbanization.[1] With unpreceded magnitude, most of the urbanization is expected to take place in globalized Asia over the next three decades. Wide spread and indeed ubiquitous urbanization throughout the world is, arguably, a typical 20th century phenomenon. The focus of change is now in Asia where urban population is expected to double in the next 30 years or even earlier crossing the critical 50 per cent mark. Ongoing fast-paced urbanization under the influence of increasing globalization especially in developing countries of Asia is like a twin-edged sword with multiple risks, and consequences of several kinds–socio-medical, cultural, economic, ecological and political. Though visible, in part, like the tip of proverbial iceberg, the bigger picture of still more risks and further consequences of this epochal demographic transition typified by urbanization spurred by globalization shall just come to the surface in phases with increasing intensity, complexity and dimensional variability in the years to come, if not in decades.

Even as the present paper addresses and posits the phenomenon of urbanization in global context with particular reference to Asia, it seeks to review and analyse certain attendant risks, and consequences of urbanization secondary to urban social stress which the authors postulate as an important aetiological risk factor to explain a broad spectrum of human morbidity and certain other social maladies universally found associated with urbanicity.

GLOBAL PERSPECTIVE

Ancient, medieval and modern times have had their share of famous cities. Cain, the son of Adam, as mythology goes, is credited with building the fabled first city. Rome founded in 753 BC was perhaps the first urban settlement to have reached one million population.[2] In 1800, only 2 per cent of the world's population was urbanized. By the year 1900, out of a total world population of close to 1.5 to 1.7 billion, only 15 per cent of it, around 250 million lived and worked in urban areas. By the year 1950, the proportion of urban to total population had risen to 30 per cent, with Europe, North America and Oceania having the highest levels of urbanization. By the year 2000, 2.8 billion people lived in urban areas making approximately 49 per cent of the world's population. While the last century witnessed unprecedented and wide-scale urbanization, the present century, by all means, belongs to Asia in so far as urbanization is concerned. At this point of time, we are at a landmark turning point in human history when far greater expansion and growth in global population shall take place in cities. In fact, cities are now home to nearly half of the world's total population and over three-quarters of the population of high income countries. By 2020, the developing world, as a whole, is likely to have become more urban than rural. The changes under way are not only a matter of percentages, but also of scale. At the beginning of the twentieth century, just 16 cities in the world–the vast majority in advanced industrial economies–contained a million people or more. Today, almost 400 cities are of this size, and about three-quarters of them are found in low- and middle-income countries.[3]

The last 50 years have been truly remarkable in terms of the number of people who have been successfully absorbed in cities in an incredibly short time period by historical standards. While the world's urban population grew by approximately 500 million between 1900 and 1950, it grew by 2.1 billion in the next 50 years; and is expected to grow by a similar magnitude in just the next 30 years. The speed of urbanization in Latin America, in the second half of the 20th century has been spectacular, vaulting from a just over 40 per cent urbanization level to 75 per cent by the end of this period which was also a period of rapid population growth and demographic transition. As may be seen (Table 1) the focus of change is now shifted to Asia.[4]

Table 1
Urban Population Growth across the Globe [4]

Region	*Urban Population*					
	In Millions	*Per Cent of Total*	*In Millions*	*Per Cent of Total*	*In Millions*	*Per Cent of Total*
	1950		*2000*		*2030*	
Africa	32	14.7	295	37.2	787	52.9
Asia	244	17.4	1376	37.5	2679	54.1
Latin America and Carribbean	70	41.9	391	75.4	608	84.0
Oceania	8	61.6	23	74.1	32	77.3
Europe	287	52.4	534	73.4	540	80.5
North America	110	63.9	243	77.4	335	84.5
Increase	501	14.8	2111	17.4	2119	13.0

In the last two centuries, cities have consistently provided the environment for institutional and technological innovation, and have often been referred to as 'engines of economic growth'; 'agents of change' and 'incubators of innovation'. Between 1960 and 2000 world output went up fourfold, while urban population almost tripled, making the world from 33 per cent urban to 47 per cent urban in 40 years (Table 2). A review of the regional dynamics of urbanization reveals interesting developments (Table 3). There has been a dramatic shift of the fulcrum of urban population away from Europe and North America to the developing regions of the world. During the period 1950-2000, the growth rate of urban population in Europe and North America was about 1.5 per cent. The share of Europe and North America in global urban population declined from about 53 per cent in 1950 to 27.5 per cent in 2000 and is expected to decline further to about 17 per cent by 2030. Africa has experienced consistent high growth in its urban population which grew at an annual rate of 4.4 per cent during 1950-2000, and its share in global urban population is expected to rise to 16 per cent by 2030 (from a paltry 4.3 per cent in 1950). Latin America has now become predominantly urban, surpassing urbanization levels in Europe and will almost be at par with North America by 2030.

Table 2
Global GDP and Growth in Urban Population [4]

Index/Parameter	1960	1970	1980	2000
World GDP (constant 1995 $ trillion)	7.9	13.5	19.5	34.3
Share of agriculture in world GDP	-	-	6.5	3.9
Share of industry in world GDP	-	-	38.0	20.8
Share of services in world GDP	-	-	55.5	66.3
World population (mm)	3020	3675	4428	6053
Per cent of urban population	33.3	36.5	39.3	46.7

Table 3
Global Urbanisation Trends [4]

Region	*Level of Urbanisation (per cent)*	
	1920	*2025*
World Total	19	61
Less developed regions	10	57
- Africa	7	54
- Asia	9	55
- Latin America	22	85
More developed regions	40	85
- Europe	46	83
- North America	52	85
- Oceania	47	75

Nearly half of the world today is urban, and the world's urban population is now growing by 60 million persons per year, about three times the increase in the rural population. In 2000, world population reached 6.1 billion, and is continuing to grow at an annual rate of 1.2 per cent, or 77 million people per year. Developing countries are urbanizing at a faster pace than what developed countries had to cope with in the past. The pace of urbanization in developing countries is now expected to be more than double that of developed countries. In 1950, 17 per cent of the population in developing countries was urban; in 2020 this population is expected to grow to 54 per cent.

The urban population in developing countries overtook that in developed countries sometime in the early 1980s. Today the urban population in developing countries is much higher than that in developed countries, leading to intensive demand for resources and skills for the efficient management of cities. This massive urbanization is taking place at much lower income levels than that witnessed in developed countries. This urbanization is also happening in regions which have different energy requirements. The centre of urban population is progressively moving from the predominantly northern latitudes of developed countries to the southern ones of developing countries; that is, the mean latitude of global urban population has been steadily moving south. This is in line with the faster rates of urbanization in developing countries. The potential energy requirements for airconditioning will therefore rise and could well be above those for heating on a per capita basis. Similarly, the requirements for other urban services such as water supply and sanitation, solid waste management and urban public transport will also rise inexorably.[5]

HIGH-PACED ASIAN URBANIZATION

Asia is too vast and heterogeneous a region to yield easily to generalization. Altogether the region contains 3.7 billion people, about three-fifths of the world's population, rising from around 1.4 billion in 1950 and 2.4 billion in 1975. Although population growth rates for Asia as a whole have been declining since the late 1960s, the enormous base populations to which these rates have been applied have resulted in very large increases in the population totals over the past 50 years.

Despite its relatively low level of urbanization (37.5 per cent in 2000), Asia is home to a staggering 1.38 billion urban residents, nearly half of the world's urban population. Since 1950, the region's urban population has increased by more than a factor of five, rising from 244 million in 1950 to 1.38 billion in 2000. By 2030, nearly 53 per cent of Asia's population is expected to be living in urban areas, a substantial increase from the current figure of just over 37 per cent. Dominated statistically by China and India, the region contains almost 200 cities with 1 million or more residents and 22 cities with 5 million or more. The most recent United Nations projections indicate that more than 1.25 billion people will be added to Asia's population by 2030, all of whom will be absorbed in the region's cities and towns. By 2015, 18 of the world's 30 largest megacities will be found in Asia.[6]

In India alone, according to its 2001 census, there are more than 300 cities of over 100,000 population and 35 with more than a million residents. For the most part, the non-Pacific Asian countries have significantly lower levels of GNP per capita than the Pacific Asian countries, but there is considerable diversity within and among countries in their economic and urban characteristics. Relative to some cities in Pacific Asia, urban growth in such cities as Mumbai, Kolkata, Delhi, Karachi, and Dhaka, for example, has probably been fueled less by economic dynamism and more by rural poverty and continued high fertility.[8]

Whereas, by 2030, Asia alone will have about 2.7 billion urban people accounting for over 50 per cent of its total population, all the other regions of the world will have a combined urban population of about 2.3 billion. Six of the 10 countries with the largest urban populations are in Asia. Urbanization in Bangladesh has been among the fastest in the world (5.6 per cent during 1950-2000). The only African country in the top 10 list, Nigeria, has also urbanized very rapidly in the past 5 decades.[9] Interestingly, by 2010, Lagos is projected to become the third largest city in the world.[10]

Moving to city level urbanization trends, the growth of urban agglomerations in developing countries has far exceeded that in developed countries. In 1950, there was only one city with a population of over 10 million people: New York City. In 2000 there were 17 cities with a population above 10 million, 22 cities with population between 5 and 10 million; 402 with a population of 1 to 5 million; and 433 in the 0.5 to 1 million category. As salient feature of urbanization in Asia has been the emergence of mega-cities–large multi-nuclear urban agglomerations of more than 10 million people. There were no such agglomerations in Asia in 1950, just two in 1975 and by 2000, 10 of the 17 global megacities emerged in Asia, and it is expected that 12 out of the 21 global mega cities in the year 2015 will be in Asia.

Of the 21 cities expected to reach 10 million plus in population by 2015, not less than 17 of them will be in developing countries in Asia and will include Dhaka, Mumbai, Delhi, Jakarta, Kolkata, Karachi, Shanghai, Metro Manila, Beijing, Istanbul, Tianjin and Tokyo. Thus, urbanization in Asia is all set to outpace countries in Latin America in the coming decades.

Presently the highest rates of economic growth are being witnessed in Asia, and hence high urban growth. This is particularly noticeable in China and India, which today have the largest rural populations but are urbanizing rapidly.[11]

At the national level, China remains a predominantly rural country with a level of GNP per capita that places it in the lower-middle-income range. But parts of China resemble the rapidly developing Pacific Asian economics. Its coastal region has witnessed very rapid urban and industrial development since 1978, when the government departed from its earlier policy of self-reliance and initiated a new "open policy" designed to attract foreign investment and technology. In the early years of this policy, foreign investment was limited to the four Special Economic Zones (SEZs)–Shenzhen, Zhuhai, Xiamen, and Shantou–which were to serve as testing grounds for a country-wide export-oriented development strategy. Gradually, other special zones have beene stablished. The result has been phenomenal economic growth for these zones and a massive increase in export-led foreign exchange earnings for China as a whole. In Shenzhen, for example, which was chosen as one of the four initial SEZs because of its close proximity to Hong Kong, the value of industrial output in 1987 was almost 70 time its 1980 value, implying an annual rate of growth of 60 per cent per annum. Similarly, Xiamen, located directly opposite the island of Taiwan, has enjoyed extraordinarily rapid export-led growth and industrialization over the last 20 years, thanks in large part to strong ties with overseas Chinese that brought an influx of FDI. Xiamen's gross domestic product (GDP) increased by a factor of 57 between 1980 and 1997, implying an average rate of growth of 23 per cent per annum. Similarly, coastal cities such as Dalian, Guangzhou, Qingdao, and Tianjin have all undergone remarkable transformations over the last 20 years since the government's open policy began.

Table 4
Emergence of Mega Cities [4]

Population of Cities with 10 million or More Inhabitants							
1950		1975		2000		2015	
New York	12.3	Tokyo	19.8	Tokyo	25.2	Tokyo	27.2
		New York	15.9	Sao Paulo	18.3	Dhaka	22.8
		Shanghai	11.4	Mexico city	18.3	Mumbai	22.6
		Mexico	10.7	New York	16.8	Sao Paulo	21.2
		Sao Paulo	10.3	Mumbai	16.5	Delhi	20.9
				Los Angeles	13.3	Mexico City	20.4
				Kolkata	13.3	New York	17.9
				Dhaka	13.2	Jakarta	17.3
				Delhi	13.0	Kolkata	16.7
				Shanghai	12.8	Karachi	16.2
				Buenos Aires	12.1	Lagos	16.0
				Jakarta	11.4	Los Angeles	14.5
				Osaka	11.0	Shanghai	13.6
				Beijing	10.8	Buenos Aires	13.2
				Rio de Janerio	10.8	Metro Manila	12.6
				Karachi	10.4	Beijing	11.7
				Metro Manila	10.1	Rio de Janerio	11.5
						Cairo	11.5
						Istanbul	11.4
						Osaka	11.0
						Tinajin	10.3

In Shanghai, the transformation is more recent but perhaps even more striking. For long the largest industrial city and the economic powerhouse of socialist China, Shanghai hade been one of the 14 cities designated open in 1984. The city initially experienced relatively modest growth, lagging well behind Guangdong, Fujian, and other parts of Southern China. The pace of urban development in Shanghai picked up after 1990, when the central government announced the development of Pudong New Area, a large area of agricultural and marginal land east of the central city. Since 1991, the growth of FDI in the city has been nothing short of astonishing. In 1985, Shanghai attracted US$759 million in FDI. By 1996, this figure had increased to $ 15.14 billion. The city is now being dramatically restructured.[12]

Even in other Asian countries where a large number of cities are witnessing high rates of economic growth, the growth in their urban population is also going to be higher. Of the 10 most populous countries, six are in Asia (Table 5). Even as more than two billion people will be added to Asia's population in the next 30 years, many of these countries will still be rapidly urbanizing. Rural population in Asia is expected to decline, in absolute terms, during 2000-2030 (yet another unprecedented historical event),whith urban population becoming double during the same period.

Table 5
Out of the 10 Most Populous Countries Six are Asian [4]

Country	*1950*		*2000*		*2030*	
	Urban Per cent	*Population (mn)*	*Urban Per cent*	*Population (mn)*	*Urban Per cent*	*Population (mn)*
China	12.5	555	35.8	1275	59.5	1485
India	17.3	357	29.0	1009	40.9	1409
US	64.2	158	77.2	283	84.5	358
Brazil	36.5	54	81.2	170	90.5	226
Indonesia	12.4	79	41.0	212	63.7	283
Nigeria	10.1	30	44.1	114	63.6	220
Pakistan	17.5	40	33.1	141	48.9	273
Mexico	42.7	28	74.4	99	81.9	135
Japan	50.3	84	78.8	127	84.8	121
Bangladesh	4.3	42	25.0	137	44.3	223

The pattern of urbanization seen in retrospect suggests that countries tend to urbanise very slowly until they a core attain urbanization level of around 25 to 30 per cent. The pace of economic growth and overall development then accelerates, with rapid structural shifts occurring in the economy, away from agriculture to industry and services. The pace of urban growth between urbanization levels of 25 to 30 per cent and 55 to 60 per cent has typically been observed to take place in a very short historical time frame of 25 to 50 years. This happened in European countries and North America at different times in the late 19th century and early 20th century, and in Latin America during the latter half of the 20th century. During this rapid phase of urbanization, the demand for urban infrastructure investment is massive and countries have usually been observed to need external savings to supplement available domestic resources to finance such investment. So far, the world has been able to somehow cope with such demands as the scene of urbanization has shifted from one region to another and the overall magnitude of increase in urban population has been manageable. What is new in the next 25 to 30 years is that three of the world's most populous countries, China, India and Indonesia, with a combined total population of about 2.5 billion will be undergoing this rapid process simultaneously, with Pakistan and Bangladesh not much far behind. The magnitude of the vertical increase in urban population in Asia in this period will be so swift that it will inevitably generate unforeseen problems as well as opportunities.[13]

India's urbanization has also been linked with economic growth in the 1990s. It appears that cities and states with faster industrialization and economic growth are indeed growing faster. From about 23 per cent of India's population being urban in 1981, this ratio increased to 29 per cent in 2001. Correspondingly, while India's industrial and service sectors contributed about 70 per cent of GDP in 1981, by 2001, these sectors accounted for just under 80 per cent of India's GDP. At the sub-national level, the more urbanized states such as Tamil Nadu, Maharashtra and Karnataka have recorded higher growth rates. Further, at the city level in India, larger cities in these faster growing states have grown rapidly–Chennai in Tamil Nadu (manufacturing and services), Bangalore in Karnataka (industries, services, information technology), Hyderabad in Andhra Pradesh (information technology), Pune in Maharashtra (manufacturing and services), and Chandigarh and Ludhiana in Punjab (manufacturing and services).[14]

URBANIZATION AND GROWTH OF SLUMS

Rapid mushrooming of squatter settlements on land pockets may be seen as a usual fallout of urbanization. The factors identified for the formation and growth of squatter settlements are poverty, absence and inadequacy of urban planning, migration, economic development of city, shortfall in existing housing stock, political reasons, refugee influx and other miscellaneous spatio-demographic reasons. While in Africa, rural-to-urban migration rates have declined over the three decades (sixties to eighties) in last century, the Asian trend is in the opposite direction : migration rate is low but rapidly increasing. In Latin America, the decline in migration began in the 1980s thus being, perhaps, a reflection of the economic crises of that decade.[15]

Slums, by definition, are heavily congested residential settlements in which satisfactory family life is impossible owing mainly to bad housing. Intrinsic to slums' own typical characteristics are overcrowding, general deterioration, insanitary conditions, absence of facilities and amenities, pollution and human abuse with devasting effects and consequences endangering public health, safety and morals.

Though problem of collection of global data on squatter settlements still eludes us, the picture in this particular area even in India is largely sketchy and inadequate. In India, slum census results are not available and for the first time, Union Ministry of Urban Employment and Poverty Alleviation is planning to ask the Registrar General to conduct a survey in all towns with population above 20,000 to get the exact data on people living in slums. Though the 2001 Census tried to collate certain information from states, there seem to be bizarre outcomes. Lucknow, for instance, registered as slum free even though Ministry is implementing slum-directed programmes in that state capital. Even Varanasi, Allahabad and Agra too did not report slums. In all, just 607 towns apparently reported slums. Slum census needs to cover 5,161 towns to reveal numbers of their slum dwellers there estimates indicates that 61.8 million people live in slums[16] Earlier reports indicated slum population in Kolkatta, Greater Mumbai, Delhi and Chennai as 43.8, 41.2, 32 and 21 lakhs in 1990-91 respectively. The same figures in 1981 were 32.8, 28.3, 18 and 13.6 lakhs respectively[17].

It may be stated that slums represent the worst of urban poverty, squalor, inequality and human misery with varied socio-economic, cultural, social, and public health dimensions related thereto. Globally, almost 1 billion people live in slums, the majority in the developing world where over 40 per cent of the urban populations are slum dwellers. Dharavi in Mumbai is the filthiest and largest slum in the world, where a captive population suffers in silence from all known dimensions of human misery. Being a typical mega-slum, it has been commented that for every centimeter of vertical poshness of the metropolitan city, there are 20 centimeters of horizontal filth. There are certain areas with garbage heaps as high as buildings nearby.[18]

The steep rise in slum growth has led to grave threats mainly to the environment, law and order and to public health besides hopelessly changing the landscape of the Indian cities, particularly metropolitan cities. To make the matter worse, squatter settlements did emerge in open spaces that were reserved for public parks, traffic routes and land marked for health and educational institutions [19].

Another study on slum population in Delhi suggested that compared to general population growth, slum population was growing at a faster rate calculated as 55 per cent per annum[20].

MAJOR RISKS AND CONSEQUENCES OF URBANIZATION

As the demographic trends unfold, the contours of urban life in almost all countries of Asia must needs be in a flux. The world is in the midst of an epochal change characterized by an ongoing fundamental economic restructuring towards ever escalating pace of urbanization, driven by globalization and the revolution in information and communication technology which in turn, impinge upon practically all spheres of human life. The magnitude of the expected increase in urban population over the next 30 years in Asia will be so rapid that it will be equivalent to the increase that took place over the last 50 years[21]. And herein lies the crux of the problem besting Asian urbanization.

The sheer speed, scale and complexity of this radical change present many challenges. Of particular concern are its varied implications and widespread ramification involving, *inter alia*, the risks to the physical environment and natural resources, to health and human well being, to social cohesion and human behaviour, and to individual rights within and across the nations. Of immediate concern is, however, the massive increase expected in the absolute numbers of the urban poor with all consequent evils and ill effects that create the miasma of urban poverty.

As cities grow and evolve, certain other paramount challenges come up like ensuring adequate urban infrastructure, its improvisation and upgradation, infrastructure investment, city management, and governance with shifted emphasis now on local government. Appropriate macro economic policies that are in tune with the rising urban demands must alone remain relevant and useful. In view of the huge challenges facing urbanizing Asia, her cities demand appropriate shifts in the national macro economic policies to ensure raising of infrastructure investment as well as facilitating fresh approach to modern planning and professional management of cities including development of effective mechanisms for crisis/disaster management.

At the second European Conference on Environment and Health held in Helsinki in June 1994, urban health was accorded a high priority. Rapid rate of urbanization brings in its wake the increasing number of environmental, economic, and social problems, that adversely affect health and well-being of city dwellers. There is a growing body of evidence on the non-medical determinants of health and disease[22]. In view of a majority of the world's population that will inhabit urban areas by 2007, two key dimensions have been suggested (i) urbanization which refers to change in size, density and heterogeneity of cities and (ii) urbanicity which refers to the impact of living in urban areas at a given time. A review of published literature suggested that most of the important factors that affect urban health can be considered within three broad themes : the social environment, the physical environment, and access to health and social services/support[23]. Moreover high prevalence disorders like anxiety, depression and substance abuse are generally known to be more common in urban than rural dwellers. Available data suggest that a variety of socio-demographic factors are often more powerful predictors of difference in prevalence than is the location of residence. In another study, influences of residential conditions in a megacity on the health levels of residents were investigated. Correlations between morbidity and specified residential-condition indictors in study areas randomly selected from the megacity Tokyo were examined. Indicators representing housing and city planning were significantly correlated with mortalities after adjusting for socio-economic differences between the communities. Urbanization upto a certain level seems to have been associated with good health: however, the most densely developed artificial urban environment seems to be associated with negative health outcomes[24]. A similar study indicted that rapid and unplanned urban growth is often associated with poverty, environmental degradation and population demands that outstrip service capacity. These conditions place human health at risk[25].

TELL-TAIL PATTERNS OF URBAN HEALTH – THE ROLE OF URBAN STRESS

Health is both an outcome and a determinant of economic development and in this way must be associated with urbanization. But while considering health in cities, can one identify a distinctive urban health profile? The concept of an epidemiological or health transition provides a starting point for discussion of this issue. Health transition is expressed as a shift from a situation in which communicable diseases are the primary causes of morbidity and mortality to one in which noncommunicable diseases predominate. It is now well-known that, the health transition is well under way in some cities, especially in the developing countries that have relatively high levels of per capita income. As the transition proceeds, urban population tends to experience relatively more chronic diseases, including cancers and heart disease; mental health will also be of growing concern. In addition to such long-standing challenges to health, some cities will face grave threats from new diseases (e.g. HIV/AIDS) and diseases that are reemerging with heightened virulence or resistance (e.g. tuberculosis and MDR tuberculosis).

The spatial proximity of urban residents and their reliance on common public resources render them more vulnerable to communicable health threats than are rural residents, who enjoy a measure of protection owing to their spatial dispersion. This "urban penalty" was first observed in the Victorian era when city dwellers died at higher rates than their rural counterparts despite their greater average incomes, but it has been in force throughout most of human history. It was only when urban population had begun to be protected by public health investment and when advances in the understanding of disease had progressed to the point that higher income could purchase effective treatments that urban population could achieve higher levels of health on average. The urban advantage that we now take for granted is a recent and possibly fragile development. Nothing locks this advantage into place. To prove our point, there must be evidence of a reemergent urban penalty. It is increasingly becoming evident that the characteristics of urban life may be expressed in health outcomes and the distribution of illness. Poverty, environment, and psycho-social problems may lead to specific psycho-somatic and other diseases or health conditions that are more common particularly in urban areas, including sexually transmitable diseases (STDs), accidents, obesity and mental disorders. In Latin America, health transition has generally appeared first in urban locations and has tended to proceed more rapidly in countries with higher levels of urbanization. A link to urbanization is seen in studies of other developing regions as well. These studies document consistently higher urban rates of cardiovascular disease, cancers, coronary heart disease, and accidents with higher rural rates of malaria malnutrition, maternal, mortality, and respiratory diseases. Evidently, urban and rural health profiles do differ. The reasons why they differ are of course complex, stemming from the many environmental, socioeconomic, and cultural changes that are associated with urbanization. Lower rates of communicable disease and urban advantages in child survival can be linked to lower urban fertility, better immunization coverage, and easier access to and greater use of health services. As communicable diseases begin to decline in urban areas, noncommunicable diseases (including the so-called "diseases of affluence") and diseases associated with social instability can be expected to rise in relative importance, particularly among adults. The growing impact of mental ill-health, violence, accidents and chronic disease is evident in disability-adjusted life year (DALY) predictions.

At least, 65 percent of the teenage pregnancies according to one study[27] were reported to have taken place in urban settings. Low birth weight (LBW) babies are mostly born to women of low socio-economic status and large number of LBW babies' birth is reported from urban slums especially in Asian countries.

Similarly, gender roles and relations put men and women at risk of different types of violence. Higher rates of homicide are reported for men, but rape and domestic violence rates are higher for women. Heise *et al* (1994) reviewed community based data for eight urban areas from different regions of the developing world and found that mental and physical abuse of women by their partners was common with damaging consequences for women's physical and psychological well-being[28].

It has been predicted that by 2030, depression, traffic accidents, and heart diseases will be the leading burdens of disease in developing countries overall, replacing the 1990 leaders, which were respiratory disease, diarrhea, and perinatal conditions[29]. And by 2020 unipolar depression is expected to account for the greatest burden of disease in developing countries. A diverse set of risk factors is implicated, including lack of control over resources, changing marital patterns and increased single parenthood and divorce rates, cultural ideology, long-term chronic stress exposure to stressful life events, and lack of social support. Anxiety and depression are typically more prevalent among urban women than men and more prevalent in poor than in nonpoor urban neighborhoods[30].

Urbanization is one of the most important demographic shifts worldwide during the last century and represents a substantial change from how most of the world's population has lived for the past several thousand years. A growing body of evidence has come to the fore showing that the characteristics of the urban environment, *ipso facto,* affects population health[31]. In the United States itself, concerns are being raised to reduce the disproportionate burden of illness and poor health borne by urban populations. Patterns of immigration, migration, change in the global economy and sharpening of income inequalities were identified as having a direct bearing upon urban health[32].

In developing countries, rapid urbanization is accompanied by diverse health problems including psychiatric complaints and disorders like anxiety, depression, insomnia, fatigue, irritability and poor memory that account for 90 percent of all mental disorders causing behavioral problems in offsprings and impede recovery from co-morbid physical ailments. Those who suffer most from common mental disorders include women, those between 15 and 49 years old and low income populations. Strong links have been established between socio-environmental factors and common mental disorders, and an urban environment has been associated with many possible risk factors for such morbidities[33]. A recent Finnish study on attempted suicides in urban settings established that socio-economic disadvantage was associated with higher rates of attempted suicide[34]. Similarly, a 2003 longitudinal study on 4.5 million Swedish population statistically proved that place of birth, socio-economic status and sex are associated with attempted suicide[35]. Again, in a longitudinal path-breaking study on 4.5 million Swedish people, it was proved that a high level of urbanization is indeed associated with increased risk of psychosis and depression for both women and men aged 25 to 64 years. Findings were attributed to adverse living circumstances amongst urban population[36].

Extensive research has been undertaken regarding the role of stress in the aetiology of many physical illnesses and fresh evidence in this area is being brought to light. Psycho-neuro-immunology offers many findings that are in favour of stress implicated in the development of physical and psychiatric ailments. Although the aetiological role played by stress in cardiovascular diseases, a number of gastro-intestinal dysfunctions and disorders, many dermatological conditions and some malignancies is of greater importance; it is also a determinant to affect the course and outcome of many other conditions including even infectious diseases[37]. Akin to early onset of premature graying of hair seen today, pre-menopausal symptoms being increasingly reported even at an early age of 30 years are attributed to urban life style, stress and exposure to pollutants[38]. Moreover as a counter part of premenopausal syndrome (PMS) seen in middle-aged ladies, a new irritable male syndrome (IMS) has been identified recently. It has been defined as a state of male hypersensitivity, anxiety, frustration and anger that occurs in males and is associated with hormonal fluctuations, stress and loss of male identity[39]. Lately, the changing gender roles in metropolitan cities has given rise to what is known as metro sexual male who on account of his inability to cope with and negotiate changing gender roles feels over stressed and becomes prone to violence against women and young ladies[40].

Though globally from 1950 to 1995, in persons of all ages, suicide rates have increased by approximately 35 percent in man and only 10 percent in women (www.who.int/whosis), suicide rates are increasing in many Asian countries. In India, the number of reported suicide during 2001 was 1,08,506; in 2002, it rose to 1,10,417. In 2003, 1,10,851 people committed suicide, which comes around 304 person ending their lives per day. Japan's grim reputation as one of the suicide capitals of the world was confirmed lately with a record of 34,427 suicides in 2003 breaking its own previous record of 33,048 in 1999. After varying for many years between 20,000 to 24,000 suicide cases per annum, the number of self harm cases in Japan rose dramatically by 35 per cent following the Asian economic crash of 1997-98 and it has stayed above 30,000 ceiling set ever since[41]. A very recent Japanese Health Ministry report highlight over 30,000 cases of child abuse and neglect (CAN) during April 2004 to March 2005 compared to 6,400 cases reported in last year.

More recently, a British study has shown that the stress of modern living for the first time resulted in mental problems overtaking physical ailments as the chief cause of long term sickness in the UK. The most marked change in the past decade is the switch of emphasis from physical to mental disorders. Alcohol dependence has also been on the increase[42]. Kleinman (1991) observed that urbanization has led to a massive increase in behavioural disturbance especially associated with breakdown of families, including abandonment of and violence to spouses, children and the elderly as well as depressive and anxiety disorders, through the latter disorders might be seen as rising owing to more accurate reporting[43]. Besides, there have been suggestions to the effect that social deviance could be traced to many of the underlying social processes accompanying urbanization, including competition, class conflict, accommodation and assimilation[44]. The fact that more depression is being recognized in developing countries reflects altered patterns of diagnosis and symptoms of depression as well as a result of global factors, knowledge obtained through media and stresses related to urbanization and industrialization, which are a consequence of globalization[45]. The current pace of Asian urbanization is spurred by globalization and in this context, it has been suggested that human species has now become a biological internet with fast connections. The bionet will only get faster in the current century – that is, more people will travel by air more often, increasing the speed at which disease move. If a tropical megacity gets hit with a new virus, New York City and Los Angeles will see it days or weeks later[46].

And to highlight the plight of poor globalizing Asian nations, Stiglitz (2002) uses another apt metaphor of dilapidated boats when he says, "Small developing countries are like small boats. Rapid capital market liberalization, in the manner pushed by the International Monetary Fund (IMF), amounted to setting them off on a voyage on a rough sea, before the holes in their hulls have been repaired, before the captain has received training, before life vests have been put on board. Even in the best of circumstances, there was a high likelihood that they would be overturned when they were hit broadside by a big wave"[47]. Thus, the gross mis-match of material and social infrastructure *vis-à-vis* the escalating popular aspirations and needs that are further enhanced by global media and urban locales will only tend to exacerbate the urban crisis by raising the urban stress beyond a certain threshold.

URBAN SOCIAL STRESS–THE KEY LINKAGE

The foregoing discussion on certain public health consequences and emerging issues in urban health unmistakably point to a universal linkage as an integral factor for explanation and close integration of the diverse kinds of urban morbidity that we encounter in typical urban settings either in Asia or elsewhere. The pathways linking the rapid phenomenon of urbanization in the unique context of globalization with the overall urban morbidity, have not yet been clarified. The authors present a unified conceptual urban stress-diathesis model, (Urbstress-Diathesis Model) which can, in most cases explicate, correlate, integrate, and predict the urban morbidity, its outcome, spectrum and risk factors in a unified and cogent manner. Urban social environment itself with its unique adverse living circumstances, low level of social cohesion, anomie, infrastructural mis-match and presence of pollutants makes for an explosive cocktail. Thus, it acts as a potent stressor, in itself, which acting singly or in concert with other stressors and the diathesis (sex, gender and class; religion/ideology, genetic endowment/ethnicity; early childhood experience, trauma/prenatal exposure to environmental, viral, and chemical insults along with individual's own innate metabolic constitution/ make up) can precipitate in an individual at the most vulnerable moment either the given morbidity or give rise to the altered/aberrant behaviour that might directly or indirectly lead to the morbid conditions (s). As to how this stressor modulates a patho-physiological and immumo-biochemical response (modulation pathway) seems to have been largely worked out for quite some time[48-50]. Full details of the authors' preliminary conceptual framework of the model with further elaboration, may be found elsewhere[51].

NOTES & REFERENCES

[It is gratefully acknowledged that in their review of global and Asian urbanization in sections II & III, the authors have largely drawn on a recent paper by Rakesh Mohan and Shubhagato Dasgupta duly included in references]

1. World Wide Fund (2005), 'Press Release-World Environment Day', June 5, 2005. WWF, Delhi.
2. Out of the copious mythological references regarding Cain, the builder of the first fabled city, vide "God the first garden made, and the first city, Cain" by Abraham Cowley (1618-67) in *The Garden*, is a poetical tribute to the first citizen Cain, the son of Adam—the first of the named Semitic prophets of God.
3. Montgomery, Mark R., Richard Stern, Barney Cohen and Holly E Reed (eds), (2004), *Cities Transformed : Demographic Change and its Implications in the Developing World*. Earthscan, London, pp.1-8.
4. Mohan, Rakesh and Shubhagato Dasgupta (2005), 'The 21st Century-Asia Becomes Urban', *Economic and Political Weekly*, Vol XL (3) pp.213-23.
5. University of Karlsruhe (2000), Global Trends : Urbanization, University of Karlsurhe (www.isl.uni-karlsruhe.de/vrl/ResEng/2000/global_trends/urbanisation/index.htm).
6. Montgomery, Mark R., Richard Stern, Barney Cohen and Holly E Reed (eds), (2004), op.cit. p.102.
7. Government of India (2001), Census of India 2001, 'Provisional Population Totals', Paper 1 of 2001, Registrar General and Census Commissioner, India.
8. Montgomery, Mark R., Richard Stern, Barney Cohen and Holly E Reed (eds), (2004), Op, cit. pp.104-105.
9. Mohan, Rakesh and Shubhagato Dasgupta (2005), op.cit., p. 215.
10. United Nations Centre for Human Settlements (UNCHS) (2001), *Cities in a Globalising World*. Earthscan, London.
11. Mohan, Rakesh and Shubhagato Dasgupta (2005), op. cit. p. 214.
12. Montgomery, Mark R., Richard Stern, Barney Cohen and Holly E Reed (eds), (2004): Op,Cit. pp. 104-105.
13. Mohan, Rakesh and Shubhagato Dasgupta (2005), op.cit., p. 216.
14. Ibid p. 215.
15. United Nations (1980), *Patterns of Urban and Rural Population Growth*, No.68 in Population Studies. United Nations, Department of International Economic and Social Affairs, New York.
16. The *Times of India*, June 7, 2005.
17. The *Times of India*, August 1, 1992.
18. *Indian Express*, January 17, 1989.
19. Ali, Sabir, S.N. Singh (1998), *Major Problems of Delhi Slums*, Uppal Publishing House, New Delhi, pp. 117-18.
20. Ibid, p.5.

21. Mohan, Rakesh and Shubhagato Dasgupta (2005), op.cit., p. 222.
22. Evans, R.G. and Greg L. Stoddart (2003), 'Consuming Research, Producing Policy? *American Journal of Public Health*, 39 (3), pp.371-79.
23. Vlahow, D. and S. Galea (2002), 'Urbanization, Urbanicity and Health,' *Journal of Urban Health* 79 (4), Supplement 1.
24. Judd, F.K. *et al* (2002), 'High Prevalence Disorders in Urban and Rural Communities,' *Australian NZ Journal of Psychiatry*, 36 (1), pp.104-13.
25. Tanaka, A *et al.* (1996), 'Health Levels Influenced by Urban Residential Conditions in a Megacity Tokyo,' *Urban Studies*, 33 (6), pp. 879-94.
26. Moore M., P. Gould and B.S. Keary (2003), 'Global Urbanization and Impact Health,' *International Journal of Hygiene and Environmental Health*, 206 (4-5) pp. 269-78.
27. *Illustrated Weekly of India*, May 7, 1989.
28. Heise *et al* (1994), 'Violence Against Women: A Neglected Public Health Issue in Less Developed Countries', *Social Science and Medicine*, 39(9), 1165-1179.
29. World Health Organization (1996), *Investing in Health Research and Development : Report of the Ad Hoc Committee on Health Research relating to Future Intervention Options*, World Health Organization, Geneva.
30. Montgomery, Mark R., Richard Stern, Barney Cohen and Holly E Reed (eds), (2004): Op,cit. p. 267.
31. Galea, S. and David Vlahov (2005), 'Urban Health Evidence, Challenges and Directions,' *Annual Review of Public Health*, 26, pp. 341-65.
32. Freudenberg, N. (2000), 'Health Promotion in the City', *Annual Review of Public Health*, 21, pp. 473-503.
33. Blue, I. and T. Harpham (1996), 'Urbanization and Mental Health in Developing Countries', *Current Issues in Public Health*, 2 (4), pp. 181-85.
34. Ostamo, A,E. Lahelma and J Lonnqvist (2002), 'Determinants of attempted suicide in urban environment', *Nordic Journal of Psychiatry*, 56 (6), pp. 451-6.
35. Westman J. *et al* (2003), 'The Influences of place of Birth and Socio-economic Factors as Attempted Suicide in a Differed Population of 4.5 Million People', *Archives of General Psychiatry*, 60 (4), pp. 409-14.
36. Sundquist, K. Golin Frank and Jan Sundquist (2004), 'Urbanization and Incidence of Psychosis and Depression', *British Journal of Psychiatry*, 184, pp. 293-298.
37. Mohit, A. (2001), 'Psychiatry and Mental Health for Developing Countries : Challenge for the 21st Century', Address Presented in 13th Congress of Pakistan Psychiatric Society (Islamabad) Jan. 25-28, 2001.
38. *The Times of India*, April 25, 2005.
39. *The Times of India*, June 6, 2005.
40. *The Times of India*, Dec. 25, 2004.
41. *The Independent* (UK), July 24, 2004.
42. *The Independent* (UK), April 8, 2005.
43. Klienman, A. (1991), Preface. In *Psychosocial Aspects of Depression*. (Eds. J.Backer & A Kleinman), London, LEA.
44. Park et al (1995), *The City*, University of Chicago Press, Chicago IL.

45. D. Bhugra and Anastasia Mastrogianni (2004), 'Globalization and Mental Disorders,' *British Journal of Psychiatry*, 184, pp. 10-20.
46. Richard Preston (2000), 'What New Things are going to kill me?' *India Today* (Special Millenium issue), October 2000, p. 122.
47. Joseph E. Stiglitz (2002), *Globalization and its Discontents*. Allen Lane, London, p. 17.
48. Selye, Hans (1956), *The Stress of Life*. McGraw-Hill New York, pp. 4-43.
49. Wali, Tariq (1983), 'Cancer', *Science Reporter* 20 (5) p. 3; also see Wali, Tariq, On Mental Illness, The Times of India November 24, 1984.
50. Shah, N.K., S. Hasnain (1983), 'Psychological Basis of Origin of Cancer, Science Reporter, 20 (2).
51. Wali, Tariq and M.Asif (2005), *Urban Stress*. (in print), Angelz (India) Trust Publication, New Delhi.

CHILD LABOUR AND WTO RULES: SURVEYS OF THE ISSUES WITH REFERENCE TO SOUTH ASIA

Kishor Sharma

INTRODUCTION

South Asian countries have experienced spectacular growth performance since the late 1980s which appears to be linked with their commitments towards market-oriented reforms. While significant reforms have taken place in trade and investment fronts, reforms in the factor markets particularly in infrastructure sector and labour market have lagged behind. Despite the half-hearted nature of reforms, liberalisation in trade policy has significantly increased the access to intermediate inputs, technologies, and reduced production costs, making their exports attractive in the world market than ever before. In addition, successful completion of the Uruguay Round of trade negotiations has increased their access to the world market.

Unfortunately, expansion of exports, particularly labour-intensive manufactured exports, has triggered a protectionist response in developed countries (DCs). Protectionist groups in DCs, argue that due to poor labour standards in developing countries, industries in their countries are unable to compete with goods manufactured in developing countries. The view that countries with poor labour standards obtain inherent comparative in international trade and investment has been widely propagated in international forums.

While Child labour is not a new issue, in recent years it has brought developed countries' attention, despite a falling child participation rate . Although the welfare of working children is a real issue, protectionist groups are trying to take advantage of this by putting pressure for trade sanctions against imports from countries with poor labour standards. However, such actions are not an effective way of dealing with the problem.

As protectionist pressure increases governments are under intense pressure to demand for the inclusion of international labour standards and a social clause in the WTO Charter. Such a clause would require WTO members to enforce certain core labour standards, including prevention of child labour. Failure to comply with the WTO rule would result in international trade sanctions. The proponents of trade sanctions believe that such actions are essential to ensure that the level playing field is fair and labour standards are improved in developing countries. When developing countries are forced to improve labour standards the demand for child labour falls which will encourage children to go to schools. But, there are three problems with this line of arguments. First, child labour exists not only in tradeable sector but also in non-tradeable and household sectors. Hence, trade sanctions will not address the welfare of working children in non-tradeable sector. Second, as the income from child workers ease, this puts pressure on their families' demand for loans. Since perfect credit markets do not exist in developing countries the ability to borrow is severely limited. Even if credit markets do exist the poor will not have collateral security to obtain loans. Third, the access to schools is limited for the poor in developing countries due to the lack of schools in remote areas. Hence, trade sanctions if introduced will fail to achieve the purpose for which they are implemented.

In this chapter we shed light on this debate using the experience from South Asia. The examination of South Asian countries is particularly interesting because about 40% of the world's child labour exists in this part of the world and there has been rapid export growth since the introduction of reforms in the late 1980s.

The paper proceeds as follows. Section II presents an overview of the issues regarding trade and child labour, while the state of child labour in South Asia is discussed in Section III. The paper concludes in Section IV with concluding remarks.

TRADE AND CHILD LABOUR: SURVEYS OF THE ISSUES

In developing countries children are deployed in a wide range of economic activities including manufacturing of carpets and garment, restaurants, farming and selling goods on street. They are also utilised in household activities including looking after small sibling and colleting water and fire wood. It is deep poverty that forces parents to employ their children in a wide range of activity rather than to send them to school. This undermines their future earnings and potential. It is estimate that about one third of household incomes in developing countries is derived by the working children. Table 1 presents regional distribution of economically active children. It apparently evident that 60% of child labour is found in the Asia-Pacific region.

Among South Asian countries the incidence of child labour is high in Bangladesh. India, Nepal & Pakistan. Hence, we limit our analysis to these countries. Child labour is not a real problem in Bhutan, Maldives and Sri Lanka.

Using international sanctions to address the problem of child labour is counterproductive because it does not address the root cause of the problem. Since the prevalence of child labour is the result of underdevelopment and poverty it is important to address this rather than to use trade restriction which are indirect and blunt (Markus, 1997 and Srinivasan, 1996). Compensation programs from wealthy countries, focused on poverty reduction and better access to education be more effective and less costly than trade restrictions.

Srinivasn (1996:10) correctly observes: 'Citizens of developed countries concerned with the welfare of working children among the poor in developing countries could influence the choices of parents away from putting their children to work altogether or at least reduce the amount of work done by their children through income transfers to parents. Such transfers relax their resource constraints.'

Table 1
Regional estimates of economically active children ages 5-14 in 2000

Region	*Number of children (in millions)*	*Work ratio (%)*
Developed economies	2.5	2
Transition economies	2.4	4
Asia and the Pacific	127.3	19
Latin America and Caribbean	17.4	16
Sub-Saharan Africa	48.0	29
Middle East & North Africa	13.4	15

Source: Every child counts: New global estimates on child labour, ILO (2002).

Since only about 5% of child labour is found in tradeable sector, trade sanctions will not tackle the problem of exploitation of children. Policies like trade sanctions in fact reduce household's income and do not encourage schooling unless they are compensated for sending their children to school. In this context, development assistance can be very useful which can be used to compensate household to send their children to school and to develop new schools in remote areas. Despite the importance development assistance in reducing the incidence of child labour, there has been a sharp decline in such assistance. For instance, in real per capita terms, net official development assistance to least developed countries has dropped by 46% during 1990 to 2000 period (UNCTAD, 2002:32).

Development assistance can be useful not only for compensating families but also improving the quality and quantity of schooling which are crucial for reducing the incidence of child labour in developing countries. Improving school quality encourages parents to send their children to school rather than to work with the hope of increasing future income of their children upon completion of school. On the other hand poor school quality might discourage parent from sending their children to schools if they perceive the future income is less than or similar to present income even after completing schooling (Krueger 1996a).

Trade sanctions are restrictions on imports and when applied benefits the firms and workers that compete with imports. Once labour standards come under the WTO rules no matter how much standards are raised it is likely that protectionist group seek to exploit the situation by demanding more. When developing countries are forced to raise their labour standards they will lose their comparative advantage in cheap labour intensive goods. This might force firms to cut the employment or use the capital intensive technology and both will reduce welfare.

The evidence suggests that standards rise as income increases. There is a very strong correlation between the involvement of child labour and per capita GDP. Krueger (1996b) finds that child labour is not completely withdrawn from the labour force until GDP reaches $5000 per capita. Hence, the international community should make every attempt to increase income levels in developing countries rather than focusing too much on labour standards. The removal of agriculture subsidies in DCs, and opening up textile and clothing markets in Europe and America is particularly important in accelerating growth in developing countries.

By improving labour standards (including elimination of child labour) developing countries might be able to gain greater access to the markets of developed countries, but the experience with trade-related intellectual property rights (TRIPs) suggests that they might regret later on (Brown et. al, 2001: 24). It is possible that labour standards might come to WTO through a number of channels as they might be considering as dumping under GATT 1994 Article VI or be interpreted as a subsidy under GATT 1994 Article XX. The eliminating child labour is in the best interest of developing countries as use of child labour today means a shortage of skill labour tomorrow. Also, there is growing evidence to suggest that improved labour standards help attract more foreign investment into the country. The evidence suggests that FDI is attracted to countries with higher rather than lower labour standards (Stern, 1998:13).

Freeman (1994) argues that a market-based solution, such as labelling requirements, may be an effective way to raise the standards in developing countries. Labelling allows consumers to make their own decision as to whether or not they prefer to buy goods produced in countries with lower labour standards. Srinivasn (1996:10) suggests that: 'By not buying products of a firm or a country that does not observe what consumers view as acceptable labour standards they can send a clear and effective signal to that firm or country to face it to choose between observing standards and retain the market or lose the market altogether. If it choose to retain the market by observing acceptable labour standards, to the extent the cost of the import goes up because of such observance, both the exporting country and the buyers of imports share the cost of improving labour standards. If it chooses to forgo the market, then while workers in the exporting industry do not gain welfare through higher standards, there is a penalty to the firm in the form of lost exports. If citizens of the developed countries are interested in raining the welfare of the workers and not in penalizing the exporting firm, they will have to compensate the firm or make income transfer to workers'.

THE STATE OF CHILD LABOUR IN SOUTH ASIA

For the past decade, South Asia has been among the world's fastest growing region, although growth performance varies significantly between countries (Table 2). For example, India recorded the highest growth rate (4% pa) in the region while Pakistan experienced the lowest growth rate (1.2% pa). In terms of export performance India has out performed all countries in the region.

Children's workforce participation rates-the number of child workers to the child population--vary from country to country. It ranged from just above 5% in India to 42% in Nepal (Table 3). The lower incidence of child labour in India appears to be mainly due to rapid economic growth in Indian economy for about a decade which has lifted millions of household out of poverty.

It must be mentioned at the outset that like many developing countries reliable data on child labour is not readily available for South Asian countries and there are huge discrepancies in data collected by various agencies. Collecting child labour data is a disincentive for countries as it shows weakness in implementing policy. Hence, our analysis is based on surveys conducted under the auspicious of ILO.

Table 2
Economic Growth and the Incidence of Child Labour in South Asia

Country	*(A) GDP Growth (1990-2001)*	*(B) Illiteracy Rate*	*(C) Total Population*	*(D) Economically Active Children*	*(E) Incidence of Child Labour (D/C)*
Bangladesh	3.1%(i)	58.4%(ii)	138,900,600(iv)	6,130,00	0.044
India	4%(i)	40.5%(ii)	1,067,421,100(iv)	23,160,000	0.022
Nepal	2.5%(i)	54.9%(ii)	25,836,100(iv)	278,000	0.011
Pakistan	1.2%(i)	56.8%(iii)	153,124,800(iv)	3,313,420	0.021

Sources: (i) UNICEF, http://www.unicef.org/infobycountry/
(ii) ILO, http://www.ilo.org/public/english/employment/gems/eeo/download/
(iii) USAID, http://www.usaid.gov/locations/asia_near_east/countries/pakistan/pakistan.html
(iv) http://www.populationworld.com.

Table 3
Child labour in South Asia

Country	*Total Population 1996 (millions)*	*Age Range*	*Number of Children in Age Range (millions)*	*Estimated Number of Child Workers in Age Range (thousands)*	*Percentage of Children Working in Age Range*
Bangladesh	122	5-14	34.5	6,584	19.1
India	945	5-14	210.0	11,285	5.4
Nepal	22	5-14	6.2	2,596	41.7
Pakistan	134	5-14	40.0	3,313	8.0
Total	1241		295.0	24,316	

Source: http://globalmarch.org/virtuallibrary/usdepartment/sweat5/chap2.htm.

The incidence of child labour tends to be higher among boys than girls and in rural areas. The higher workforce participation rate for boys is due to the fact that girls work in informal sector (such as at home) which are harder to capture by statistics. Children often work alongside other family members. Urban children often work in garment, carpet and textile related activities, small business and bidi industry (hand-rolled cigarette) together with their parents while children in rural areas tend to work with their families in agriculture, fishing, forestry or small family enterprises.

Child labour represents 12% of the total labour force in Bangladesh. Of the children engaged in economic activities, 22.92% are seller/vendors, 16.10 % are factory workers 5.72% are brick/stone breakers, 4.77% agricultural worker, 2.27% are in craft, 0.65% in fish processing and 0.44% beggars (ILO-IPEC, 1996). It is estimated that 80% of child labour in India are employed in agriculture sector and 8% of the work force in the hand knotted carpet industry are child labours. In Nepal, 94.7% of child labours perform agriculture and household work and the remaining 5% are engaged in non-agriculture activities, including manufacturing and service industries (ILO-IPEC, 1999). Of those involved in non-agriculture, 1.6% are in construction, transportation and communication, 0.8% work as general technical workers and another 0.8% work as production workers and 0.4% as sales workers. In Pakistan, 67% of child labour are found in agriculture, 11% in manufacturing and remaining 22% work in service related activities (FBS, ILO and IPEC, 1996). These working children are exposed to danger in most instances. In agriculture, large numbers of children are exposed to harmful pesticides, while in construction and manufacturing they are exposed to toxic substances such as asbestos, benzene and mercury. There is no doubt that these work hazards affect children physical and mental development during their formative years, but they are forced to work due to wide spread poverty.

Except for India, all South Asian countries have ratified, either the ILO conventions on Minimum Age Convention, 1973 (Convention 138) or the Worst Forms of Child Labour Convention, 1999 (Convention 182) or both. Although employment of child labour is regulated in each country, child labour practices remain a major concern and work age of children varies between countries. For example, in Bangladesh minimum age for employment is 12 years, while in India and Pakistan, the minimum work age of 14 applied only to certain specific occupations and processes. In Pakistan, the Employment of Children Act 1991 prohibits the employment of children under 15 in dangerous or hazardous activities. Procedures are also established for implementation of and enforcement of the Act, such as the requirement that all employers maintain a register of particulars regarding the employment of any children under the age of 15. In Nepal, the minimum work age of 14 does not apply to certain activities, such as plantation and brick kilns. Table 4 presents the ratification status among the South Asian countries.

Table 4

Ratification Status of Minimum Age Conventions (C138) and Worst form of Child Labour Convention (C182) in South Asia

Country	*Minimum Age Convention (C138)*	*Worst Forms of Child Labour Convention (C 182)*
Bangladesh	Not yet ratified	Ratified (12/3/2001)
India	Not yet ratified	Not yet ratified
Nepal	Ratified (30/5/1997)	Ratified (3/1/2002)
Pakistan	Not yet ratified	Ratified (11/10/2001)
Sri Lanka	Ratified (111/2/2000)	Ratified (1/3/2001)

Source: ILO Web site.

Since inception in 1919, ILO has approved 174 Conventions. Once a Convention is ratified, the country in question is expected to introduce to enforce it through law. The ILO does not have enforcement power and it relies on voluntary compliance with ratified Conventions. There is a significant variation in the ratification coverage of conventions by country. For example, India has ratified 36 as against 11 by the United States.

CONCLUSION

Global trade liberalisation, together with reforms in domestic fronts, has made exports from South Asia attractive in the world market than ever before. Unfortunately, this has triggered a protectionist response in developed countries. Protectionist groups are trying to take advantage of this by putting pressure for trade sanctions against imports from countries with poor labour standards. As protectionist pressure increases governments are under intense pressure to demand for the inclusion of international labour standards and a social clause in the WTO Charter. Such a clause would require WTO members to enforce certain core labour standards, including prevention of child labour. Failure to comply with the WTO rule would result in international trade sanctions. The proponents of trade sanctions believe that such actions are essential to ensure that the level playing field is fair and labour standards are improved in developing countries. However, such action will increase poverty and deteriorate welfare. If people in DCs are concern with the welfare of children in developing countries, the best way to address this is through transfer payment.

Also, overloading WTO with non-trade issue can be very costly and can slow down the pace of multilateral trade liberalisation. While ILO is responsible for managing the labour standard issues, it has no enforcement power. The best way to handle this issue is to make ILO more effective in handling labour issues and improve its monitoring mechanism. Over burdening WTO with non-trade issues will not only attract criticism but undermine its existence.

REFERENCES

Amarsinghe, S.W. (2002), Sri Lanka The Commercial Sexual Exploitation of Children: A Rapid Assessment, Report prepared for the ILO.

Bachman, S.L. (2000), A New Economics of Child Labour: Searching for Answers behind the Headlines, *Journal of International Affairs*, 53 (2), pp. 545-572.

Bhagwati, J. (2000), Free Trade Today, Princeton: Princeton University Press.

Brown, D.K., Deardorff, A.V. and R.M. Stern (2001), Pros and Cons of Linking Trade and Labour Standards', paper presented at the Murphy Institute Conference on the Political Economy of Policy Reform, Tulane University, Nov. 9-10, 2001.

Fallon, P. and Tzannatos, Z. (1998), Child labour: Issues and Directions for the World Bank, Monograph (Washington, DC: World Bank).

Krueger, A.B. (1996a), Observations on International Labour Standards and Trade, NBER Working Paper 5632.

Krueger, A. (1996b) 'International Labour Standards and Trade', in Michael Bruno and Boris Pleskovic (eds.) Annual World Bank Conference on Development Economics, (Washington, D. C.: The World Bank), pp. 281-302.

Markus, Keith (1997), 'Should Core Labour Standards be Improved Through International Trade Policy', World Bank Policy Research Working Paper No. 1817, August.

Weiner, M. (1991), Child Labour and the State in India, Princeton, N. J.: Princeton University Press.

ILO (1996a), *Economically Active Population Estimates and Projections, 1950-2010.* Geneva: ILO.

ILO (1996b), 'Child Labour: What is to be Done', Document for Discussion at the Informal Tripartite Meeting of the Ministerial Level, ILO Geneva Available at http:\\www.ilo.org\public\english\standards\ipec\publ\policy\what\index.htm.

ILO-IPEC (International Labour Organisation-International Program on Elimination of Child Labour (1996), Rapid Assessment of Child Labour Situation in Bangladesh, Report.

ILO-IPEC (1999), Country Paper: Nepal.

Federal Bureau of Statistics (FBS), Ministry of Labour, Manpower and Overseas Pakistanis International Labour Organisation (ILO) and International Programme on the Elimination of Child Labour (IPEC) (1996), Summary of results of Child Labour Survey in Pakistan (1996), Islamabad, Pakistan.

Freeman, R. B. (1994), 'A hard-heard look at labour standards', in U.S. Department of Labour, Bureau of International Labour Affairs, International Labour Standards and Global Economic Integration: Proceedings of a Symposium. Washington, D.C.

Jafarey, S. and Lahiri, S. (1999), Will Trade Sanctions Reduce Child Labour? The Role of credit market, Department of Economics, University of Essex, Discussion paper No. 500.

Suwal, B.R., K.C., B.B. and Adhikari, K.P. (1997), Child Labour Situation in Nepal (Report from Migration and Employment Survey, 1995/96), Kathmandu, Nepal.

Stern, R.M. (1998), Labour Standards and International Trade, The University of Michigan, Ann Arbor, Discussion Paper No. 430.

Department of Census and Statistics (1999), Child Activity Survey Sri Lanka 1999, Colombo, Sri Lanka.

Sen, R.K. and Dasgupta, A. (2003), Problems of Child Labour in India, Deep and Deep Publications: New Delhi.

UNCTAD (2003), 'The Least Developed Countries Report, 2002', Overview, Geneva: UN.

PARTICIPATORY WATERSHED APPROACH IN WASTE LAND DEVELOPMENT PROGRAMME–AN EXPERIENCE OF SOUTH INDIAN PROVINCES

S. Ramesh

INTRODUCTION

Waste lands are defined as degraded lands which can be brought under vegetative cover with reasonable efforts and which are currently under utilized and also the lands which are deteriorating due to lack of water and soil management. Andhra Pradesh (A.P.) has geographical area of 2,75,068 sq.kms. Of this an area of 51,750 sq.kms., accounting for 18.8 per cent is considered wastelands in A.P. The national average accounting for wastelands is 20.2 per cent of the total geographical area. Although the wasteland development initiatives were taken up in during early 90's, it gained momentum with launching of Integrated Wasteland Development Programme (IWDP). The scheme is implemented on watershed basis in accordance with the common guidelines for watershed development since 01 April, 1995. This programme is implemented by Department of Land Resources (DoLR) under Ministry of Rural Development. IWDP is centrally sponsored scheme and the cost norm Rs. 4000/- per ha. It has been revised to Rs. 6000 per hectares w.e.f. 1.4.2000. The increase of Rs. 2000 is to be shared between the central and State Govts. in the ratio of 75:25. Thus the funding pattern of the scheme has been revised from 100% Central grant to sharing in the ratio of 11:1 between the (Federal) Central Govt. and the State Govts., i.e., Rs. 5500 is borne by the Central Government and Rs. 500 is shared by the State Government.

Since 1995-96 till date (31 March, 2004), 48 projects were completed covering 4,27,912 hectares. This is the highest area covered in any state of the country. Andhra Pradesh ranks No.1 in terms of achievements under IWDP in developing the wastelands on watershed basis. An amount of Rs. 1,290 millions were released and spent during the period from 1995-96 to 2003-04 which is highest amount spent by any state in the country. Thus, the achievements of IWDP in Andhra Pradesh for developing wastelands on watershed basis were highly admired.

The study was taken up in Visakhapatnam district of Andhra Pradesh for evaluating watershed projects funded under IWDP. The agriculture profile of the district indicates higher concentration of small and marginal farmers eking out livelihoods from their small holdings rearing one or two cattle/buffaloes with or without sheep and goat which provide subsidiary income in addition to getting income from off-farm sources. The principal crops grown in the district are paddy, grams, oil seeds and millets. Green gram is cultivated in rabi season while paddy/millets are cultivated in kharif season. The total number of cows, buffaloes, bulls/bullocks, goat, sheep and poultry birds in the district were 1,64,000, 1,64,000, 3,55,000, 1,31,000, 2,08,000 and 1,54,000 respectively. The higher concentration of breedable cows and buffaloes indicate higher dependency on small farm diary holding systems. The district is also marked by higher concentration of (82.8%) rural population, of whom 10% and 9% belong to Scheduled Caste (SC) and Scheduled Tribe (ST) population.

In the district, watershed development was taken up through funds from Integrated Wasteland Development Programme (IWDP), Employment Assurance Scheme (EAS) and Rural Infrastructure Development Fund (RIDF) of National Bank for Agriculture and Rural Development (NABARD). IWDP was introduced with 100% central assistance on a pilot basis in isolated patches during 1990-91. However, the impetus of IWDP watersheds gained movement from 1995-96 following the recommendation of Dr. Hanumanth Rao's committee report.

In this section an analysis was made on the watershed development programmes taken up during the year 1998 & 1999 such that they would be nearing completion by 2003 & 2004. This facilitated scope for evaluating the programmes effectively.

METHODOLOGY

The Visakhapatnam district of Andhra Pradesh was selected with a view to study the impact of watershed development programme funded under IWDP. A structured schedule was developed which was emphasized for making indepth case studies on watershed projects. In Visakhapatnam division, Pedapalli Watershed Project, Kokkirapalli Watershed Project, Mondigedda Watershed Project, Teeda Watershed Project of Kassim Kota Mandal and Baliya Guda Watershed of Araku Valley were studied. Focus group discussions were held with community organization such as User Groups (UGs), Self-Help Groups (SHGs), Watershed Committee (WC), Watershed Association (WA) as well as with Programme Implementing Agency (PIAs) and Watershed Development Team (WDTs) for eliciting the information in depth from all the five projects. In addition, information was collected from secondary sources like progress reports, office records and registers. The findings of the study are presented in the ensuing sections.

STATUS OF IWDP WATERSHED PROGRAMMES IN VIZAG DISTRICT

Under IWDP-II, 10 Watershed Projects were sanctioned for treatment of 5000 Hectares with financial outlay of Rs. 29.19 million for a period of 5 years from

2002-03 to 2006-07. Out of Rs. 29.19 million, a specific pattern of fund release is adopted. As per this the 1st year and final year 15% and 10% of the above outlay is released while 25% each released during the remaining years.

These watersheds are being implemented at Mandal level by Mandal Agricultural Officers as WDT members under the technical supervision of Assistant Directors of Agriculture (Soil Conservation Wing).

An amount of Rs. 4.336 million was released during the year 2002-03 and the same was spend for execution of Water Conservation works in these watersheds.

During the Year 2003-04, an amount of Rs. 3.907 million were released by the Government during the month of October 2003 for implementation of the Programme, out of which an amount of Rs. 3.90 million expenditure incurred and balance are available under this project. Of the total Area projected for treatment 5000 Hect., only an area of 1089 Hect., was treated.

The Soil Conservation measures such as Continuous Contour Trenching, Farm Ponds, Percolation Tanks and Gully control works were taken up in the watershed by involving Agricultural Officers as WDT members under the technical supervision of Assistant Director Agriculture (Soil Conservation).

Under IWDP–III, 12 Watershed Projects were sanctioned during the year 2003-04 covering 7 Projects in Agency Mandals and 5 Projects in Plain Mandals. Preparatory Activities like Conduct of PRA exercises, formation of community organization is under Progress. During the month of March 2004 an amount of Rs. 4.950 million are released for implementation of the Programme as per Hariyali Guidelines. According to the Hariyali Guidelines, Gram Panchayat will plan, manage and monitor the project and Gram Panchayat Sarpanch and Village Secretary will operate the funds.

FIELD REALITIES

1. Selection Process

There are two distinct government PIAs in Vizag district. In Arakuu Valley the Project Director Integrated Tribal Development Agency (ITDA), Paderu is responsible for implementation of watersheds in the district while in the rest of the divisions District Water Management Agency (DWMA) is responsible for execution of watershed programmes. The Panchayat takes active role by passing resolution to take up the soil and moisture conservation works in the villages suitable selecting the land/catchment area. While doing so in the gram sabha the Chairman and Secretary of the association would be elected and the members present are enrolled for watershed association and also for self-help groups. The resolutions passed are submitted to either Project Director, ITDA or to the DWMA office. The district authorities would consider the resolution from the watershed committees and funds would be allotted duly selecting the PIAs. In the organization structure PIA holds the top position, WDT middle position and WC in the lower rung. The WDT comprises of agriculture officer, horticulture officer, forest range officer as members of the WDT and the WDT team works in consultation with UGs, SHGs and WC.

2. Institutional Arrangements

At State level, the Commissioner of Rural Development, Government of Andhra Pradesh, Hyderabad is the overall authority for implementation of the watershed development programmes. At the District level the Project Director (DWMA) would be monitoring the project. PIA works under the technical guidance of MDT, an agency of DWMA. At Project level, Assistant Directors (Soil Conservation) of the concerned area act as PIA for implementation of the project. The agriculture officers of the concerned Mandal act as WDT for the watershed.

3. Planning Process

In order to mobilize the community for the need to involve them actively in the programme, methods for awareness generation were followed. A district level workshop was organized and at project level, gram sabha, inviting all the sections of the community. Posters, pamphlets were distributed and displayed in the meeting halls. Sensitization workshops were also undertaken discussing with Ryot Mithra, SHGs, UGs, People's representatives and Watershed Committee. Information was also passed on to media for effective dissemination among wider public.

The Sarpanch of village panchayats were in many cases the Chairman of the Watershed Association. The gram sabha select 11 members from different categories comprising (1) Backward Caste Community; (2) Members of Development of Women and Child in Rural Areas (DWCRA)-1, SC women-1; Chief Minister Employment Yojana CMEY-1, SHG-2 and UGs-4. These 11 members would form the watershed committee.

After conducting Participatory Rural Appraisal (PRA) exercise, the treatment plans were prepared. Based on the identified works, the beneficiaries of such works were formed into groups which are designated as User Groups (UGs). On an average the Self-Help Groups (SHGs) ranging from 10-15 were identified in each watershed. Brick making, tailoring, Adda leaf plate making are some of the economic activities taken up by them.

Rapport Building Measures

In the district by and large, digging of farm pond and distribution of high yielding varieties of vegetable seeds were taken up as an Entry Point Activity (EPA). It should be noted here that the scheme of Rythu Bazar was very successful in this district. Many of the farmers showed keen interest in vegetable cultivation for augmenting their household incomes. The villagers are satisfied with the EPA. The officers gained the credibility and confidence of the people which later helped in seeking their active involvement in implementation of the watershed programmes.

Beneficiary Contribution

Mostly UGs, and SHGs were less income groups hence could not be expected of contributing in terms of cash. However, 5-10% of the wage work generated under the programme is collected through Shramdan and partly in cash also.

Owing to unprecedented consecutive droughts, condition during last three years there has been rural misery due to failure of crops.

Capacity Building

Curriculum of the technical training imparted included horticulture, conservation measures, and adoption of cover crops such as cowpea, horse gram, pulses and dolichos. Agronomic practices like deep ploughing, vermi composting, green manuring, kitchen garden crops etc. The professional training covered fodder development activities, training to Gopala Mithra on artificial insemination and first aid, Adda leaf plate making, brick making, sheep and goat rearing, vegetable cultivation etc.

The department PIAs were imparted training on low cost structures of SMC works, and WDT members (3 persons) were trained at Watershed Training Centres Padmanabham in Ahmednagar under Ingo German Project. The Water Association Members of 350 were trained which helped in better communication and for preparation of posters, charts and lamination of photos. 11 members of WC were imparted two technical training programmes at Watershed Training Centre Padmanabham. The Secretaries/Volunteers numbering 5 attended 6 trainings on Soil and Moisture Conservation (SMC) works. The UGs numbering 62 participated in 4 technical trainings which helped them in resolving the problems, preparation of plans and estimates and maintenance of structures. Lastly, SHGs numbering 72 attended 4 technical training programmes mostly relating to income generating activities such as dairy farming and fodder cultivation.

4. Project Planning Process

Participatory Rural Appraisal (PRA) techniques were employed for eliciting village information from village elders, UGs, SHGs and WA members. This generated interest among the villagers in sharing their information and expressing their views freely on their preferences and their needs. In such meetings elites officials and non-officials, village elders, Panchayat people were present. While on technical aspects the decision were taken by PIA and WDTs and in selection and identification the villagers views of the WA were considered and were incorporated in the planning.

Preparation of Perspective Plan

The UGs and SHGs participated in PRA and expressed their views, preferences/interests. The works were also identified by the UGs and SHGs in the presence of the PIA/WDT. The plans prepared by the SHGs and UGs were discussed by the WC and approval is sought for taking up the said works. The DWMA approves the plan scrutinized and forwarded by the WDT. The agency, having got staff like draftsman who can verify the plans and develop maps help in formulation of the plan. The other supporting staff (Engineering staff) will verify and check whether the estimates were technically correct and whether or not they exceed the norms/department rates specified. The plan thus approved is finally sent back to WC and WDT for execution. Usually, after conducting PRA exercise, planning (treatment plan) is done survey number wise for 550 hectares of treatable area.

Preparation of Action Plan and Activity Plan

A five-year action plan showing year-wise breakups is prepared. Activity plan has been prepared by taking holistic approach of treating the area viz., SMC works, Afforestation, Horticulture, Modern techniques in Agriculture/ Horticulture crops, dairying and other income generating activities, bee keeping, poultry, small scale industries like brick making, vegetable growing.

5. People's Participation

Although it is desired that the programme should be clientele centered its seems that still the officials enjoy the privilege of sanctions and approvals in implementation (control) of the programme. Although the PRA is conducted, it is doubtful how far the reflections and the villagers needs, preferences, priorities were taken to cognizance. The plans seems to have been prepared scrupulously in accordance with the administrative regime. While the decisions are to be taken by the villagers themselves in the distribution of benefits also, it is doubtful whether villagers are provided information on benefit sharing mechanism/usufructs especially in the SMC works taken up in the JFM area using IWDP watershed funds. Members of WA were members of VSS (leave alone members) even the President SHG, Malivalasa Mahila Group was not aware of the provisions/entitlements, usufructs mechanism of sharing the benefits (mature plantations). However, the members of community organizations felt empowered, enthused and enjoyed elevated status in their community.

6. Project Implementation Process

Implementation plan, activity plan and action plan were prepared on the basis of the identified activities through PRA exercise after EPA. The sequence of such activities taken up included (i) PRA exercise, (ii) Identification of works by UGs + SHGs, (iii) Preparation of plans and estimates by UGs and WDT, (iv) Approval of WC, (v) Submission of plans to PIA through WDT, (vi) Sanction of plans and estimates by PIA and (vii) Execution of plans by UGs and SHGs under the guidance of WC. Before appreciating the implementation process perhaps it is instructive to understand the roles and responsibilities assigned to the UGs, SHGs, WC and Secretary in the implementation mechanism.

Roles and Responsibilities of UGs, SHGs, WC, WA and Secretary in Execution of Plan

UGs are assigned with the task of community mobilization and creation of awareness. (1) Mobilization and creation of awareness among the public; (2) Assessment of resources and inventory for preparation of plans/estimates with the help of volunteers; (3) Resolve disputes within/between groups; (4) Assets creation and (5) Maintenance of assets created are the multifarious responsibilities assigned to the UGs in implementation of the watershed activities/projects under the overall guidance of WC.

The role of SHGs in implementation of the WDP is (1) Organization of social mobilization with the help of PR department officials; (2) Participation in the small savings and (3) Overall development of poor by farming groups and thrift groups, income generating activities.

WC is an executive body at village level involved in preparation of action plan with the help of watershed members, technical committee and user groups. It assists UGs in preparation of plan estimates, helps in payment, and in execution of works. It is responsible for coordination and liaisoning with gram panchayat and WDT for ensuring smooth implementation.

WA will meet 4 times in a year to monitor and review the progress, statement of accounts, formation of UGs and SHGs, approve arrangements for collection of donations and contributions, lay down procedures for operation and maintenance of created assets, approval of activities and takes decisions involving the entire community.

Secretary is joint account holder assigned with the tasks of social mobilization, money disbursement, execution of identified works and plan preparation. The WDT guides WC which in turn directs the UGs in execution of SMC works. The mode of implementation as could be understood from the reflections is through work contract system wherein not many of the SHGs got the assigned minimum wage of Rs. 52/- per day. As against this, it is reported that they got a wage rate of Rs. 30-35 per day per male person and Rs. 25-30 for female persons per day in Malivalasa village, Arakuu Mandal.

The types of conservation works carried out included loose boulders, rockfill dams, water harvesting structures, graded bunding, field canals, field bunds, diversion weir, farm ponds, tanks, Continuos Contour Trench (CCT), etc. The production related works included paddy cultivation, vegetable cultivation, cashewnut plantation and cultivation of ragi (minor millet). It is also observed that horticulture, teak plantation and pasture development works were also taken up in many of the Govt. PIA managed watershed areas.

The Problems faced

It was reported that due to deficient rainfall for last 3 years the benefits accrued could not be noticed despite good work done. Coordinating different activities of line departments becomes difficult with frequent transfers particularly in Agency areas. The political interference and groupism in the villages divided on party lines did not enable to propose certain community benefiting projects like establishment of a cashew factory on cooperative lines which could have transformed the economic scenario of the Pedapalli and Kokkiralapalli watershed projects. Similarly large scale plantations of Jeelugu a sort of drink which is fetching Rs. 2000 annually per tree would enable the livelihood security of the tribal poor farmers belonging to konda dora, malli, konda kummari and valmiki sects of people living in the fragile eco systems of Araku valley. In order to promote the livelihoods further economic activities such as procurement of Chebula (kArakukaya), collection of addakulu (leaf plate making), collection of soap nuts, imili (tamarind) processing, emblica aficinalis (usuri) processing should be taken up. However, the income generating activities taken up under the programmes included brick making, dairy and fodder development, pottery, poultry and adda leaf making.

The other developmental activities implemented for synergy included girl-child protection scheme, construction of lavatories, supply of farm machinery, organization of infertility camps, formation of rythu mithra groups, green manuring and seed production programmes.

7. Fund Management

(A) Project Fund

As stated earlier the amounts are released in different proportions every year. However, the projects initiated under IWDP-II & III vary slightly in their proportions. It was found that not much difficulty is faced in flow of funds when the money is spent properly and utilization certificates sent promptly. On an average around 7.5 lakh out of the total outlay of 30.0 lakh was released and spent for a watershed development project initiated in 2003-04 which indicates that the fund is released in a smoother fashion without much hassles. On an average of the Rs. 7.5 lakhs spent, of which an amount Rs. 20,000 was spent on training, Rs. 30,000 for afforestration and the rest Rs. 7.0 lakhs towards SMC works.

An outlay of Rs. 291.90 lakhs was sanctioned for treatment of 5000 hectares under IWDP-II to Vizag district for a period of 5 years from 2002-03 to 2006-07. Of the total outlay of Rs. 291.90 lakhs, an amount of Rs. 43.36 lakhs was released for the year 2002-03 and an additional amount of Rs. 39.07 lakhs released by October 2003. Further an amount of Rs. 49.5 lakhs were released for implementation of 12 watershed projects, as per Hariyali guidelines sanctioned during the year 2003 to 2004 under IWDP-III. It is reported that efforts are being made by DWMA to constitute gram panchayat functional committees who will monitor the project at panchayat level and Gram Panchayat Sarpanch and Village Secretary will operate the funds.

(B) WDF Fund

The WC took active part in mobilizing the stakeholders and collecting contribution from the UGs and deposited in a separate account for maintenance of the project even after its completion. It amounted only Rs. 2500/- in Thida watershed of Kasim Kota Mandal of Vizag district.

The problems encountered in mobilizing the WDF fund was the poverty of the members coupled with unprecedented chronic drought effecting the economy of the entire state during the past 3 years.

8. Maintenance, Protection and Utilization of Assets Created

The modus operandi of fund utilization included money withdrawal procedure through joint account with WDT and Secretary, payment procedure effected by WC, accounting through cash-book maintenance and auditing of funds is done by (1) internal audit, (2) by Charted Accountant, (3) Accountant General audit and (4) social audit.

Maintenance of Records

The WDT maintain the records such as Resolution Book , Well Inventory, Cash Book , Assets Register, Pass Book, Plantation Register, M' Book and plans and Estimates Register

9. Monitoring

Periodic monitoring for assessing the progress and also taking corrective measures to keep tract of the project inline with the objectives and in accordance with the action plan is mandatory for effective implementation of any development programme. Watershed Development Programmes cannot be exception to this. A weekly review meeting of the WC by the PIA and a fortnight review by MDT DWMA and a monthly meeting by the Project Director to each of the watershed is stipulated. PIA and WDT supervise the ongoing SMC works and they check the watershed committees. WDT maintains the records and the reports were sent periodically to PIA and PD, DWMA. Process documentation is also done through maintenance of asset register and photo album. Information also is furnished to Commissioner Rural Development, Hyderabad and PD, DWMA in the prescribed format. In addition to the auditing procedures such as A.G. audit and internal audit the concept of social audit is appreciated. The statement of accounts and the registers were kept in the general body of the WA for transparency to avoid suspicion and confidence building measure. The PIA is the controlling authority and inspects the organizations of the watershed.

10. Steps taken for Post Project Management

As stated earlier, efforts were made to raise the WDF fund which would be utilized for post project management and for institutional backup aimed at sustaining the programme even after withdrawal of the PIA seems to be doubtful. In other words the sustainability of the programme and the post project management unless taken care by panchayat seems to be uncertain. Even the capacity building efforts to enable the organizations such as UGs, SHGs, WC and WA may not yield the results required for taking over on a self sustaining basis.

IMPACT OF WATERSHED PROJECTS

1. Institutional Arrangements

The project initiated during the year 1998 and 1999 funded under IWDP were taken up by Project Director, DRDA. However, District Water Management Agency like in other districts of Andhra Pradesh, was established in Visakhapatnam district also during the year 2001, for monitoring the programmes like Neeru Meeru and watershed programmes. The Project

Director (PD), DWMA is supported by Deputy Executive Engineer, Assistant Executive Engineer, Assistant Engineer and Agriculture Officer, who are deputed from other state government departments. The capacity building particularly the skills imparted in training for enabling the UGs and SHGs for planning the watershed programmes through conduct of PRAs could only provide basic understanding of planning concepts and the intricacies involved in such exercises. The NGO-PIAs were not many. There is a one reputed NGO, Bhagawathula Charitable Trust, Yellamanchali which used to act as PIA. However, they were busy and engrossed in their own activities. They were unable to take up these works. The WDT members were capable and have profound expertise to guide the community organizations involved in planning and management of these watersheds.

2. People's Participation

The involvement of community organizations such as UGs, SHGs, WA, WC in watershed management is in primitive stage in the district compared to several of the Drought Prone Area Programme (DPAP) districts. Moreover, the information management system seems to be inadequate to mobilize the poor illiterate small and marginal farmers to participate in the programme for their advantage. By far, the elite in the village and the progressive farmers dominate the management of watershed programmes and it is continuing unabated. The weaker sections and the participation of female members except for the wage earning is invisible. The synergy expected in dovetailing in other rural development programmes for the benefiting the SHGs has not taken place. The political support required for establishing a processing centre for efficient utilization of the cashew-nut fruit which hither to going waste is missing. It may be noted that the majority of the watershed areas are marked by large-scale mango and cashew plantations. Lack of a cashewnut processing unit and by product utilization units poses greater threat to the economy of small and marginal farmers who are majority in this region. Establishment of such units in cooperative lines under professional management hold key for the development of the region in order to make the impact of the watershed development programme visible in this region. In Arakuu area (Paderu division) where the River Valley Project (RVP) operates, the agro-ecological setting is totally different. Despite the development efforts, illiteracy, ill health and the belief system makes the livelihoods miserable. The dominant tribal sects in the area are konda dora, malli, konda kummari and valmiki who still believe in superstitions which workout against the development process itself. Large-scale awareness building efforts, establishment of agro-processing units for value addition to the raw produce particularly the Non Timber Forest Produce (NTFP) would help to offset the above listed constraints in these watershed areas. It was found that in many cases the kith and kin of the Sarpanch were invariably the Chairman/President of the WA/WC/Vana Samrakshana Samithi (VSS). As a result the benefits of many of the development programmes in general also did not percolate to the masses at large. The watershed development programme in Paderu division in Araku

Valley was not an exception to this. In many cases the participation of the people in the development programmes is passive negligible.

3. Physical Changes

- Following implementation of watershed development programmes perceptible physical changes were noticed. As a result of improvement of ground water levels the recharging the wells improved. This facilitated greater access to drinking water as well as water to animals. The villagers of Sitarampur were ecstatic over the thrilling experience of having the dream of drinking water facility even in summer months. This was unheard in the history of Sitarampur village under Mondigedda Watershed of Payakaraopeta block to realize the dream of access to drinking water right in the village without having to walk 2 km distance. The drinking water problem for both human beings and livestock is solved permanently.
- Positive impact was reported with regards to in situ moisture conservation, prevention of runoff and creation of water harvesting structures.
- Some of the failed wells got recharged owing to percolation effects in the valley as well as in the ridge region.
- The number of dug wells and tube wells increased by 33.3 and 23.5 per cents respectively.
- An area of 120 acres was brought under double cropping. Area under horticulture also increased by 25.0 per cent. Area under afforestation increased by 75.0 per cent.
- There was 111.1% increase in the area under irrigation. This helped to switch over to paddy cultivation.
- The arable land brought under agriculture increased by 14.5 per cent through creation of water harvesting structures which facilitated better percolation.
- There was an improvement in the yields of green gram, groundnut and black gram. The area under green and black gram cultivation increased.
- First time, dhalva paddy was cultivated in the village of Sitarampur which was considered as historic event for the village.
- There was an increased in bio-mass production including natural grass availability. The availability of water increased by 40.0 per cent.
- There was an increase in the milk production to tune of 60.0 per cent due to more availability of fodder resulting from change in cropping pattern as well as availability of range grass.
- There was substantial improvement in the employment generation. It was to the tune of 66.6 per cent in the watershed areas.
- The value of the agricultural land increased by 50.0 per cent.

4. Socio-economic Changes

It was reported that migration was lessened to more than 50% due to availability of work in the village itself and also due to extension of area brought under cultivation. As a result of higher crop yields the farmers could get more income. This facilitated them to send their children to the schools for primary education. This in turn helped them their participation in immunization programmes taken up in the schools. Table-1 provides the detailed description of impact of watershed on agro-socio economic parameters. The affordability of the small and marginal farmers increased marginally to have better clothing for their children and even to repay the personnel loans/debts. The income from livestock also improved due to availability of fodder in summer months also (table 2). The participation of the households in watershed development programmes provided greater opportunity for developing cosmopolite behaviour. Some of the exposure visits taken up by the PIAs helped to build more awareness and changed their mental disposition favourably to certain enterprises. The community organizations such as UGs, SHGs, WC, WA improved their communication and managerial skills due to their active involvement in the management of watershed development programmes.

Table 1
Impact of Watershed on Agriculture and Allied Activities

Sl. No.	*Particulars*	*Pre-Project Period*	*Post Project Period*	*% increase*
1.	Arable land	380	435	14.5
2.	Non Arable land	120	65	
3.	Area irrigated	45	95	111.1
4.	No. of Dug wells	12	16	33.3
5.	No. of Tube wells	34	42	23.5
6.	Water Harvesting Structures (types)	-	8	-
7.	Gully Controls measure (No.) - LBS RFDs	--	1589	-
8.	Area under Afforestation	120	210	75.0
9.	Pasture Development	-	50 acres	-
10.	Area under Double Crops	-	120 acres	-
11.	Area under Horticulture	1200 acres	1500 acres	25.0
12.	Milk Yield per day per animal	5 ltrs.	8 ltrs.	60.0
13.	Availability of fodder/grass (months in a year)	5	7	40.0
14.	Availability of water in wells in general	No water during summer	Water available during summer	-
15.	Availability of water in well during summer (in days)	-	2 months i.e., 60 days	-
16.	Employment availability (mandays in a year)	90	150	66.6
17.	Land value (Rs.)	60,000/ acres	90,000/ acre	50.0

CONCLUSION

Watershed approach for development of natural resources once again proved as an appropriate measure for sustainable resource conservation particularly for soil and water conservation preventing soil erosion and runoff and providing protection to the biosphere. Despite the constraints of lack of active participation of the people, the achievements particularly in terms of conservation of soil and water, increased area brought under agriculture,

Table - 2
Impact of watershed–Select Socio-economic parameters

Sl. No.	Particulars	Pre-Period	Past Project Period	% increase Period
1.	Income from different sources			
	(a) Daily labour wage (Rs.)	40	60	50.0
	(b) Agriculture annual income (average in Rs.)	4000/acre	5000/acre	25.0
	(c) Income from livestock	Rs. 50/- per day per animal	Rs. 70/- per day per animal	40.0
	(d) Income form Non farm activities	-	-	-
2.	Migration	Regular 50-55%	Regulated 25-30%	
3.	Creation of Institutions (with examples)	-	-	-
4.	Creation of Assets (eg. Community Hall, Drinking water facility, water tanker, approach road, etc.)	-	8 new borewells are dug for drinking water	-
5.	Participation of women in development programme	Marginal	Increased	-
6.	Saving habit	-	Increased with formation of DWCRA and User Groups	-

increased food grain production, milk production and improvement in living conditions needs to be appreciated. The administrative innovation in bringing about institutional dovetailing mobilizing the community through organizations such as UGs, SHGs, WA and WC indeed paid much dividends as it rightly deserved. The experience of DWMA in conserving soil and water through involving people by community organizations helped to bring in synergy with the ongoing Swarna Jayanthi Gram Swarajgar Yojana (SGSY), a massive self employment programme aiming at social mobilization on self help principle working in group approach on cluster basis. It is in other words to conclude the expected outcomes in terms of the (1) amount of benefit supposed to be derived from the programme by the target groups (WA), (2) the transparency and the managerial efficiency expected to provided to the DWMA from the WDT staff concerned, and the efforts of the community organizations such as UGs, SHGs, WA and WC in mobilizing the people for associating and involving them at various stages, to be achieved have, however being fulfilled to a greater extent considering the agro-ecological and social setting of the district.

In sum, it can be concluded that involvement of multiple stake holders paid dividends in making the programme people's centered and also with accrual of benefits , though not to the desired extent, as envisaged in the programme. It could throw light on "What is usually not appreciated" i.e the potential of the watershed approach in arresting run off and prevention of soil erosion of the already wasted lands and their development.

TRENDS IN INTER-REGIONAL POVERTY AND ECONOMIC INEQUALITY IN INDIA

I. Sundar

INTRODUCTION

Poverty being a concrete reality has affected the Indian society for the past several decades. In India poverty is not a present phenomenon. Ample evidence of its incidence among the masses is found in the literal and descriptive accounts of the precolonial and colonial times. In order to eradicate poverty and economic inequality, the government of India has implemented a lot of development programmes from time to time. The economic polices of India continues to undergo changes in the form of shifting the focus from economic growth to poverty and inequality reduction in accordance with the changing needs of the society over a period of time. The mounting pressure on poverty compelled the government to undertake special poverty alleviation programmes under different heads. These special poverty eradication programmes are mostly supplementary to the main five-year plans. Significant among them are the food-for-work programme, undertaken in the year 1987 with the main objectives of providing man with days of work. Integrated Rural Development Programme of the 1978 with the objective of providing financial assistance to weaker sections, Rural Landless Employment Guarantee Programme of 1983 with the objective of providing employment guarantee to the landless agricultural labour in rural areas, National Rural Employment Programme of 1980 with the objective of providing employment to the rural people and progrmme of self employment for educated youth in the year 1983 with the main objectives of encouraging the educated unemployment youth to undertake self employment ventures in India. As a result of restructuring Indian economy, the IRDP and allied programmes including million-wells-scheme started as single self employment programme called Swarna Jayanthi Gram Swarozgar Yojana in the year 1999, which aims at promoting micro-enterprises and helping the rural poor to form self help groups. Further Jawahar Gram Samridhi Yojana was introduced in the year 1994 as successor to Jawahar Rozgar Yojana with the main objective of creation of durable productive community assets. The other poverty eradication programmes such as national social assistance programme of 1995, employment of assurance scheme of 1993, Pradhan Mantri Gramodaya Yojana of 2000 Swarna Jayanthi Shahari Rozgar

Yojana and provision of basic needs viz, education, health, nutrition, water supply and housing play a considerable role in eradication of poverty and economic inequality in the country.

REVIEW ON THE SUBJECT

Many studies have been conducted to examine the poverty in India. Hence there is a need to review a few studies for the purpose of present analysis. Subramanian (1986) in his study on "Poverty and Inequality in Tamil Nadu by using NSS data for 11 years ending 1983, observes that the proportion of the population in poverty has been consistently high in both the rural and the urban areas, and also showed that the trends in the number of people in poverty had also, by and large, been extremely discouraging. Bardhan (1973) estimated poverty line at Rs. 15/- per capita per month for the rural households and Rs. 18/- per capita per month for the urban households at 1960-62 prices.

Minhas (1974) estimated the poverty line at Rs. 200, per capita per annum for the rural areas and Rs. 240/- per capita per annum for the urban areas at 1960-61 prices. As against this Ojha, (1971) estimated in 1967-68, 289 million persons lived below the poverty line in 1967-68. As compared to 52 per cent in 1960-61, 70 per cent of rural population was below the poverty line in 1967-68. Mundel (1983) estimated poverty line for the State of Tamil nadu as Rs. 57/- per capita in 1973-74 prices based on a nutritional intake norm of 2435 calories per head per day.

Da Costa (1971) measured the extent of poverty in India for the year 1963-64. He divided the poverty stricken people into the poor, the destitute, and the seriously destitute. Rao and Chandrasekhar (1984) have examined the inter-state and inter-temporal dimensions of the incidence of poverty in urban area for the period 1963-64 to 1973-74. A study by Sastry (1981) examined the incidence of poverty and its inter-relationship with economic development, inequality and poverty in the three sub-regions of Andhra Pradesh (Coastal Andhra, Rayalaseema and Telengana) and its districts.

Bhatty's (1993) study revealed that the inequality in the distribution of per capita consumption expenditure was uniformly less than the inequality in the distribution of income. The study by Saith (1991) investigated the relationship between rural poverty, prices and agricultural production in India for the period 1956-57 to 1973-74 on the basis of secondary data. Rajaraman (1975) studied the changes in rural poverty and inequality in Punjab on the basis of the N.S.S. consumption expenditure data 16th – 1960-61, 17th – 1961-62 and 25th 1970-71 rounds.

The character of poverty among the rural poor in the West Godavari district of Andhra Pradesh was examined by Parthasarathy Elliott al (1995). Thankurtha (1980) estimated the extent of poverty in the Calcutta city (for the period 1950-72) on the basis of the family budget enquiries undertaken by the Bureau of Applied Economics and Statistics, West Bengal.

Thus many studies have analysed poverty in various levels over a period of time. This paper analyses poverty during post liberalization period on the basis of data relating to three points of time.

RESULTS AND DISCUSSION

A careful analysis of trends in rural poverty reveals the following facts. It is observed from table 1 that the number of people living below poverty line was 2519.5 lakhs in 1983 and the number decline to 1932.43 lakhs in 1999-2000, showing 30.38 per cent of decline in rural poverty in India. In 1983 the poverty line was fixed at Rs. 89.5 per cent rural poverty and it rose to 327.56 rupees 1999-2000 showing 100.21 per cent of increase and it is mainly due increase in the price of goods and services in consequence of inflation. More than 100 per cent of poverty reduction is observed in some states and UTS viz., Goa (954.54%), Jammu and Kashmir 9341.42%), Kerala (289.23%), Tamilnadu (125.57%), Delhi (528.77%), Lakshadweep (200%), Pondicherry (143.75%) in terms of absolute numbers and also percentage terms. These states record a steady decline in poverty level.

Table 1
Trends in Rural Poverty in India

State	*No of Persons Living Below Poverty Line, Persons in Each*				*Poverty Line Interms of Fixed Rupees*			
	1983	*1993-94*	*1999-2000*	*Growth Rate*	*1983*	*1993-94*	*1999-2000*	*Growth Rate*
Andhra Pradesh	114.34 (26.53)	79.49 (15.92)	58.13 (11.05)	-96.69	72.66	163.02	262.94	72.36
Arunachal Pradesh	2.70 (42.60)	3.62 (45.01)	3.80 (40.04)	+28.94	98.32	232.05	365.43	73.09
Assam	73.43 (42.60)	94.33 (45.01)	92.17 (40.04)	+20.33	98.32	232.05	365.43	73.09
Bihar	417.70 (64.37)	450.86 (58.21)	376.51 (44.30)	-10.94	97.48	212.16	333.07	70.73
Goa	1.16 (14.81)	0.38 (5.34)	0.11 (1.35)	-954.54	88.24	194.94	318.63	72.30
Gujarat	72.88 (29.80)	62.16 (22.18)	39.80 (13.17)	-83.11	83.29	202.11	318.94	73.88
Haryana	22.03 (20.56)	36.56 (28.02)	11.94 (8.27)	-84.50	88.57	233.79	362.81	75.58
Himachal Pradesh	7.07 (17.00)	15.40 (30.34)	4.84 (7.94)	-46.07	88.57	233.79	367.45	75.89
Jammu & Kashmir	13.11 (26.04)	19.05 (30.34)	2.97 (3.97)	-341.42	91.75	233.79	367.45	75.03
Karnataka	100.50 (36.33)	95.99 (29.88)	59.91 (17.38)	-67.75	83.31	186.63	309.59	73.09
Kerala	81.62 (39.03)	55.95 (25.76)	20.97 (9.38)	-289.23	99.35	243.84	374.79	73.49
Madhya Pradesh	215.48 (48.90)	216.19 (40.64)	217.32 (37.06)	+0.84	83.59	193.10	311.34	73.15
Maharashtra	193.75 (45.23)	193.33 (37.93)	125.12 (23.72)	-35.42	88.24	194.94	318.63	72.30
Manipur	4.76 (42.60)	6.33 (45.01)	6.53 (40.04)	+27.10	98.32	232.05	365.43	73.09
Meghalaya	5.04 (42.60)	7.09 (45.01)	789 (40.04)	+36.12	98.32	232.05	365.43	73.09

Contd...

State	No of Persons Living Below Poverty Line, Persons in Each				Poverty Line Interms of Fixed Rupees			
	1983	1993-94	1999-2000	Growth Rate	1983	1993-94	1999-2000	Growth Rate
Mizoram	1.58 (42.60)	1.64 (45.01)	1.40 (40.04)	-12.85	98.32	232.05	365.43	73.09
Nagaland	3.19 (42.60)	4.85 (45.01)	5.21 (40.04)	+38.77	98.32	232.05	365.43	73.09
Orissa	164.65 (67.53)	140.90 (49.72)	143.69 (48.01)	-14.58	106.28	194.03	323.92	67.18
Punjab	16.79 (13.20)	17.76 (11.95)	10.20 (6.35)	-64.60	88.57	233.79	362.68	75.57
Rajasthan	96.77 (33.50)	94.68 (26.46)	55.06 (13.74)	-75.75	80.24	215.89	344.03	76.67
Sikkim	1.24 (42.60)	1.81 (45.01)	2.00 (40.04)	+38.00	98.32	232.05	365.43	73.04
Tamilnadu	181.61 (53.99)	121.70 (32.48)	80.51 (20.55)	-125.57	96.15	196.53	307.64	68.74
Tripura	8.35 (42.60)	11.41 (45.01)	12.53 (40.04)	+33.35	98.32	232.05	365.43	73.09
Uttar Pradesh	448.03 (46.45)	496.17 (42.28)	412.01 (31.22)	-8.75	83.85	213.01	336.88	75.10
West Bengal	268.60 (63.05)	209.90 (40.80)	180.11 (31.85)	-49.13	105.55	220.74	350.17	69.85
Andaman & Nicobar	0.84 (53.99)	0.73 (32.48)	0.58 (20.55)	-44.83	96.15	196.53	307.64	68.75
Chandigarh	0.09 (23.79)	0.07 (11.35)	0.06 (5.75)	-50.00	101.03	253.61	388.15	73.97
Dadra & Nagar Haveli	0.16 (14.81)	0.72 (51.95)	0.30 (17.57)	+46.67	88.24	194.94	318.63	72.30
Daman & Diu	-	0.03 (5.34)	0.01 (1.35)	-200.00	-	194.94	318.63	38.81
Delhi	0.44 (7.66)	0.19 (1.90)	0.07 (0.40)	-528.57	88.57	233.79	362.68	75.57
Lakshadweep	0.09 (39.03)	0.06 (25.76)	0.03 (9.38)	-200.00	99.35	243.84	374.79	73.49
Pondicheery	1.56 (53.99)	0.93 (32.48)	0.64 (20.55)	-143.75	96.15	196.53	307.64	68.74
All India	2519.57 (45.65)	2440.31 (32.27)	1932.43 (27.09)	-30.38	89.5	205.84	327.56	100.21

Source: Planning Commission, Government of India.
Figures in parentheses denote percentages

The factors that have contributed to rapid decline in poverty in these states increase effective implementation of poverty alleviation schemes such as Jawahar Rozgar Yojana, Swarna Janaynthi Gram Swarozgar Yojana, National social assistance programme, employment assurance scheme, Pradhan Mantri Gramodaya Yojana, Swarna Jayanthi Shahari Rozgar Yojana and effective provision of basic minimum needs such as education, health, nutrition water supply and housing.

More than 50 per cent of decline in poverty population is found in the states such as Andhrapradesh (96.69%), Gujarat (83.11%), Haryana (84.50%), Karnataka (67.75%), Punjab (64.60%), Rajasthan (75.75%) and Haryana during 1983 and 1999-2000. It is significant to note that there is an increasing trend in number of poor people in Arunachal Pradesh (28%), Assam (20.33%), Madhya Pradesh (0.84%), Manipur (27.10%), Meghalaya (36.12%), Nagaland (38.77%), Sikkim (38%), Tripura (33.35%) and Dadra and Nagar Haveli. However, in terms of percentage analysis they show a marginal decline. This is due to increase in population. It could be noted that poverty increase can be noted in absolute number, but relative sense a sharp decline and 2.2 per cent of population growth in responsible for this situation.

Some states record 25 per cent of reduction in number of people living below poverty line. During 1983 and 1999-2000. These include Bihar (10.94%), Mizoram (12.85%), Orissa (4.58%) and Uttar Pradesh (8.75%). These states are backward and their attempt to reduction of poverty is not upto the mark of expectation. The remaining states have shown about 25-50 per cent of reduction in number of people living below poverty line. There is a wide variation with respect to fixation of poverty line. Almost all states and UTs shows more than 70 per cent increase in poverty line fixed amount. The amount prescribing poverty line is low in Andhra Praesh, as it is Rs. Below 300 in 1979-2000 than those of remaining states in India. In general states such as Tripura (40.04%), Sikkim (40.4%), Orissa (48.01%), Manipur (40.4%), Bihar (44.30%) and Arunachal Pradesh have more proportion of below poverty people in 1999-2000.

A keen observation of data in table 2 indicates the state wise trends in urban poverty in India during 1983 and 1999-2000. In 1983, 769.4 million people constituted 40.79 per cent of them were lived below poverty line and the number decreased to 670.07, constituted 23.62 per cent in 1999-2000, showing 15.86 per cent of shortfall during the period. However, inter-state analysis presence different situations. The states such as Andhra Pradesh (17.47%), Arunachal Pradesh (33.33%), Bihar (9.72%), Madhya Pradesh (23.06%), Maharashtra (5.57%), Mizoram (17.77%), Orissa (34.40%), Dadra and Nagar Haveli (33.33%) and Pondicherry (2.82%) have shown an increasing trend with respect to absolute number of people living below poverty line. However, these states and UTs have shown a declining trend in terms of percentage estimate and it is due to a general increase in population size during the period of analysis.

Jammu and Kashmir records highest shortfall in urban poverty situation and it could be noted that its urban poverty was 17.76 per cent in 1983 and it declined to 1.98 per cent in 1999-2000, showing 689.65 per cent of decline, showing effective implementation of urban poverty eradication programme. In Punjab 11.85 million people were lived below poverty line in 1983 and it declined to 4.29 million in 1999-2000, recording 176.22 per cent of decline during the period of analysis. A decline of 200 per cent is observed in urban poverty in Daman and Diu during 1983 and 1999-2000 and it is 144.44 per cent in the case of Chandigarh.

Table 2
Trends in Urban Poverty in India

State	*No of Persons Living Below Poverty Line, Persons in Each*				*Poverty Line Interms of Fixed Rupees*			
	1983	*1993-94*	*1999-2000*	*Growth Rate*	*1983*	*1993-94*	*1999-2000*	*Growth Rate*
Andhra Pradesh	50.24	74.47	60.88	+17.47	106.43	278.14	457.40	76.73
	(36.3)	(38.33)	(26.63)					
Arunachal Pradesh	0.12	0.11	0.18	+33.33	97.51	212.42	343.99	71.65
	(21.73)	(7.73)	(7.47)					
Assam	4.26	2.03	2.38	-78.99	97.51	212.42	343.99	71.65
	(21.73)	(7.73)	(7.47)					
Bihar	44.35	42.49	49.13	+9.72	111.80	238.49	379.78	70.56
	(47.33)	(34.50)	(32.91)					
Goa	1.07	1.53	0.59	-81.35	126.47	328.56	539.71	76.56
	(27.00)	(27.03)	(7.52)					
Gujarat	45.04	43.02	28.09	-60.34	123.22	297.22	474.41	74.02
	(39.14)	(27.89)	(15.59)					
Haryana	7.57	7.31	5.39	-40.44	103.48	258.23	420.20	75.37
	(24.15)	(16.38)	(9.99)					
Himachal Pradesh	0.34	0.46	0.29	-17.24	102.26	253.61	420.20	75.66
	(9.43)	(9.18)	(4.63)					
Jammu & Kashmir	2.49	1.86	0.49	-689.65	99.62	253.61	420.20	76.29
	(17.76)	(9.18)	(1.98)					
Karnataka	49.31	60.46	44.49	-10.83	120.19	302.89	511.44	76.49
	(42.82)	(40.14)	(25.25)					
Kerala	25.15	20.46	20.07	-25.31	122.64	280.54	477.06	74.29
	(45.68)	(24.55)	(20.27)					
Madhya Pradesh	62.49	82.33	81.22	+23.06	122.82	317.16	481.65	74.50
	(53.06)	(48.38)	(38.44)					
Maharashtra	97.14	111.90	102.87	+5.57	126.47	328.56	539.71	76.56
	(40.26)	(35.15)	(26.81)					
Manipur	0.89	0.47	0.66	-34.84	97.51	212.42	343.99	71.65
	(21.73)	(7.73)	(7.47)					
Meghalaya	0.57	0.29	0.34	-67.65	97.51	212.42	343.99	+71.65
	(21.73)	(7.73)	(7.47)					
Mizoram	0.37	0.30	0.45	+17.77	97.51	212.42	343.99	+71.65
	(21.73)	(7.73)	(7.47)					
Nagaland	0.31	0.20	0.28	-10.72	97.51	212.42	343.99	+71.65
	(21.73)	(7.73)	(7.47)					
Orissa	16.66	19.70	25.40	+34.40	124.81	298.22	473.12	+73.62
	(49.15)	(41.64)	(42.83)					
Punjab	11.85	7.35	4.29	-176.22	101.03	253.61	388.15	+73.97
	(23.79)	(11.35)	(5.75)					
Rajasthan	30.06	33.82	26.78	+12.24	113.55	280.85	465.92	+75.62
	(37.94)	(30.49)	(19.85)					
Sikkim	0.10	0.03	0.04	-150.00	97.51	212.42	343.99	+71.65
	(21.73)	(7.73)	(7.47)					
Tamilnadu	78.46	80.40	49.97	-57.01	120.30	296.63	475.60	+74.70
	(46.96)	(39.77)	(22.11)					
Tripura	0.60	0.38	0.49	-22.44	97.51	212.42	343.99	+71.65
	(21.73)	(7.73)	(7.47)					
Uttar Pradesh	108.71	108.28	117.88	+7.77	110.23	258.65	416.29	73.52
	(49.81)	(35.39)	(30.89)					

Contd...

State	*No of Persons Living Below Poverty Line, Persons in Each*				*Poverty Line Interms of Fixed Rupees*			
	1983	*1993-94*	*1999-2000*	*Growth Rate*	*1983*	*1993-94*	*1999-2000*	*Growth Rate*
West Bengal	50.09 (32.32)	44.66 (22.41)	33.38 (14.86)	-50.05	105.91	247.53	409.22	74.11
Andaman & Nicobar	0.26 (46.96)	0.33 (39.77)	0.24 (22.11)	-8.33	120.30	296.63	475.60	74.70
Chandigarh	1.10 (23.79)	0.73 (11.35)	0.45 (5.75)	-144.44	101.03	253.61	388.15	73.97
Dadra & Nagar Haveli	0.02 (27.00)	0.06 (39.93)	0.03 (13.52)	+3.33	126.47	328.56	539.71	76.56
Daman & Diu	-	0.15 (27.03)	0.05 (7.52)	-200.00	-	328.56	539.71	39.12
Delhi	17.95 (27.89)	15.32 (16.03)	11.42 (9.42)	-57.18	123.29	309.48	505.45	75.60
Lakshadweep	0.10 (45.68)	0.08 (24.55)	0.08 (20.27)	-25.00	122.64	280.54	477.06	74.29
Pondicheery	1.72 (46.96)	2.38 (39.77)	1.77 (22.11)	+2.82	120.3	296.63	475.60	74.70
India	709.4 (40.79)	763.37 (32.36)	670.07 (23.62)	-15.86	115.65	281.35	454.11	74.53

Source: Planning Commission, Government of India, Cited in National Human Development Report, 2001, pp. 166-169.
Figures in parentheses denote percentage.

In Sikkim 21.73 per cent of people were lived below poverty line in 1983 and it declined to 7.47 per cent in 1999-2000, showing 150 per cent of decline in urban poverty in the period of analysis. Assam state shows 78.99 per cent of decline in urban poverty as it's decreased from 21.73 in 1983 to 7.47 in 1999-2000. In the case of Goa state the decline in urban poverty is observed from 27 per cent in 1983 to 7.52 per cent in 1999-2000. In the same period Gujarat records 60.34 per cent of decline in urban poverty. In Meghalaya state 0.57 million people were lived below poverty in 1983 and the number declined to 0.34 in 1999-2000, showing 67.65 per cent of decline in the period of analysis. Tamilnadu state shows 57.01 per cent of decline in urban poverty during the period of analysis and it is 50.5 per cent in the case of West Bengal.

Urban poverty in New Delhi shows 57.18 per cent of decline during 1983 and 1999-2000. The states such as Orissa, Haryana and Manipur have show 25.50 per cent of decline in urban poverty in the period of analysis. The remaining states and UTs show below 25 per cent of decline in urban poverty during the period of analysis.

An analysis of poverty line in terms of fixed Rs. Indicates the following facts. In general all the state and union territories show an increase of above 70 per cent in terms of poverty line fixed rupees. The states such as Arunachal Pradesh, Assam, Manipur, Meghalaya, Mizoram, Nagaland, Sikkim and Tripura had poverty line fixed Rs. 97.51 in 1983 and it rose to 343.99 in 1999-2000. The states and UTs like Goa, Karnataka, Maharashtra, Dadra and Nagar

Haveli, Daman and Diu and Delhi have above Rs. 500 as fixed poverty line per month.

A keen observation of data in table 3 indicates the trends combined poverty in India. At the national level 3228.97 million people were lived below poverty line in 1983 and it decreased to 2602.50 in 1999-2000, showing 24.07 per cent of decline. This is due to progressive implementation of anti-poverty programme in the country. In Goa there were 2.23 million poor people in 1983 and the number declined to 0.70 million in 1999-2000, showing 218.57 per cent of decline in absolute number and in terms of percentage it declined from 18.90 to 4.40 in the same period. Though there is a marginal decline in percentage of people living below poverty line in Arunachal Pradesh (29.14%), Assam (17.83%), Madhya Pradesh (6.89%), Manipur (21.42%), Meghalaya (31.71%), Nagaland (36.24%), Sikkim (54.4%), Tripura (31.25%) and Dadra and Nagar Haveli (45.45%) their number of below poverty population increased during 1983 and 1999-2000.

Table 3
Trends in Combined Poverty in India

State	*No of Persons Living Below Poverty Line in Lakhs*			
	1983	*1993-94*	*1999-2000*	*Growth Rate*
Andhra Pradesh	164.58	153.97	119.01	-38.29
	(28.91)	(22.19)	(15.77)	
Arunachal Pradesh	2.82	3.73	3.98	+29.14
	(40.88)	(39.35)	(33.47)	
Assam	77.69	96.36	94.55	+17.83
	(40.47)	(40.86)	(36.09)	
Bihar	462.05	493.35	425.64	+8.55
	(62.22)	(54.96)	(42.60)	
Goa	2.23	1.91	0.70	-218.57
	(18.90)	(14.92)	(4.40)	
Gujarat	117.92	105.19	67.89	-73.69
	(32.79)	(24.21)	(14.07)	
Haryana	29.60	43.88	17.34	-70.70
	(21.37)	(25.05)	(8.74)	
Himachal Pradesh	7.41	15.86	5.12	-44.72
	(16.40)	(28.44)	(7.63)	
Jammu & Kashmir	15.60	20.92	3.46	-350.86
	(24.24)	(25.17)	(3.48)	
Karnataka	149.81	156.46	104.40	-43.49
	(38.24)	(33.16)	(20.04)	
Kerala	106.77	76.41	41.04	-160.16
	(40.42)	(25.43)	(12.72)	
Madhya Pradesh	277.97	298.52	298.54	+6.89
	(49.78)	(42.52)	(37.43)	
Maharashtra	290.89	305.22	227.99	-27.58
	(43.44)	(36.86)	(25.02)	
Manipur	5.65	6.80	7.19	+21.42
	(37.02)	(33.78)	(28.54)	
Meghalaya	5.62	7.38	8.23	+31.71
	(38.81)	(37.92)	(33.87)	
Mizoram	1.96	1.94	1.85	-5.95
	(36.00)	(25.66)	(19.47)	

State	*No of Persons Living Below Poverty Line in Lakhs*			
	1983	*1993-94*	*1999-2000*	*Growth Rate*
Nagaland	3.50	5.05	5.49	+36.24
	(39.25)	(37.92)	(32.67)	
Orissa	181.31	160.60	169.09	-7.22
	(65.29)	(48.56)	(47.15)	
Punjab	28.64	25.11	14.49	-57.65
	(16.18)	(11.77)	(6.16)	
Rajasthan	126.83	128.50	81.83	-54.99
	(34.46)	(27.41)	(15.28)	
Sikkim	1.35	1.84	2.05	+54.14
	(39.71)	(41.43)	(36.55)	
Tamilnadu	260.07	202.10	130.48	-99.32
	(51.66)	(35.03)	(21.12)	
Tripura	8.95	11.79	13.02	+31.25
	(40.03)	(39.01)	(34.44)	
Uttar Pradesh	556.74	604.46	529.89	-5.06
	(47.07)	(40.85)	(31.15)	
West Bengal	318.69	254.56	213.49	-49.27
	(54.85)	(35.66)	(27.02)	
Andaman & Nicobar	1.11	1.06	0.82	-35.36
	(52.13)	(34.47)	(20.99)	
Chandigarh	1.19	0.80	0.51	-133.33
	(23.79)	(11.35)	(5.75)	
Dadra & Nagar Haveli	0.18	0.77	0.33	+45.45
	(15.67)	(50.84)	(17.14)	
Daman & Diu	-	0.18	0.06	-200.00
		(15.80)	(4.44)	
Delhi	18.39	15.51	11.49	
	(26.22)	(14.69)	(8.23)	-60.05
Lakshadweep	0.19	0.14	0.11	-72.72
	(42.36)	(25.04)	(15.60)	
Pondicheery	3.28	3.31	2.41	-36.09
	(50.06)	(37.40)	(21.67)	
All India	3228.97	3203.68	2602.50	24.07
	(44.48)	(35.97)	(26.10)	

Source: Planning Commission, Government of India.
Figures in parentheses denote percentages.

It is significant to note that some states and UTs show a more than 100 per cent decline in number of people living below poverty line during 1983 and 1999-2000. These include Daman and Diu (200%), Chandigarh (133.33%), Kerala (160.16%), Jammu and Kashmir (350.86%) and Goa (218.57%). A 50 to 100 per cent of decline in overall poverty is observed in Gujarat (73.69%), Haryana (70.70%), Punjab (57.65%), Rajasthan (54.99%), Sikkim (54.14%), Tamilnadu (99.32%), Delhi (60.05%) and Lakshaweep (72.72%). Some states and UTs record low level of reduction in below poverty population.

These include Mizoram (5.95%), Orissa (7.22%) and Uttar Pradesh (5.06%). The remaining states have reduced their poverty population in the range of 25-50 per cent. The reduction in below poverty people shows a progressive increase in the well beings of Indian population.

Table 4 presents data on trends in per capita consumption expenditure in India. A study of trend in inequality in per capita consumption expenditure examines the following facts. At the national level the per capita consumption was Rs. 328.18 per capita per month in 1993-94 and it rose to 590.98 in 1999-2000, showing 44.46 per cent of increase in per capita consumption expenditure. In general, urban per capita consumption is greater than rural per capita consumption expenditure. In 1999-2000 urban per capita consumption expenditure is Rs. 854.96 and rural 486.06, showing much difference between the two. The urban per capita consumption expenditure shows 46.43 and real per capita consumption expenditure shows 42.10 per cent of growth rate during 1993-94 and 1999-2000.

Table 4
Per Capita Consumption Expenditure

State	Rural			Urban			Combined		
	1993-94	*1999-2000*	*Growth Rate*	*1993-94*	*1999-2000*	*Growth Rate*	*1993-94*	*1999-2000*	*Growth Rate*
Andhra Pradesh	288.7	453.61	36.35	408.6	773.52	47.17	322.28	550.53	41.46
Arunachal Pradesh	316.85	647.92	51.09	494.11	765.91	35.48	343.75	672.31	48.87
Assam	258.11	426.12	39.42	458.6	814.12	43.66	280.42	473.42	40.76
Bihar	218.3	384.72	43.25	353	601.89	41.35	236.78	417.18	43.24
Goa	487.24	868.77	43.91	519.33	1155.45	55.05	501.4	1014.78	50.59
Gujarat	303.3	551.33	44.98	454.2	891.68	49.06	356.87	678.27	47.38
Haryana	385	714.37	46.10	473.9	912.07	48.04	407.67	767.89	46.91
Himachal Pradesh	350.63	684.5	48.77	746.92	1242.93	39.90	386.23	737.82	47.65
Jammu & Kashmir	363.31	677.23	46.35	541.58	952.85	43.16	406.84	746.74	45.51
Karnataka	269.4	499.78	46.09	423.1	910.99	53.55	318.47	638.81	50.14
Kerala	390.4	765.7	49.01	493.8	932.61	47.05	419.08	816.76	48.68
Madhya Pradesh	252	401.5	37.23	408.1	693.56	41.15	289.83	478.92	39.48
Maharashtra	272.7	496.77	45.10	529.8	973.33	45.56	371.54	697.42	46.72
Manipur	299.57	537.79	44.29	319.55	707.77	54.85	305.59	596.36	38.64
Meghalaya	356.98	563.64	36.66	530.55	971.87	45.40	390	639.13	38.97
Mizoram	389.55	721.83	46.03	549.51	1056.64	47.99	472.59	935.53	49.48
Nagaland	441.45	941.3	53.10	510.02	1242.39	58.95	454.48	1005.99	54.82
Orissa	219.8	373.17	41.09	402.5	618.48	34.92	245.94	413.71	40.55
Punjab	433	742.43	41.67	510.7	898.82	43.18	456.59	792.07	42.35
Rajasthan	322.4	548.88	41.26	424.7	795.81	46.63	346.6	611.19	43.29
Sikkim	298.72	531.68	43.81	518.44	905.69	42.75	321.12	559.97	49.79
Tamilnadu	293.6	513.97	42.87	438.3	971.61	54.88	344.31	681.37	49.46
Tripura	343.93	528.41	34.91	489.94	876.59	44.10	367.43	589.5	37.67
Uttar Pradesh	273.8	466.68	41.33	389	690.68	43.67	297.62	516.99	42.43
West Bengal	278.8	545.49	48.88	474.2	866.6	45.28	333.36	571.66	41.68
Andaman & Nicobar	495.9	780.21	36.44	907.19	1114.27	18.58	608.07	873.28	30.36
Chandigarh	463.03	989.2	53.19	1028	1435.36	28.38	975.18	1382.87	29.48
Dadra & Nagar Haveli	234.28	561.18	58.25	441.86	1207.34	63.40	253.4	636.82	60.20
Daman & Diu	452.48	901.48	49.80	474.98	979.43	51.50	463.33	976.04	52.52
Delhi	605.22	917.21	34.01	794.95	1383.46	42.53	777.01	1316.3	40.97
Lakshadweep	526.32	876.19	39.93	507.63	1018.25	50.14	515.17	967.35	46.74
Pondicheery	347.96	597.63	41.77	419.84	784.28	46.46	396.53	731.9	45.82
All India	281.40	486.08	42.10	458.00	854.96	46.43	328.18	590.98	44.46

Source: NSS 38th, 50th and 55th Rounds on Household Consumption Expenditure.

Chandigarh occupies the first position in India with respect to its per capita consumption expenditure per month at combined level. Its per capita consumption expenditure was Rs. 915-18 in 1993 and it rose to 1382.89 in 1999-2000 showing 29.48 per cent increase. In general its urban per capita consumption expenditure is greater than its rural. The growth of rural consumption expenditure is greater than its urban, indicating the better prosperity of agricultural and its allied activities. Delhi comes to next position in its percentage consumption expenditure to the aggregate level and it is worked out Rs. 1316.3 in 1999-2000. Its growth during 1993-94 and 1999-2000 is 40.97 per cent at the overall level. Goa takes the third position in its per capita consumption expenditure at the national level and it shows 50.59 per cent of growth during 1993-94 and 1999-2000 and Nagaland states come to next position in its per capita consumptin expenditure with 54.82 per cent of absolute growth level. The states such as Daman and Diu, Andaman and Nicobar Island Mizoram and Kerala have per capita consumption expenditure in the range of Rs. 800-1000. Among them Andaman and Nicobar Islands record low growth rate (30.36%) at the absolute level. In all the states and union territories rural urban difference exists with respect to per capita consumption expenditure. In general, per capta consumption expenditure is greater in urban areas than rural area. Some states and union territories like Pondicherry, Dadra and Nagar Haveli, Tamilnadu, Rajasthan, Meghalaya, Maharashtra, Karnataka, Jammu and Kashmir, Himachal Pradesh, Haryana, Gujarat and Arunachal Pradesh have per capita consumption expenditure in the range of Rs. 600-800 in 1999-2000. The per capita consumption expenditure is quite low in Assam, Bihar, Madhya Pradesh and Orissa as they have below Rs. 500 per month.

It is significant to note that more than 50 per cent of growth in per capita consumption expenditure is observed in Nagaland, Dadra and Nagar Haveli, Daman and Diu, Goa and Karnataka during 1993-94 and 1999-2000 in absolute sense. The growth of real per capita consumption expenditure is quite impressive in Arunachal Pradesh, Chandigarh and Dadra and Nagar Haveli as they record above 50 per cent in the period of analysis. More than 50 per cent increase is observed in urban per capita consumption expenditure in Nagaland, Tamilnadu, Lakshaweep, Dadra and Nagar Haveli, Manipur, Karnataka and Goa, some states and union territories record below 40 per cent of increase in per capita consumption expenditure. These include Manipur, Meghalaya, Tripura, Andaman and Nicobar Islands and Chandigarh.

Data presented in table 5 indicate the growth of composition of per capita consumption expenditure during 1993-94 and 1994-2000. At the overall level rural per capita food consumption expenditure was 63.18 percent in 1993-94 and but it declined to 59.41 per cent in 1999-2000, indicating 6.66 per cent of growth rate in the period of analysis. In general rural per capita food consumption expenditure is more than 60 per cent in Lakshadweep, Dadar and Nagar Haveli, Andaman and Nicobar Islands, West Bengal, Tripura, Orissa, Meghalaya, Manipur, Bihar, Assam and Andhra pradesh in 1999-2000. The rural per capita food consumption expenditure's growth rate is quite low in Andhra Pradesh, Meghalaya, Mizoram, Tripura, West Bengal, Andaman

Table 5
Composition of Per Capita Consumption Expenditure

State	Rural Composition of Percapita Consumption Expenditure						Urban Composition of Percapita Consumption Expenditure					
	Food Consumption			Non-Food Consumption			Food Consumption			Non-Food Consumption		
	1993-94	1999-2000	Growth Rate	1993-94	1999-2000	Growth Rate	1993-94	1999-2000	Growth Rate	1993-94	1999-2000	Growth Rate
Andhra Pradesh	59.58	60.5	1.52	40.42	39.5	2.32	53.84	47.44	13.49	46.16	52.56	12.17
Arunachal Pradesh	61.63	55.6	10.84	38.37	44.4	13.58	60.82	57.65	5.49	39.18	42.35	7.48
Assam	72.26	67.63	6.84	27.74	32.37	14.30	59.68	53.38	11.80	40.32	44.62	9.63
Bihar	71	66.54	6.70	29	33.46	13.32	62.92	57.24	9.92	37.08	42.76	13.28
Goa	56.62	54.2	4.46	43.38	45.8	5.28	59.09	51.33	15.11	40.91	48.67	15.94
Gujarat	67.1	59.82	12.16	32.9	40.18	18.11	58.41	49.58	17.80	41.59	50.42	17.51
Haryana	60.05	55.51	8.17	39.95	44.49	10.20	53.87	45.87	17.44	46.13	54.13	14.77
Himachal Pradesh	60.02	56	7.17	39.98	44	9.13	42.45	45.34	6.37	57.55	54.66	5.28
Jammu & Kashmir	61.78	62.6	1.30	38.22	37.4	2.19	56.41	55.51	1.62	43.59	44.49	2.02
Karnataka	61.95	59.08	4.85	38.05	40.92	7.01	55.71	46.32	20.27	44.29	53.68	17.49
Kerala	60.45	53.7	12.56	39.55	46.3	14.57	53.93	49.04	9.94	46.07	50.96	9.59
Madhya Pradesh	61.19	58.09	5.33	38.81	41.91	7.39	52.85	47.6	11.02	47.15	52.4	10.01
Maharashtra	59.48	54.71	8.72	40.52	45.29	10.53	53.02	45.31	17.01	46.98	54.69	14.09
Manipur	67.48	63.12	6.90	32.52	36.88	11.82	63.82	56.4	13.15	36.18	43.6	17.01
Meghalaya	60.83	60.44	0.64	39.17	39.56	0.98	56.38	47.02	19.90	43.62	52.98	17.66
Mizoram	61.24	59.36	3.16	38.76	40.64	4.62	54.14	52.04	4.03	45.86	47.96	4.37
Nagaland	64.99	58.93	10.28	35.01	41.07	14.75	58.85	47.64	23.53	41.15	52.36	21.40
Orissa	68.06	64.11	6.16	31.94	35.89	11.00	57.79	56.95	1.47	42.21	43.05	1.95
Punjab	57.92	52.29	10.76	42.08	47.71	11.80	53.03	47.12	12.54	46.97	52.88	11.17
Rajasthan	62.28	59.5	4.67	37.72	40.5	6.86	56.65	50.85	11.40	43.35	49.15	11.80
Sikkim	65.65	56.78	15.62	34.35	43.22	20.52	55.18	47.53	16.09	44.82	52.47	14.57
Tamilnadu	62.84	58.74	6.97	37.16	41.26	9.94	54.6	45.61	19.71	45.4	54.39	16.52
Tripura	64.85	65.2	0.53	35.15	34.8	1.00	56.96	56.18	1.38	43.04	43.82	1.78

State	Rural Composition of Percapita Consumption Expenditure						Urban Composition of Percapita Consumption Expenditure					
	Food Consumption			Non-Food Consumption			Food Consumption			Non-Food Consumption		
	1993-94	1999-2000	Growth Rate	1993-94	1999-2000	Growth Rate	1993-94	1999-2000	Growth Rate	1993-94	1999-2000	Growth Rate
Uttar Pradesh	61.47	57.42	7.05	38.53	42.53	9.51	55.99	50.49	10.89	44.01	49.51	11.10
West Bengal	66.82	65.9	1.39	33.18	34.1	2.69	55.93	52.28	6.98	44.07	47.72	7.65
Andaman & Nicobar	63.28	61.56	2.79	36.72	38.44	4.47	43.78	51.26	14.59	56.22	48.74	15.34
Chandigarh	56.08	47.82	11.27	43.92	52.18	15.82	35.79	38.82	7.80	64.21	61.18	4.95
Dadra & Nagar Haveli	65.46	60.09	8.93	34.54	39.91	13.45	62.68	47.72	31.34	37.32	52.28	28.61
Daman & Diu	62.11	53.76	15.53	37.89	46.24	18.05	62.79	53.7	16.93	37.21	46.3	19.63
Delhi	63.46	44.41	42.89	36.54	55.59	34.26	48.58	41.04	18.37	51.42	58.96	12.78
Lakshadweep	64.49	62.09	3.86	35.51	37.91	6.33	67.14	60.03	11.84	32.86	39.97	17.78
Pondicheery	61.37	56.61	8.40	38.63	43.39	10.97	57.71	51	13.15	42.29	49	13.69
All India	63.18	59.41	6.66	36.82	40.59	9.33	54.65	48.06	13.71	45.35	51.94	12.68

Source: NSS 38th, 50th and 55th Rounds on Household Consumption Expenditure.

and Nicobar Islands and Lakshaweep since their growth rate is below 5 per cent during 1993-94 and 1999-2000.

Regarding urban per capita consumption expenditures growth a more than 10 per cent increase is observed in Pondicherry (10.97%), Delhi (34.26%), Daman and Diu (18.65%), Dadar and Nagar Haveli (13.45%), Chandigarh (12.82%), Sikkim (20.52%), Punjab (11.80%), Orissa (11%), Nagaland (14.75%), Assam (14.30%), Bihar (13.32%), Haryana (10.20%), Kerala (14.57%), Maharashtra (10.53%), and Manipur (11.82%). An analysis of pattern of urban per capita consumption expenditure examines the following facts. At the national level food consumption expenditure in urban area was 54.65 per cent in 1993-94, but it declined 48.06 per cent in 1999-2000 showing 13.71 per cent of shortfall during the period.

The per capita food consumption expenditure proportion is below 50 per cent in Delhi, Chandigarh, Dadar and Nagar Haveli, Tamilnadu, Sikkim, Punjab, Nagaland, Meghalaya Maharashtra Madhya Pradesh, Kerala, Karnataka, Himachal Pradesh, Haryana, Gujarat and Andhra Pradesh. The urban per capita food consumption expenditure growth rate is quite low in Jammu and Kashmir (1.62%), Arunachal Pradehs (5.49%), Mizoram (4.03%), Orissa (1.47%) and Tripura (1.38%) in relation to other states and union territories in India.

Regarding position of urban non-food consumption expected a more than 55 per cent is observed in Chandigarh 61.18 per cent and Delhi (58.96%). The growth of non-food consumption expenditure is quite low in Jammu and Kashmir (2.02%), Mizoram (4.37%), and Orissa (1.95%) as it is below 5 per cent during 1993-94 and 1999-2000. The growth of urban non-food consumption is quite impressive in Dadar and Nagar Haveli (28.61%), Nagaland (21.40%), Karnataka (17.49%), Daman and Diu (19.63%), Lakshadweep (17.98%), Meghalaya (17.66%) and Tamilnadu (16.52%). The rapid growth of non-food consumption expenditure is a sign of development.

CONCLUSION AND POLICY SUGGESTIONS

It could be seen clearly from the above discussion that though there was about 25 per cent decline in poverty during 1983 and 1999-2000, it points to an increasing trend in poverty in terms of absolute number in some states and union territories such as Sikkim, Dadar and Nagar Haveli, Tripura, Nagaland, Meghalaya, Manipur, Madhya Pradesh, Bihar, Assam and Arunachal Pradesh. Among these states poverty increase in terms of percentage estimate is noted in Dadar and Nagar Haveli. In the states mentioned above though the percentage of decline in poverty line is noted, the absolute number of poor people increased because of the general increase in population. The decline in rural poverty is quite remarkable in Jammu and Kashmir, Kerala, Goa, Delhi, Lakshadweep and Pondicherry which is indicative of effective implementation of anti-poverty programme in these states. Regarding trend in per capita consumption expenditure more than 40 per cent increase was observed during 1993-94 and 1999-2000. The per capita consumption is quite high in Delhi, Chandighar, Nagaland and Goa and it is quite low in Assam, Bihar, Madhya

Pradesh and Orissa. The increase in per capita consumption expenditure is quite note worthy in Dadar and Nagar Haveli, Nagaland, Mizoram, Karanataka and Goa. In general, rural per capita consumption expenditure is lesser than urban per capita consumption expenditure both at the national level and at the state level. Regarding consumption of per capita consumption expenditure more increase was observed in non-food consumption than food consumption during 1993-94 and 1999-2000. This is more particular in Dadar and Nagar Haveli, Tamilnadu, Nagaland, Meghalaya and Haryana. This paper identifies some problems and defect in the implementation of anit-poverty programme in different parts of the country as per the evidence of statistical data analysis. In order to reduce poverty and economic inequality in India the following suggestions can be considered.

1. Efforts should be made to reduce the number of poor people in rural areas of Arunachal Pradesh, Assam, Madhya Pradesh, Manipur, Meghalaya, Sikkim, Tripura and Dadar and Nagar Haveli by allocation of more funds to implement anti-poverty programmes.
2. Steps should be taken to reduce the incidence of urban poverty in Andhara Pradesh, Arunachal Pradesh, Bihar, Madhya Pradesh, Maharasthra, Mizoram, Dadar and Nagar Haveli and Pondicherry by implementing urban oriented anti poverty programmes.
3. Women self-help groups should be promoted to avail themselves of rural credit particularly in backward states and northeastern hill states where the incidence of poverty is high.
4. Efforts should be made to increase the per capita food consumption expenditure with a view to increase the living conditions through effective participation of people in development programme.
5. Population growth should be controlled in some states where increase in number of poor people is noticed, despite the decline in reduction of poverty in terms of percentage estimate.
6. Micro-entrepreneurial activities should be promoted in a massive level in backward and poor states and union territories through effective involvement of NGOs and other voluntary agencies.
7. Wide spread region inequality in India with respect to per capita consumption expenditure. Hence this gap can be reduced through proper income redistribution programme.
8. Effects should be made to reduce the regional variation in spread of poverty through effective government intervention programmes.
9. Effects should be made to revise the poverty line fixed rupees in par with increase in the cost of living in different parts of the country.
10. Despite implementation a massive level of anti-poverty programmes, the prevalence of below poverty people, indicates the inadequate planning mechanism to implement the same. Hence, proper administrative arrangements should be made to identify the target groups and their needs.

11. The prevalence of spill our funds in implementation of anti-poverty programmes is a sign of improper and inadequate implementation of anti-poverty programmes in different parts of the country. Hence, proper steps should be made to implement the anti-poverty programmes.

REFERENCES

Bardhan (1974), "The pattern of Income Distribution in India: A review". In Srinivasan T.N., and Bardhan, P.K. (Ed.) Poverty and Income Distribution in India, Culcutta, Statistical Publishing Society.

Bhatty, I.Z. (1993), Inequality and poverty in Rural India in T.N. Srinivasan and P.K. Bardhan, Op.Cit, p. 291-336.

Da Costa, E.P.W. (1971), "A Portrait of Indian Poverty" in A.J.Fonseca (Ed.) Challenge of Poverty in India, Delhi, Vikas Publications.

Minhas (1986), "Planning and the Poor" New Delhi, Sultan Chand and Company.

Mundel (1983), "Agricultural Production and Pros on incidence of Rural Poverty, Economic and Political Weekly 18 (26) p. 257.

Ojha, P.D. (1970), "A configuration of Indian Poverty: Inequality and levels of living "Reserve Bank of India Bulletin, (January).

Parthasarathy (1995), "Public Intervention and Rural Poverty Case of Non-Sustainable reduction in Andhra Pradesh "Economic and Political Weekly: (October) pp.14-21.

Rajaraman, Indira (1975), "Poverty Inequality and Economic Growth: Rural Punjab, 1960-61 to 1970-71". Journal of Development Studies. 10:3 (March) pp. 278-290.

Rao, V.G. and Chadra Shekar, H. (1984), "Inter-state Variations in Urban Poverty, Margin (April) Vol. 16, No. 3.

Saith (1991), "Asian Rural Industrialisation Context, Features, Strategies" in Janbreman and Sudipto Mundle (eds) op.cit.

Sastry, S.A.R. and Suryanaryana, T. (1981), "Optimum Diet and Poverty Lines", Anvesak Vol. XI(1), pp. 97-116.

Subramaniam (1986), "Poverty and Inequality in Tamil Nadu Working papers Madras Institute of Development Studies, No. 74.

Thakurtha Guha, B.K. (1980) "Poverty in Culcutta, 1950-1972" Arthavijnana, Vol. 22, No. 4, December pp. 565-575.

INDONESIAN ECONOMIC AND BUSINESS DEVELOPMENT

Sofyan S. Harahap

INTRODUCTION

Business and economic development of Indonesia can be studied since the colonization years of Dutch and Japanese occupation. The Dutch colonized Indonesia around 350 years and Japan over 35 years. Dutch colonization put Indonesian economy as its source of raw material for industry and economy. Indonesia was ruled by the Dutch to realize its colonial economic interest. Japan also came to take resources to finance its war ambition. Then, based on the colonial economic structure, after its independence in 1945, Indonesia had to follow the model of Dutch economic development. At the initial period of its administration, the Indonesian government developed and nationalized the agricultural sector, especially plantation and mining. Chinese merchants filled the trading sector during the colonial era. After Soeharto took power in 1967 the government opened doors to foreign companies. Japan, USA and other countries came and brought money to invest in many sectors, especially in mining, manufacturing, and banking. For many years, Japan became the biggest foreign investor in Indonesia.

In 1997, Asian crisis hit Indonesian economy and become a disaster and went to deep political crisis. The new leader could not control the euphoria of democracy. The economy worsened. In 2004, Indonesia for the first time conducted a direct presidential election and Susilo Bambang Yudhoyono was elected as the first President chosen directly by people. The elected president is expected to be a strong leader to raise Indonesian economy as a miracle as it was during 1970-mid 1990.

This paper aims on discussing the development of economic and business in Indonesia. In this regard, the following sections will discuss the form of government, structure of population, state of the economic by macroeconomic and business indicators. In the end, the paper will discuss the relationship between Indonesia and Taiwan. The attachment provides the Procedures & Requirements to Establish Limited Liabilities Company under the Framework of Foreign Investment in Indonesia.

GENERAL INFORMATION

General

Indonesia is the largest archipelago in the world, having 13,667 islands, 300 tribes, and 336 ethnic groups. They speak more than 250 different languages and dialects. Indonesia is located between two oceans-the Pacific and the Indian Oceans. The main islands are Sumatra, Java, Kalimantan (Borneo), Sulawesi (Celebes) and Papua (formerly Irian Jaya). Indonesia stretches some 5,500 kilometers from east to west and 1600 kilometers from north to south. Indonesia is divided into 31 provinces with Jakarta the capital city, more than 241 Kabupaten (districts), and 3625 Kecamatan (sub districts). It is the fifth most populous country in the world. In 1997 Indonesia had a population of more than and a growth rate of 1.9%. (Leong and Lim, 1992; Mann, 1994). Unlike Europe, America or Australia, which have four seasons, Indonesia has only dry and rainy seasons. Indonesia has an equatorial climate with temperatures ranging between 25 - 35 degree Celsius. In 1996 Indonesian earned US$ 50 per year and 60% of the population lived in absolute poverty (Tambunan, no year).

Population

Indonesia is the most populous Muslim country in the world. The country in 2000 had a population of 206.264.595 and the estimated population in 2003 was 210 million. 87.3% of this population is Muslim (See attachment 1 population of Indonesia by province 1971-2000). The percentage of Moslems and other religions in 1990 are:

Table 1
The Percentage of Population According to Sex and Religions 1990

Sexes	*Religions*					
	Islam	*Catholics*	*Christian/ Protestant*	*Hindu*	*Buddha*	*Others*
(1)	(2)	(3)	(4)	(5)	(6)	(7)
Male	87.1	3.6	6.1	1.8	1.1	0.3
Female	87.3	3.6	6.0	1.8	1.0	0.3
Male + Female	87.3	3.6	6.0	1.8	1.0	0.3

Source: Indonesian Statistics Bureau 1990.
Note: The detailed population based on regions can be seen from appendices Table 1.

Even though quantitatively Muslims are the majority, qualitatively, especially in politics, and in business, Muslims cannot do much to implement their teachings. Since Independence, there has been a conflict between secular and religious supporters and until now the economy and politics have been controlled by non-Muslims, or at least by non-Islamic way of life. Unlike Malaysia where Islam is a formal state religion, in Indonesia Islam is not a state religion. Indonesia has Pancasila, or Five Basic Principles, as the state ideology.

The basic principles consist of: 1. Belief in one God; 2. Unity of Indonesia. The state is governed by secular ideology. The implementation of Islamic Law (the Shariah) depends on individuals or groups and is not enforced by the state. Because Indonesia formerly was not really a democratic state, social initiatives always came from the top or government elites. Government and political elites were dominated by secular ideology. Even though Muslims proposed to start Islamic banks before independence, the existence of Islamic banks could not be realized until the support of political elite was obtained.

The form of Government

Indonesia was a Dutch colony for 350 years. She then became a colony of Japan for 3 ½ years. Many political and cultural analysts argue that the colonial era affected Indonesian culture. Indonesia proclaimed its independence in 1945. Since that period, Indonesia has had different government structures. Firstly, between 1945 and 1959, Indonesia had a parliamentary democracy and was governed by different Prime Ministers. During this time period Indonesia had 7 cabinets and was led by 6 Prime Ministers. One Prime Minister, Mr. Ali Sastroamidjojo led the government twice. During this era, the President held only a symbolic position. The first Indonesian general election after its independence was conducted in 1955.

Secondly, between 1959 and 1965, the form of government became a presidential system, in which President Soekarno led the government. Soekarno became a strong leader and was enshrined as life-long president. This period came to be known as "Demokrasi Terpimpin" or the "guided-democracy" system. During this time the President led government administration. The period from Independence Day until 1966 is termed the Old Order Era, or "Orde Lama" (ORLA). Thirdly, from 1966 to 1998 (Mei 21 1998), Indonesia was governed by the New Order or Orde Baru (ORBA), led by Soeharto, an army General. This period is called Demokrasi Pancasila, that is democracy guided by 5 basic principles. During this era Indonesia held 6 general elections, firstly in 1971, followed by 9 political parties and one Golongan Karya. In 1973, Soeharto's government had coalition with 2 political parties besides Golongan Karya. In 1997, the last election in New Order the Golkar won 75%. In 1998, Habibie replaced Soeharto as President, marking the reformation era. Habibie'S government called a new general election in 1999 with the coalition of 49 political parties.

Because the parliament rejected his accountability, Habibie decided not to join the rally for the next presidency, he resigned and Abdurrahman Wahid succeeded him in 1999. In 2001, the then Vice-President Megawati Soekarnoputri replaced Abdurrahman Wahid by Parliament's initiative. In the 2004 general election that followed with 24 political parties and with 5 presidential candidates, Susilo Bambang Yudhoyono defeated Megawati, becoming the first directly elected new president.

The form of government in the Third World is mostly centralized, authoritarian, and paternalistic (Hikam, 1996). Some authors argue that this form of government is appropriate to enable them develop their economies (Widjaya, 1988). A centralized and authoritarian government influences every sector of social life in the country (King, 1982; Rasyid, 1998). The government has a significant role in shaping the people's customs, culture, behavior and ethics. Thus, understanding the form of government may help to further understand the economic and business development in Indonesia.

ECONOMIC DEVELOPMENT

Economic Indicators

In 1969, Indonesia under her New Order led by President Soeharto, started the five year economic development plan. Economic development at that time emphasized industry and agriculture. During Soeharto's era, the economic growth averaged 7% and economic condition changed dramatically. Indonesia was named as an economic miracle. During 1970-1990 economic growth reduced poverty from 60% to 15.2%. At the same time, China reduced poverty from 33% to 10%, Malaysia from 18% to 6% and Republic Korea from 23% to 8%. (Tambunan, undated).

The share of major sectors in Indonesia's GDP in 2002 are: Agriculture, 17.5%; Industry 44.5%; and Services 38.1%. The growth rates of Indonesian GDP by total and industry are as follows:

Table 2
The growth rate of Indonesia GDP and industry

No	*1997*	*1998*	*1999*	*2000*	*2001*	*2002*
GDP	4.7%	- 13.1%	0.8%	4.9%	3.4%	3.7%
Industry	5.2%	- 14.0%	2.0%	5.9%	3.3%	3.7%

Source: Tambunan (2004) from Asian Development Bank.

The growth rate of Indonesia in 1988 was negative due to the Asian financial and economic crisis. However, between 2003 and 2004 the economic growth was around 6-7%.

Compared to other ASEAN countries Indonesia did not rank among the strongest economies in ASEAN, the growth rate of output by industries and total GDP were much lower than those for Cambodia, Laos, and Myanmar. Total trade as a percentage of GNP was also lower. The export performance of Indonesia was also relatively weaker compared Singapore, Malaysia and Thailand (Tambunan, 2004).

Indonesian main important Manufactured Goods are lumber and woods products, Pulp, Textile and its products, Footwear and head gear, article of stone, plaster cement, asbestos, pearls, precious stones, metals, base metals and its products, machinery equipment, mechanical appliance, electrical equipment, transportation equipment, musical instrument, arms and ammunition. In 2001 the top three in export values are Machinery, mechanical appliance and electrical (US$ 8,650.- US$ 1 Million), Textile and its products (US$ 7,675.- US$ 1 Millions), and wood and its products (US$3,832.approx.).

According to Tambunan (2004) ASEAN is not the major target of Indonesia's export compared to the rest of the world and the share of Indonesia to ASEAN market has been developed slowly. The important markets for Indonesia are European Union, Japan and USA.

Another important thing to be noted is Manpower Export. Total export of manpower since 2001-2004 (September) are as follows:

Table 3
Manpower Export to Overseas

Countries	*2001*	*2002*	*2003*	*2004 (Sep)*
Asia Pacific	217,555	238,324	109,722	67,817
Middle East and Africa	121,180	241,961	183,770	176,788
USA	228	40	171	16
Europe	29	68	31	3
Total	338,992	480,912	293,694	244,624

Source: Department of Labor, RI.

The high unemployment rate in Indonesia compels manpower to search jobs overseas. However due to corrupt administrative practices some of them go abroad illegally and face a terrible life. Malaysia was the second top target country in 2004. Malaysia then enforced strict immigration law so that immigrant workers can be under the protection of government. According to the Department of Labor, migrant labor has remitted USD 907,67 Millions in 2002. Saudi Arabia is the top contributor followed by Hong Kong, Taiwan, Kuwait, Malaysia and South Korea.

Asian Crisis

Indonesia experienced economic miracle between 1970-mid 1997. In 1997, Indonesia faced a domino effect of economic crisis from Thailand and other Asian countries. Initially, an exchange rate crisis was followed by capital market crisis, banking crisis, eroding public confidence and then an unprecedented political crisis. The economic crisis retarded Indonesia's economic development.

Banking crisis adversely affected the state budget, which otherwise should have enabled the government to recapitalise the banking industry. Almost US$ 80 billions had to be paid by government to recapitalized its banking industry and US$ 8 billion had to be paid yearly as interest cost on bond issued to save the banking industry. So far, government has closed and frozen up as many as 90 banks from 240 to 150 banks (Siswanto, 2001). Indonesian GDP declined to 13.1% after the crisis (see table 2 above). During the economic crisis in 1997 the outflow of funds was estimated at US $ 80 billions.

Tsuname in 2004 hit the Indonesian economy hard. Tsuname took away 120,000 lives and caused huge destruction of economic facilities and infra structure, especially in Aceh and North Sumatra. The total cost of Tsunami is expected to be US$ 20 billions.

Inflation Rate

Some economic indicators (inflation and interest rates 2000 to 2002) of certain industrial countries compared to Indonesia can be seen in Table 4, as follows:

Due to political risk, and Indonesian economic situation, the inflation rate and interest rate remained higher compared to other industrial and developing countries. This fact could be one of the reasons why the investors discourage to invest their funds in Indonesia.

Table 4
Inflation Rate In Indonesia and some Industrial Countries

Country	*2000*	*2001*	*2002*
Inflation rate:			
Industrial Countries	2.2	1.4	1.7
Developing Countries	5.7	5.6	6
Country in Transition	15.9	11.3	8.8
Indonesia	9.35	12.55	10.03
Interest rate (short term)			
USA	3.7	2.1	3.2
Japan	0.2	0.1	0.1
Europe Union	4.1	3.4	3.8
Indonesia	14.53	17.62	12.93

Source: Indonesian Statistic Board 2002 and BI 2000's annual report.

In line with economic recovery, the inflation rate also declined. Inflation stood at oger 10 % in 2002. Between 2003 and 2005, the rate went down to one digit level. Monthly Inflation rate in 2003 ranged between 5.16% and 8.68%. In 2004 it ranged between 4.60% and 7.20 %. Between January and March 2005 inflation rate ranged between 7.15% and 8.81%. The improving inflation rate is a sign of better economic condition ahead.

Interest Rates on Saving Deposit in Commercial Banks since 2001-2004 were as follows: 19%, 8.96%, 5.14% and 4.37%. The trend is down. The same situation happened with the rate of interest of Bank Indonesia Certificates (Sertifikat bank Indonesia or SBI). In May 2002 the rate was 16.29%; by December 2002 it declined to 13.12%, to 8.38% in December 2003 and 7.30% in December 2004.

Foreign Exchange

Before the crisis in 1997, the average exchange rate of the Rupiah against the dollar was US$ 1 = Rp 2,500.-. Since the economic crisis in 1997 the Rupiah's exchange rate has been very volatile, fluctuating from Rp 9,000,- to Rp. 16,000. Per US $ 1. The average exchange rates against US Dollar were as follows: in 2000, Rp 8,403.-; in 2001. 10,255.; and in 2002, Rp. 9,316. Since Megawaty's government until now the exchange rate ranged between Rp. 9,200 and 9,600.- Indonesia's Foreign Debt, as of December 2002, based on Bank Indonesia's annual Report 2002 is as follows (US$ million):

Table 5
Government and Private Debt

Government Debt	US $ 74.197
Private Debt	US $ 55.230
Total	US $ 120.897

Source: Bank Indonesia Annual Report.
Foreign Debt in 2004 is US$ 136.14042 in millions.

Foreign Investment

In 1967, after Soeharto took power, he opened doors to foreign investment flows. The flow of foreign investment entering Indonesia until 1997 was abundant.

Since 1997, when President Soeharto signed a letter of intent asking for help from the IMF, Indonesia's economy has been controlled and monitored by IMF, even though there is public demand to exit from the IMF program, due to its failure to revive Indonesia's economy. IMF, as argued by some scholars, has failed and only concentrates on the interest of industrial countries and MNCs, rather than serving the interest of Indonesia (Stiglitz, 2002). In a recent study-by agreement IMF's own Independent Evaluation Office (IEO) it was stated that the IMF has blundered in helping Indonesia, Brazil and Korea (Khanna, 2003). Indonesian economic growth in 2002 was around 4% and according to the government senior minister the growth is expected to be around 5% in 2003.

As a member of AFTA (established 1992) Indonesia attracted the foreign investments, especially in the manufacturing sector, which is to enjoy special privileges, such as income tax exemption, full foreign equity ownership, duty free import of capital goods, domestic market access, and at least 30 years long-term lease for industrial land. The Procedures and Requirements to Establish Limited Liabilities Company under the Framework of Foreign Investment in Indonesia can be seen in attachment 6.

BUSINESS INDICATORS

The Structure of Indonesia's Financial System

The structure of financial systems from country to country varies slightly. In the developed countries, the role of banking sectors is decreasing in importance; however in the developing countries it is most influential. In a country where the domination of the banking sector is significant, the role of the central bank is vitally important (Zurianto, 1996). Financial institutions include:

(a) banking institutions such as commercial banks, savings banks, development banks.

(b) non-banking financial institutions such as security companies, leasing companies, insurance firms, factoring.

(c) capital market (Binhadi, 1995:171) .

In terms of assets and number of offices, the core of the Indonesian financial sector is its banking system, at least before 1997 crisis (Nasution, 1995, 1996; Cole and Slade, 1996). Indonesia's banking system consists of BI, all commercial banks (of which 5 out of 141 in Indonesia are state-owned banks), and People's Credit Banks. In 1994, Nasution maintained that BI and all commercial banks in 1997 held over 90% of the gross assets of Indonesia's financial assets, consisting of 21.3% by BI and 78.7% by all other commercial banks. The situation has not changed much in the post-crisis. Almost 46.4% of the total of Indonesia's commercial banks' gross assets were dominated by the state owned banks (BI, 2002). This percentage highlights the important role of the banking sector in Indonesia's financial system. The development of Indonesia Reserve Requirement for the last 5 years in US$ millions between 2000 and 2004 are as follows: $22,522.5, $20,497.1, $24,455.17, $28,011.12, $27,476.15.

Capital Market

Capital market was established in 1976. Indonesia now has two capital markets Bursa Efek Jakarta (BEJ) or Jakarta Stock Exchange (JSX) and Bursa Efek Surabaya (BES) or Surabaya Stock Exchange. The history of Indonesian capital market started in 1880, from the colonialist era. Based on the book of Effectengids that was published by Verreniging Vor de ffectenhandel. In 1912, Amsterdamse Effecteunbeurse established its branches in Batavia (Jakarta). Due to World War II, all activities of the capital market was closed by the colonial government.

After Indonesian Independence historical change can be divided into two kinds: The first one comprised the Old Order (1945-1966).The development of capital market in this era was insignificant. After Soeharto took power, the New Order rebuilt the capital market. In 1976, Indonesian government established the Capital Market Supervisory Body (BAPEPAM) and in 10 August 10, 1977, based on the Presidential Decree No 52 / 1976, the new capital market was launched. Many companies were "went public" and sold their stock at the Jakarta Stock Exchange. The capital market also opened up to foreign investors who could buy upto 49% of the shares of domestic companies.

In 1992, the Indonesian capital market was privatized and its operation using Jakarta Automated Trading System (JATS). There are 332 company were listed in the Jakarta Stock Exchange. Value Trading in JSX between 2000 and 2004 were as follows, respedctively: US$ 4,465.12, $ 6,614.1; $ 10,200.4, $ 16,746.6, $ 30,052.8, $ 35,213.9. Combined Stock price Indexes between 2000 and 2004 were as follows: 416,32, 392,03, 424,94, 679,3 and 1000,23.

Even though the share of capital market was still below the banking industry as the source of capital for the economy, the development of the market is significant. The government continuously improved the regulation and supervision. Indonesia is expected to have one-roof supervisory board to govern over all financial institutions: capital market, banking and non-banking financial institution, called OJK (Otoritas Jasa Keuangan). The Board of Security Exchange Supervisory or Badan Pengawas Pasar Modal has been established since JSX established and become a very independent supervisory board.

Some Problems on the Economic and Business Development

The new government still faces a lot of problems in pursuing economic and business development of Indonesia. The legacy of colonial era and the previous government still hold out as barriers against acceleration of economic and business development. The lack of qualified human resources, the foreign debt, corruption, Asian Crisis effects, legal aspect, and Indonesian cultures, the euphoria of democracy and international pressure are some problems that faced by new government. The process of general election of President, governors, major, head of district (Bupati) is having positive and negative effects. The new process is expected to select a qualified and competent leader but at the same time there is a problem of money politics and the expensive process and the possibility of social conflicts among the people. The legacy of previous government especially on the structure of economy, foreign debt, corruption and the dependency on the foreign intervention are a main barrier of economic and business development.

Some new rules have been set up by the Parliament as well as the President, e.g giving autonomy to the local governments, fighting corruption, freeing press, reducing subsidies to some commodities, negotiating foreign debt, cooperation with other countries, liberalization of financial markets, encouraging foreign investments. However, those ideal rules are not enough if bureaucrats and people do not support the government initiatives. The government, private sectors, people and international community must cooperate hand to hand to achieve the economic and business development.

The Indonesian culture is different from western culture, some of the policies and their implementation do not consider this contingent factors and as a result there was a failure in the implementation of the policies. Due to the spread of corruption in all level of bureaucracies there is hindrance in the achievement and effectiveness of good policies and goals. The lack of qualified educational sector is also another barrier for economic and business development. The management of economic development needs a global and qualified human resources, so far some strategic developments are taken by foreign experts.

TAIWAN AND INDONESIA ECONOMIC RELATIONSHIPS

Taiwan and Indonesia has been a long story and have a very good economic cooperation. The trade, export and import goods and service and other form of economic cooperation can be seen below.

Trade Volume & Commodities

Compared to ASEAN countries Sakakibira and Yamakawa (2003) noted that Trade Intensity Index (1998-2000) Indonesian and Taiwan equalled 4.1. The higher ones were Vietnam 7.6, Philippines 7.2 and the lower indexes were Brunei 0.7 and Laos 0.8. Trade index between Taiwan and Indonesia was 1.6, which is low compared to the rest of the world. The highest indexes were of USA 21.7, Japan 18.2. Taiwan has no trade index with China, Brunei, Cambodia, Laos, and Myanmar. Trade index between Taiwan and Vietnam was 0.7. From this figure we can argue that the trade relation between Taiwan and Japan still can be developed.

The biggest value of export for Indonesia is in Oil and Gas, Since 1989 the total Total Trade Volume between Taiwan and Indonesia was US$ 3.2 billion (2002). There are 23 main export commodities from Indonesia to Taiwan: Crude Rubber, synthetic Rubber, Oil, Coal, Bracket, Mining products, Logging, textile, Communication equipment, steel, copy paper, beer, lamp holder from sea shell, coconut flour, meal and powder, polyester texture yarn, coffee, cigar, plastic table cloth, confectionery, PE and PP woven fabric, writing paper & newsprint, tire, urea & diammonum phosphate, wooden furniture, detergent powder, handicraft, petroleum, coconut, pearl (SeeAttachment 5 on Indonesian Main Important Manufactured Goods). The biggest export items are machinery and wood and its products. (See attachment 5 for detailed on Indonesian main important Manufactured goods).

Indonesia also sends human labor to Taiwan. Based on the data from the Ministry of Manpower in Indonesia, human labor entered Taiwan since 1986 and almost 478.000 Indonesian labor work in Taiwan. In August 2004 total manpower works in Taiwan was 19.000. Majority of them are working in informal sector.

Investments

Total Investment of Taiwan to Indonesia developed very rapidly. Total investment 2001-2004, respectively are as follows in million US$ 18.2, US$ 8.7, US$ 1.6, US$ 19.2 and US$ 1.5 (Bank Indonesia, 2004)

Taiwan vs Indonesia

The comparison of economic indicators between the two countries can be seen in the following data:

Table 6
Economic Indicators of Taiwan and Indonesia

No.	*Indicators*	*Taiwan*	*Indonesia*
1.	GDP 2004	US$ 576,2 billion	US$ 827,4 billion
2.	GDP Growth	6%	4.9%
3.	Agriculture from GDP (2002)	1.7%	17.5%
4.	Industry from GDP (2002)	30.9%	44.5%
5.	Services from GDP (2002)	67.4%	38.1%
6.	Population below proverty line	1%	16.6%
7.	Inflation rate	1.7%	9.3%
8.	Interest rate		20%
9.	Labor force	10.22 million	111,5 million
10.	Unemployment rate	4.5%	9.2%
11.	Yearly Revenue Budget	US $ 67.41 billion	US$ 52,13 billion
12.	Yearly Expenditure Budget	US $ 76.70 billion	US$ 55,88 billion
13.	Public debt from GDP	32.4%	56.2%
14.	Current Account	US $ 21.16 billion	US$ 7,338 billion
15.	Export	US$ 170.5 billion	US$ 69,86 billion
16.	Import	US$ 165.4 billion	US$ 45,07 billion
17.	Reserve		US$ 27,48 billion

CONCLUSIONS

The economic and business development of Indonesia has fluctuated since 1945. The form of government and the political climate have significantly affected since the independence. The Asian Miracle and the Asian Tigers have put some Asian countries as exemplary success stories of economic development. But the 1997 crisis deeply ravaged the economic, banking, and political climate.

Indonesian reform has shown good signs toward stable economic growth. But she has much homework to do after the colonial era, Soekarno and Soeharto eras. The first directly elected President has a strong mandate to lead Indonesian people to build economic welfare and achieved a sustained and prosperous society. This is a main social capital to be ground the global society. The economic indicators have shown that Indonesia, with abundant natural resources, may achieve her track record as an economic miracle. Some of obstacles facing Indonesia should be resolved if Indonesia would like to resume her economic miracle.

The economic relationship between Taiwan and Indonesia appears not to be optimum.We may have room to maximize economic cooperation. Both countries may have to set their economic, business and other social educational relationships in order to benefit both government and people of both countries. The two countries either private or government bodies can set a prospective relationships that may encourage the economic, business and social educational growth. In the era of globalization no border and barrier of cooperation should be exist.

As academics we encourage the flourishing of economic cooperation between the two countries. Such cooperation ought to proceed in the fields of education and human resource development. Human resource is the core of economic development. The more human resources there are the higher the economic growth. The heart of education is in the university. We may arrange a more intensive cooperation between our universities in this field.

REFERENCES

Bank Indonesia (2002), Annual Report of Bank Indonesia.

Bank Indonesia (2003), Annual Report of Bank Indonesia, Jakarta: BI

Bank Indonesia (2004), Data Stalistick.

Bapepam, Indonesia, Sejarah Pasar Modal, *www.bapepam.go.id*

Binhadi, (1995), Financial Sector Deregulation, Banking Development, and Monetary Policy, Jakarta Institute of Banker.

Bursa Efek Jakarta, Sejarah BEJ, *www.jsx.co.id.*

CIA, The World Factbook, Indonesia & Taiwan (2005), *www.cia.gov.*

Cole, David C. and Slade, Betty F. (1996*), Building a Modern Financial System, The Indonesian Experience,* Cambridge, University Press.

Ecip, S. Sinansari, Syu'bah Asa, Avesina (2002), Ketika Bagi Hasil Tiba, Perjalanan 10 tahun Bank Muamalat, Jakarta: Bank Mumalat Indonesia.

Econit (1997), *"Pemerintah Perlu Segera Susun UU Baru Soal Bank Sentral" waspada,* Monday, October, 27, *http://www.waspada.com/*

Harahap, Sofyan S. (1999), The Central Bank and Commercial Bank Control Relationship in Indonesia, PhD Dissertation at the University of Adelaide, 1999.

——(1997), Akuntansi Islam (Islamic Accounting), Jakarta: Bumi Aksara.

——(2001), The Disclosure of Islamic values through Annual Report, A Case Study of BMI Annual Report. A Paper Presented at the International Conference on Information System and Islam, IIU, K. Lumpur.

Hikam, Muhammad A.S. (1996), Demokrasi dan Civil Society, Jakarta: LP3ES.

KBRI, Attaché Trade Department KBRI Taipei (2002), Trade and Volume of Indonesia's Export to Taiwan, July 2002.

King, D. (1982), "*Indonesia's New Order as a Bureaucratic Polity, a New Patrimonial Regime or Bureauratic Authoritarian Regime: What difference does it make?*" in Anderson, Benedict and Kahin, Audrey (eds) *Intrepreting Indonesia's Politic: Thirteen Contributions to the Debate,* Ithaca, USA, Publication No. 62, Cornell: Modern Indonesia's Project.

Leong, Tan Cheng and Terence T.S. Lim (1992), Indonesia. Business and Investment Opportunities, Singapore: Cassia Communication PTE Ltd.

Mann, Richard I. (1994), The Culture of Business in Indonesia, Canada: Gateway Book.

Nasution, Anwar (1995), *Financial Sector Development in Indonesia", in Zahid, Shahid N. (ed.) Financial Sector Development in Asia, Country Srudies,* Asian Development Bank.

Nasution, Anwar (1996), *"The Banking System and Monetary Aggregates Following Financial Sector Reform, Lessons from Indonesia, Helsinki, Finland, UNU World Institute for Development Economic Research".*

Rahardjo, Dawam D.K.K. (1996), *Perjalanan Sejarah BI.*, Jakarta, LP3ES.

Rasyid (1998), "*Sistem Kita Terlalu Sentralistik*", Panjimas, Vol. 53, November 4, *http://www.panjimas.co.id/*

Saludo (1996), "*Power 50*", Asiaweek, Vol. 22, No. 27, July 5, pp. 34-49.

Siswanto, Achmad (2001), Dilema Upaya Merger Dan Kredibiltas Perbankan, Pemeriksas No. 82 November 2001.

Stgilitz, Joseph (2002), *Globalization and Its Discontent,* New York.

Tambunan, Tulus (no year), Some Evidence on the Impact of Economic Growth on Poverty Reduction in Indonesia, Unpublished paper.

—— (2004), The Important of ASEAN Trade/Economic Integration from the Indonesian Perspective, presented in ISEI Seminar, December 2004.

Tim InfoBank (2003), Rating 135 Bank di Indonesia per December 2002, InfoBank, No 289, June 2003.

Widjaya, Albert (1988), "*Budaya Politik dan Pembangunan Ekonomi*", Jakarta, LP3ES.

Zurianto, Toto (1996), "*Bank Sentral Perdebatan yang Tidak Pernah Selesai*", *Pengembangan Perbankan,* No. 62, November-Desember, pp. 56-60.

ATTACHMENTS

Attachment 1
Population of Indonesia by Province1971, 1980, 1990, 1995 and 2000

Province	*Population*				
	1971	*1980*	*1990*	*1995*	*2000*
Nanggroe Aceh Darussalam	2,008,595	2,611,271	3,416,156	3,847,583	3,930,905
Sumatera Utara	6,621,831	8,360,894	10,256,027	11,114,667	11,649,655
Sumatera Barat	2,793,196	3,406,816	4,000,207	4,323,170	4,248,931
Riau	1,641,545	2,168,535	3,303,976	3,900,534	4,957,627
Jambi	1,006,084	1,445,994	2,020,568	2,369,959	2,413,846
Sumatera Selatan	3,440,573	4,629,801	6,313,074	7,207,545	6,899,675
Bengkulu	519,316	768,064	1,179,122	1,409,117	1,567,432
Lampung	2,777,008	4,624,785	6,017,573	6,657,759	6,741,439
Kep. Bangka Belitung	-	-	-	-	900,197
DKI Jakarta	4,579,303	6,503,449	8,259,266	9,112,652	8,389,443
Jawa Barat	21,623,529	27,453,525	35,384,352	39,206,787	35,729,537
Jawa Tengah	21,877,136	25,372,889	28,520,643	29,653,266	31,228,940
DI Yogyakarta	2,489,360	2,750,813	2,913,054	2,916,779	3,122,268
Jawa Timur	25,516,999	29,188,852	32,503,991	33,844,002	34,783,640
Banten	-	-	-	-	8,098,780
Bali	2,120,322	2,469,930	2,777,811	2,895,649	3,151,162
Nusa Tenggara Barat	2,203,465	2,724,664	3,369,649	3,645,713	4,009,261
Nusa Tenggara Timur	2,295,287	2,737,166	3,268,644	3,577,472	3,952,279
Kalimantan Barat	2,019,936	2,486,068	3,229,153	3,635,730	4,034,198
Kalimantan Tengah	701,936	954,353	1,396,486	1,627,453	1,857,000
Kalimantan Selatan	1,699,105	2,064,649	2,597,572	2,893,477	2,985,240
Kalimantan Timur	733,797	1,218,016	1,876,663	2,314,183	2,455,120
Sulawesi Utara	1,718,543	2,115,384	2,478,119	2,649,093	2,012,098
Sulawesi Tengah	913,662	1,289,635	1,711,327	1,938,071	2,218,435
Sulawesi Selatan	5,180,576	6,062,212	6,981,646	7,558,368	8,059,627
Sulawesi Tenggara	714,12	942,302	1,349,619	1,586,917	1,821,284
Gorontalo	-	-	-	-	835,044
Maluku	1,089,565	1,411,006	1,857,790	2,086,516	1,205,539
Maluku Utara	-	-	-	-	785,059
Papua	923,44	1,173,875	1,648,708	1,942,627	2,220,934
Indonesia	119,208,229	147,490,298	179,378,946	194,754,808	206,264,595

Source: Indonesian Statistic Bureau, 2000 (30 Province)

Attachment 2
Value Growth of Foreign Trade with Main Partner Countries, Indonesia, 2003 - 2004

Partner Country	*2003*		*2004*		*Growth (%)*	
	Export	*Import*	*Export*	*Import*	*Export*	*Import*
ASIA						
1. Japan	13 603.5	4 228.2	57 646.4	6 081.6	323.76	43.83
2. Republic of Korea	4 323.8	1 527.9	25 275.0	1 942.6	484.56	27.14
3. China	3 802.5	2 957.5	12 631.9	4 101.3	232.20	38.67
4. Taiwan	2 233.1	877.1	24 074.9	1 240.3	978.09	41.41
5. Singapore	5 399.7	4 155.1	18 390.9	6 082.8	240.59	46.39
6. Malaysia	2 363.9	1 138.2	10 509.7	1 681.9	344.59	47.77
AUSTRALIA & OCEANIA						
1. Australia	1 791.6	1 648.4	4 724.4	2 214.9	163.70	34.37
2. New Zealand	156.1	153.7	999.5	223.7	540.29	45.54
AMERICA						
1. United States	7 373.7	2 694.8	7 371.0	3 225.4	-0.04	19.69
2. Canada	382.1	321.8	245.4	551.8	-35.78	71.47
EUROPE						
1. United Kingdom	1 135.8	463.7	1 534.8	703.2	35.13	51.65
2. Netherlands	1 401.5	369.6	3 987.0	474.6	184.48	28.41
3. France	652.8	453.2	718.5	544.2	10.06	20.08
4. Germany	1 416.8	1 181.2	1 550.0	1 734.0	9.40	46.80
5. Italy	843.9	323.7	6 072.5	473.3	619.58	46.22

Note: Export in FOB, Import in CIF.
Source: Indonesian Statistic Bureau (2004).

Attachment 3
Quantity and Value of Oil and Gas Export Indonesia, 1989-2002

Year	*Oil and Gas*				*Total Export*	*% of Oil and Gas To Total*
	Crude Oil	*Oil Products*	*Gas*	*Total*		
		FOB Value (million USD)				
1989	5,140.4	919.9	2,618.4	8,678.7	22,158.9	39.2
1990	6,219.9	1,183.9	3,667.3	11,071.1	25,675.3	43.1
1991	5,695.7	1,018.7	4,180.5	10,894.9	29,142.4	37.4
1992	5,397.7	1,221.2	4,052.0	10,670.9	33,967.0	31.4
1993	4,778.4	914.7	4,052.7	9,745.8	36,823.0	26.5
1994	5,071.6	932.9	3,689.1	9,693.6	40,053.4	24.2
1995	5,145.7	1,296.9	4,022.0	10,464.6	45,418.0	23.0
1996	5,711.8	1,516.1	4,493.9	11,721.8	49,814.8	23.5
1997	5,480.0	1,302.5	4,840.1	11,622.5	53,443.6	21.8
1998	3,348.6	708.1	3,815.5	7,872.2	48,847.6	16.1
1999	4,517.3	917.9	4,357.0	9,792.2	48,665.4	20.1
2000	6,090.1	1,651.6	6,624.9	14,366.6	62,124.0	23.1
2001	5,714.7	1,189.4	5,732.2	12,636.3	56,320.9	22.4
2002	5,227.6	1,307.5	5,577.6	12,112.7	57,158.8	21.2
2003	5,621.0	1,553.8	6,476.9	13,651.7	61,058.3	22.4

Source: Indonesian Statistic Bureau 2003.

Attachment 4
Indonesian Main Important Manufactured Goods
(million US $)

Main Products	*1985*	*1995*	*1998*	*1999*	*2000*	*2001*
Wood & its product	1209	5092	2947	3707	3709	3832
Pulp	27	1452	2115	2441	3002	2598
Textiles	545	6064	5024	6853	8204	7675
Footwear	14	2113	1255	1685	1780	1607
Articles of Stone, Plaster cement, as Bes	14	340	235	529	639	607
Base metals & its Products	658	1798	1701	1900	2346	2036
Transportation equpment	3	483	710	564	587	553
Instruments-measuring & musical	69	278	282	339	488	520
Arms & ammunition	–	0	7554	1110	19	18
Machinery	90	3399	3965	4785	10311	8650

Source: ADB (2003).

Attachment 5
Key Economic Indicators of ASEAN 10 Countries

No.	*Country*	*Total Area (sq km)*	*Population 2003 in 000*	*686,276Share of Industry*	*GDP 2003 (million US$)*
1.	Brunei	5,765	363	na	4,715
2.	Cambodia	181,035	13,588	28,0	4,215
3.	Indonesia	1,890,754	214,519	44,5	208,492
4.	Laos, PDR	236,800	5,637	24,7	2,043
5.	Malaysia	330,257	24,711	48,7	103,161
6.	Myanmar	676,577	53,515	10,5	9,605
7.	Philippines	300,000	81,453	32,5	80,359
8.	Singapore	682	4,353	33.6	91,355
9.	Thailand	513,254	62,553	42,5	143,308
10.	Vietnam	330,363	81,095	38,5	39,021
	ASEAN	4,465,487	541,787		686,276

Source: ASEAN Finance & Macroeconomic Surveillance Unit (FMSU) Database.

Attachment 6
The Procedures & Requirements to Establish Limited Liablities Company Under The Framework of Foreign Investment In Indonesia

A. Legal Basis

Save the certain area which is governed under specific regulations (such as mining, banking, and finance), in general direct foreign investment activities is governed by the foreign Capital Investment Law, Law No 1 of 1967 as amended by Law No 11 of 1970 (Foreign Investment Law).

Pursuant to the Foreign Investment Law, the Foreign Investment shall be conducted by forming a foreign investment company (" PMA Company"). In the form of a limited liability company, abbreviated as "PT" (Which is governed by the Limited Liability Company Law, Law No 1 of 1995- "Company Law"). As a limited liability company, a PMA company shall have at least 2 founders or shareholders.

Without prejudice to the prevailing implementing regulations, a PMA Company can be set up by way of :

(a) Establishing a new PT by way of joint venture with other foreign investor(s) (100% foreign owne); or

(b) Establishing a new PT by way of joint venture with Indonesian partners; or

(c) Purchasing shares in existing PT (could be a PMA company, a company establish under framework of Domestic Investment Law (" PMDN Company") or non PMA Company and PMDN company)

In this memorandum, the explanation set out herein is limited only to the establishment of a new PT either by way of joint venture with other of foreign investor(s) (100% foreign owned) or bya way joint venture with Indonesian partner (s).

All PMA companies are fallen under the coordination of the Capital Investment Coordinating Board (" BKPM"). Therefore all applications related to the establishment of PMA Companies and its amendment thereafter are managed by BKPM.

BKPM was established as a "one-stop-shop" in 1973 for foreign investors wishing to set up PMA company. The intention of BKPM was that a Potential foreign investor would need to obtain one license from BKPM, instead of being requirement to approach each Indonesian government which may have jurisdiction over relevant areas of investment for approval engage in activities in particular areas. Application for investment may be made both in Indonesia, and following recent law, offshore through an Indonesia Embassy or Consulate.

B. Negative List and Activities which require a partnership with a small scale enterprise

A PMA company may only be created or formed for business activities which are open for foreign investment. In this regard, the Indonesian Government under the Presidential Decrees, namely the Presidential Decree No 98 of 2000 as amended with Presidential Decree No 118 of 2000, have issued the list of activities which are (i) closed for foreign investment, (ii) 100% opened and (iii) opened under certain requirements among others, the requirement to have partnership with the local party.

In addition to the negative list, the Indonesian government under the Presidential Decree, namely the Presidential Decree No 127 0f 2001, have also issued the list of activities which are required to have a partnership arrangement with an Indonesioan small-scale enterprise. In this regard, the Indonesian government permits the partnership with the small-scale enterprise under any of the following schemes:

(a) Nucleus-Plasma scheme (Inti plasma)

In the nucleus-plasma scheme, the PMA company shall act as the nucleus and the small-scale enterprise as the plasma. The PMA Company shall carry out the fostering activities ranging from the provision of production means, technical guidance to the marketing of products. The PMA company as the nucleus shall foster and develop the small-scale enterprise as the plasma in:

- Providing and preparing the land.
- Providing the production means.
- Providing the technical guidance in business and production management.
- Achieving, controlling and enhancing the required technology.
- The financing and.
- Providing other assistance needed for increasing the business efficiency and productivity.

(b) Sub- Contract scheme

In the sub-contract scheme, the small-scale enterprise shall procedure the components needed by the PMA company as part of its product. The PMA company shall foster and develop the small-scale enterprise in:

- Proceeding part of the production and components
- Procuring the raw material used for the continuous production at reasonable quantities and prices.
- The guidance & technical skill on the production and management
- Achieving, controlling and enhancing the required technology
- The financing

(c) General Trading Scheme

In the general trading scheme, the PMA company shall market the products of the small-scale enterprise or the small-scale enterprise shall supply the need required by the PMA company. In the general trading scheme the partnership between the PMA company and the small-scale enterprise can take place in the forms of joint marketing, provision of business location, or the receipt of supplies from the small-scale enterprise, to meet the needs required by the PMA company.

(d) The Franchise Scheme

In the franchise scheme, the PMA company as the grantor of the franchise shall give the rights to use the license, trademark, and business distribution channels to the small-scale enterprises along with the managerial guidance assistance.

(e) The agency scheme, the small-scale enterprise shall be given special rights to market the products of the PMA company.

(f) The Share Participation Scheme.

In the share participation scheme, the PMA company/the founders of the PMA company shall establish a partnership with the small-scale enterprises by way of inviting the small-scale enterprise jointly invest in a new project/company or through a share purchase at reasonable prices with convenient payment system which does not inflict the small-scale enterprise.

C. Procedures for Establishment of a PMA Company

1. *Capital Adequacy*

No formal minimum capital requirements exist for establishing a PMA company. BKPM will, however, conduct its own examination as to the capital adequacy of the project based on the commercial feasibility of the proposal.

There is nit any formal debt to equity ratio for establishing a PMA company. BKPM has however a general policy that the maximum debt to equity ratio of the PMA company is 75%: 25%.

2. *Foreign Investment Application*

The application for the foreign capital investment shall be made using type 1/PMA application form, as attached hereto and accompanied with the following documents:

(a) For Foreign participant:

(1) Copy of articles of association of the foreign company in English or Indonesian language; and or

(2) Copy of the valid passport for foreign individual

(b) For Indonesian participant:

(1) Copy of articles of Association of the company and its amendment or identity card for individual; and

(2) Copy of tax identification number ("NPWP")

(c) Flowchart of The production process and Raw materials requirements for processing industries.

(d) Explanation of Business activities for services sector.

(e) Power of attorney to sign and manage the application if the participant(s) are represented by another party

(f) Other requirements from the relevant sector, minister of the proposed activity, as the case may be;

(g) If the proposal activity is required to have a cooperation with the small scale enterprises:

(1) Copy of the agreement between the small-scale enterprises and the founders/shareholders of the proposed PMA company (For the interest of the PMA company);

(2) Letter of statement from the small-scale enterprises stating that the small scale enterprises fulfills the criteria-scale enterprises pursuant to the prevailing regulations.

(3) BKPM Approval

Based on the application, BKPM will review and further decide whether the application will be approved or not. If the application is approved, BKPM will issue an approval which will be valid as in-principle business license maximum valid for 3 years. The issuance of the BKPM approval in practice may take up to one month, although the prevailing regulation provides a 10 working days as from the complete and accurate application is received by BKPM as a deadline for BKPM to give its decision.

3. *Incorporation*

After obtaining the BKPM approval, the founders/shareholders of the PMA Company shall conduct the incorporation process of the PMA company by executing Dead Of

Establishment (DoE) that containing the articles of association of the PMA Company before a Notary Public..

In relation to the establishment of new PMA Company, after executing the DoE, the Shareholders of the PMA company shall then undertake the following actions; Obtaining Letter Of Domicile for the PMA Company. The letter of domicile is obtained from the relevant Head Of Sub District/Kelurahan which has the jurisdiction over the office of the PMA Company. In issuing the letter of domicile, the Kelurahan shall require the following documents (a) copy of the DoE of the PMA company, (b) copy of identity card of the President Director of the PMA company, (c) letter of domicile issued by the building owner which the office of the PMA company located.

(a) Obtaining NPWP for the PMA company from the relevant Tax Office

In order to obtain the NPWP, the PMA Company shall submit an application using a from with has been provided by the Tax Office, accompany with the following documents (a copy of the DoE of the PMA company, (b) copy of Identity Card of one of the Directors of the PMA Company (in case the Director is the foreigner, it is also require to submit letter of his/her domicile issued by Kelurahan), (c) copy letter of domicile of the PMA company which is issued by the Kelurahan.

(b) Injecting capital to the PMA company's account

Further, the Director (s) of the PMA Company shall open an account in a Bank Located in Indonesia. After the account has been established then the relevant founders / shareholders of the PMA Company in exchange for the issuance of shares by the PMA Company to the relevant shareholders.

4. *Minister of Justice Approval*

The DoE shall be filled by Notary Public to the Minister Of justice and Human Rights of this Republic for its approval accompany with the following documents:

(i) Receipt of Money transfer given a bank in relation to the PMA Company's Account

(ii) Copy to the BKPM approval

(iii) Copy to the NPWP; and

(iv) Copy of the Letter of Domicile.

As from the approval of the Minister of Justice to the DoE, the PMA company shall become as a legal entity.

5. *Registration and Publication*

After obtaining the Minister Of Justice approval, within 30 days, the DoE shall be registered with the Register of Enterprises Office at the Regional Office of the Department of trade & Industry.

Following such registration, the relevant DoE shall be Published in State Gazette of Republic.

HEALTH INSURANCE FOR THE POOR IN INFORMAL SECTOR

Siddhartha Sarkar

INTRODUCTION

In India the informal sector employs more than 90 per cent of workforce, most if not all, are covered by meaningful social security schemes. The term social security in developing countries is used in much broader sense than that used in developed countries (Ahmad *et al.* 1991, Guhan 1994, Prabhu 2001). It has been further recognised that the neglect of social opportunities due to lack of adequate progress in social security has been detrimental to the economic and social development in the developing countries including India (Datta 1998: L-2). The informalised workforce is unprotected labour, which imply labour that does not have any socio-economic safety. The protection that a society provides to individuals and households to ensure access to wage and working conditions in a comprehensive sense, in matters of security of employment, health care, maternity benefits, provident fund, retirement benefits, is an essential element of the safety nets that keeps working people and their families from falling into poverty (Sarkar 2004 a: 122).

The informal sector represents an important part of the economy and certainly of labour market in many countries, especially developing countries and poses a challenge to policy makers with regard to issues relating to improvement of the working condition and social protection of the workers engaged in the informal sector. In the developing economies a substantial share of employment is indeed in informal category and women in all age groups depend on the informal sector more heavily than men. Women are over represented in this sector in the sense that their share in the sector is higher than their share in total labor force. Most women tend to be own account workers and only a few are heads of micro enterprises. Relatively lower level of education among women, compared to men, seems to explain, in part, this gender differential in informal employment. Discrimination in the labour market also explains in part the disproportionate concentration as it limits women's access to formal and wage employment. Women also face additional constraints because of their homemaking and childcare responsibilities, which limits their participation in formal employment. Even within the informal sector more women than men seem to be in poor quality employment. The causes for participation in the informal sector can be economic and non-economic. Economic reasons are related to unemployment and an inflexible formal labour market, a declining real price of capital and the high cost of formal production. Besides, non-economic causes are concerned with a greater flexibility and satisfaction in work, a complete use of workers professional qualifications and increased leisure time. There are two groups of factors, which determine the decision to become active in the informal sector, more specifically, the structural as well as opportunity factors. The structural factors consist of financial pressure, socio-psychological pressure and institutional constraints. The opportunity factors consist of individual background, skills, education, living condition or non-individual components, environment, values, standards etc. (Sarkar 2004 b: 366).

The realisation that mere existence of health care facilities does not necessarily mean that they are readily accessible to the poorest section in the informal economy, tend to the evolution of a unique health insurance scheme, with contribution according to individual capacity. Health insurance protects against the cost of illness, mobilises funds for health services, enhances the efficiency of mobilisation of funds and provision of health services, and achieves certain equity objectives by continuously benchmarking. Previously insurance was not considered as an option for the poor in informal sector. They were regarded to be too poor to save and pay premium. It is being gradually recognised that even low-income group can make tiny contribution to health insurance schemes. Health insurance for the poor can take different forms namely, community based or non-community based insurance policy of the government. In recent years community health insurance has gained as a possible means of improving access to health care among the poor and protecting the poor from indebtedness and hardship resulting from medical expenditures. Non-governmental organisations (NGOs) play an important role in the delivery of affordable health services to the poor but their coverage has always remained diminutive (Table 1 and 2). This paper examines several health insurance schemes catering to the informal sector as well as some critical issues with regard to extending health insurance coverage to poor households in general and those working in the informal sector in particular.

EXISTING HEALTH INSURANCE SCHEMES

The various health care programmes are presently operating for the informal sector in developing countries. In India community and self-financing schemes, and micro-credit linked health insurance schemes are the important intermediate steps in the evolution of an equitable health financing mechanism for the workers in informal sector.

Various other terms are used with regards to community health insurance (CHI), including micro health insurance and local health insurance. The benefit of CHI lies in keeping transaction cost low, in formulating a scheme suited to community needs, in influencing health behaviour through health education, and affecting the supply health care. CHI programmes offer best aspiration for cutting down financial burden caused by sickness to a large segment of

Table 1
Salient Characteristics of Selected NGOs Managed Health Insurance Schemes

Voluntary Organisations/Location	*Date Started*	*Service Provided*	*Health Service Delivery/Organisation*	*Population Served*	*Total Annual Cost (Rs.)*
Sevagram/ Wardha, Maharasthra	Hospital, 1945 Community health programme 1972	1. 500 bed hospital 2. Out reach community health programme	- - Trained male VHW provides basic curative, preventive and promotive health care. Mobile with doctor and ANM provides care every 2 months	- - 19,457	- - 69,459
Bombay Mother and Child Welfare Society (BMCWS)/ Chawl in Bombay	1947	Health activities, Two maternity hospitals (40 beds each) with child welfare centres, Non-health activities, Day care centres, convalescent home	• Outpatient and inpatient maternity care • Outpatient pediatric care including immunization		120175 (health and non health combined)
Raigarh Ambikapur Health Association (RAHA)/ Raigarh, Madhya Pradesh	1969 Community health services started 1974	Federation of 3 referral hospitals and 65 independent health centres with outreach community care	• RAHA functions include management of insurance scheme, training and support for health centres. • health centres staffed by nurse provide outpatient care run MCH clinic • VHWs provide community based care	400,000	30,000-50,000 (cost range of individual health centres of which there are 65)
Christian Hospital/ Bissamaucuttak, Orissa	Hospital 1954, out reach community care 1980	120 bed hospital, community project currently not operational	Outpatient/inpatient care, specialties include obstetrics, gynecology, surgery, ophthalmology	-	1,911,740 (hospital only)

Voluntary Organisations/Location	*Date Started*	*Service Provided*	*Health Service Delivery/Organisation*	*Population Served*	*Total Annual Cost (Rs.)*
UPASI Coonoor, Tamil Nadu	19th century CLWS -1971	Association of tea growers run comprehensive labour welfare scheme (CLWS)	CLWS provides training, management support to health programmes of individual tea estates. Tea estates have small cottage hospital and outreach care provided by local workers	250,000	300,000
Goalpur Co-operative Health Society/Shanti-niketan, West Bengal	1964	Dispensary, periodic community health services	Doctor provides outpatient care twice weekly	1,247	32,000
Students health home/ West Bengal	1955	Polyclinic plus 28 regional clinics	Polyclinic has 20 beds provides outpatient and inpatient care; Regional clinics, outpatient care only, health education campaigns, blood donation camps	550,000	2,950,745
Saheed Shabsankar Saba Samithi (SSSS)/ Burdwan, West Bengal	1978	Dispensary occupational health activities, rural health programme, school health programme, fair price medicine shop	Doctors provide outpatient care weekly MCH clinic	-	87,780
Arvind eye hospital/ Madurai, Tamil Nadu	1976	2 urban hospitals (100 beds), 2 rural hospitals (500 beds), outreach programme	Outpatient and inpatient eye care Regular eye camps organized	-	10,987,700
Tribovandas Foundation/ Anand, Gujarat	1980	Community based health programme linked with milk cooperatives, regional rehabilitation centres, Balwadis women's income generating scheme	Community health workers (CHWs) Ws provide basic curative, preventive, and promotive care; field, supervisors provide support to CHWs milk society building used as base for coordinating health services.	300,000	1,080,000 (health and non-health combined)

Contd...

Voluntary Organisations/Location	*Date Started*	*Service Provided*	*Health Service Delivery/Organisation*	*Population Served*	*Total Annual Cost (Rs.)*
SEWA/ Ahmedabad, Gujarat	Union 1972, health programme 1984	Union of self-employed women. Helps organize women into cooperatives of various traders, provides credit facilities. Provides health care as a support, which stocks rational generic drugs.	Health centres in urban slums and rural villages. CHWs provide basic care, doctors provide support twice weekly.	63,000	391,850 (health programme only)
CINI/ Daulatpur, West Bengal	1975	Community based health programmes, dispensary and outreach rehabilitation centre. Other activities: income generating schemes, farm, health training, research	CHWs provide MCH care through Mahila Mandals, doctors run daily OPD, weekly MCH clinic, supplementary feeding	70,000 (Community health project)	1,900,000

Source: Dave [1991]

Table 2
Prepayment and insurance mechanisms in selected NGOs managed health insurance schemes

Features	*Sevagram*	*RAHA*	*Tribovandas Foundation*	*Goalpara Home*	*Students Health*	*SSSS*
Coverage provided	Household	Individual	Household	Household	Institutional and individual	Individual
Annual subscription fee	8 payali sorgham (Landless) and 2 payali sorgham per acre extra (land holders), or equivalent cash	Rs. 5 or Rs. 2 rice	Rs. 10	Rs. 18 in cash or in kind (rice or labour)	Rs. 2 Institutions Rs. 6- Individuals	Rs. 2 or Rs. 5
Number of members	At least 75% of households (23 villages covered) Total insured 14,390	75,000	Approximately 1/5 to 1/6 of all households in villages, (319 villages covered) 150 out of 175 households	150 out of 175 households in village	630 institutes total 350,000 students covered	6800
Member entitlement	Community care: free CHW services, drugs, and mobile (doctor +ANM) services. Hospital: free care for unphased illness episodes, 25% subsidy for anticipated illness episodes, e.g., pregnancy and chronic ailments	Community care: free CHW services and drugs. Free health centre services including MCH clinic. Hospital: free care after paying entrance fee up to ceiling of Rs. 1000	Community care: free services , subsidized drugs. Hospital: 50% subsidy	Dispensary: Free doctor consultations, drugs at cost. Free periodic public health activities	Polyclinic/ regional clinics: free consultations, drugs, diagnostic tests, operations, bed stay at nominal charges	Outpatient clinic: free consultations, drugs at cost, free MCH care

Contd....

Features	*Sevagram*	*RAHA*	*Tribovandas Foundation*	*Goalpara Home*	*Students Health*	*SSSS*
Non-member entitlement	Non-members not entitled to use community health services	Non-members charged for drugs (over cost), not entitled to attend MCH clinic	Non-members have same emoluments to community services as members but not hospital care	Non-members charged for drugs (over cost)	Non-members not entitled to avail of services	Non-members are not entitled to avail the services
Management of fund	VHW responsible for membership collections, Collections once a year at harvest time. Compulsory that 75% of villages covered.	Individual health centres respon-sible for membership collections. Collections once a year. New members waiting period 2 months before services entitlements Rs. 3 retained by centre, Rs. 2 to RAHA for referral fund.	VHW services responsible for membership collections. Collected once a year at times-bonus payments distributed (non-adult society members can also enroll in scheme)	Village health communities-funds collections once a year.	Institutions enrolled once a year. Individuals ongoing (no waiting period)	Able to enroll through the year. No waiting period between enrollment and service entitlements.

Source: Dave [1991]

the low-income groups. This scheme is purely based on non-profit making motive, which is intended for the workers of informal sector and involves repayment and the pooling of resources to cover the cost of health related matters. Often the schemes are operated by a hospital and intended at households of the surrounding area and membership is voluntary rather than compulsory. A survey of existing literature on health insurance suggested approaches to community financing. The conventional method to community financing was considered to be inapt and forced *Sewagram* to fashion its responses in the light of its own observations and experiences (Table 3).

Table 3
Approaches to Community Financing

Conventional Approach	*Sewagram Experience*
It does little to promote equally, can place great burden on the poor and the sick, and suffers from poor selection.	The principle of contribution according to capacity, but services according to need, developed an egalitarian system, which does not suffer from poor selection.
It lacks stability and needs some external support to mobalise and sustain community efforts.	The acceptability and affordability of the scheme resulted in stability of revenue and willing community involvement on a sustainable basis.
It favours the creation of those health facilities for which there is high local demand, rather than meeting professionally perceived needs.	Doctors prefer not to over-medicate as the hospital has to raise 25 per cent of its own expenditure. Also as the remaining 75 per cent of the funds is assured to the professionals, they do not succumb to whimsical local demands for tonics and injections.
It carries the danger of an excessive use of facilities.	The facilities are primarily controlled by professionals and not by the people, thus avoiding chance of excessive use.
It is never easy to sell the concept among poor people.	The need for and affordability of the scheme are strong selling points.
It tends to benefit the community more than individual and hence there could be greater reluctance to participate.	Sewagram's insurance scheme is oriented more towards individual as there is an element of risk sharing and hence there is little reluctance to participate.

Source: Jajoo [2000].

Several NGOs and governments have initiated micro-credit schemes for vulnerable groups to crash the vicious circle of poverty, malnutrition, disease, low productivity, and low income. Micro-credit is now considered not only an effective tool for poverty reduction but also used as an instrument for empowerment of the poor, particularly the women. This operation creates income to the poor by extending them small credits for self-employment and other economic activities. However, it was soon realised that loan repayments by these groups were much below the expected level. The experience suggested that ill health and expenditure on treatment and associated consumption needs were the prime reasons for defaulting on repayments. To plug the erosion of income of borrowers on health care needs, some NGOs (such as Grameen Bank in Bangladesh and the Self-Employed Women Association (SEWA) in India) have initiated health insurance schemes for their members. The Grameen Bank Health Programme was started in 1994 with the objectives to adopt preventive measures against diseases, to arrange for treatment at minimum cost, and to build a non-profit primary health care system. Under this scheme the borrowers pay a fixed annual amount of 60 *Taka* per family as premium and a very petty sum at the time of using the facility. The scheme over time has proven to meet the desired objectives (Rahman 2000). In India, SEWA is a trade union of 215,000 women workers of the informal sector. It organises them towards the goals of full employment and self-reliance at the household level. Full employment includes social security, which in turn incorporates insurance. SEWA's experience repeatedly revealed that despite women's efforts to come out of poverty through enhanced employment opportunities and increased income, they were still vulnerable to various crises in their lives. These prevented them from leading a life free of poverty. The crises they continue to face are death of a breadwinner, accidental damage to and destruction of their homes and work equipment, and sickness. Maternity too often becomes a crisis for a woman, especially if she is poor, malnourished, and lives in a remote area. One of the SEWA studies observed that women identified sickness of themselves or a family member as the major stress event in their lives. It was also a major cause of indebtedness among women. The health insurance programme was, from the start, linked to SEWA's primary health care programme, which include occupational health services. Thus, insured members also have access to preventive and curative health care with health education. Health insurance accounts for the majority of claims and for 50 per cent of the premium paid out to the insurance programme by SEWA members. The scheme was introduced by the SEWA Bank in March 1992 with an initial enrolment of 7000 women from Ahmedabad city (Chatterjee and Vyas 1997). Later on it was extended to cover rural woman members from nine districts of Gujarat. Now its enrolment is 30,000 women, of which 50 per cent is from rural areas. Health insurance is an integral part of the insurance programme of SEWA. The major motivation behind the initiation of a health insurance scheme for women is that maintenance of an active health seeking behaviour is a vital component for ensuring a good quality life and women tend to place a low priority to their health care needs. The poor women's health is most vulnerable both because of their unhygienic living conditions as well as the burden of bearing children. And persistent poor health of such workers costs them in terms of loss of working days and the corresponding incomes. The coverage of the SEWA health insurance programme includes maternity coverage, hospitalisation coverage for a wide range of diseases, and insurance for occupational health related illnesses and other diseases specific to women (Table 4). SEWA's health insurance scheme functions in co-ordination with Life Insurance Corporation of India (LIC) and New India Assurance Company (NIAC). SEWA has integrated the schemes of LIC and NIAC into a comprehensive health insurance package to address women's basic needs. The claimants are the needy health-benefits seekers and as the insurance is an additional benefit, the beneficiaries willingly pay the premium. Most of the insurers opt for fixed deposit of Rs. 500 or Rs. 700 (depending upon the type of coverage) with the SEWA Bank and the interest accrual goes towards annual payment of premium. It is the large membership and assets of the SEWA Bank that has made possible the provision of the insurance coverage at low premium.

Table 4
Type of coverage under SEWA scheme

Provider	*Description of Coverage*	*Coverage Amount (Rs.)*	*Premium (Rs.)*
New India Assurance	Accidental death of the woman member		
	Loss of assets	10,000	3.50
	Accidental death of a member's husband	10,000	3.50
SEWA	Loss during riots, fire, floods, theft, etc.:		8.00
	(a) of work equipment	2000	
	(b) of the housing unit	3000	
	Health Insurance (Including coverage for:	1200	30.00
	(a) gynecological ailments		(10)
	(b) occupational health related diseases)		(5)
	Maternity Benefits	300	-
Life Insurance Corporation of India	Natural death	3000	15.00
	Accidental death	25,000	

Note: Total premium for the entire package is Rs. 60 plus Rs. 5 as service charge.

The comprehensive review of the existing health insurance schemes for informal sector in India describes that several programmes indulge to economically lower segment of the population. The voluntary health insurance plan, which covers only hospitalisation expenses, is too expensive for the informal sector workers to get enrolled. There are various community-based and self-financing schemes but, given the massive health care needs, the coverage of population by them is just not adequate. The proportion of population covered by any health insurance scheme is minute, let alone those employed in informal sector. The market for health insurance is growing at a substantial rate, though. At this stage, it may be worthwhile to abridge the experience with health insurance of select Asian and Latin American countries to understand what lessons can be learnt by India. There have been commendable efforts in developing health insurance models by these countries whose per capita incomes are well below those of the developed countries. The specific experiences of China, Thailand, Indonesia, Sri Lanka, Chile, Uruguay, Colombia, Brazil, and Argentina are worth mentioning. China stands out as an example where insurance has been successful in covering a large part of the population both in rural and urban areas. The Chinese expenditure is characterised by high total expenditure, low government expenditure and heavy dependence on insurance financing. There are two kinds of coverage which are in practice in China namely, labour insurance medical coverage for state-owned enterprise workers and retired persons, and free medical service which caters to workers and retired persons of government agencies and parties and non-profit institutions. A noteworthy feature of China's health care system is the coverage of rural population through various kinds of schemes, which have been designed in accordance with the local economic conditions and public opinion. China's system of health care certainly scores better compared to some of its Asian counterparts like India and Indonesia. Thailand has four different kinds of health care financing programmes namely, voluntary health schemes, mandatory schemes, social welfare schemes, and fringe benefit schemes. The target population of each of these schemes varies in terms of their place of residence (rural/urban) and employment status (formal sector/ informal sector). The coverage of population in the informal sector, especially in rural areas is, however, far from a enviable level. In fact, 41 per cent of the population, which is not covered by health insurance scheme largely, consists of subsistence farmers, self-employed, rural workers, and urban dwellers engaged in informal sector activity such as street vending and small-scale commercial undertakings. Despite this under-coverage, the experiment with the health card scheme seems to have worked. The health-card scheme is designed for delivering health care services to the workers in the informal sector where assessing incomes is problematic. The health-card scheme was initiated primarily with the objective of improving health among the rural population. Indonesia, with a very low level of government expenditure and negligible insurance spending, fares the worst (among the countries under comparison) as far as health outcomes are concerned. In the Asian group of countries, Sri Lanka too (like China) emerges as a good performer. However, the pattern of health care expenditure between the two greatly varies. While China relies substantially on insurance spending, Sri Lanka's health care expenditure is characterised by high government, low private, and low insurance expenditures. The pattern of health care expenditure in Latin American countries varies according to the size of the country (both in terms of population and geographical size) and the income level. Taking a larger perspective, there are mainly two types of managed competition, which are emerging in this region where government is the sponsor and where private employers are playing the role of sponsor. The former type is followed in countries like Chile, Uruguay, and Colombia. In Chile, for instance, 73 per cent of the population is covered by public health care whereas the remaining 27 per cent are enrolled into the ISPRAE, a private insurance plan. Colombia too has a system of mixed public funding and managed competition, which has not only increased the coverage but also made the system more equitable. In fact, Colombia's health care system has been hailed as one of the most successful ones in the region. Brazil has three distinct systems being availed of by three different income classes namely, public system primarily by informal sector and low-income workers, private supplementary medicine by formal sector and middle-income workers, and direct out-of-pocket payments by high-income workers. Argentina's health delivery system is mixed and a large number of private insurance plans. While the broad goals and objectives of the health care system in the reviewed countries remain equity and efficiency in the delivery of health care, yet there are variations in the design of programmes, role of government, etc. In the Asian group of countries, China and Sri Lanka, with their success in the health arena, do pose as examples worth emulating but it needs to be noted that each of them follows a different pattern. In Sri Lanka, there is a dominance of government spending in the health sector whereas insurance spending is substantial in China. In the Indian case, the effort can be two-directional. Government health spending can be improved in terms of the amount spent as well as efficiency of expenditure. The latter is, however, more important. The widespread introduction of low user fees in government hospitals can improve the provision of basic health services. A mix of government expenditure as well private insurance is possible but the amount of premium to be collected from workers in the informal sector remains a moot question. This becomes all the more important when the share of informal sector workers is more than 90 per cent and it is not easy to make an assessment of their income. The Chinese model throws some light on how risk sharing can be made workable even in rural areas where incomes are not too low. The India-China comparison has always been a subject of debate because of their similarities in terms of geographical size, population, and low levels of income. China has exceeded India as far as the achievements in the area of health are concerned. China's basic indicators of infant mortality rate, life expectancy, and maternal mortality are far more favourably placed as compared to those of India. Thailand's health-care scheme has been another pioneering attempt towards promoting grass-root participation and management skills (Gumber 2002).

EXTENDING HEALTH INSURANCE COVERAGE

There are several important issues concerning formulating, designing and operationalising an affordable health insurance scheme for the poor in informal sector. Before introducing a unique plan, wide-ranging designs in different settings can be tried out on a pilot basis. The critical points and steps to be considered in this process are as follows (Gumber 2002).

Defining Benefit Package

The types of benefits to be included are: (i) inpatient care: the event is unpredictable but rare and the cost of treatment is either unaffordable or payment pushes people, even the better off, into indebtedness and poverty. (ii) outpatient care: Insurance is generally not well suited to routine ambulatory care because its requirements tend to be reasonably predictable and are of relatively low cost and people might be expected to meet these costs out of their pockets as they go along without too much hardship. Most people, however, do prefer the inclusion of at least those services (diagnostic and clinical) having a bearing on their pockets. (iii) chronic care: Insurance is also poorly placed to meet the needs of chronic care as such conditions, although of high cost, are not unpredictable. As long as members of a scheme may be willing to subsidise others in rare times of extreme need, they may be unwilling to heavily subsidise them on a regular basis. This is not to say that providing protection for those with chronic illness is not important, but just that insurance is not the best way of doing it. (iv) maternity care: Another area that generates considerable discussion is that of the possible inclusion of deliveries in the package. It is possible to argue that while mothers have nine months to plan to meet the financial costs of normal delivery and should be expected to do so themselves, a scheme might include emergency deliveries which are rarer but expensive. If schemes do decide to include outpatient care and chronic care they must expect premiums to rise. Also, experience tends to suggest that women groups do want deliveries to be included. If so, the costs of the scheme may rise and again a future requirement might be to include all antenatal care. Individual schemes may wish to deviate from these broad principles. One option might be to offer greater protection to the poorest in the group by perhaps offering them greater benefits, i.e. to cover the cost of ambulatory care where this benefit is not enjoyed by better off members. Alternatively, schemes could decide to meet the non-medical costs of treatment (e. g. transport costs) or they may even wish to extend benefits beyond just health care to cover loss of income, though this is unlikely and should only be considered when there is a demonstrated record of financial sustainability and ability to pay. Another possible approach is to consider whether referrals to the more specialized facilities are to be included. Should a scheme's benefits be restricted to secondary hospitals or should referral for, say, specialist cancer treatment or heart surgery be allowed? This could potentially be very high cost and could drain the scheme, resources. What is an appropriate role for the State? The government would presumably wish to give some freedom to determine the benefit package but may wish to insist that certain elements be included, e.g. inpatient and preventive care. Also a minimal benefit package should be defined so as to ensure delivery of only cost-effective services.

Deciding on a Panel of Providers

If services are free there is little point in getting insurance. If most of the costs are in the form of unofficial fees, again health insurance can do little to help. Health insurance only makes sense when fees are being charged and this may rule out involvement with government facilities. However, fees may differ significantly from government facilities, where services may be free, to NGO providers to expensive for-profit providers. Obviously the higher the fees, the higher will be the premiums needed for a scheme to break even, but also the greater are potential benefits from health insurance. The question is whether the services should be restricted to just one provider or whether members should have choices. This depends largely on what members want and where they are currently getting their services but the decision does have some implications as set out below. In some areas, especially rural and hilly areas, there may be little choice. Such an approach is perhaps easier to implement, although lack of competition reduces any pressure on the provider to improve the services. In urban areas, there may be a number of potential providers. Dealing with a larger number may be more difficult from a managerial point of view but does offer better potential for driving up quality. A scheme offering a choice of providers must include incentives for members to access the quality of care they need in the cheapest setting. One way to do this is to charge higher co-payments for higher cost providers.

Type of Membership and Population Coverage

This includes whether the scheme would cover just the villagers, slum dwellers, poor, occupation groups, thrift and credit groups (e.g. DWCRA), select geographic unit, workers, women, or adult groups. Unit costs will differ if switching over from individual to household memberships because children and other dependents (elderly) have different health needs than the working population. Clearly, on the one hand the more are the people that are covered, the higher are the premiums per household, but on the other hand there is a reduction in adverse selection.

Reducing Moral Hazard and Preventing Adverse Selection

Although the ultimate decision should be down to the group itself it is advisable that unless the majority of members join (ideally all) there are likely to be problems. Ideally one should cover the entire village or panchayat or settlement and make the scheme compulsory while covering minimal benefit package. If services are free to members once they have paid a premium they have a strong incentive to use services even if their need is not great. One-way of preventing such overuse (also called moral hazard) is to charge co-payments - a small amount charged when services are used. Although far less than the user fees, this would at least provide a deterrent to unnecessary use. Also, on the provider side there are incentives for over treatment and also the possibility of fraudulent practices as numbers and providers collaborate to falsify claims. One should aim at creating incentives for cost-effective treatment, i.e. preventing unnecessary use of services and ensuring services are of the appropriate quality provided at reasonable cost. Approaches exist to contain, if not prevent, such practices totally. Members themselves would be expected to monitor the use themselves through peer pressure; it may also be possible to compare utilisation between groups to identify areas where overuse may be possible. Any managing organisation could monitor this issue.

Organisational Arrangements

Management will be important at all stages of preparation, design, implementation, and evaluation. One approach might be to contract an NGO to take on this role. They might carry out the initial groundwork and be responsible for monitoring schemes, perhaps even for negotiating special discounted rates with providers. If the groups are small, the managing agency may wish to introduce an additional element of risk pooling by taxing schemes and redistributing these funds to schemes in need. The role of evaluation would, of course, be given to another institution. A managing institution, however, would require special skills in the areas of community participation/ community liaison/marketing, bookkeeping and financial analysis, monitoring, access to medical expertise (to validate treatment decisions), and possibly in providing preventive care directly (funded through premiums).

Payment Systems

There are a number of options here. In short, the approach should be as simple as possible and not open to fraud. Funds could be retained within the age group or held at the facility (if they can be trusted). Members might be given a card with their photograph on it and be exempted at the facility with the scheme reimbursing the provider afterwards. Alternatively, the member might be expected to make payment up front and be reimbursed by the scheme later-though this may present a significant barrier to some.

The Task of Government

A number of important roles emerge for government in the development of a health insurance scheme, which include financing, management, training, monitoring, and evaluation. First of all, it would be important to carry out a mapping exercise which would include the following: identifying the nature and activities of the target groups; assessing their knowledge of, and interest in, health insurance and carry out advocacy and training as necessary through workshops and door-to-door campaigns; identify interested groups for the pilot project; carry out willingness-to-pay survey and design the cost benefit package; carry out a baseline survey on current health practices in the pilot project area and also in control groups to obtain approximate initial administration costs. It might be reasonable to provide schemes with government funds to meet the initial start-up costs. Those would not be significant as the approach would be paper based. Although an ongoing subsidy is probably unwarranted - schemes would be expected to be self-supporting with the benefit package tailored to meet what people are willing to pay - in the short term a subsidy might be justified. Government can also stimulate the interest in the schemes and guarantee interest so that the people can learn the benefits of insurance, a concept many will be unfamiliar with. It can also provide an extra incentive to well designed schemes - the subsidies may be made available to schemes which incorporate elements of best practices. (One approach may be to cover 50 per cent of premiums for a fixed period of two years).If government wishes to evaluate schemes with a view to their replication it is important that the schemes are developed in a variety of settings (urban/rural with varied access to types of health facilities and socio-economic population groups). Otherwise they will leave themselves open to criticism that they only work in particular circumstances. It is also important to be clear about what the schemes are intended to achieve so that there can be some basis for evaluation.

CONCLUDING REMARKS

Health insurance has gained amplified importance as a financing tool in meeting health care facilities to the poor in the informal sector. Community based health insurance is more useful mechanism for providing insurance to the poor. However the approach of the government is to support voluntary insurance rather than to widen the existing social insurance schemes. Social insurance may be better way of providing health protection to the low-income groups but alternative straight forward approaches to the people below the poverty line is needed.

REFERENCES

Ahmad, E., Dreze, J. and Sen, A. (eds.) (1991), Social Security in Developing Countries. Clarendon Press, Oxford.

Chatterjee, M. and Vyas, J. (1997), Organizing Insurance for Women Workers: the SEWA Experience. Self-Employed Women's Association (SEWA), Ahmedabad.

Datta, R.C. (1998), Public Action, Social Security and Unorganised Sector. Economic and Political Weekly, XXXIII (22): L2-L5.

Dave, P. (1991), Community and Self-Financing in Voluntary Health Programmes in India. Health Policy and Planning, 6 (1): 20–31.

Guhan, S. (1994), Social Security Options for Developing Countries. International Labour Review, 133(1): 35-53.

Gumber, A. (2002), Health Insurance for the Informal Sector: Problems and Prospects. Working Paper No. 90. Indian Council for Research on International Economic Relations, New Delhi.

Jajoo, U.N. (2000), Health Insurance for the Poor: Innovations in Primary Health Care. In: R. Jhabvala et. al. (eds). The Unorganised Sector: Work Security and Social Protection. Sage Publications, New Delhi.

Prabhu, K.S. (2001), Economic Reforms and Social Development. Sage Publications, New Delhi.

Rahman, K. (2000), Poverty, Micro-Credit and Health: What Role can WHO Play? WHO Regional Health Forum, 4 (1 & 2): 68–80.

Sarkar, S. (2004a), Extending Social Security Coverage to the Informal Sector in India. Social Change, 34 (4): 122-130.

Sarkar, S. (2004b), Theorising in Informal Sector: Concept and Context. Social Action, 54(40): 359-373.

INDEX